Silver Burdett Ginn
Mathematics

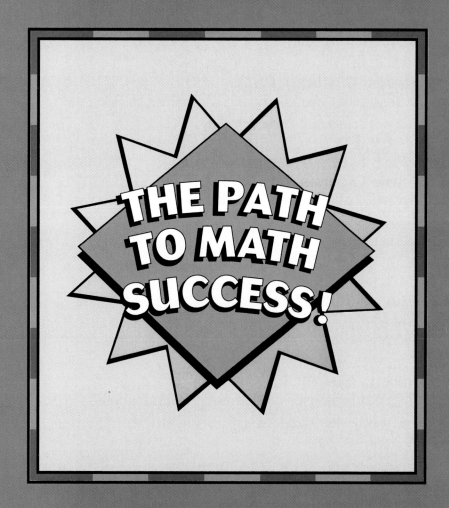

THE PATH TO MATH SUCCESS!

Silver Burdett Ginn

Parsippany, NJ

Atlanta, GA • Deerfield, IL • Irving, TX • Needham, MA • Upland, CA

Program Authors

Francis (Skip) Fennell, Ph.D.
Professor of Education and Chair, Education Department

Western Maryland College
Westminster, Maryland

Joan Ferrini-Mundy, Ph.D.
Professor of Mathematics

University of New Hampshire
Durham, New Hampshire

Herbert Ginsburg, Ph.D.
Professor of Psychology and Mathematics Education

Teachers College, Columbia University
New York, New York

Carole Greenes, Ed.D.
Professor of Mathematics Education and Associate Dean,
 School of Education

Boston University
Boston, Massachusetts

Stuart J. Murphy
Visual Learning Specialist

Evanston, Illinois

William Tate, Ph.D.
Assistant Professor of Mathematics Education

University of Wisconsin-Madison
Madison, Wisconsin

Acknowledgements appear on page 522, which constitutes an extension of this copyright page.

ISBN 0-382-34894-X

4 5 6 7 8 9 10 WC 06 05 04 03 02 01

Silver Burdett Ginn
299 Jefferson Road, P.O. Box 480
Parsippany, NJ 07054-0480

Grade Level Authors

Jennie Bennett, Ed.D.
Instructional Mathematics Supervisor

Houston Independent School District
Houston, Texas

Charles Calhoun, Ph.D.
Associate Professor of Elementary
  Education Mathematics

University of Alabama at Birmingham
Birmingham, Alabama

Lucille Croom, Ph.D.
Professor of Mathematics

Hunter College of the City University
  of New York
New York, New York

Robert A. Laing, Ph.D.
Professor of Mathematics Education

Western Michigan University
Kalamazoo, Michigan

Kay B. Sammons, M.S.
Supervisor of Elementary Mathematics

Howard County Public Schools
Ellicott City, Maryland

Marion Small, Ed.D.
Professor of Mathematics Education

University of New Brunswick
Fredericton, New Brunswick, Canada

Contributing Authors

Stephen Krulik, Ed.D.
Professor of Mathematics Education

Temple University
Philadelphia, Pennsylvania

Donna J. Long
Mathematics/Title 1 Coordinator

Metropolitan School District of
  Wayne Township
Indianapolis, Indiana

Jesse A. Rudnick, Ed.D.
Professor Emeritus of Mathematics
  Education

Temple University
Philadelphia, Pennsylvania

Clementine Sherman
Director, USI Math and Science

District Office of Dade County Public Schools
Miami, Florida

Bruce R. Vogeli, Ph.D.
Clifford Brewster Upton Professor of
  Mathematics

Teachers College, Columbia University
New York, New York

Contents

Chapter 2

Adding and Subtracting Whole Numbers and Money

Chapter Theme: Fun and Games
Real Facts: Number of Calls to TV Show 38
Real People: Magda Liolis Moshova and Melinda Toporoff,
Game Show Creators. 38

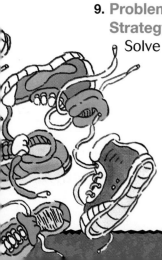

Chapter 3

Multiplication and Division Facts

Chapter Theme: Collections

Chapter 4

Using Data and Probability

Chapter 5

Multiplying by One-Digit Numbers

Chapter Theme: Communications

Chapter 7

Time and Measurement

Chapter Theme: World Records
Real Facts: Heights of Mountains 248
Real People: Ashrita Furman, World-Record Holder 248

Chapter 8 — Dividing by One-Digit Divisors

Chapter Theme: Performing Arts
Real Facts: Number of Television Episodes Broadcast 296
Real People: Michael Westmore, Makeup Designer 296

Chapter 9 Fractions

Chapter Theme: Hobbies
Real Facts: Lengths of Toy Animals 336
Real People: Mary Rodas, Toy Inventor 336

Decimals

Chapter Theme: On the Road

Chapter 11

Geometry

Chapter Theme: A World of Shapes

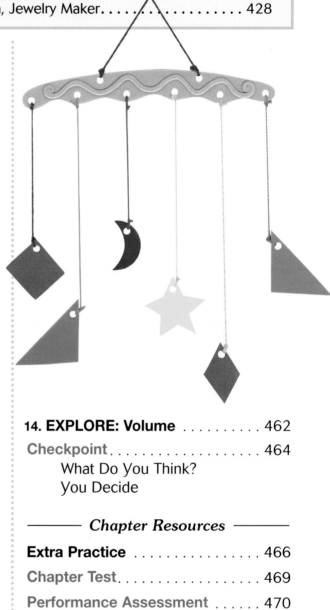

Chapter 12

Dividing by Two-Digit Divisors

Chapter Theme: Fairs and Rides

Place Value

Chapter Theme: NUMBERS

REAL-WORLD Math

·····················Real Facts·····················

Some of the world's tallest buildings are in Chicago, Illinois. The chart below lists the five tallest buildings in that city.

Chicago's Tallest Buildings		
Building	**Height in Feet**	**Stories**
Amoco Building	1,136	80
AT & T Corporate Center	1,007	60
John Hancock Center	1,127	100
Sears Tower	1,450	110
Two Prudential Plaza	978	64

- What is the tallest building listed? the shortest?

- How can you use place value to put the buildings in order from tallest to shortest?

·····················Real People·····················

Meet Jack Catlin, an architect. He designs all kinds of structures, such as offices and schools. Architects draw diagrams with exact measurements for builders. The students in the picture at the right are using numbers in many ways as they build their model.

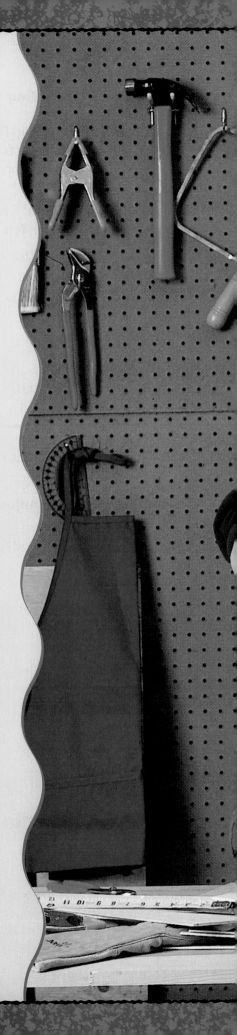

Time for Lunch!

Base-ten blocks can help you explore place value.

Learning About It

On the first day of school, all the fourth-grade students left their lunch boxes on the playground. Alexis was looking for hers in the pile of 125 lunch boxes.

Step 1 Work with a partner to model 125.

- Use hundreds, tens, and ones blocks.

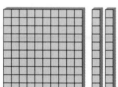

- How many of each block did you use?

- How did you decide the number of blocks you needed?

Step 2 Make a model that shows 2 hundreds 12 tens 14 ones. To find what number these blocks show, you need to think about regrouping.

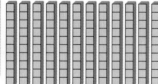

- How many ones make a ten? Regroup 10 ones. What blocks do you have now?

- How many tens make 100? Regroup 10 tens. What blocks do you have now?

- What number does your model show?

What You Need

For each pair:
  base-ten blocks
  1 thousand
  4 hundreds
  13 tens
  16 ones

125

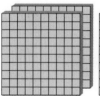

Step 3 Look at the model to the right.

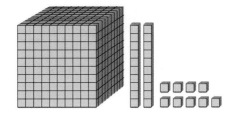

- What number is modeled?

- What blocks are not needed in this model?

Think and Discuss Why must you show 0 in the hundreds place when you write the digits for the number modeled above?

Practice

1. **Describe** How can you model 326 using base-ten blocks?

2. Ben says he can model 531 without using any tens.

   a. Describe what his model would look like.

   b. Explain why you would not write 0 in the tens place.

Copy this chart.

Place	Thousands	Hundreds	Tens	Ones
Number	3	3	3	3
Value	3 thousands or 3,000			

3. Complete the chart to show the value of the 3s in 3,333.

4. How can you describe the relationship between the values of the 3s as you move from right to left on the chart?

5. Enlarge the chart to include a four-digit number of your own choosing. Include the written values for your number.

Lots of Peanuts!

Place value helps you read and write numbers.

Learning About It

The average fourth grader eats enough peanut butter in one year to make about 29 sandwiches. It takes about 2,200 peanuts to make the peanut butter for those sandwiches.

A place-value chart can help you read and write numbers.

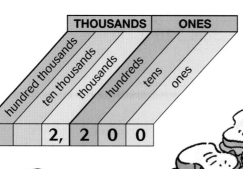

THOUSANDS			ONES		
hundred thousands	ten thousands	thousands	hundreds	tens	ones
		2,	2	0	0

Each group of three numbers is called a **period**.

THERE'S ALWAYS A WAY!

You can write this number in different ways.

- **word form:** two thousand, two hundred

- **short word form:** 2 thousand, 200

- **standard form:** 2,200

- **expanded form:**

  2 in the thousands place means 2,000.
  ↓
  2,200 = 2,000 + 200
      ↑
  2 in the hundreds place means 200.

Word Bank

period
word form
short word form
standard form
expanded form

What if every elementary and high school student in West Virginia brought a peanut butter sandwich to school on the same day? They would bring 315,406 peanut butter sandwiches.

THOUSANDS			ONES		
hundred thousands	ten thousands	thousands	hundreds	tens	ones
3	1	5,	4	0	6

THERE'S ALWAYS A WAY! You can write 315,406 in different ways.

- **word form:** three hundred fifteen thousand, four hundred six

- **short word form:** 315 thousand, 406

- **standard form:** 315,406

- **expanded form:** 300,000 + 10,000 + 5,000 + 400 + 6

Think and Discuss Look at the number 2,200 on page 4. Why does the expanded form of 2,200 not have any tens or ones?

Try It Out

Write each number in short word form and standard form.

1. four thousand, twenty-two

2. nine hundred five thousand

3. sixty-three thousand, five hundred seven

4. one thousand, five

Write the value of each underlined digit.

5. 2̲66

6. 4,5̲68

7. 7̲05,326

8. 2̲6,759

9. 850̲,367

10. 75,00̲5

11. 8̲6,016

12. 19̲,486

13. 10̲1

14. 64,7̲21

15. **Analyze** Which 8 in 888,287 has the greatest value? How do you know?

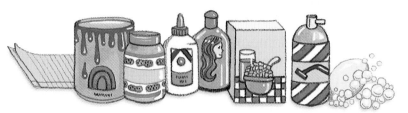

◄ **Science Connection** George Washington Carver, who lived from 1864 to 1943, discovered more than 300 uses for peanuts. Some of the peanut-based products he developed are peanut butter, glue, shampoo, paper, cereal, paint, and shaving cream.

INTERNET ACTIVITY
www.sbgmath.com

Practice

Write each number in standard form.

16. five thousand, five hundred ten

17. ninety-two thousand

18. 4,000 + 800 + 20

19. 800,000 + 700

20. 3,000 +1

Write each number in expanded form. Then write the value of the underlined digit.

21. 6,4<u>0</u>6   **22.** 47,<u>4</u>00   **23.** 819,2<u>6</u>6   **24.** <u>7</u>5,002   **25.** <u>3</u>40,000

26. 5<u>1</u>,338   **27.** 8,2<u>5</u>6   **28.** <u>9</u>85,586   **29.** <u>2</u>2,587   **30.** 5,<u>7</u>00

Using Algebra **Use place value to continue each pattern.**

31. 25,345; 26,345; 27,345; ▨ ; ▨ ; ▨

32. 100; 110; 120; ▨ ; ▨ ; ▨

33. 7,461; 8,461; 9,461; ▨ ; ▨ ; ▨

34. 438; 448; 458; ▨ ; ▨ ; ▨

Problem Solving

Use the table to solve.

35. What state produces six hundred seventy-five thousand tons of peanuts?

36. **Analyze** Which two states together produce as many peanuts as Texas? What strategy did you use to solve the problem?

37. **Create Your Own** Use the table to write a problem.

Peanut Production	
State	**Tons of Peanuts**
Alabama	200,000
Florida	94,000
Georgia	675,000
New Mexico	25,000
North Carolina	175,000
Oklahoma	100,000
Texas	275,000

38. How many states produce more peanuts than North Carolina?

39. How many states produce less than 200,000 tons of peanuts?

Review and Remember

Add or subtract.

40.	4 + 5	**41.**	10 − 4	**42.**	8 − 2	**43.**	5 + 6	**44.**	13 − 7

45.	23 − 9	**46.**	18 − 10	**47.**	25 + 15	**48.**	14 − 7	**49.**	32 − 7

50.	8 2 + 2	**51.**	3 2 + 6	**52.**	6 3 + 0	**53.**	9 2 + 5	**54.**	6 2 + 4

Time for Technology

Using a Calculator

Quick Changes!

You can use place value and addition or subtraction to change the value of a number being displayed.

1. Change 35,892 to 35,992. What did you do?

2. Change 6,258 to 5,258. What did you do?

3. Change 868,426 to 878,426. What did you do?

Use a calculator to find the number that is

4. 10,000 less than 45,621

5. 100,000 less than 187,762

6. 100,000 more than 360,529

7. 1,000 more than 49,533

8. Predict How will 48,532 change if you add 1,000 and subtract 100? Check by using your calculator.

For Extra Practice, see Set A, page 32.

Survey Says...

You can put numbers in order by comparing them.

Learning About It

What is your favorite ice cream? Mr. Scotto's class took a survey on their Internet home page. Here are the votes for the top four flavors.

Which flavor got more votes, vanilla or chocolate?

Compare 1,357 and 1,382.

> **Step 1** Line up the numbers to compare the digits.

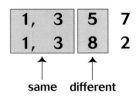

same   different

The thousands and hundreds are the same. The tens are different.

> **Step 2** Compare the tens.

5 is less than 8, so 1,357 is less than 1,382.

You can write 1,357 < 1,382 or 1,382 > 1,357.

> ◄ **Math Note**
>
> < means *is less than*
> > means *is greater than*

Chocolate got more votes than vanilla.

Connecting Ideas

Use what you've learned about comparing numbers to write the numbers from the ice-cream survey in order from least to greatest.

STRAWBERRY 1,092

CHOCOLATE 1,382

MINT 955

VANILLA 1,357

- 955 is the least number. It has no thousands.

  955, __?__, __?__, __?__

- Compare 1,092 with 1,357.

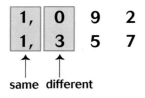

same different

0 hundreds < 3 hundreds. So 1,092 < 1,357.
955; 1092; __?__; __?__

- Compare 1,357 with 1,382.

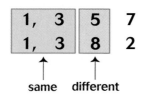

same different

▼ **Social Studies Connection**
Ice cream cones were first served at the 1904 World's Fair in St. Louis, Missouri.

5 tens < 8 tens. So 1,357 < 1,382.

Ordered from least to greatest, the numbers are 955; 1,092; 1,357; 1,382.

Think and Discuss Explain how to write 3,675; 3,072; 1,967; and 2,498 in order from greatest to least.

Try It Out

Compare. Use > or < for ⬤.

1. 389 ⬤ 398

2. 860,452 ⬤ 860,568

3. 4,287 ⬤ 3,287

4. 5,681 ⬤ 5,679

5. 5,401 ⬤ 897

6. 365 ⬤ 392

Order each set from least to greatest.

7. 2,520 791 235 709   **8.** 22,568 23,497 22,526

9. Analyze Comparing the ones place in the numbers below will tell which is greater. So what do you know about the other digits? ■, ■ ■ 2   ■, ■ ■ 6

Practice

Compare. Use > or < for ●.

10. 4,304 ● 4,345   **11.** 7,690 ● 954   **12.** 13,287 ● 23,287

13. 52,688 ● 62,689   **14.** 105,740 ● 201,430   **15.** 68,204 ● 6,924

16. 1,200 ● 1,201   **17.** 14,817 ● 14,820   **18.** 102,100 ● 102,200

Order each set from greatest to least.

19. 873 859 964 961   **20.** 32,750 3,762 32,075

21. 7,421 7,562 7,419 7,577   **22.** 42,015 42,125 41,995 42,650

23. Find the numbers in the cloud that match the letter points on the number line.

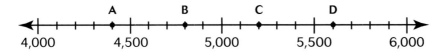

Use the numbers in the cloud to answer Exercises 24–27.

24. Which numbers are less than 5,525?

25. Which numbers are greater than 9,999?

26. Which numbers are between 4,250 and 8,740?

27. Using Estimation Which two numbers have a sum of about 16,000? How can you check that your answer is reasonable?

5,200 10,260 5,600 1,339 4,400 8,741 4,800

Problem Solving

Use the information in the table for Problems 28–31.

28. In which month was the most vanilla ice cream sold?

29. **Analyze** How many strawberry ice-cream cones were sold in June? What strategy did you use to get your answer?

30. Order the total monthly sales from least to greatest.

31. **You Decide** If cones come in boxes of 200, how many boxes would you order for September? Explain your reasoning.

32. **Using Algebra** How can you find the number that the stands for in $25 + \blacksquare = 35$?

Ice-Cream Cone Sales

Flavor	May	June	July	August
Vanilla	875	910	1,070	1,120
Chocolate	980	1,125	1,315	1,275
Strawberry	650		1,135	1,010
Total	**2,505**	**2,840**	**3,520**	**3,405**

Review and Remember

Using Algebra Use the pattern to find the missing numbers.

33. 20, ▓ , 40, ▓ , 60

34. 3, ▓ , 9, 12, ▓

35. ▓ , 115, 130, 145, ▓

36. 4, 8, ▓ , 16, ▓

37. 250, ▓ , 350, 400, ▓

38. 25, 50, ▓ , 100, ▓

Money $ense

What's the Scoop?

Daria has $6.00 to spend on ice cream cones for herself and 2 friends.

1. Pick 3 cones she could buy. Add toppings if you like! What is the total cost?

2. Suppose Daria has a five-dollar bill and 4 quarters. What money should she give the clerk? What should her change be?

Single	$1.49
Double	$1.99
Triple	$2.49
Nuts	10¢
Sprinkles	5¢

For Extra Practice, see Set B, page 33.

Developing Skills for Problem Solving

First read for understanding and then focus on whether numbers are exact or estimates.

READ FOR UNDERSTANDING

Mount Rushmore National Memorial, the famous sculpture of 4 American presidents, was started in 1927. It was finished 14 years later and cost almost $1,000,000 to make! Mount Rushmore is over 5,500 feet high. Each head is about 60 feet tall.

1. In what year was the sculpture started?

2. How tall is each president's head?

3. How many presidents are on Mount Rushmore?

▲ **Social Studies Connection**
Mount Rushmore National Memorial is in the Black Hills of South Dakota.

THINK AND DISCUSS

MATH FOCUS

Exact Numbers or Estimates Estimates are not exact numbers. To identify estimates, look for numbers that have been rounded, or look for word clues such as *almost*, *over*, or *about*.

Reread the paragraph at the top of the page.

4. Is the year 1927 an exact number or an estimate? How do you know?

5. Is it correct to say that the sculpture cost exactly $1,000,000 to make? Why or why not?

6. In what year was the sculpture completed? Is your answer an exact answer or an estimate?

7. Why is it important to be able to know if numbers are exact or if they are estimates?

Show What You Learned

Answer each question. Give a reason for your choice.

Mount Rushmore National Memorial is off Highway 244 and is about 25 miles from Rapid City, South Dakota. The memorial is open 24 hours a day. Each year, more than 2,500,000 people come to view the sculpture.

1 Which number below is used as an estimate?

  a. 2,500,000 visitors

  b. Highway 244

  c. 24 hours a day

2 Which number below is used as an exact number?

  a. 2,500,000 visitors

  b. 25 miles

  c. 24 hours a day

3 How many miles is Mount Rushmore from Rapid City?

  a. exactly 25 miles

  b. about 25 miles

  c. 244 miles

4 Which of the following is true?

  a. The memorial is closed at night.

  b. The memorial is never closed.

  c. The memorial is open only during the day.

About 17 miles south of Mount Rushmore is the Crazy Horse Memorial. Crazy Horse was a Lakota chief who led and won two famous battles in 1876 for the Lakota homeland.

5 Which number below is used as an estimate?

  a. 17 miles

  b. two battles

  c. 1876

▲ **Social Studies Connection**
Crazy, in the Lakota language, means "spirited." This model of the *Crazy Horse Memorial* shows how the finished sculpture on the mountain in the background will look.

6 **Explain** How do you know that your answer to Problem 5 is an estimate?

7 **Journal Idea** When might the number 30 be used as an exact number in everyday life? When might it be used as an estimate?

Checkpoint

Understanding Place Value

Write each number in short word form and standard form. (pages 4–7)

1. one thousand four hundred thirty-six

2. eight hundred thirty thousand, thirty-eight

3. five thousand, two hundred seventy-nine

4. forty-nine thousand, six hundred seventy-three

5. four hundred sixty-three thousand, nine hundred twenty-two

What do you think?
When comparing two numbers, when must the left-most digits be compared first?

Write the value of each underlined digit. (pages 4–7)

6. 8,<u>4</u>05   7. 1<u>6</u>,296   8. <u>3</u>26,915   9. <u>4</u>5,678   10. 6,3<u>2</u>5   11. 6<u>8</u>7,312

Using Algebra **Use place value to continue the pattern.** (pages 4–7)

12. 236; 336; 436; ▧ ; ▧ ; ▧

13. 4,721; 5,721; 6,721; ▧ ; ▧ ; ▧

14. 22,453; 23,453; 24,453; ▧ ; ▧ ; ▧

15. 132,600; 142,600; 152,600; ▧ ; ▧ ; ▧

16. 75,600; 74,600; 73,600; ▧ ; ▧ ; ▧

Compare. Use > or < for ⬤. (pages 8–11)

17. 378 ⬤ 392   18. 88,452 ⬤ 88,542   19. 713,564 ⬤ 713,518

20. 30,945 ⬤ 3,945   21. 14,678 ⬤ 114,524   22. 6,184 ⬤ 6,129

Order these numbers from least to greatest. (pages 8–11)

23. 15,672   26,931   19,542   24. 763   1,053   673

25. 83,036   83,003   81,936   26. 1,672   354   245   1,762

Problem Solving

Use the table for Problems 27–29.

27. List the states in order of population from the least to the greatest.

29. Which two states have a population between 600,000 and 650,000?

30. **Analyze** Write the least number you can make using the digits 6, 3, 7, 1, and 4, each only once. Explain how you know the number is the least.

Journal Idea

List examples of newspaper articles that include numbers in word or standard form.

28. **Social Studies Connection** Which state's population is exactly 100,000 greater than Alaska's?

State Populations	
State	**Population**
Alaska	606,000
Vermont	580,000
Wyoming	476,000
South Dakota	721,000
North Dakota	638,000
Delaware	706,000

Critical Thinking Corner

Visual Thinking

Counting on an Abacus

Social Studies Connection The abacus was first used in China over 1,800 years ago. To show a number on the abacus, beads are pushed toward the crossbar.

- Beads above the crossbar are worth 5.

- Beads below the crossbar are worth 1.

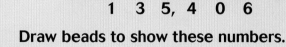

1 3 5, 4 0 6

What numbers are shown below?

1.

2.

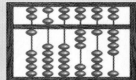

Draw beads to show these numbers.

3. 575

4. 10,251

5. 562,048

6. 4,792

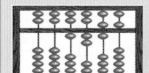

5

How Big Is a Million?

You can use a thousand to estimate a million.

Learning About It

Can you picture a million of something? Try to picture a million sneakers lined up heel to toe. If the line of sneakers started in Washington, D.C., it would stretch to Philadelphia, more than 125 miles away!

Work with a partner. Explore a million.

Step 1 You can use paper clips as a way to picture about a million of something.

- Place a box of 100 paper clips on a desk.

- Collect enough boxes of 100 paper clips from other groups to make 1,000 paper clips. Place the boxes in a row.

- How many boxes of 100 make 1,000?

What You Need

For each pair:
 box of 100 paper clips
 reading book
 calculator

1,000,000

16

Step 2 How many rows of these paper-clip boxes do you need to have 1,000,000 paper clips?

• To find out, copy and complete a chart like the one below.

Row of Paper-Clip Boxes	Number of Paper Clips
1 row	1,000
10 rows	10,000
100 rows	
1,000 rows	

Think and Discuss How many 1,000s make 1,000,000? Explain how you know.

Practice

Work with a partner and a reading book.

1. Guess how many words are in your reading book. Then use these hints to make an estimate.

    • About how many words are on one page?

    • How many pages would add up to 1,000 words?

    • How many 1,000-word groups are in your book?

2. How many books would it take to contain a million words?

    • Remember, a million is 1,000 thousands.

    • How many books like yours would contain 1,000 thousand-word groups?

3. **Language Arts Connection** What is meant by these commonly used expressions?

    • "I have a million things to do!"

    • "They must be millionaires!"

    • "You look like a million dollars!"

    • "Your chances are one in a million!"

Did You Know?

• A factory can produce 300,000 pairs of sneakers daily.

• About 74,000,000 pairs of sneakers are sold each year in the United States.

• Americans spend almost $2 billion a year for sneakers.

Popping Millions

You can read and write numbers in the millions.

Learning About It

The largest box of popcorn was filled by students at the Beauclerc School in Jacksonville, Florida. The box contained about 25,334,000 pieces of popcorn!

25,334,000

MILLIONS			THOUSANDS			ONES		
hundred millions	ten millions	millions	hundred thousands	ten thousands	thousands	hundreds	tens	ones
	2	5,	3	3	4,	0	0	0

Say: 25 million, 334 thousand

THERE'S ALWAYS A WAY! You can write a number in different ways.

- **word form**: twenty-five million, three hundred thirty-four thousand

- **short word form**: 25 million, 334 thousand

- **standard form**: 25,334,000

▲ Kid Connection
Beauclerc School students popped corn and filled the world's largest popcorn box. They estimated the number of pieces in the box and the student with the closest guess won a bicycle.

Think and Discuss Each period in the chart has the same pattern of place-value names. What is the pattern? How does the pattern help you to read the numbers?

Try It Out

Write each number in word form and short word form.

1. 7,549,437   **2.** 56,700,000   **3.** 120,000,550

▲ Students took 6 days to pop all that corn. Most of it was donated to charities. Some of the popcorn was taken by a truck to a pig farm to feed the pigs.

Practice

Write the standard form for each number.

4. fifty-seven million, forty thousand, thirty

5. two hundred sixty-nine million

6. five million, two hundred thousand

7. four hundred fifteen thousand

Write the word form and the short word form.

8. 13,440,000   **9.** 5,675,110   **10.** 240,000,000   **11.** 1,001,000

Give the value of the 2 in each number.

12. 2,454,867   **13.** 35,421,756   **14.** 726,000,000   **15.** 3,040,002

16. 8,466,278   **17.** 1,247,563   **18.** 263,554,735   **19.** 856,125

Problem Solving

Use the table to answer Problems 20–22.

20. Which states sold between 4 million and 8 million pounds of popcorn?

21. Order the amounts of popcorn sold from the least amount to the greatest. List the states in the same order.

22. Create Your Own Write a problem by using the information in the table.

Pounds of Popcorn Sold in 1995	
State	**Pounds of Popcorn**
Illinois	4,959,000
Kentucky	9,422,360
Nebraska	5,723,399
Ohio	2,252,430

Review and Remember

Choose a Method Use mental math or paper and pencil to solve. Tell why you chose the method you used.

23. $\begin{array}{r} 18 \\ + 9 \\ \hline \end{array}$ **24.** $\begin{array}{r} 15 \\ - 7 \\ \hline \end{array}$ **25.** $\begin{array}{r} 22 \\ + 3 \\ \hline \end{array}$ **26.** $\begin{array}{r} 41 \\ - 3 \\ \hline \end{array}$ **27.** $\begin{array}{r} 35 \\ + 6 \\ \hline \end{array}$ **28.** $\begin{array}{r} 14 \\ - 5 \\ \hline \end{array}$

For Extra Practice, see Set C, page 33.

Number Search

Place value can help you describe some number patterns.

Learning About It

Work with your partner.

Step 1 Arrange your base-ten blocks as shown below.

- What numbers do each of these models show?

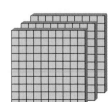 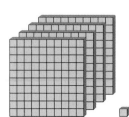

- What is the same about these models? What is different?

- Describe the pattern that these numbers follow. Use your blocks to model the numbers in this pattern that come before 201 and after 401.

- Do you think 1,001 is part of the pattern? Explain.

Step 2 Now model 104, 214, and 324.

- What is the same about each model?

- Look for differences and patterns. How do the hundreds change? How do the tens change?

Think and Discuss How would you make the next three numbers in the pattern?

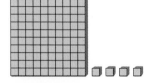 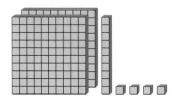 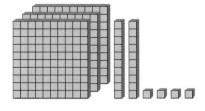

What You Need

For each pair:
  base-ten blocks
  6 hundreds
  12 tens
  12 ones

Practice

Use only tens and ones blocks.

1. Think of a number pattern. Model the first four numbers in your pattern. List the numbers.

2. **Predict** What are the next three numbers in your pattern?

Look at the numbers in the cloud.

3. What is the same about these numbers? What is different?

4. List the numbers in the cloud in order from least to greatest. Then fill in the numbers that are needed to complete the pattern.

2,999
5,999
6,999
1,999

Critical Thinking Corner

Logical Thinking

Pattern Search

Using Algebra Find the patterns. Then write the missing numbers.

1. 1, 4, 3, 6, 5, ▪, ▪

2. 5, 6, 4, 5, 3, ▪, ▪

3. 50, ▪, 40, 45, 30, 35, ▪

4. 100, 98, 97, 95, 94, ▪, ▪

Problem Solving
Find a Pattern

Finding a pattern can help you solve problems.

A fluffy chick grows from a single cell in a chicken egg. The cell divides into two cells. The two cells divide into four cells. The four cells divide into eight cells and so on. How many cells are there after eight divisions?

 UNDERSTAND

What do you need to find?

You need to find the total number of cells after eight cell divisions.

 PLAN

How can you solve the problem?

You can **find a pattern**. Look at the number of cells there are each time the cells divide.

 SOLVE

Look at the numbers in the pattern.

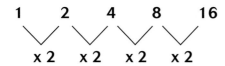

The cell doubles each time there is a cell division. So the pattern for eight divisions will look like this.

1   2   4   8   16   32   64   128   **256**

After 8 cell divisions, there will be 256 cells.

LOOK BACK

Is there another way to describe the pattern above?

Start
1 cell

1st Division
2 cells

2nd Division
4 cells

3rd Division
8 cells

4th Division
16 cells

Using the Strategy

Find a pattern to help you solve each problem.

1 **What If?** Suppose the pattern in the wall below continues? How many bricks will be in the fifth layer?

2 Suppose you have 28 shells. How many rows can you make if you continue the pattern shown below?

3 Tom lines up 16 rocks in his rock collection. The rocks follow this pattern: big, little, little, big, little, little, and so on. Is the last rock big or little?

4 **Analyze** Suppose you save $1.00 in January, $2.00 in February, and $3.00 in March. If you continue this pattern, how much money will you have saved in a year?

5 Marta's number pattern begins with 1, 3, 6, 10, 15. What are the next four numbers in her pattern?

6 Each house on a street has an odd number. If the first house is number 1, what number is the eighth house?

Mixed Strategy Review

Try these or other strategies to solve each problem. Tell which strategy you used.

THERE'S ALWAYS A WAY!

Problem Solving Strategies

- *Find a Pattern*
- *Guess and Check*
- *Draw a Diagram*
- *Solve a Simpler Problem*

7 Together, Jill and Keesha have 17 shells. Jill has 5 more shells than Keesha. How many shells does each girl have?

8 Jeremy writes these numbers: 1,290; 1,379; 1,468; 1,557. If he continues the pattern, what will the next three numbers be?

9 **Analyze** Clint makes a square array with 4 rows and 4 columns of rocks. He takes some rocks away. What is the least number of rocks he could take away and still have a square array?

In the Round

When you report amounts, you can often use rounded numbers instead of exact amounts.

Learning About It

Buttons have been ordered for the Juneteenth volunteers. So far, 37 students have signed up. About how many students is that, rounded to the nearest ten?

Round 37 to the nearest ten. Use a number line.

37 is between 30 and 40.

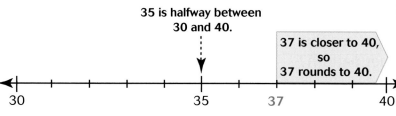

35 is halfway between 30 and 40.

37 is closer to 40, so 37 rounds to 40.

About 40 students have volunteered.

What if only 34 students volunteered? About how many students would that be, rounded to the nearest ten?

34 is between 30 and 40.

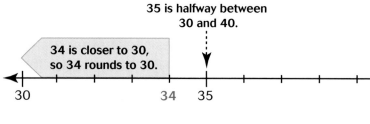

35 is halfway between 30 and 40.

34 is closer to 30, so 34 rounds to 30.

About 30 students would have volunteered.

Think and Discuss Thirty-five is halfway between 30 and 40. How does knowing the halfway point between tens help you round?

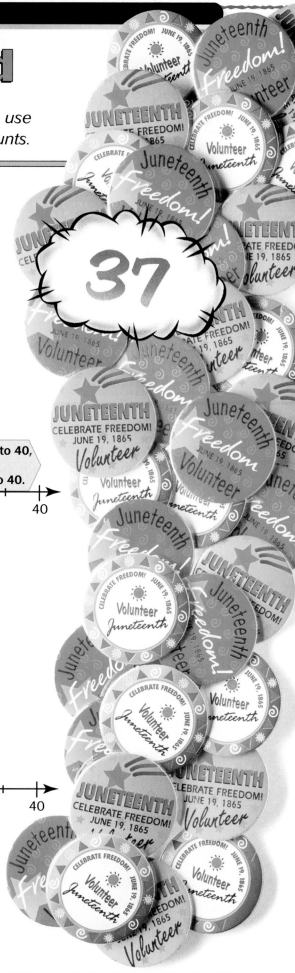

More Examples

Round 750 to the nearest hundred.

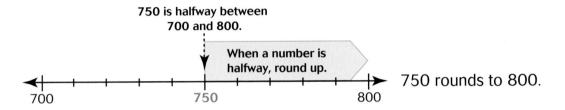

750 is halfway between 700 and 800.

When a number is halfway, round up.

700   750   800

750 rounds to 800.

Round 52,382 to the nearest thousand. 52,382 is between 52,000 and 53,000.

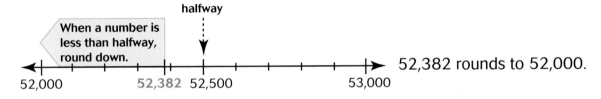

halfway

When a number is less than halfway, round down.

52,000   52,382 52,500   53,000

52,382 rounds to 52,000.

Connecting Ideas

You can also round numbers without using a number line.
You can use the rounding rule.

Round 478 to the nearest hundred.

Step 1 Find the rounding place.	**Step 2** Look at the digit to its right. If it is 5 or more, round up.
<u>4</u>78	<u>4</u>78 478 rounds to 500.

Round 7,263 to the nearest thousand.

Step 1 Find the thousands place.	**Step 2** Look at the digit to its right. If it is less than 5, round down.
<u>7</u>,263	<u>7</u>,263 7,263 rounds to 7,000.

Try It Out

Name the two tens, hundreds, or thousands that each number is between.

1. 53   **2.** 15   **3.** 79   **4.** 512   **5.** 3,644

Round each number to the nearest ten, nearest hundred, and nearest thousand.

6. 4,854   **7.** 8,243   **8.** 9,425   **9.** 7,912   **10.** 4,869

Round each number to the underlined place.

11. <u>7</u>6   **12.** 8<u>3</u>3   **13.** 9<u>8</u>9   **14.** <u>3</u>50   **15.** <u>6</u>,801

Practice

Round to the underlined place.

16. <u>7</u>4   **17.** <u>5</u>8   **18.** <u>8</u>5   **19.** <u>8</u>3   **20.** <u>9</u>3

21. <u>3</u>1   **22.** <u>9</u>7   **23.** <u>7</u>9   **24.** <u>7</u>5   **25.** <u>8</u>8

26. <u>1</u>23   **27.** <u>8</u>62   **28.** <u>3</u>15   **29.** <u>6</u>96   **30.** <u>4</u>85

31. <u>4</u>53   **32.** <u>7</u>78   **33.** <u>6</u>89   **34.** <u>2</u>33   **35.** 7<u>1</u>3

36. <u>1</u>,715   **37.** 5,<u>4</u>75   **38.** <u>6</u>,562   **39.** <u>3</u>,470   **40.** 9,<u>0</u>25

41. 4<u>8</u>,253   **42.** 6<u>1</u>,744   **43.** 10<u>3</u>,502   **44.** 239,8<u>7</u>5   **45.** 186,<u>0</u>93

46. Journal Idea A number rounded to the nearest ten is 70. What numbers might you have rounded?

Problem Solving

Use the table to fill in the rounded numbers for Problems 47–50. Explain why your answers are reasonable.

47. Total attendance at the Juneteenth celebration was about ___?___.

48. About ___?___ people went on the Multicultural Trail Ride.

Juneteenth Celebration	
Activity	**Number of People**
Multicultural Trail Ride	75
Sunken Garden Theater	715
African American Art Exhibit	1,099
Total Attendance	1,889

49. At least ___?___ people enjoyed the African American Art Exhibit.

50. Storytelling in the Sunken Garden had an audience of about ___?___.

51. **What If?** Suppose an additional 755 people came to a concert in the Sunken Garden. Is this about 700 or about 800 people? Why?

52. At the Juneteenth celebration, 1,225 ears of corn were served. About how many ears is that, rounded to the nearest hundred?

53. **Analyze** What is the greatest two-digit whole number that will round to a two-digit number when rounded to the nearest ten?

54. **Using Algebra** Use these clues to find the mystery number.

- It is greater than 100 and less than 151.

- It is 200 when rounded to the nearest hundred.

55. Round the numbers in the cloud to their greatest places. Then add the rounded numbers and subtract 1,000. What is left?

▲ **Fine Arts Connection**
The *Purple Quilt* shown above, was created by Faith Ringgold, an artist who uses paintings and quilted fabrics to tell stories. She has used many of her quilts to illustrate her books, such as the award-winning *Tar Beach.*

108   77
532
12   11
256

Review and Remember

Write the value of each underlined digit.

56. 7<u>6</u>8 **57.** <u>3</u>05 **58.** 6,90<u>7</u> **59.** <u>9</u>,743 **60.** 5,1<u>2</u>8 **61.** 1,0<u>2</u>5

62. 8,5<u>4</u>3 **63.** 5,78<u>9</u> **64.** 2,<u>8</u>00 **65.** <u>3</u>,400 **66.** 7,0<u>9</u>0 **67.** 7,<u>1</u>9

68. <u>7</u>4 **69.** 1<u>8</u>6 **70.** <u>4</u>,007 **71.** 5,1<u>1</u>9 **72.** <u>8</u>41 **73.** 9<u>4</u>

74. 1<u>0</u>,000 **75.** 48<u>7</u> **76.** <u>7</u>,213 **77.** 1<u>1</u>1 **78.** 3<u>8</u> **79.** <u>9</u>75

Problem Solving
Using a Bar Graph

You can use the information from a bar graph to solve a problem.

Some dog owners were asked what kinds of dogs they own. The results of the survey are shown in the graph. How many more people own retrievers than spaniels?

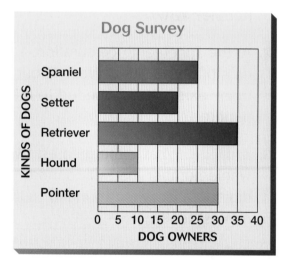

Dog Survey

KINDS OF DOGS — Spaniel, Setter, Retriever, Hound, Pointer

DOG OWNERS — 0 5 10 15 20 25 30 35 40

 UNDERSTAND

What do you need to find?

You need to find the difference between the number of people who own retrievers and the number of people who own spaniels.

 PLAN

How can you solve the problem?

Find the two bars you need to compare. Read the number scale for each bar. Subtract to compare the numbers.

 SOLVE

The bar for retriever owners shows 35. The bar for spaniel owners shows 25.

$35 - 25 = 10$

So, 10 more people own retrievers.

 LOOK BACK

Could you have solved this problem without subtracting? Explain why or why not.

Show What You Learned

Use the bar graph on page 28 for Problems 1–4.

1 Which kind of dog was owned the least?

2 **What If?** Suppose half of all the hounds that people owned were tan. How many people owned tan hounds?

3 Do more people own spaniels or pointers? how many more?

4 **Analyze** Twice as many people own setters as own hounds. Is this statement correct? Explain why or why not.

Retriever   Hound   Spaniel

Use the bar graph at the right for Problems 5–8.

5 Which dog food is most popular? least popular?

6 How many more dog owners use dry cereal than use moist cereal?

7 **Analyze** How many dog owners answered the survey?

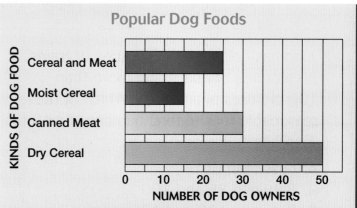

8 **Create Your Own** Use the information in the graph to write a problem about what dog owners like to feed their pets. Ask a classmate to solve the problem.

Problem Solving

★ ★ ★ ★ ★ **Preparing for Tests**

Practice What You Learned

Choose the correct letter for each answer.

1 Kelly's town has about 25,000 people. Sue Ann's town has about twice as many people as Kelly's town. Which of these represents a reasonable number for the number of people in Sue Ann's town?

A. 5,000
B. 25,000
C. 50,000
D. 500,000

Tip

Sometimes you can eliminate some answer choices. Why can you eliminate Choices A and B in this problem?

---

2 Tim made ten tickets for a drawing. He numbered the first five tickets this way: 101, 121, 141, 161, 181. If he continues this pattern, what will be the numbers of the next three tickets?

A. 201, 221, 241
B. 191, 211, 221
C. 191, 201, 211
D. 182, 183, 184

Tip

You can use the *Find a Pattern* strategy to help you solve this problem.

---

3 Juan has collected 59 pictures of trains, 26 pictures of boats, and more than 100 pictures of airplanes. Which of these is reasonable for the total number of pictures Juan has collected?

A. Less than 85
B. Between 85 and 100
C. Between 100 and 185
D. More than 185

Tip

Words like *more than*, *almost*, and *about* tell you that numbers are estimated, not exact.

4 Paula has a collection of 58 blue marbles, 29 red marbles, and 12 green marbles. **About** how many marbles does she have in all?

A. 90
B. 100
C. 110
D. 120

5 Ruth is taller than Jake. Jake is shorter than Sally. Carlos is taller than Ruth. Which of the following is a reasonable conclusion?

A. Ruth is the tallest.
B. Carlos is taller than Jake.
C. Sally is shorter than Jake.
D. Carlos is the shortest.

6 Maria measured two ribbons. One ribbon was 620 cm long and the other was 260 cm long. Which number sentence can be used to find the difference in the lengths of the ribbons?

A. 260 cm − 620 cm = ▩
B. 620 cm − 260 cm = ▩
C. 260 cm + 620 cm = ▩
D. 260 cm + 260 cm = ▩

7 Lee's car travels about 39 miles on one gallon of gas. **About** how far can the car travel on 3 gallons of gas?

A. 40 miles
B. 80 miles
C. 120 miles
D. 140 miles

8 In a 500-piece jigsaw puzzle, 84 pieces are green and 129 pieces are blue. How many pieces are **NOT** blue?

A. 213
B. 287
C. 371
D. 381

Use the graph for Problems 9 and 10.

This graph shows how students get to school each day.

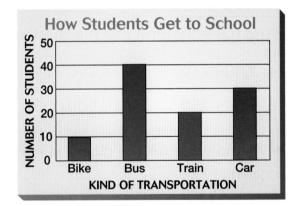

9 How many more students take a bus to school than ride bikes to school?

A. 30
B. 25
C. 20
D. 15

10 On rainy days, students who usually ride bikes to school come by car instead. How many students come to school by car on rainy days?

A. 10
B. 20
C. 30
D. 40

✔ Checkpoint

Place Value Through Millions

Vocabulary

Match each number with its name in the Word Bank.

1. 1,000,000 + 400,000 + 70,000

2. nine million, two hundred seven thousand, six hundred twelve

3. 50,503,742

Word Bank

expanded form
standard form
word form

Concepts and Skills

Write the word form and the short word form. (pages 18–19)

4. 2,400,210
5. 12,290,124
6. 23,110,000
7. 125,000,000

8. 1,005,250
9. 10,000,000
10. 113,007
11. 900,950

Write the value for the digit 1 in each number.
(pages 18–19)

12. 4,387,164
13. 12,847,629
14. 158,984,635
15. 1,473,984

Round to the underlined place. (pages 24–27)

16. 6̲3
17. 9̲5
18. 8̲4
19. 3̲6
20. 9̲9
21. 5̲9

22. 89̲2
23. 6̲74
24. 1̲23
25. 81̲5
26. 9̲60
27. 41̲5

28. 1,4̲63
29. 4̲,598
30. 1,0̲98
31. 9,3̲51
32. 9̲99
33. 2̲48

Mixed Practice

Write each number in short word form and standard form.

34. five thousand, two hundred thirty-six

35. one million, four hundred seventy thousand

36. one hundred sixty thousand, two hundred twenty-five

What do you think?
How does knowing the halfway number help you to round to the nearest ten or hundred?

Problem Solving

37. A picture puzzle has 2,475 pieces. How many pieces does the puzzle have, rounded to the nearest thousand? the nearest ten?

38. Explain If someone said, "I couldn't do that in a million years," would they mean exactly 1,000,000? What would they mean?

39. Analyze The Rose Bowl seats 103,839 people. The Sugar Bowl seats 80,895. Round both numbers to their greatest place. Then estimate how many more seats there are in the Rose Bowl than in the Sugar Bowl.

40. The highest mountains in Japan, Canada, and the United States are Mt. Fuji, 12,385 feet; Mt. Logan, 19,844 feet; and Mt. McKinley, 20,300 feet. List these three mountains from the highest elevation to the lowest.

Journal Idea

Write down your telephone number. How many digits are in the number? What number does your telephone number make? Write the number in word form.

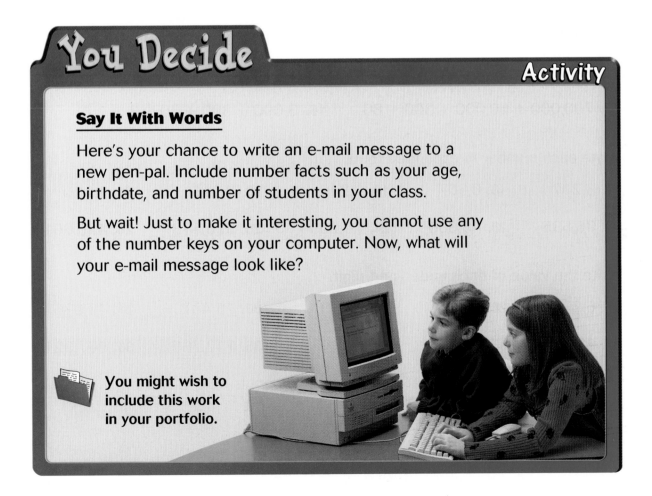

You Decide

Activity

Say It With Words

Here's your chance to write an e-mail message to a new pen-pal. Include number facts such as your age, birthdate, and number of students in your class.

But wait! Just to make it interesting, you cannot use any of the number keys on your computer. Now, what will your e-mail message look like?

You might wish to include this work in your portfolio.

Extra Practice

Write each number in standard form.

1. four thousand, two hundred twenty-two

2. sixty-five thousand

3. ten thousand, six hundred five

4. one thousand, four hundred twelve

5. seven hundred eighty-five thousand

6. four hundred fifty thousand, five

7. $6,000 + 500 + 20 + 2$

8. $2,000 + 10$

9. $5,000 + 400 + 60$

10. $600,000 + 2,000 + 400$

11. $4,000 + 300 + 4$

12. $300,000 + 10,000 + 600 + 9$

13. $30,000 + 3,000 + 200 + 70 + 5$

14. $10,000 + 7$

15. $700,000 + 60,000 + 300 + 80$

16. $3,000 + 300 + 30 + 3$

Write each number in expanded form.

17. 3,217   18. 6,507   19. 1,249   20. 8,016   21. 7,120

22. 35,535   23. 48,600   24. 70,209   25. 516,573   26. 430,001

Write the value of each underlined digit.

27. 6,<u>2</u>93   28. <u>2</u>,176   29. 5,79<u>8</u>   30. <u>1</u>5,437   31. 49,0<u>3</u>6

32. 68,<u>7</u>03   33. <u>3</u>3,491   34. <u>5</u>76,439   35. 1<u>1</u>2,786   36. 807,<u>9</u>21

37. Georgia produces about 175,000 tons of peanuts each year. Write this number in word form, short word form, and expanded form.

Extra Practice

Set B (pages 8-11)

Compare. Use > and < for ⬤.

1. 5,672 ⬤ 5,665
2. 4,532 ⬤ 492
3. 7,064 ⬤ 7,345

4. 31,735 ⬤ 51,357
5. 345,238 ⬤ 345,392
6. 76,497 ⬤ 7,407

7. 675,432 ⬤ 75,948
8. 26,755 ⬤ 26,759
9. 905 ⬤ 950

Order each set from least to greatest.

10. 702   891   640   752
11. 652   675   631   644

12. 3,215   3,346   3,129   3,285
13. 54,769   53,896   51,703

14. 9,075   9,175   9,005   9,705
15. 78,076   76,067   77,165

16. Write six four-digit numbers using the digits 2, 4, 6, and 8. Each number should begin with the digit 2. Then order the numbers from greatest to least.

Set C (pages 18-19)

Write each number in standard form.

1. four million, two hundred forty thousand

2. three hundred ten million

3. fifty-four million, five hundred thousand, two hundred

4. ten million, three hundred twenty-five thousand, six hundred five

5. eight million, four hundred thirty-two thousand, one hundred seventy-five

Write the value of the 5 in each number.

6. 3,256,017
7. 10,536,422
8. 5,438,978

9. 54,100,342
10. 36,783,546
11. 526,723,784

12. Illinois sold 4,959,000 pounds of popcorn in 1995. What is the value of each 9 in the number?

Extra Practice

Set D (pages 24–27)

Write the two tens, hundreds, or thousands
that the number is between.

1. 26   2. 83   3. 240   4. 678   5. 6,587

6. 4,920   7. 892   8. 55   9. 592   10. 3,782

Round to the nearest ten.

11. 63   12. 89   13. 75   14. 223   15. 548

16. 36   17. 609   18. 533   19. 7   20. 66

Round to the nearest hundred.

21. 652   22. 589   23. 328   24. 2,276   25. 6,089

26. 7,899   27. 3,481   28. 979   29. 430   30. 1,206

31. 85   32. 462   33. 1,702   34. 549   35. 8,215

Round to the nearest thousand.

36. 801   37. 7,099   38. 18,505   39. 9,775   40. 4,295

41. 6,452   42. 2,103   43. 5,675   44. 3,524   45. 8,078

46. 3,501   47. 7,817   48. 4,600   49. 1,399   50. 7,633

51. Suppose 1,672 people came to a Juneteenth celebration.
About how many people attended, rounded to the
nearest ten? Rounded to the nearest hundred?

52. Suppose about 100 people bought hot dogs. If you made
this estimate an exact number, what is the least number
and the greatest number of hot dogs sold?

Chapter Test

Write each number in standard form.

1. seventy-six thousand

2. thirty-five thousand, four hundred ten

3. six million, two hundred thousand

4. one hundred twenty-two thousand

5. three hundred fifty million

6. six thousand, four hundred sixty-five

Order each set from least to greatest.

7. 673   681   679   670

8. 3,247   3,374   3,241   3,369

9. 41,620   4,620   41,026

10. 75,003   74,302   75,032

Write the value of 5 in each number.

11. 1,659   **12.** 25,137   **13.** 156,748   **14.** 5,703,216   **15.** 7,563

Write the next three numbers in the pattern.

16. 909   808   707   **17.** 214   324   434   **18.** 2,155   3,255   4,355

Round to the underlined place.

19. 7̲5   **20.** 6̲84   **21.** 34̲2   **22.** 2,4̲67   **23.** 4̲,327

Solve.

24. Write six four-digit numbers, using the digits 1, 2, 3, and 4. Each number should begin with the digit 1. Then order the numbers from greatest to least.

25. Suppose you went into the bean bag business. It takes 1,000 beans to fill each bean bag. How many beans would you need to fill 1,000 bean bags?

 Self-Check

To find out if you understand place value, write the number 1,234,567. Read the number aloud. Then name the value of each digit.

Performance Assessment

Show What You Know About Numbers

1 Use the numbers 4,606 and 6,440.

a. Write the lesser number in as many ways as you can.

b. Round the greater number to the nearest thousand.

Self-Check Did you remember to look at the hundreds place when you rounded the greater number?

2 Find the mystery number. Use the following clues.

a. It's a four-digit number with a 4 in the ones place.

b. The tens place is twice the ones place.

c. The ones place and the thousands place are the same number.

d. The thousands place is twice the hundreds place.

Self-Check Does your answer work with all four clues?

3 Write two stories that include numbers. In the first story, make 500 a lesser number. In the second story, make 500 a greater number.

Self-Check Did you read over your stories to check that they made sense?

 For Your Portfolio

You might wish to include this work in your portfolio.

Extension

Roman Numerals

The ancient Romans used these seven letters to write numbers. Numbers written with these letters are called Roman numerals.

You add to find the number of some Roman numerals.

II	VII	XII	LX	DC
1 + 1	5 + 1 + 1	10 + 1 + 1	50 + 10	500 + 100
2	7	12	60	600

$I = 1$
$V = 5$
$X = 10$
$L = 50$
$C = 100$
$D = 500$
$M = 1,000$

You subtract to find the number for other Roman numerals.

IV	IX	XL	XC	CD
5 − 1	10 − 1	50 − 10	100 − 10	500 − 100
4	9	40	90	400

Here are some other examples.

III	XIV	XLV	XCV	CDII
1 + 1 + 1	10 + 4	40 + 5	90 + 5	400 + 2
3	14	45	95	402

Write the standard number.

1. VIII   **2.** LX   **3.** XV   **4.** XX   **5.** MD

6. XXXV   **7.** XIII   **8.** MC   **9.** XXIV   **10.** CLX

Write the Roman numeral.

11. 6   **12.** 17   **13.** 55   **14.** 26   **15.** 71

16. 40   **17.** 700   **18.** 95   **19.** 1,300   **20.** 1,600

Cumulative Review

★ ★ ★ ★ ★ **Preparing for Tests**

Choose the correct letter for each answer.

Number Concepts	**Operations**

1. What number is equal to forty-nine thousand, six hundred seventy?

   A. 4,967
   B. 49,670
   C. 490,067
   D. 490,607

2. What is 569 rounded to the nearest ten?

   A. 500
   B. 560
   C. 570
   D. 600

3. Which shaded region does **NOT** represent $\frac{1}{2}$?

   A.   **C.**

   B.   **D.**

4. What is 5,854 rounded to the nearest hundred?

   A. 6,000
   B. 5,900
   C. 5,800
   D. 5,000

5. Martin has 4 quarters and 2 dimes. How much will he have left if he spends a quarter?

   A. $0.42
   B. $0.59
   C. $0.95
   D. $1.20

6. Marisa bought two boxes of crackers for 99¢ each and a pound of grapes for $1.29. **About** how much did she spend?

   A. $1.00
   B. $1.50
   C. $2.00
   D. $3.00

7. Sam practices the piano 2 hours every day. How many hours does he practice in 7 days?

   A. 21
   B. 14
   C. 9
   D. 5

8. What is the difference between 4,000 and 532?

   A. 3,578
   B. 3,568
   C. 3,472
   D. 3,468

Patterns, Relationships, and Algebraic Thinking	Measurement

9. If 3 times a number is 27, which expression could be used to find the number?

A. 3 × 27
B. 27 ÷ 3
C. 3 + 27
D. 27 − 3

10. Which number sentence is in the same family of facts as 6 × 4 = 24?

A. 24 − 6 = 18
B. 4 + 6 = 10
C. 24 × 4 = 96
D. 24 ÷ 6 = 4

11. What is the missing number in this number pattern?

3, 6, 9, 12, ■, 18, 21

A. 13
B. 15
C. 16
D. 23

12. What is the missing number?

Number of Birds	Number of Legs
1	2
2	4
3	6
4	■

A. 4
B. 7
C. 8
D. 10

13. Tony has a toy robot that is 1 foot 6 inches tall. How many *inches* tall is that? (Hint: 1 foot equals 12 inches.)

A. 12 in.
B. 18 in.
C. 20 in.
D. 24 in.

14. Look at the thermometer. What is the temperature?

A. 23°C
B. 24°C
C. 25°C
D. 27°C

15. What is the best estimate of the *area* of the shaded region?

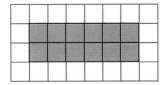

A. 2 square units
B. 6 square units
C. 12 square units
D. 16 square units

16. Tim left school at 3:05 P.M. It took him 17 minutes to get home. What time did Tim get home?

A. 3:12 P.M.
B. 3:17 P.M.
C. 3:22 P.M.
D. 3:25 P.M.

Chapter 2

Adding and Subtracting Whole Numbers and Money

Chapter Theme: FUN AND GAMES

....................**Real Facts**...................

On the TV game show *Figure It Out,* players stump a celebrity panel to win prizes! The number of phone calls and letters the show gets helps the producers decide how popular the program is. The graph below shows four months of calls for *Figure It Out.*

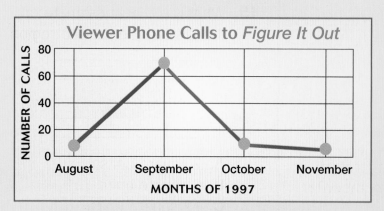

Viewer Phone Calls to *Figure It Out*

NUMBER OF CALLS

MONTHS OF 1997

- During which month did *Figure It Out* receive the most phone calls? the least?

- Based on the graph, how many phone calls do you predict the show will receive in December?

........**Real People**...................

Meet Magda Liolis Moshova (left) and Melinda Toporoff (right), two of the creators of *Figure It Out.* They enjoy coming up with ideas their audience will like.

Checkers Champ

*You can use a related fact or other facts that you know
to help you add and subtract basic facts.*

Learning About It

The object of checkers is to capture
or block the other person's pieces.
Tyler and Megan are playing a
game of checkers. Each
person started with
12 pieces. Tyler has
lost 7 pieces.
How many pieces
does he have left?

$12 - 7 = \blacksquare$

**Pieces Megan
won from Tyler**

- **One way** to find the answer is to use
a basic fact you already know.

  If you know that $12 - 6 = 6$,

  then $12 - 7$ is one less, or 5.

- **Another way** to find the answer is to
use a related fact.

  If you know $5 + 7 = 12$,

  then you know that $12 - 7 = 5$, because
it is a related fact.

Tyler has 5 pieces left.

Connecting Ideas

Fact families, showing related addition and subtraction facts, help you remember basic facts.

A fact family is two addition facts and two subtraction facts that use the same numbers.

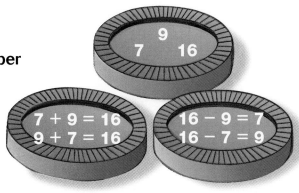

Think and Discuss How many facts would be in a fact family if two numbers were the same? Why?

INTERNET ACTIVITY
www.sbgmath.com

Try It Out

Add or subtract.

1. $3 + 4$ **2.** $8 + 7$ **3.** $9 - 5$ **4.** $17 - 9$ **5.** $5 + 6$

6. $\begin{array}{r} 9 \\ + 8 \\ \hline \end{array}$ **7.** $\begin{array}{r} 15 \\ - 9 \\ \hline \end{array}$ **8.** $\begin{array}{r} 17 \\ - 8 \\ \hline \end{array}$ **9.** $\begin{array}{r} 16 \\ - 7 \\ \hline \end{array}$ **10.** $\begin{array}{r} 6 \\ + 7 \\ \hline \end{array}$

Using Algebra **Find each sum or difference.**

11. $5 + 3 = \blacksquare$
$3 + 5 = \blacksquare$
$8 - 3 = \blacksquare$
$8 - 5 = \blacksquare$

12. $6 + 7 = \blacksquare$
$7 + 6 = \blacksquare$
$13 - 7 = \blacksquare$
$13 - 6 = \blacksquare$

13. $9 + \blacksquare = 12$
$\blacksquare - 3 = 9$
$12 - 9 = \blacksquare$
$3 + \blacksquare = 12$

14. $\blacksquare + 5 = 9$
$5 + \blacksquare = 9$
$\blacksquare - 5 = 4$
$9 - 4 = \blacksquare$

Practice

Add.

15. $2 + 4$ **16.** $5 + 2$ **17.** $7 + 1$ **18.** $3 + 4$

19. $\begin{array}{r} 9 \\ + 6 \\ \hline \end{array}$ **20.** $\begin{array}{r} 7 \\ + 8 \\ \hline \end{array}$ **21.** $\begin{array}{r} 7 \\ + 0 \\ \hline \end{array}$ **22.** $\begin{array}{r} 4 \\ + 6 \\ \hline \end{array}$

23. $\begin{array}{r} 5 \\ + 7 \\ \hline \end{array}$ **24.** $\begin{array}{r} 6 \\ + 5 \\ \hline \end{array}$ **25.** $\begin{array}{r} 3 \\ + 9 \\ \hline \end{array}$ **26.** $\begin{array}{r} 5 \\ + 8 \\ \hline \end{array}$

Social Studies Connection Each year, a national ➤ checkers championship is held at the International Checkerboard Hall of Fame in Mississippi. The hall has the world's largest floor-checkerboard.

Add.

27.   9
   + 9

28.   6
   + 8

29.   7
   + 9

30.   4
   + 4

31.   3
   + 0

Subtract.

32. $6 - 6$ **33.** $8 - 5$ **34.** $9 - 4$ **35.** $8 - 0$ **36.** $7 - 3$

37. 13
   − 9

38. 15
   − 6

39. 11
   − 5

40. 13
   − 8

41. 11
   − 1

42. 16
   − 8

43. 12
   − 9

44. 16
   − 7

45. 13
   − 6

46. 11
   − 3

47. 14
   − 6

48. 15
   − 8

49. 14
   − 8

50. 18
   − 9

51. 10
   − 4

Using Algebra Find each sum or difference.

52. $8 + 5 = \blacksquare$
$13 - \blacksquare = 5$
$5 + \blacksquare = 13$
$13 - 5 = \blacksquare$

53. $5 + \blacksquare = 9$
$\blacksquare - 5 = 4$
$4 + 5 = \blacksquare$
$9 - 5 = \blacksquare$

54. $15 - 7 = \blacksquare$
$\blacksquare + 7 = 15$
$15 - \blacksquare = 8$
$8 + 7 = \blacksquare$

55. $9 + \blacksquare = 15$
$15 - \blacksquare = 6$
$6 + 9 = \blacksquare$
$\blacksquare - 6 = 9$

Write the fact family.

56. 6, 8, 14   **57.** 9, 16, 7   **58.** 12, 9, 3   **59.** 5, 5, 10

◄ **Social Studies Connection**
In Senegal, Africa, people play on a checkerboard of 10-by-10 squares instead of 8-by-8 squares. Each player has 20 checkers instead of 12. Each piece may be moved backward as well as forward.

Problem Solving

60. At the end of a checkers game, Megan had won all 12 of Tyler's checkers. Tyler had won 9 of Megan's checkers. How many more checkers did Megan win than Tyler?

61. Megan's school had a checkers tournament. The first day Megan played 8 games. She played 7 games on the second day. How many games did she play in all?

62. **What If?** Suppose Megan won all but 6 of the games she played in the tournament. How many games did she win?

63. Players sat in groups of 4. Each player played 1 game with all group members. How many games did a group play? Explain your strategy to find the answer.

64. **Analyze** Each of the 8 rows on a checkerboard has 8 squares. Half of the squares are black, and half are red. How many black squares are on the checkerboard?

Review and Remember

Write the place value for the digit 3 in each number.

65. 132

66. 13,658

67. 3,265

68. 356,847

69. 3,485,261

70. 5,340

71. 403

72. 273,798

73. 35,147

74. 2,435,896

75. 3,045

76. 930

Critical Thinking Corner

Logical Thinking

Mystery Digits

Using Algebra Find the missing digits.

1.
```
   ▌2▌
+  4▌6
  775
```

2.
```
   5▌▌
+ ▌27
  932
```

3.
```
   3▌8
+ 25▌
  ▌32
```

4.
```
   ▌53
+ 5▌▌
 1,182
```

For Extra Practice, see Set A, page 76.

Bull's-Eye!

You can estimate sums and differences by rounding.

Learning About It

Jesse and Nora keep a running score as they play darts. So far, Jesse has scored 52 points, and Nora, 28. Estimate how many points they have scored altogether.

52
+ 28

Round to the nearest ten.

Add
50
+ 30
80

Jesse and Nora have scored about 80 points.

About how many more points has Jesse scored than Nora?

52
− 28

Round to the nearest ten.

Subtract
50
− 30
20

Jesse has scored about 20 more points than Nora.

52
Jesse's score

28
Nora's score

More Examples

A. Round to the nearest hundred.

343 ⇒ 300
+ 176 ⇒ + 200
500

476 ⇒ 500
− 325 ⇒ − 300
200

B. Round to the nearest dollar.

$4.67 ⇒ $5.00
+ 2.41 ⇒ + 2.00
$7.00

$8.17 ⇒ $8.00
− 2.68 ⇒ − 3.00
$5.00

Think and Discuss The sum of two numbers rounds to 50. One of the numbers is 23. What could the other number be?

Try It Out

Estimate by rounding to the greatest place value.

1.	37 + 21	**2.**	52 − 37	**3.**	86 − 43	**4.**	$5.29 + 3.76	**5.**	763 − 214

Practice

Estimate by rounding to the nearest ten.

6.	53 − 29	**7.**	66 − 17	**8.**	47 + 33	**9.**	84 − 46	**10.**	73 + 24

Estimate by rounding to the nearest hundred.

11.	631 + 167	**12.**	591 + 318	**13.**	534 − 423	**14.**	874 − 382	**15.**	372 + 244

Estimate by rounding to the nearest dollar.

16.	$6.57 − 2.16	**17.**	$9.34 − 4.69	**18.**	$7.17 + 1.75	**19.**	$5.42 + 2.35	**20.**	$10.73 − 5.14

Problem Solving

21. When Jesse finished playing darts, he had 195 points. Nora finished with 265. Estimate how many more points Nora scored.

22. Jesse wants to buy a new dart board and a box of target balls. Estimate what they will cost him altogether.

23. Journal Idea When would it be appropriate to find an estimated sum or difference instead of an exact answer? Explain your thinking.

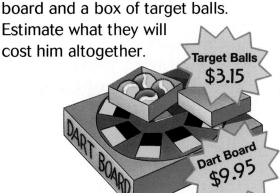

Target Balls
$3.15

Dart Board
$9.95

Review and Remember

Add or subtract.

24. 9 + 4

25. 12 − 8

26. 16 − 7

27. 8 + 6

28. 14 − 9

29. 10 + 10

30. 9 + 8

31. 9 − 9

For Extra Practice, see Set B, page 76.

Developing Skills for
Problem Solving

First read for understanding and then focus on whether you need an exact answer or an estimate to solve a problem.

READ FOR UNDERSTANDING

Smith School held a board-game tournament to raise money. Twenty-one teams each paid a fee of $22.00 to play. Eighteen girls and 19 boys volunteered to help run the event. Eighty-nine students each paid $2.00 to watch.

1. How many teams played in the tournament?

2. How much did each team pay to play in the tournament?

3. How many students paid to watch the event?

THINK AND DISCUSS

MATH FOCUS

Is an Estimate Enough? Sometimes you only need to estimate to solve a problem. If you are asked to find "about how many," or to decide "if there are enough," often you can estimate.

Reread the paragraph at the top of the page.

4. Would you estimate or find an exact answer to tell how much money the teams paid altogether to be in the tournament? Explain.

5. The school has 45 volunteer badges. Is that enough for all the volunteers? Can you estimate to solve this problem? Explain.

6. Why is it helpful to be able to solve a problem by using an estimate rather than an exact answer?

Show What You Learned

Answer each question. Give a reason for your choice.

One of the games at the tournament is a word game. Read the rules at the right. Yoshi picked 5 letters: *H, W, Y, E* and *N*. She could make either of the words shown below the rules.

RULES

Take turns.

Pick 5 letter tiles.

Make a word.

Add the points for each letter in your word. The points for each letter are shown on the tile.

The sum of the points in your word is your score.

1 What is the best way for Yoshi to decide which word will give her the most points?

   a. Round the points of each letter to the greatest place value. Then add the rounded points for each word.

   b. Add the total number of points of all 5 letters that Yoshi picked.

   c. Find the exact number of points for each word and compare.

2 Which of the following best shows how Yoshi should decide which word to make?

   a. $20 + 10 + 10 + 10 = 20 + 10 + 20$

   b. $23 + 8 + 5 + 14 < 23 + 8 + 24$

   c. $23 + 8 + 5 + 14 + 24 = 74$

At the tournament refreshment stand, a taco costs $2.75 and a drink costs $0.95. You want to buy 2 tacos and 2 drinks. You have $10.00. Do you have enough money?

3 What are you asked to find?

   a. the cost of the tacos and drinks

   b. if you have enough money to purchase the tacos and drinks

   c. the change you will receive from the $10.00

4 What do you need to know?

   a. about how much the tacos and drinks will cost

   b. exactly how much money you will have left

   c. how much more a taco costs than a drink

5 **Explain** Do you need to find an exact answer or an estimate to solve the problem? Explain.

Marble Mania

You can use basic facts and regrouping to add two- and three-digit numbers.

Learning About It

Josh's favorite marble game is called Ringer. At the beginning of summer, Josh had 176 marbles. By the end of summer he had won 148 marbles. How many marbles did Josh have by the end of summer?

Josh had 176 marbles.

Josh won 148 marbles.

$$176 + 148 = \blacksquare$$

Estimate first: **200 + 100 = 300**

Step 1 Add ones. Regroup 14 ones as 1 ten 4 ones.	**Step 2** Add tens. Regroup 12 tens as 1 hundred 2 tens.	**Step 3** Add hundreds.
$\begin{array}{r} 1 \\ 176 \\ +\ 148 \\ \hline 4 \end{array}$	$\begin{array}{r} 1\ 1 \\ 176 \\ +\ 148 \\ \hline 24 \end{array}$	$\begin{array}{r} 1\ 1 \\ 176 \\ +\ 148 \\ \hline 324 \end{array}$

Josh had 324 marbles at the end of summer.

Compare the answer with your estimate.
Do they make sense?

More Examples

A. $\begin{array}{r} 1 \\ 75 \\ +\ 46 \\ \hline 121 \end{array}$

B. $\begin{array}{r} 1 \\ 306 \\ +\ 129 \\ \hline 435 \end{array}$

C. $\begin{array}{r} 1\ 1 \\ 325 \\ 132 \\ +\ 74 \\ \hline 531 \end{array}$

D. $\begin{array}{r} \$1.25 \\ +\ 2.08 \\ \hline \$3.33 \end{array}$

▲ Ringer is a game in which 13 marbles are placed in an X shape in the center of a circle. The first player to hit seven marbles from the circle wins.

Think and Discuss How do you know when you need to regroup ones or tens? When don't you need to regroup?

Try It Out

Estimate first. Then add to find each sum.

1. 57
    + 33

2. 73
    + 59

3. 436
    + 29

4. 508
    + 376

5. 425
    212
    + 178

Practice

Find each sum.

6. 23
    + 26

7. 58
    + 37

8. $0.34
    + 0.29

9. 314
    + 72

10. 465
     + 226

11. 529
     + 345

12. 209
     + 36

13. $3.41
     + 2.35

14. 765
     + 176

15. 498
     + 375

16. 627
     + 296

17. 309
     + 275

18. 38
     27
     + 19

19. 54
     49
     + 3

20. 325
     243
     + 157

Problem Solving

21. Every June, children 8 to 14 years old compete in the National Marbles Tournament in Wildwood, New Jersey. One year, 32 boys and 31 girls competed in the contest. How many children competed altogether?

22. **Create Your Own** You have 70 marbles and want to have 100. Write a short story in which you play a number of games and win the number of marbles that you need. Make sure your winnings total 100.

▲ **Kid Connection** Sarah and Nicole Rohrbaugh are twins from West Virginia. In 1996, they competed against 80 boys and girls from 18 states at the National Marbles Tournament.

Review and Remember

Compare. Write > or < for ● .

23. 1,289 ● 1,364

24. 5,706 ● 5,702

25. 29,671 ● 29,692

26. 115,279 ● 117,382

For Extra Practice, see Set C, page 76.

Marco Polo!

You know how to use basic facts to add three-digit numbers.
Now use them to add four- and five-digit numbers.

Learning About It

Marco Polo is a computer game in which points are earned for getting Marco safely to China. Hector is good at helping Marco Polo survive the dangers of travel. In two games, he scored 15,986 and 13,539 points. How many points did Hector score in all?

$$15,986 + 13,539 = \blacksquare$$

Estimate first: $20,000 + 10,000 = 30,000$

Game 1	15,986
Game 2	13,539

THERE'S ALWAYS A WAY!

• **One way** is to use paper and pencil.

Add each column. Regroup if necessary.

Step 1 Add ones and tens.	**Step 2** Add hundreds.	**Step 3** Add thousands and ten thousands.
$\begin{array}{r} {\scriptstyle 1\ 1} \\ 15{,}986 \\ +\ 13{,}539 \\ \hline 25 \end{array}$	$\begin{array}{r} {\scriptstyle 1\ 1\ 1} \\ 15{,}986 \\ +\ 13{,}539 \\ \hline 525 \end{array}$	$\begin{array}{r} {\scriptstyle 1\ 1\ 1} \\ 15{,}986 \\ +\ 13{,}539 \\ \hline 29{,}525 \end{array}$

• **Another way** is to use a calculator.

Press: ① ⑤ ⑨ ⑧ ⑥ ⊕ ① ③ ⑤ ③ ⑨ ═

Display: ⟨ *29525* ⟩   Place a comma in your answer: 29,525.

Hector's total score was 29,525 points. The estimate was 30,000, so the answer is reasonable.

More Examples

A.
```
  1 1 1
  3,564
+   758
  4,322
```

B.
```
    1 1 1
    7,638
+   3,879
   11,517
```

C.
```
    1 2 1
    2,375
    4,680
+   1,276
    8,331
```

Think and Discuss What number would you add to 299,992 to make a sum of 300,000? Explain your answer.

Try It Out

Estimate first. Then find each sum.
Check that your answers are reasonable.

INTERNET ACTIVITY
www.sbgmath.com

1.
```
  6,354
+ 1,243
```

2.
```
  5,672
+ 3,856
```

3.
```
  24,316
+ 13,452
```

4.
```
  47,865
+ 26,527
```

5.
```
  1,215
+ 2,695
```

6.
```
    725
  1,548
+ 1,492
```

7.
```
  3,807
    691
+   425
```

8.
```
  9,450
  4,525
+ 6,110
```

9.
```
    315
  7,106
  2,423
+ 3,201
```

10.
```
  1,245
  3,162
  4,391
+ 2,146
```

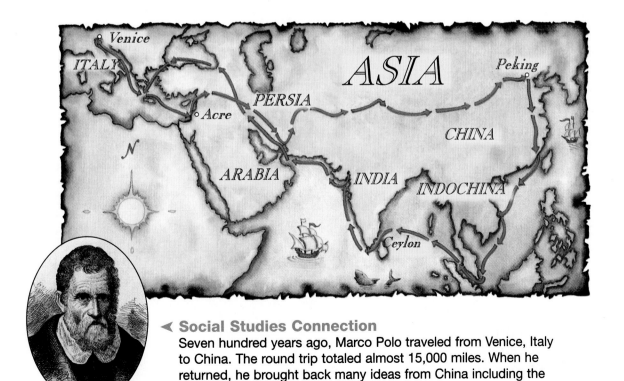

◄ **Social Studies Connection**
Seven hundred years ago, Marco Polo traveled from Venice, Italy to China. The round trip totaled almost 15,000 miles. When he returned, he brought back many ideas from China including the compass, papermaking, printing, and coal for fuel.

Practice

Estimate first. Then find each sum.

11. 5,345
     + 2,284

12. 6,784
     + 2,137

13. 4,657
     + 972

14. 25,461
     + 32,327

15. 36,395
     + 45,220

16. 3,275
     + 1,543

17. $69.95
     + 7.52

18. 68,125
     + 46,596

19. $225.32
     + 194.85

20. 17,106
     + 3,352

 Add. Use a calculator.

21. 78,356
     + 47,143

22. 25,214
     36,170
     + 2,456

23. $575.31
     287.25
     + 306.17

24. 37,607
     12,513
     4,051
     + 25,638

25. 42,173
     5,609
     812
     + 12,463

Problem Solving

Hector recorded the scores for six of his Marco Polo games. Use his table to answer Problems 26–32.

26. What was Hector's highest score? lowest score?

27. What was Hector's combined score for Games 3 and 4?

28. What was Hector's total score for Games 5 and 6? Were these scores higher than those for Games 3 and 4?

29. About how many more points did he score in the first game than in the second?

30. **Using Estimation** About how many thousand points did Hector score in all six games?

> **Hint** Round each score to the nearest thousand and add.

Game Scores

Game	Score
Game 1	15,986
Game 2	13,539
Game 3	32,562
Game 4	41,376
Game 5	23,765
Game 6	31,450

31. Explain Hector's goal is to score 50,000 points in one game. If he had scored another 8,000 points in the fourth game, would he have made his goal? Explain your reasoning.

32. What If? Suppose Hector plays a seventh game. He scores 9,036 more points than he did in Game 6. About how many points would he score in Game 7? Explain why your answer is reasonable.

Review and Remember

Write each number in standard form.

33. five hundred twenty-six thousand, four hundred five

34. two million, nine hundred fourteen thousand, two hundred eleven

35. twenty-seven million, one hundred twelve thousand, two hundred ten

36. two hundred seventy-two million, six hundred forty thousand

37. one million, one thousand, one

38. four hundred thousand, twenty

39. $3{,}000{,}000 + 500{,}000 + 10{,}000 + 600 + 20 + 9$

40. $40{,}000{,}000 + 1{,}000{,}000 + 60{,}000 + 2{,}000 + 800 + 4$

41. $600{,}000{,}000 + 80{,}000{,}000 + 200{,}000 + 90{,}000 + 7{,}000 + 90 + 2$

Time for Technology

Using a Calculator

Finding Number Patterns

Using Algebra Use a calculator to find n. Then look for patterns and solve the Challenge.

$$120 - 12 + 3 = n$$
$$1{,}230 - 123 + 4 = n$$
$$12{,}340 - 1{,}234 + 5 = n$$
$$123{,}450 - 12{,}345 + 6 = n$$

The Challenge

Write the number sentence that comes next and find n.

✔ Checkpoint

Adding Whole Numbers

Use basic facts to add or subtract. (pages 40–43)

1. $8 - 2$ **2.** $3 + 4$ **3.** $6 + 7$ **4.** $7 - 1$

5. $8 + 4$ **6.** $17 - 8$ **7.** $7 + 8$ **8.** $12 - 4$

9. $7 + 7$ **10.** $6 + 9$ **11.** $15 - 8$ **12.** $14 - 6$

Estimate by rounding to the greatest place value. (pages 44–45)

13.	**14.**	**15.**	**16.**	**17.**
71	36	89	65	735
+ 18	+ 23	− 32	− 29	+ 198

18.	**19.**	**20.**	**21.**	**22.**
$ 8.17	572	$ 9.43	642	$ 12.74
+ 2.54	+ 367	− 4.78	− 413	− 8.16

Find each sum. (pages 48–49)

23.	**24.**	**25.**	**26.**	**27.**
56	78	$0.47	417	$ 5.28
+ 31	+ 17	+ 0.29	+ 231	+ 2.37

28.	**29.**	**30.**	**31.**	**32.**
305	298	$ 6.74	54	325
+ 469	+ 536	+ 2.98	33	172
			+ 29	+ 286

Add. (pages 50–53)

33.	**34.**	**35.**	**36.**
6,789	$ 36.75	14,723	47,286
+ 2,092	+ 27.36	+ 12,175	+ 35,437

37.	**38.**	**39.**	**40.**
27,762	$ 459.23	38,502	57,684
17,596	734.72	12,351	8,296
+ 13,965	+ 235.91	6,798	795
		+ 25,960	+ 32,517

Mixed Practice

Estimate by rounding to the greatest place value.
Then add.

41. 93
+ 34

42. 473
+ 246

43. $5.46
+ 3.84

44. 745
+ 254

45. 367
+ 129

46. $12.76
+ 8.45

47. 643
+ 317

48. $14.92
+ 5.13

Problem Solving

49. You scored 12,345 points playing your favorite computer game. In the next game you scored 24,689 points. How many total points did you win in both games altogether?

50. **Explain** You started with 132 marbles. You bought 24 more. Then you won 43. How many marbles did you have in all? Explain the method you would use to find out.

What do you think?
How does knowing basic facts help you add greater numbers?

Journal Idea

Add the 7 digits of your phone number. Write down the sum. Then add the sum of the first 3 digits to the sum of the last 4 digits. What answer do you get? Explain why you got the answers that you did.

Critical Thinking Corner

Logical Thinking

Magic Square

The sum of the numbers in the shaded part of this magic square is 34. How many other squares of 4 numbers can you find that have a sum of 34?

7	12	1	14
2	13	8	11
16	3	10	5
9	6	15	4

Jump Rope!

You can use basic facts and regrouping to subtract two- and three-digit numbers.

Learning About It

A world record was set at the Double Dutch Championships in South Carolina in June 1996. The winning team jumped 447 times in 2 minutes. Another team jumped 298 times in 2 minutes. How many more jumps did the winning team make?

$$447 - 298 = \blacksquare$$

Estimate first: $400 - 300 = 100$

National Sports News

Double Dutch Record Set: 447 Jumps In Two Minutes

Step 1 Subtract the ones. Regroup 1 ten as 10 ones.	**Step 2** Subtract the tens. Regroup 1 hundred as 10 tens.	**Step 3** Subtract the hundreds.
$\begin{array}{r} \overset{3\ 17}{4\cancel{4}\cancel{7}} \\ -\ 298 \\ \hline 9 \end{array}$	$\begin{array}{r} \overset{13}{\underset{3\ \cancel{3}}{4}\cancel{4}\cancel{7}} \\ -\ 298 \\ \hline 49 \end{array}$	$\begin{array}{r} \overset{13}{\underset{3\ \cancel{3}}{4}\cancel{4}\cancel{7}} \\ -\ 298 \\ \hline 149 \end{array}$

The winning team made 149 more jumps.

More Examples

A. $\begin{array}{r} \overset{4\ 10}{5\cancel{0}} \\ -\ 27 \\ \hline 23 \end{array}$ B. $\begin{array}{r} \overset{5\ 10}{6\cancel{0}8} \\ -\ 274 \\ \hline 334 \end{array}$

Think and Discuss When do you regroup a ten for ones? a hundred for tens?

▲ **Health and Fitness Connection**
In Double Dutch, jumpers quickly jump through two ropes which turn in opposite directions. This game is great exercise for fun or competition.

Try It Out

Estimate first. Subtract. Add to check each answer.

1. 42
    − 27

2. 60
    − 32

3. 568
    − 85

4. 709
    − 247

5. 523
    − 146

Practice

Subtract.

6. 63
    − 32

7. 78
    − 5

8. 96
    − 18

9. 468
    − 146

10. $0.84
    − 0.57

11. 592
    − 146

12. $0.75
    − 0.47

13. 507
    − 234

14. 781
    − 35

15. $0.93
    − 0.77

16. 90
    − 34

17. $ 4.72
    − 1.34

18. 630
    − 325

19. 534
    − 476

20. 706
    − 230

21. 812
    − 57

22. 83
    − 19

23. $ 5.31
    − 1.85

24. 927
    − 259

25. $ 8.20
    − 3.47

Problem Solving

26. **Kid Connection** In 1995, Joy Hiller from South Carolina won the Double Dutch World Invitational Championships. Joy jumped 351 times in 1 minute. Another contestant jumped 298 times in 1 minute. How many more times did Joy jump in 1 minute than the other contestant?

27. **Explain** A jump-rope competition began with 350 contestants. There were 25 contestants eliminated in each round. How many contestants were left after 3 rounds? Explain how you know.

▲ Joy Hiller is a Double Dutch champion. She has been jumping rope since she was 4.

Review and Remember

Round to the nearest ten.

28. 84

29. 172

30. 58

31. 185

32. 1,162

For Extra Practice, see Set E, page 77.

Space Quest

Use basic facts to subtract four- and five-digit numbers.

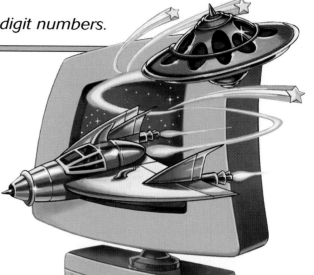

Learning About It

Space Quest is a computer adventure game for two people. In one game, Emma scored 36,248 points and Scott scored 19,563 points. By how many points did Emma win?

$$
\begin{array}{r}
36{,}248 \\
-\ 19{,}563 \\
\end{array}
$$

THERE'S ALWAYS A WAY!

○ **One way** is to use paper and pencil.

Step 1 Subtract ones and tens.	**Step 2** Subtract hundreds.	**Step 3** Subtract thousands and ten thousands.
$$\begin{array}{r} \overset{1\ 14}{36{,}2\cancel{4}8} \\ -19{,}563 \\ \hline 85 \end{array}$$	$$\begin{array}{r} \overset{11}{\overset{5\ \ \cancel{1}14}{3\cancel{6}{,}2\cancel{4}8}} \\ -19{,}563 \\ \hline 685 \end{array}$$	$$\begin{array}{r} \overset{15\ 11}{\overset{2\ \cancel{5}\ \ \cancel{1}14}{\cancel{3}\cancel{6}{,}2\cancel{4}8}} \\ -19{,}563 \\ \hline 16{,}685 \end{array}$$

○ **Another way** is to use a calculator.

Estimate first: $36{,}000 - 20{,}000 = 16{,}000$

Then enter the numbers and operations.

Press: ③ ⑥ ② ④ ⑧ ⊖ ① ⑨ ⑤ ⑥ ③ ⊜

Display: ▢ *16685* ▢ Place a comma in your answer: 16,685.

Emma won by 16,685 points.

More Examples

A.
$$
\begin{array}{r}
\overset{15}{\overset{3\ \cancel{9}\ \cancel{5}13}{4{,}0\cancel{6}\cancel{3}}} \\
-\ 2{,}795 \\
\hline
1{,}268
\end{array}
$$

B.
$$
\begin{array}{r}
\overset{14}{\overset{2\ 17\ 5\ \cancel{4}12}{\cancel{3}\cancel{7}{,}6\cancel{5}\cancel{2}}} \\
-\ 28{,}475 \\
\hline
9{,}177
\end{array}
$$

C.
$$
\begin{array}{r}
\overset{16}{\overset{4\ \cancel{6}\ 9\ 13}{\cancel{5}7{,}0\cancel{3}\cancel{6}}} \\
-\ 29{,}872 \\
\hline
27{,}164
\end{array}
$$

Think and Discuss Explain how you could find the answer to 39,999 subtracted from 40,005.

Try It Out

Estimate first. Then subtract.

1. 5,875 − 2,375	**2.** 8,026 − 4,753	**3.** 47,892 − 21,545	**4.** 64,238 − 56,457	**5.** 85,036 − 37,564

Practice

Subtract.

6. 5,641 − 2,375	**7.** 7,435 − 3,596	**8.** 6,053 − 3,568	**9.** 45,734 − 12,356	**10.** 62,539 − 27,645
11. 30,576 − 12,759	**12.** 45,921 − 38,417	**13.** 72,065 − 28,431	**14.** 96,132 − 43,857	**15.** 9,056 − 4,097
16. 9,806 − 6,978	**17.** 83,214 − 57,479	**18.** 62,593 − 58,729	**19.** 7,056 − 6,079	**20.** 50,347 − 40,985

Problem Solving

21. Scott's score for his first Space Quest game was 27,986 points. On his second game, he scored 36,762. How much better did Scott score on his second game?

22. Emma and Scott played against two friends. Emma's score was 28,745 points. Scott's score was 27,056 points. What was their combined score?

23. The top score in Space Quest is 64,976. Emma has 49,584 points. How many more points must she score to reach the top score?

24. **Create Your Own** Write a word problem about a computer game that uses subtraction of greater numbers. Exchange problems with a classmate.

Review and Remember

Using Algebra Give the next three numbers in each pattern.

25. 23, 26, 29, 32, . . .   **26.** 91, 82, 73, 64, . . .   **27.** 132, 142, 152, 162, . . .

28. 10, 11, 13, 16, . . .   **29.** 30, 25, 20, 15, . . .   **30.** 150, 125, 100, 75, . . .

Are You Puzzled?

Now you can regroup to subtract with zeros.

Learning About It

Amy's new jigsaw puzzle has a total of 3,000 pieces. So far, Amy has used 1,675 pieces. How many more pieces must she use to complete the puzzle?

$$3,000 - 1,675 = \blacksquare$$

Estimate first: **3,000 − 2,000 = 1,000**

Step 1 There are no ones, tens, or hundreds to subtract. Regroup 1 thousand as 10 hundreds.	**Step 2** Regroup 1 hundred as 10 tens.
$$\begin{array}{r} \overset{2\ 10}{\cancel{3},000} \\ -\ 1,675 \end{array}$$	$$\begin{array}{r} \overset{9}{\underset{2\ 10\ 10}{\cancel{3},\cancel{0}00}} \\ -\ 1,675 \end{array}$$
Step 3 Regroup 1 ten as 10 ones.	**Step 4** Subtract.
$$\begin{array}{r} \overset{9\ 9}{\underset{2\ 10\ 10\ 10}{\cancel{3},\cancel{0}\cancel{0}0}} \\ -\ 1,675 \end{array}$$	$$\begin{array}{r} \overset{9\ 9}{\underset{2\ 10\ 10\ 10}{\cancel{3},\cancel{0}\cancel{0}\cancel{0}}} \\ -\ 1,675 \\ \hline 1,325 \end{array}$$

Amy has 1,325 more pieces to use.

Think and Discuss

Which exercise requires more regrouping? Explain.

a. $\begin{array}{r} 2,222 \\ -\ 200 \end{array}$ **b.** $\begin{array}{r} 2,000 \\ -\ 222 \end{array}$

Try It Out

Estimate first. Then subtract.

1. $\begin{array}{r} 800 \\ -\ 479 \end{array}$ **2.** $\begin{array}{r} 4,000 \\ -\ 1,265 \end{array}$ **3.** $\begin{array}{r} 8,000 \\ -\ 472 \end{array}$ **4.** $\begin{array}{r} 4,000 \\ -\ 1,763 \end{array}$ **5.** $\begin{array}{r} 70,907 \\ -\ 56,746 \end{array}$

Practice

Subtract.

6. 300
− 120

7. 603
− 368

8. 800
− 509

9. 430
− 75

10. 700
− 470

11. 6,080
− 2,270

12. 3,000
− 1,270

13. 5,600
−   431

14. 8,000
− 4,892

15. 4,000
− 1,074

16. 50,080
− 27,865

17. 78,000
− 57,892

18. 40,008
− 10,547

19. 80,096
− 6,874

20. 90,900
− 32,790

21. 7,000
− 3,006

22. 90,105
− 2,763

23. 30,007
− 12,006

24. 9,000
− 3,060

25. 69,004
− 57,622

Problem Solving

26. Sam is working on a 500-piece whale puzzle. He has 175 unused pieces. How many pieces has Sam used in the puzzle so far?

27. The García family is working on completing a 5,000-piece world-map puzzle. Marisa has joined 1,309 pieces to the puzzle. Her sister Susana has joined 975 pieces. Estimate how many pieces they have to join to finish the puzzle.

28. Explain Miss Johnson's class is working on a 1,500-piece puzzle. Every week, each of her 28 students puts 10 pieces in the puzzle. How many pieces will be left after 3 weeks? Explain the strategy you used.

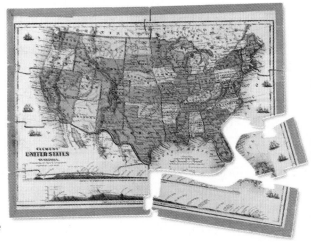

▲ **Social Studies Connection**
Jigsaw puzzles began as a way to teach geography in the 1760s in England. Later, one type of puzzle even had two sides. One side had a map and the other showed a scene.

Review and Remember

Using Algebra Find the missing number.

29. $\$7.15 - \$1.49 = n$ **30.** $49 \div n = 7$ **31.** $5 \times 3 = n$ **32.** $747 + 465 = n$

For Extra Practice, see Set G, page 78.

Problem Solving
Solve a Simpler Problem

Sometimes you can solve a difficult problem by first solving a simpler problem.

Sixty-four students play in pairs in a Mancala tournament. If players lose, they are out of the tournament. If players win, they play another game. Winners play until one winner is left. How many games must be played before there is a winner?

 UNDERSTAND

What do you need to find?

You need to find the number of games that must be played to find a winner.

 PLAN

How can you solve the problem?

First solve a simpler problem. How many games would be played if there were 2 players? if there were 3 players? 4 players?

A Social Studies Connection
Mancala is an African game played with stones. It has been played in Africa and the Middle East for over 3,000 years.

 SOLVE

2 players would need to play 1 game.
3 players would need to play 2 games.
4 players would need to play 3 games.

The number of games is always 1 less than the number of players.

If there are 64 players, 63 games must be played.

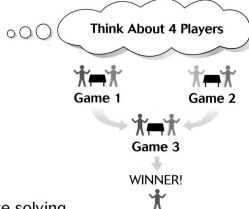

 LOOK BACK

How did solving a simpler problem make solving this problem easier?

Using the Strategy

Solve Problems 1–4 by first solving a simpler problem.

1 The tournament is set up in the school gym. Several games are played at once. A rope barrier separates different playing areas. To make the barrier the rope is cut into 15 equal parts. How many cuts are made?

2 The pieces of rope are hooked to posts as shown at the right. How many posts are needed for the 15 pieces of rope?

3 The students involved in the tournament are served lunch at long tables. These tables are made by placing 16 of the tables shown at the right end to end. How many students can sit at one long table?

4 A local bakery is donating dessert for the tournament. The organizers want to be sure that everyone has enough, so they order 5 desserts for every 3 players. How many desserts are needed for 15 players?

Mixed Strategy Review

Try these or other strategies to solve each problem. Tell which strategy you used.

Problem Solving Strategies

- Write a Number Sentence
- Find a Pattern
- Draw a Picture
- Solve a Simpler Problem
- Guess and Check
- Work Backwards

5 At the Mancala tournament, 3 games are played at each table. How many tables are needed for 20 games?

6 Round 1 of the tournament began at 9:00 A.M., Round 2 at 9:45 A.M., and Round 3 at 10:30 A.M. At what time will Round 6 begin?

7 You buy a hamburger platter for $3.89, 2 cartons of milk for $0.65 each, and a fruit cup for $0.55. How much change should you receive from a $10 bill?

8 **Analyze** A popular board game can be played by 2, 3, or 4 players. What are the fewest games needed for 25 people to play? Explain.

Quick! Think!

Sometimes you can use mental math to find the answers to addition and subtraction problems.

$$\begin{array}{cc} 40 & 8 \\ +\,20 & +\,6 \\ \hline 60 & +\,14 = 74 \end{array}$$

Learning About It

To make the game called Quick! Think!, you write addition and subtraction examples on cards. Then you turn one card over at a time. The first person to get the correct answer keeps the card. The player with the most cards wins. But there is a catch. You must use mental math!

The first card reads

48 + 26 = ▨

You can get the answer by **breaking apart** the numbers in the problem.

Word Bank

**breaking apart
compensation**

> Think $48 = 40 + 8$ $26 = 20 + 6$

Start with the tens. Add 40 and 20.	Then add the ones.	Next, add the sums of the tens and ones.
$\begin{array}{r} 40 \\ +\,20 \\ \hline 60 \end{array}$	$\begin{array}{r} 8 \\ +\,6 \\ \hline 14 \end{array}$	$\begin{array}{r} 60 \\ +\,14 \\ \hline 74 \end{array}$

Breaking apart also works for subtraction.

57 − 34 = ▨

> Think $57 = 50 + 7$ $34 = 30 + 4$

Subtract the tens.	Subtract the ones.	Add the differences of the tens and ones.
$\begin{array}{r} 50 \\ -\,30 \\ \hline 20 \end{array}$	$\begin{array}{r} 7 \\ -\,4 \\ \hline 3 \end{array}$	$\begin{array}{r} 20 \\ +\,3 \\ \hline 23 \end{array}$

More Examples

You can also break apart greater numbers.

A. 214 + 132 = ■

$$\begin{array}{r} 200 \\ +\,100 \\ \hline 300 \end{array} + \begin{array}{r} 10 \\ +\,30 \\ \hline 40 \end{array} + \begin{array}{r} 4 \\ +\,2 \\ \hline 6 \end{array} = 346$$

Add the sums.

B. 545 − 132 = ■

$$\begin{array}{r} 500 \\ -\,100 \\ \hline 400 \end{array} + \begin{array}{r} 40 \\ -\,30 \\ \hline 10 \end{array} + \begin{array}{r} 5 \\ -\,2 \\ \hline 3 \end{array} = 413$$

Add the differences.

Connecting Ideas

Compensation is another method you can use to add or subtract mentally.

Add. 58 + 34 = ■

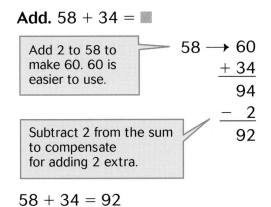

Add 2 to 58 to make 60. 60 is easier to use.

$$58 \rightarrow \begin{array}{r} 60 \\ +\,34 \\ \hline 94 \\ -\;\;2 \\ \hline 92 \end{array}$$

Subtract 2 from the sum to compensate for adding 2 extra.

58 + 34 = 92

Subtract. 76 − 37 = ■

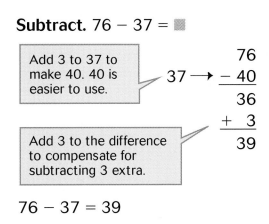

Add 3 to 37 to make 40. 40 is easier to use.

$$37 \rightarrow \begin{array}{r} 76 \\ -\,40 \\ \hline 36 \\ +\;\;3 \\ \hline 39 \end{array}$$

Add 3 to the difference to compensate for subtracting 3 extra.

76 − 37 = 39

More Examples

You can use compensation with greater numbers.

A. 436 + 199 = ■

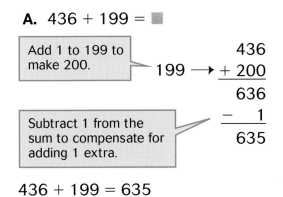

Add 1 to 199 to make 200.

$$199 \rightarrow \begin{array}{r} 436 \\ +\,200 \\ \hline 636 \\ -\;\;\;1 \\ \hline 635 \end{array}$$

Subtract 1 from the sum to compensate for adding 1 extra.

436 + 199 = 635

B. 4,500 − 2,995 = ■

Add 5 to 2,995 to make 3,000.

$$2{,}995 \rightarrow \begin{array}{r} 4{,}500 \\ -\,3{,}000 \\ \hline 1{,}500 \\ +\;\;\;\;\;5 \\ \hline 1{,}505 \end{array}$$

Add 5 to the difference to compensate for subtracting 5 extra.

4,500 − 2,995 = 1,505

Think and Discuss Would you use mental math or paper and pencil to find the answer to 361 − 174? Explain.

Try It Out

Add or subtract mentally. Use breaking apart.

1. 29 + 37   **2.** 97 − 24   **3.** 469 − 323   **4.** 335 + 447

Add or subtract mentally. Use compensation.

5. 38 + 17   **6.** 86 − 28   **7.** 593 − 299   **8.** 698 + 123

Practice

Add or subtract mentally. Use breaking apart.

9. 33 + 15   **10.** 56 + 23   **11.** 74 − 31   **12.** 96 − 63

13. 89 − 62   **14.** 254 + 315   **15.** 437 + 196   **16.** 678 − 352

17. 3,479 − 363   **18.** 7,146 + 547   **19.** 5,423 + 1,182

Add or subtract mentally. Use compensation.

20. 47 + 29   **21.** 58 + 23   **22.** 43 − 9   **23.** 61 − 29

24. 62 − 38   **25.** 483 + 198   **26.** 548 − 196   **27.** 497 + 456

28. 2,678 − 398   **29.** 6,723 − 3,995   **30.** 7,995 + 1,178

31. 99 + 17   **32.** 571 − 295   **33.** 4,768 − 2,998

Problem Solving

Use mental math.

34. Alana's Quick! Think! game has 16 addition cards and 14 subtraction cards. How many cards are there altogether?

35. When the card with the example 576 − 298 turned up, Jay got the answer right away. What answer did he give? What strategy do you think he used?

576 − 298 = ▨

36. Alana wrote a new card for Quick! Think! that she thought was a challenge. The example she wrote was 361 + 527. What is the answer and what strategy did you use?

361 + 527 = ▨

37. To break a tie between John and Marsha, they each took a subtraction card. The one with the greatest difference won the game.

John took 657 − 312.
Marsha took 798 − 526.
Who won?

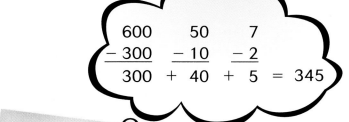

$$\begin{array}{ccc} 600 & 50 & 7 \\ -\,300 & -\,10 & -\,2 \\ \hline 300 & +\;40 & +\;5 \;=\; 345 \end{array}$$

38. Explain Suppose you are playing Quick! Think! The card turned up is 3,995 + 1,736. What answer would you give? What method would you use? Why?

Review and Remember

Write each set of numbers in order from least to greatest.

39. 4,863; 5,279; 5,066; 4,684; 5,134

40. 10,321; 10,198; 9,764; 9,789; 10,165

41. 138,476; 139,212; 139,098; 137,207; 140,176

Money $ense

Mental Money

Use mental math to find how much money is in each group. Which group has more money?

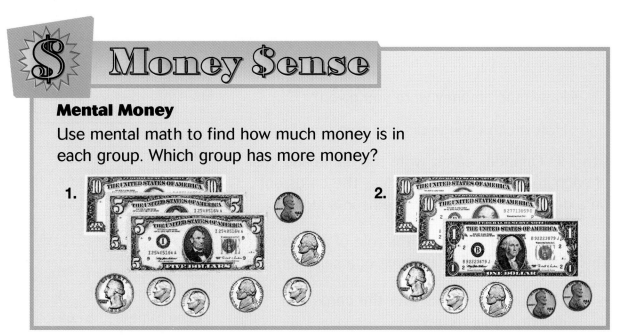

For Extra Practice, see Set H, page 78.

Count Your Change

*Counting with play money can help you
explore making change.*

Learning About It

An easy way to make change is to count on from the
cost of the item.

Work with a partner.

Step 1 You sold a jump rope to your partner for
$3.54. You were paid with a five-dollar bill. Use play
money to make the change.

What You Need

For each pair:
  index cards
  markers
  play money
    4 five-dollar bills
    10 one-dollar bills
    *5 each—quarters,
    dimes, nickels, and
    pennies*

Making Change

Start with the cost.   Count on the least valuable coin first.   End with the amount you were given.

$3.54 + 🪙 + 🪙 + 🪙 + 🪙 + 💵

$3.55 ⟶ $3.65 ⟶ $3.75 ⟶ $4.00 ⟶ $5.00

• How much money were you given?

• How much change did you give back?

Step 2 On index cards, write the name and cost
of each item in the table. Then lay the cards out
on a desktop. Use them like items in a store.

Step 3 One person takes the role of a customer.
The other person takes the role of a salesperson.

• The customer looks over the cards and
decides what to buy.

Price List	
Item	Cost
Dice	$0.52
Marbles	$0.73
Checkers	$1.64
Card game	$1.70
Picture puzzle	$2.66
Dominoes	$2.78
Dart game	$3.88
Board game	$4.53
Video game	$7.69

- Then the customer decides what bills to use to pay for the item. Payment must be made only with bills. The money is handed to the salesperson along with the card.

- The salesperson takes the card and money and counts out the customer's change.

- Switch roles and play again. Continue to buy several items.

Think and Discuss Do you think it is easier to make change by counting on or by subtracting? Explain.

Practice

1. Make up a price for an item and write it on an index card. Give your partner the card and enough bills to pay for the item. Have your partner count out the change.

2. An item costs $4.76. How many different ways can the salesperson make change if you pay for the item with a $5.00 bill?

3. **Explain** Suppose you buy an item that costs $3.10. Why might you give the salesperson $5.10?

4. **Explain** How can you check to be sure that you got the right amount of change?

Critical Thinking Corner

Number Sense

What's Missing?

Using Algebra Find each missing addend.

1. Their difference is 1.

Addend	Addend	Sum
■	+ ▲	= 15

2. Their difference is 3.

Addend	Addend	Sum
■	+ ▲	= 11

Piñata Party

Sometimes one method of solving a problem works better than another.

Learning About It

Carlos is filling a piñata with treats for his sister's party. So far, he has 135 fruits and nuts and 98 toys. How many treats does he have altogether?

135 + 98 = ■

98 is close to 100, so Carlos can use mental math.

$135 + 100 = 235$ $235 - 2 = 233$

Carlos has 233 piñata treats.

Anita has 168 picture cards and 247 roasted nuts for another piñata. How many little gifts has she in all?

168 + 247 = ■

135 fruits and nuts   98 toys

Anita should use paper and pencil or a calculator.

She chooses to use a calculator.

 1 6 8 + 2 4 7 = 415

Anita has 415 piñata treats.

Think and Discuss Carlos had 356 piñata treats and used 187. What calculation method can he use to find the number of treats he has left? Explain your method.

Try It Out

Choose a Method Use paper and pencil, a calculator, or mental math. Write the solution and the method you used.

1. 365 + 167   **2.** 298 + 172   **3.** 496 − 123   **4.** 562 − 279

5. 1,999 + 2,176   **6.** 967 − 589   **7.** 5,672 − 1,995   **8.** 932 + 789

Practice

Choose a Method Use paper and pencil, a calculator, or mental math. Write the solution and the method you used.

9. 98 + 37   **10.** 76 − 39   **11.** 562 − 431   **12.** 429 + 298

13. 569 + 372   **14.** 726 − 389   **15.** 398 + 325   **16.** 562 − 295

17. 709 + 124   **18.** 3,000 − 299   **19.** 798 + 462   **20.** 912 − 376

21. 825 − 486   **22.** 543 − 296   **23.** 961 + 198   **24.** 4,000 − 399

25. 3,124 + 1,998   **26.** 5,004 − 1,276   **27.** 2,341 + 1,235   **28.** 6,753 − 3,521

29. 1,250 − 250   **30.** 498 + 152   **31.** 777 − 444   **32.** 475 + 218

Problem Solving

Write the solution and the calculation method you used.

33. Some piñatas are larger than others. If one piñata holds 234 tiny treats and another holds 279, how many more treats does the second piñata hold?

34. Imagine that one piñata holds 116 prizes and another holds 276. How many prizes are there in all?

35. Anita had 345 little gifts to use in piñatas. Eduardo had 198 gifts. How many more piñata gifts did Anita have than Eduardo?

▲ **Social Studies Connection** Piñatas are clay pots filled with party favors, covered with papier mâché, and decorated. The finished piñata is hung from a rope, and blindfolded guests try to break it open with a stick.

Review and Remember

Write the standard form for each number.

36. 5 hundreds
8 tens
6 ones

37. 2 thousands
9 hundreds
0 tens
4 ones

38. 8 thousands
5 hundreds
4 tens
0 ones

39. 1 ten thousand
5 thousands
0 hundreds
9 tens
6 ones

For Extra Practice, see Set I, page 78.

Problem Solving
Using Money

You can add and subtract money to solve problems.

Coupons can be used to buy games for less than full price at Game World. The amount on the coupon is subtracted from the price of the game. Game prices and coupons are shown at the right. Which of the games will cost less than $18.00 if bought with a coupon?

$24.25

$19.95

$19.75

 UNDERSTAND

What do you need to know?

You need to know which games cost less than $18 when bought with a coupon.

Stepping Stones	Memory Lane
$6.75 Discount	$2.25 Discount

Boiling Point
$1.50
Discount

 PLAN

How can you solve the problem?

You can subtract the amount on each coupon from each game price. Then you can compare the new price to $18.00.

 SOLVE

Stepping Stones	Memory Lane	Boiling Point
$24.25	$19.95	$19.75
− 6.75	− 2.25	− 1.50
$17.50 < $18.00	$17.70 < $18.00	$18.25 > $18.00

Stepping Stones and Memory Lane cost less than $18.00 when they are bought with a coupon.

 LOOK BACK

How could you use addition to check your subtraction?

Show What You Learned

Use the information below to answer Problems 1–6.

$16.25

$14.99

$9.95

$18.99

Raceway $2.50 Discount

LEAPIN' LIZARDS $4.25 Discount

COMET TRAIL $1.00 Discount

Mystery Mountain $3.25 Discount

1. How much does Raceway cost with a coupon?

2. Is $15.00 enough to buy Mystery Mountain with a coupon? Explain.

3. Which games cost $12.00 or less with coupons?

4. **Analyze** Which game costs less with a coupon, Raceway or Leapin' Lizards? without a coupon?

5. Mallory bought one of each game shown above. If she used a coupon for each game, how much money did she save by using the coupons?

6. **Create Your Own** Write a problem that involves buying games and using discount coupons. Give your problem to a classmate to solve.

Use the chart to solve Problems 7–10.

Goofy Games toy store records the price of each game they sell. Then they compare this sale price to the price they paid to buy the game from a manufacturer. The difference between the prices is the money Goofy Games made by selling the game.

Game	Selling Price of the Game	Price Paid to Manufacturer	Money the Store Made
A	$19.95	$12.50	$7.45
B	$6.85	$4.75	?
C	$11.99	$7.15	?
D	$22.25	?	$6.40
E	?	$21.75	$9.15

7. How much money did the store make on Game B? on Game C?

8. How much did the store pay the manufacturer for Game D?

9. What price did Goofy Games charge customers for Game E?

10. **Analyze** Which game made the most money for the store?

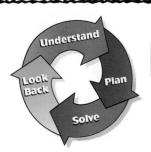

Problem Solving

Practice What You Learned

Choose the correct letter for each answer.

1 Georgia uses 20 inches of wood around the edges of a rectangular frame. If the frame is 6 inches long, how wide is it?

A. 4 in.
B. 8 in.
C. 12 in.
D. 14 in.

Tip

Try drawing a picture to solve this problem.

---

2 A bird watcher counted 324 wrens and 465 sparrows. Which number sentence could be used to find how many more sparrows than wrens were counted?

A. $324 + 465 = $ ■
B. $465 + 465 = $ ■
C. $324 - 465 = $ ■
D. $465 - 324 = $ ■

Tip

Sometimes you can eliminate an answer choice. Why can you eliminate Choice C in this problem?

---

3 There are 4 people at a party. Each person shakes the hand of each of the other people once. How many handshakes are there?

A. 4
B. 6
C. 7
D. 8

Tip

You can use the *Act It Out* strategy to help you solve this problem.

4 Jenny has 2 pets and Kyle has 7 pets. Nina has more pets than Jenny but fewer pets than Kyle. Which is reasonable for the number of pets Nina has?

A. 1
B. 2
C. 5
D. 8

5 Will played three dart games. His scores were 297, 186, and 302. Which is the best estimate of his total score for the three games?

A. 500
B. 700
C. 800
D. 900

6 Alice arranges boxes of greeting cards in a store window. She puts 8 boxes on the bottom row, 6 boxes on the next row, and so on. There are 2 boxes on top. How many boxes does Alice arrange in the display?

A. 16
B. 20
C. 21
D. 36

7 Bill has $3.00. He wants to buy 2 tacos for 99¢ each and a drink for $1.99. **About** how much more money does he need?

A. $0.50
B. $1.00
C. $1.50
D. $4.00

8 Victor bought apples, pears, and peaches at the market. He bought twice as many pears as apples. He bought 2 more peaches than apples. What other information is needed to determine the total number of fruits Victor bought?

A. The number of pears he bought
B. The weight of the fruit
C. The cost of the fruit
D. The size of the apples

Use the graph for Problems 9 and 10.

This graph shows how some people learn about the news.

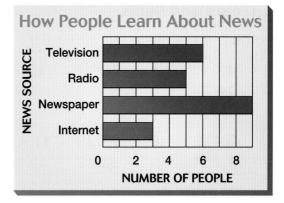

How People Learn About News

9 Which is the most popular way to learn about the news?

A. Television
B. Radio
C. Newspaper
D. Internet

10 How many more people use television than the Internet to learn about the news?

A. 1
B. 2
C. 3
D. 6

✓ Checkpoint

Subtracting Whole Numbers

Vocabulary

Complete. Use the words from the Word Bank.

1. If you add 58 + 34 by adding 50 + 8 + 30 + 4, you are using a strategy called __?__ .

2. If you add 58 + 34 by thinking 60 + 34 − 2, you are using a strategy called __?__ .

3. If you round the numbers before you add or subtract, you get an __?__ .

> **Word Bank**
>
> breaking apart
> compensation
> estimate

Concepts and Skills

Subtract. (pages 56–57; 58–59; 60–61)

4. 43 − 29	**5.** 70 − 54	**6.** $0.92 − 0.32	**7.** 86 − 17	**8.** 526 − 135
9. 3,479 − 1,254	**10.** 7,029 − 3,642	**11.** 8,000 − 5,461	**12.** 50,000 − 17,932	**13.** 9,765 − 893

Use break apart to find each answer mentally. (pages 64–67)

14. 32 + 64   **15.** 57 − 36   **16.** 76 − 23   **17.** 78 + 17

18. 433 + 221   **19.** 795 − 352   **20.** 598 − 376   **21.** 781 + 103

Use compensation to find each answer mentally. (pages 64–67)

22. 57 + 39   **23.** 63 − 9   **24.** 78 + 13   **25.** 61 − 38

26. 475 + 198   **27.** 798 + 137   **28.** 828 − 398   **29.** 621 − 395

Use mental math to add or subtract. (pages 64–67)

30. 87 − 26   **31.** 479 − 362   **32.** 198 + 72   **33.** 4,251 + 2,999

34. 471 − 195   **35.** 93 + 75   **36.** 72 − 29   **37.** 536 + 261

Problem Solving

38. You jumped 237 times in your first jump-rope contest. In the second contest, you jumped 316 times. How many more times did you jump the second time?

39. You and a friend played a computer game. You scored 5,000 points. Your friend scored 3,765 points. How many more points did you score?

40. **Explain** You have 198 gifts for one piñata and 281 for another. How many gifts do you have altogether? Explain the method you used to find out.

Journal Idea

Look at any page near the back of your math book and write down the page number. Look at a page near the front of the book and write down its page number. How many pages are between these two pages? Briefly explain how you found the answer.

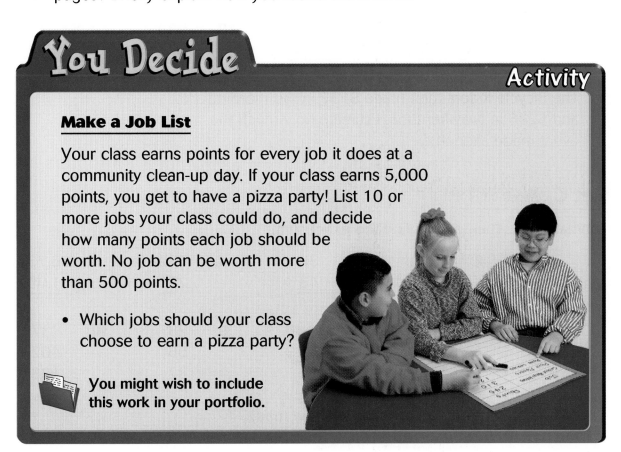

You Decide

Activity

Make a Job List

Your class earns points for every job it does at a community clean-up day. If your class earns 5,000 points, you get to have a pizza party! List 10 or more jobs your class could do, and decide how many points each job should be worth. No job can be worth more than 500 points.

- Which jobs should your class choose to earn a pizza party?

You might wish to include this work in your portfolio.

> **What do you think?**
> How does counting on help you make change?

Extra Practice

Set A (pages 40–43)

Find the sum or difference.

1. $9 + 8$ 2. $7 + 6$ 3. $16 - 7$ 4. $15 - 8$ 5. $6 + 7$

6. $18 - 9$ 7. $8 + 6$ 8. $9 + 3$ 9. $17 - 9$ 10. $12 - 8$

11. At the end of a checkers game, you had captured all 12 of your opponent's pieces. Your opponent had captured 7 of your pieces. How many more pieces did you capture than your opponent?

Set B (pages 44–45)

Estimate by rounding to the greatest place value.

1. 42 2. 59 3. 72 4. $\$5.28$ 5. 862
   $+ 17$ $+ 33$ $- 34$ $+ 2.76$ $- 217$

6. $\$6.78$ 7. 330 8. $\$13.78$ 9. 934 10. $\$11.13$
   $- 1.59$ $+ 476$ $+ 1.32$ $- 376$ $- 2.74$

11. The Bicycle Ride-a-thon made $132 in the morning and $296 in the afternoon. Estimate how much the event made altogether.

Set C (pages 48–49)

Estimate first. Then add to find the exact sum.

1. 76 2. 45 3. 89 4. 532 5. $\$6.73$
   $+ 23$ $+ 19$ $+ 43$ $+ 256$ $+ 1.09$

6. 436 7. 617 8. $\$5.46$ 9. 28 10. 237
   $+ 91$ $+ 296$ $+ 3.29$ 56 462
                                          $+ 37$ $+ 108$

11. Pete has 42 marbles. Sally has 37. How many marbles do they have altogether?

Extra Practice

Set D (pages 50–53)

Find each sum.

1. 6,715 + 1,263	**2.** 5,624 + 3,295	**3.** 9,506 + 792	**4.** 3,197 + 4,658	**5.** 17,236 + 21,503
6. 32,750 + 17,625	**7.** 56,179 + 27,618	**8.** 41,758 + 36,593	**9.** 2,173 1,201 3,562 + 1,010	**10.** 35,312 125 1,042 + 13,226

Set E (pages 56–57)

Subtract.

1. 74 − 21	**2.** 96 − 79	**3.** $0.53 − 0.17	**4.** 90 − 47	**5.** 692 − 378
6. 809 − 492	**7.** $6.52 − 3.85	**8.** 975 − 382	**9.** 520 − 176	**10.** 723 − 465

11. You entered a speed-walking competition. You walked 536 feet in the first race before time ran out. You walked 398 feet in the second race. How much farther did you walk in the first race?

Set F (pages 58–59)

Subtract.

1. 6,478 − 3,165	**2.** 8,927 − 4,768	**3.** 5,407 − 1,862	**4.** 7,463 − 2,874	**5.** 9,876 − 697
6. 37,564 − 12,352	**7.** 89,372 − 56,734	**8.** 50,439 − 40,986	**9.** 75,672 − 27,564	**10.** 87,673 − 8,524

Extra Practice

Set G (pages 60–61)

Subtract.

1. 400 − 128	**2.** 800 − 609	**3.** 500 − 321	**4.** 700 − 260	**5.** 8,000 − 5,376
6. 5,000 − 2,760	**7.** 9,000 − 7,214	**8.** 7,000 − 2,076	**9.** 50,000 − 26,781	**10.** 80,000 − 37,680

11. A jump-rope competition began with 600 contestants. There were 247 contestants eliminated after the first round. How many contestants were left?

Set H (pages 64–67)

Add or subtract mentally, using breaking apart or compensation.

1. 47 + 12 **2.** 76 − 34 **3.** 53 − 28 **4.** 78 + 13

5. 475 + 198 **6.** 896 − 532 **7.** 458 + 231 **8.** 4,853 − 1,998

9. You are playing a mental math game and you are given this problem: 498 + 362. What answer will you give? What method did you use?

Set I (pages 70–71)

Choose a Method Choose paper and pencil, a calculator, or mental math. Write your solution and the method you chose.

1. 78 + 26 **2.** 96 − 49 **3.** 472 − 236 **4.** 762 + 239

5. 5,764 + 3,287 **6.** 698 + 172 **7.** 6,785 − 2,431 **8.** 9,321 − 6,784

9. 1,998 − 498 **10.** 613 + 488 **11.** 977 − 38 **12.** 780 + 205

13. The large piñata contains 235 small gifts. The small piñata holds 178 gifts. How many more gifts does the large piñata contain? What calculation method did you use?

Chapter Test

Find the sum or difference.

1. $14 - 8 = n$ **2.** $9 + 7 = n$ **3.** $8 + 5 = n$ **4.** $15 - 7 = n$

Estimate by rounding to the greatest place.

5.   56
      − 23

6.   73
      − 37

7. $5.78
      − 1.98

8.   435
     + 243

9.   362
     + 533

Add.

10.   47
      + 36

11.   574
     + 368

12. $3.57
      + 4.86

13.   4,564
     + 2,671

14.   6,072
     + 5,184

Subtract.

15.   83
      − 49

16.   732
     − 356

17. $6.63
      − 3.95

18.   800
     − 463

19.   7,536
     − 2,784

**For Questions 20–23, tell whether you would use
paper and pencil, calculator, or mental math.
Explain the reasons for your choices.**

20. $198 + 137$ **21.** $7,632 - 3,967$ **22.** $593 - 251$ **23.** $32,578 + 17,986$

24. A video store sells a computer game for $15.79. It
sells another game for $9.98. What is the total price
for both games?

25. The high score for a computer game that you are
playing is 75,635. You score 52,786. How many
more points do you need to tie the high score?

 Self-Check Explain how you would subtract
731 − 294. Then explain how you would use
addition to check your answer.

Performance Assessment

Show What You Know About Addition and Subtraction

1 Make a spinner like the one shown.

a. Spin the pointer twice. Find the sum and difference of the numbers that you spun.

b. Which two numbers would give you a sum closest to 450?

Self-Check Did you use the two numbers that you spun in both an addition and a subtraction sentence?

What You Need

blank 6-part spinner
paper clip
base-ten blocks

2 Tricia has three $10 bills to buy gifts at the game store. She wants to buy 3 games. The table shows the choices Tricia has. You may use base-ten blocks, pictures, numbers, or words to show your computation.

a. Which games can Tricia buy?

b. How much change will she get?

c. What is the least number of bills and coins that she can get for change?

d. Will she have enough money left over to buy a game for herself?

Self-Check Did you check that Tricia was able to buy three games in all?

Price List	
Game	**Cost**
Magic Land	$15.86
Teaser	$12.47
Potato Catch	$10.15
Leap Toad	$19.95
Purple Palace	$4.50

For Your Portfolio

You might wish to include this work in your portfolio.

Extension

Front-End Estimation

You want to buy a game of checkers that costs $4.70. You also want to buy a bag of marbles that costs $2.23. How can you estimate the total cost quickly?

You can use front-end estimation.

Front-end estimation is a way of estimating by adding the digits with the greatest value—the front-end digits. Then you use the rest of the numbers to make your estimate more accurate.

Step 1 Add the front-end digits.	**Step 2** Use the cents to make your estimate more accurate.	**Step 3** Add the two amounts.
$4.70 + 2.23 $4.00 + $2.00 = $6.00	$4.70 + 2.23 $0.70 plus $0.23 is about $1.00 more	$6.00 + $1.00 = $7.00

The total cost is about $7.00. The estimate is more than the exact sum.

Use front-end estimation. Tell if the estimate is more than or less than the exact sum.

1. $3.74 + 3.30	**2.** $5.59 + 3.32	**3.** $4.41 + 2.07	**4.** $5.38 + 3.15	**5.** $5.23 + 4.26
6. $1.15 + 1.33	**7.** $3.76 + 2.19	**8.** $2.73 + 5.15	**9.** $2.98 + 2.05	**10.** $4.88 + 2.95

Cumulative Review

★ ★ ★ ★ ★ **Preparing for Tests**

Choose the correct letter for each answer.

Number Concept	Operations

Number Concept

1. What is the value of the 5 in 51,768?

   A. 5 ones
   B. 5 tens
   C. 5 thousand
   D. 50 thousand

2. What is 14,865 rounded to the nearest hundred?

   A. 14,800
   B. 14,870
   C. 14,900
   D. 15,000

3. Which is a set of even numbers?

   A. 2   8   12   16
   B. 3   9   12   20
   C. 4   6   7   14
   D. 2   5   8   13

4. The parents at Smith School are having a bake sale. At the end of the day, they decide to round all their prices to the nearest 10¢. If an item originally cost 75¢, what will it cost now?

   A. 60¢
   B. 70¢
   C. 80¢
   D. $1.00

Operations

5. Cal has 24 marbles. He bought 4 bags of new marbles. Each bag has 8 marbles. How many marbles does he have now?

   A. 24
   B. 32
   C. 40
   D. 56

6. Inez has 4 pairs of socks. If she buys one more pair, how many socks in all will she have?

   A. 12
   B. 10
   C. 8
   D. 5

7. What is the quotient of $45 \div 9$?

   A. 9
   B. 8
   C. 6
   D. 5

8. Fran read one book that had 88 pages and another that had 69 pages. **About** how many pages did she read in all?

   A. 160
   B. 170
   C. 190
   D. 200

Patterns, Relationships, and Algebraic Thinking	Geometry and Spatial Reasoning

Patterns, Relationships, and Algebraic Thinking

9. Which number makes this number sentence true?

$16 \div \blacksquare = 4$

A. 20
B. 12
C. 6
D. 4

10. Which number sentence is in the same family of facts as $35 \div 7 = 5$?

A. $20 + 15 = 35$
B. $5 \times 7 = 35$
C. $7 + 5 = 12$
D. $35 - 7 = 28$

11. Which number pair completes the last row of the table?

Number of Bikes	Number of Wheels
2	4
4	8
■	■

A. 8, 4
B. 6, 3
C. 5, 12
D. 6, 12

12. What is the missing number in the number pattern?

63, 54, 45, ■, 27

A. 18
B. 32
C. 36
D. 40

Geometry and Spatial Reasoning

13. How many sides does a quadrilateral have?

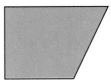

A. 3
B. 4
C. 5
D. 6

14. How many corners does a hexagon have?

A. 3
B. 4
C. 5
D. 6

15. How many faces does a cube have?

A. 3
B. 4
C. 5
D. 6

16. Which shows a line of symmetry?

A.

B.

C.

D.

Chapter 3

Multiplication and Division Facts

Chapter Theme: COLLECTIONS

REAL-WORLD Math

............Real Facts...................

Your favorite toy may someday be a collector's item! Many collectible toys can be found for under $50.00, but rare toys may be worth thousands of dollars. The graph below shows how much some toys now cost.

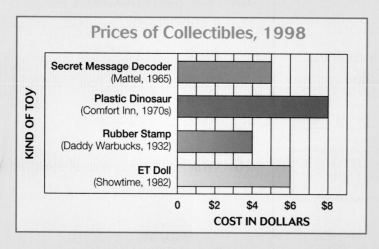

Prices of Collectibles, 1998

KIND OF TOY

Secret Message Decoder (Mattel, 1965)
Plastic Dinosaur (Comfort Inn, 1970s)
Rubber Stamp (Daddy Warbucks, 1932)
ET Doll (Showtime, 1982)

0    $2 $4 $6 $8
COST IN DOLLARS

• Suppose you wanted to buy 3 Secret Message Decoders. How much money would you need?

• Suppose you have $10. If you buy only the toys shown in the graph, what could you buy?

.............Real People...................

Meet Louise Mesa. She owns the Frog Fantasies Museum in Eureka Springs, Arkansas. For only $1.00, you can buy a ticket to see her family's collection of more than 6,000 frogs.

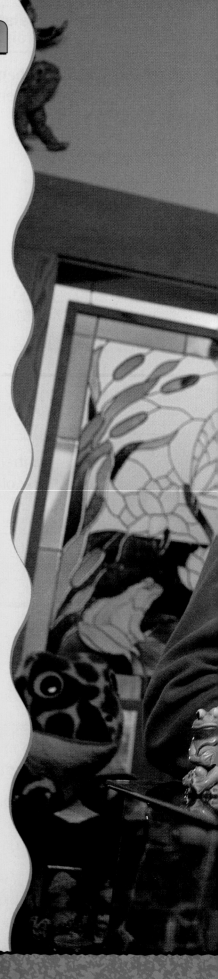

Using Algebra

Shell It Out

*Collecting shells helps you explore
how multiplication and division are related.*

Learning About It

Three friends went to the beach together. They each collected 4 shells. Use counters to explore how many shells they had altogether.

Work with a partner.

Step 1 Draw circles on a piece of paper to represent the 3 friends. Put 4 counters in each circle to represent the shells each friend collected.

Step 2 How many counters are there altogether?

Since each friend collected the same number of shells, a multiplication sentence can help you find the total.

Number of friends	$\times$	Number of shells for each	$=$	Total number of shells
3	$\times$	**4**	$=$	**12**

Step 3 Copy the chart below.
The chart shows 3 friends with 4 shells each.

What You Need

For each pair:
20 counters

3 friends
4 shells each

Number of Friends	Number of Shells per Friend	Drawing	Total Number of Shells	Multiplication Sentence
3	4	⊙⊙⊙	12	$3 \times 4 = 12$

Use counters to help you fill in your chart for each of these.

- 4 friends, 3 shells each
- 3 friends, 5 shells each
- 6 friends, 2 shells each
- 5 friends, 1 shell each

Use counters to explore how multiplication is related to division. If you want to divide 12 shells equally among 3 friends, how many shells would each friend get?

12 shells

Step 4 Make 3 circles. Divide 12 counters equally among them. How many counters are in each circle?

Since you are making equal groups, a division sentence can help you.

3 friends share 12 shells

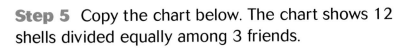

Total number of shells	÷	Number of friends	=	Number of shells per friend
12	**÷**	**3**	**=**	**4**

Step 5 Copy the chart below. The chart shows 12 shells divided equally among 3 friends.

Number of Shells	Number of Friends	Drawing	Number of Shells per Friend	Division Sentence
12	3	⊙⊙⊙	4	12 ÷ 3 = 4

Use counters to help you fill in your chart for each.

- 18 shells in all, 6 friends
- 20 shells in all, 5 friends

Think and Discuss How did working with counters help you to understand how multiplication and division are related?

Practice

1. Use counters or drawings to decide how many different ways 12 shells can be divided into equal groups.

2. **Explain** Compare the following: $3 \times 4 = 12$ and $12 \div 3 = 4$. Explain how they are alike and how they are different.

3. **Describe** Tell how multiplication and division are related.

Tie Up Loose Ends

Doubles can help you remember the facts for 2 and 4.

Learning About It

You and a friend are each making a friendship bracelet. If each bracelet uses 5 threads, how many threads will you need altogether?

$2 \times 5 = \blacksquare$

$2 \times 5 = 10$ threads altogether

What if four of you were making bracelets with 5 threads each? How many threads would you need altogether?

$4 \times 5 = \blacksquare$

THERE'S ALWAYS A WAY!

● **One way** to find the answer is to use doubles. 4 is the double of 2.

Since $2 \times 5 = 10$,

then $4 \times 5 = 10 + 10$ 4×5 ⟹ $\begin{bmatrix} 2 \times 5 = 10 \\ 2 \times 5 = 10 \end{bmatrix}$ ⟹ 20

or $4 \times 5 = 20$

● **Another way** is to add.

$5 + 5 + 5 + 5 = 20$

You need 20 threads altogether.

Think and Discuss An even number can be divided into equal groups. An odd number cannot. When you multiply a number by 2 or 4, will the product be even or odd? Explain.

Try It Out

Complete the first fact in each pair. Then use doubles
to complete the second fact.

1. 2 × 5
4 × 5

2. 2 × 4
4 × 4

3. 2 × 9
4 × 9

4. 2 × 7
4 × 7

5. 2 × 3
4 × 3

Practice

Find the product. Use doubles if you wish.

6.   9
× 2

7.   4
× 2

8.   6
× 4

9.   6
× 2

10.   4
× 4

11.   3
× 4

12.   8
× 4

13.   7
× 2

14.   7
× 4

15.   5
× 2

16. 3 × 2

17. 8 × 2

18. 9 × 4

19. 2 × 4

20. 5 × 4

21. Explain How does knowing 2 × 8
help you find the product of 4 × 8?

Problem Solving

22. Salita wants to make Raksha Bandhan
bracelets for her 4 brothers. She is using
6 threads for each bracelet. How many
threads does she need?

23. What If? Your class sold 48 bracelets at
$1.00 each. You spent $2.10 for thread
and $6.40 for beads. How much money
did your class earn after expenses?

24. Create Your Own Write a multiplication
problem about friendship bracelets.
Trade with a partner and solve.

▲ **Social Studies Connection**
During the Raksha Bandhan festival
in India, sisters tie thread bracelets
around their brothers' wrists. The
thread bracelet is a symbol of the
bond between brother and sister.

Review and Remember

Add or subtract.

25.   521
− 183

26.   235
+ 407

27.   96,784
+   8,400

28.   40,091
− 30,131

For Extra Practice, see Set A, page 124.

Collecting Properties

The properties of multiplication help you find products.

Learning About It

Multiplication properties help you remember facts. Numbers that are multiplied to give a **product** are called **factors**.

Word Bank

product

factor

Commutative Property

The order in which factors are multiplied does not change the product.

$5 \times 3 = 15$ $3 \times 5 = 15$

Associative Property

The way in which factors are grouped does not change the product.

$(2 \times 2) \times 3 = 12$ $2 \times (2 \times 3) = 12$
$\quad 4 \quad \times 3 = 12$ $2 \times \quad 6 \quad = 12$

Property of One

When you multiply any number by 1, the product is that number.

$5 \times 1 = 5$

Zero Property

When you multiply any number by 0, the product is 0.

$2 \times 0 = 0$

Think and Discuss Which multiplication properties are like the addition properties? Which are different? Give examples to explain your answers.

Try It Out

Use properties to solve.

1. 0×4

2. 1×121

3. 0×8

4. $1 \times 2{,}589$

5. 0×543

6. $3 \times 2 = 2 \times \blacksquare$

7. $4 \times \blacksquare = 7 \times 4$

8. $(3 \times 2) \times 4 = 3 \times (2 \times \blacksquare)$

Practice

Using Algebra Find the missing number. Name the property that helps you find each missing number.

9. $1 \times \blacksquare = 6$

10. $4 \times 8 = 8 \times \blacksquare$

11. $(\blacksquare \times 2) \times 7 = 8 \times (2 \times 7)$

12. $\blacksquare \times 9 = 0$

13. $\blacksquare \times 2 = 2 \times 5$

14. $2 \times (\blacksquare \times 1) = (2 \times 2) \times 1$

15. $10 \times 0 = \blacksquare$

16. $\blacksquare \times (\blacksquare \times 6) = 6$

17. $(1 \times \blacksquare) \times 3 = 1 \times (5 \times 3)$

Problem Solving

18. Journal Idea The product of two numbers is 0. Can you name one of the factors? Explain.

19. Explain The product of two numbers is 17. What do you think the numbers are? Explain.

Review and Remember

Add or subtract.

20. $\begin{array}{r} 275 \\ -\ 69 \end{array}$

21. $\begin{array}{r} 700 \\ +\ 596 \end{array}$

22. $\begin{array}{r} 3{,}450 \\ +\ 1{,}006 \end{array}$

23. $\begin{array}{r} \$\ 5.54 \\ -\ 2.83 \end{array}$

24. $\begin{array}{r} \$\ 28.43 \\ -\ 10.67 \end{array}$

Money $ense

Money Riddles

Solve each money riddle below.

1. Jo has 6 coins which equal 22¢. If she has 4 of one kind of coin and 2 of another kind of coin, what coins does Jo have?

2. Kurt has 6 equal piles of coins. If he adds a dime to each pile, the value doubles. How much money did he start with?

For Extra Practice, see Set B, page 124.

Cool Cars

Using Algebra

Doubles also help you remember the facts for 3 and 6.

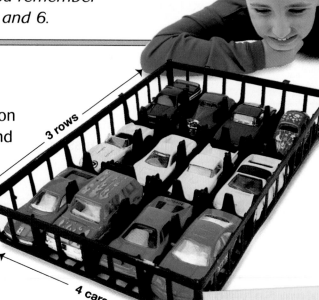

3 rows

4 cars

Learning About It

Josh stores his minicar collection in trays. The trays have rows and columns that form **arrays**. Each tray has 3 rows with 4 cars each. How many cars does each tray hold?

$$3 \times 4 = \blacksquare$$

What if a tray had 6 rows? How would Josh find out how many cars he has?

Word Bank

array

THERE'S ALWAYS A WAY!

- **One way** is to use doubles. 6 is the double of 3.

  Since $3 \times 4 = 12$
  then $6 \times 4 = 12 + 12$
  or $6 \times 4 = 24$

- **Another way** is to add.

  $$4 + 4 + 4 + 4 + 4 + 4 = 24$$

Each tray holds 24 cars.

Think and Discuss When you multiply a number by 3, will the product be even or odd? Explain.

Try It Out

Complete the first fact. Then use doubles to complete the second fact.

1. 3×3	**2.** 3×2	**3.** 3×5	**4.** 3×7	**5.** 3×6
6×3	6×2	6×5	6×7	6×6

Practice

Multiply. Use doubles if you wish.

6. 2
× 3

7. 5
× 6

8. 7
× 6

9. 5
× 3

10. 6
× 6

11. 6
× 3

12. 3
× 6

13. 3
× 3

14. 8
× 6

15. 7
× 3

16. 9
× 3

17. 8
× 3

18. 9
× 6

19. 4
× 3

20. 4
× 6

21. **Explain** How can you use 3 × 7 to help you solve 6 × 7?

Problem Solving

Use the table at the right to solve Problems 22–25.

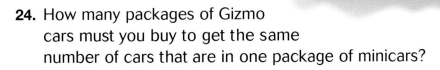

Type of Car	Number of Items per Package
Gizmo cars	3
4 x 4 trucks	2
Minicars	6

22. How many Gizmo cars are in 3 packages? in 6 packages?

23. How many trucks will you get if you buy 5 packages?

24. How many packages of Gizmo cars must you buy to get the same number of cars that are in one package of minicars?

25. **You Decide** You bought several packages of cars. Altogether you end up with a total of 30 cars. Which packages and how many did you buy?

Review and Remember

Add or subtract.

26. $3.11
−0.52

27. $4.36
+ 9.87

28. 5,532
+ 4,140

29. $12.44
− 7.50

30. 649
−506

31. $ 4.01
+ 9.49

32. $0.36
+ 0.22

33. $6.57
− 5.50

For Extra Practice, see Set C, page 124.

Counting Coins

Skip counting can help you remember your 5s and 10s facts.

Learning About It

You can organize coins into a collection. The coins can be arranged by date, design, or mint mark.

How much are 6 nickels worth? **6 × 5 = ▨**

To find 6 × 5, you can count by 5s until you have said six numbers.

$$6 \times 5 = 30$$

6 nickels are worth 30¢.

How much are 6 dimes worth? **6 × 10 = ▨**

To find 6 × 10, count by 10s until you have said six numbers.

$$6 \times 10 = 60$$

6 dimes are worth 60¢.

Think and Discuss How can the product of a 5s fact also be the product of a 10s fact?

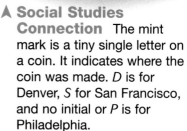

▲ **Social Studies Connection** The mint mark is a tiny single letter on a coin. It indicates where the coin was made. *D* is for Denver, *S* for San Francisco, and no initial or *P* is for Philadelphia.

INTERNET ACTIVITY

www.sbgmath.com

Try It Out

1. 10 × 1　　**2.** 5 × 3　　**3.** 10 × 3　　**4.** 5 × 5　　**5.** 10 × 2　　**6.** 5 × 2

Practice

Find each product.

7. 2
    × 10

8. 3
    × 5

9. 2
    × 5

10. 1
     × 5

11. 4
     × 5

12. 3
     × 10

13. 10
     × 5

14. 9
     × 5

15. 7
     × 10

16. 5
     × 5

17. 6
     × 10

18. 10
     × 10

Using Algebra Compare. Use >, < , or = for ●.

19. 5 × 4 ● 10 × 4

20. 6 × 5 ● 10 × 3

21. 10 × 4 ● 5 × 10

22. 5 × 8 ● 10 × 3

23. 10 × 6 ● 5 × 10

24. 10 × 3 ● 6 × 5

25. **Create Your Own** Make up an example like those in Exercises 19–24. Ask a classmate to solve it.

Problem Solving

Use the table to solve Problems 26–28.

Coin Values		
Country	**5-Unit Value**	**10-Unit Value**
Gambia	5-bututs coin	10-bututs coin
Mexico	5-centavos coin	10-centavos coin
Japan	5-yen coin	10-yen coin

◄ **Social Studies Connection**
There are other countries besides the United States where money comes in units of 5 and 10.

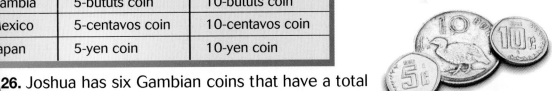

▲ butut (boo TOOT) and centavo (sen TAH voh) coins

26. Joshua has six Gambian coins that have a total value of 45 bututs. How many 5-bututs coins and how many 10-bututs coins does he have?

27. Nicolai has seven 10-centavos coins and four 5-centavos coins. What is the total value of these coins in centavos?

28. **Analyze** You have 5 nickels. You need 3 times that many more to finish filling a nickel board. How many nickels fit on the board?

Review and Remember

Using Estimation Estimate each sum or difference. Check the reasonableness of your answers.

29. 488
    − 361

30. 5,167
    + 3,485

31. 9,826
    − 5,999

32. 872
    + 994

33. 6,234
    + 4,102

For Extra Practice, see Set D, page 125.

Using Algebra

Putting the Pieces Together

Patterns on the multiplication table can help you learn 7s, 8s, and 9s.

Learning About It

Look at the multiplication table below. The 9 empty squares stand for the facts you haven't learned yet.

The Property of One When you multiply any number by 1, the product is that number. For example, $1 \times 9 = 9$. So, you know all the 1s facts.

You already know the facts for 2, 3, 4, 5, and 6.

x	1	2	3	4	5	6	7	8	9
1	1	2	3	4	5	6	7	8	9
2	2	4	6	8	10	12	14	16	18
3	3	6	9	12	15	18	21	24	27
4	4	8	12	16	20	24	28	32	36
5	5	10	15	20	25	30	35	40	45
6	6	12	18	24	30	36	42	48	54
7	7	14	21	28	35	42			
8	8	16	24	32	40	48			
9	9	18	27	36	45	54			

The Commutative Property The order in which factors are multiplied does not change the product. For example, $6 \times 8 = 48$ and $8 \times 6 = 48$. This property helps you know all these other facts, too.

Which facts do you still have to learn?

Step 1 Use the pattern to learn the other 7s facts.

$7 \times 1 = 7$
$7 \times 2 = 14$
$7 \times 3 = 21$
$7 \times 4 = 28$
$7 \times 5 = 35$
$7 \times 6 = 42$

Each product is 7 more than the product that comes before.

So $7 \times 7 = 49$
$7 \times 8 = 56$
$7 \times 9 = 63$

x	1	2	3	4	5	6	7	8	9
1	1	2	3	4	5	6	7	8	9
2	2	4	6	8	10	12	14	16	18
3	3	6	9	12	15	18	21	24	27
4	4	8	12	16	20	24	28	32	36
5	5	10	15	20	25	30	35	40	45
6	6	12	18	24	30	36	42	48	54
7	7	14	21	28	35	42	49	56	63
8	8	16	24	32	40	48	56	64	72
9	9	18	27	36	45	54	63	72	81

A **multiple** of 7 is any product that has 7 as a factor.

Step 2 Use the table to find the pattern for the 8s facts. What are these products?

$8 \times 7 = \blacksquare$
$8 \times 8 = \blacksquare$
$8 \times 9 = \blacksquare$

Step 3 Look at the 9s facts. What is the sum of the digits of each product? What other patterns can you find in the 9s facts?

$9 \times 1 = 9$
$9 \times 2 = 18$
$9 \times 3 = 27$
$9 \times 4 = 36$
$9 \times 5 = 45$
$9 \times 6 = 54$
$9 \times 7 = 63$
$9 \times 8 = 72$
$9 \times 9 = 81$

$8 - 1 = 7$

Example: $9 \times 8 = 72$

$7 + 2 = 9$

Think and Discuss What other patterns can you find in the multiplication table?

Try It Out

Find each product.

1. 7×7 **2.** 9×8 **3.** 7×8 **4.** 1×7 **5.** 8×4

6. 9×6 **7.** 7×3 **8.** 8×7 **9.** 5×9 **10.** 9×7

Practice

Multiply.

11. 7
     × 8

12. 5
     × 7

13. 1
     × 9

14. 6
     × 7

15. 9
     × 7

16. 4
     × 8

17. 7
     × 9

18. 0
     × 7

19. 8
     × 10

20. 2
     × 7

21. 3
     × 9

22. 6
     × 9

23. 5
     × 9

24. 4
     × 9

25. 9
     × 8

26. 8
     × 8

27. 6
     × 8

28. 2
     × 8

29. 9×10

30. 3×8

31. 2×9

32. 9×9

33. 5×8

34. 9×8

35. 7×1

36. 10×7

37. 9×0

38. 7×7

39. 1×8

40. 3×7

Find each missing number.

41. $3 \times 7 = n$

42. $n \times 5 = 45$

43. $n \times 2 = 16$

44. $8 \times 8 = n$

45. $n \times 8 = 56$

46. $8 \times n = 64$

47. $8 \times n = 80$

48. $n \times 8 = 56$

Problem Solving

The Southside Birdwatchers kept a six-month record
of the seed they put out for the birds. Use their
graph to answer Problems 49–52.

49. In what month did the birds
eat the most seed?

50. How much more seed was
eaten in November than in
October?

51. Did the birds eat more seed
during the first 3 months or
the last 3 months?

52. What month used three
times as much seed as
September?

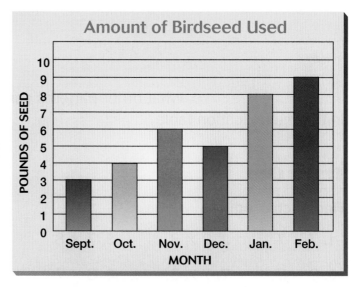

53. If you were a birdwatcher and you sighted 8 different birds every day for one week, how many different birds would you see altogether?

54. There are 9 teams with 7 people on each team in a birding contest. How many people have entered the contest?

55. You worked on your Junior Ranger badge for 2 hours. Each hour you sighted 9 different birds, 7 different reptiles, and 8 different mammals. How many animals did you sight in all?

56. José saw 3 different woodpeckers each day for 5 days. He saw 5 different ducks each day for 3 days. Did he see more ducks or woodpeckers?

57. Nine friends each saw 9 catbirds last week. How many catbird sightings were made in all?

58. **Analyze** The product of two numbers is 35. Their sum is 12. What are the numbers? What strategy did you use to find the answer?

Review and Remember

Using Algebra Find the rule. Then complete each table.

59. Rule: _____

Input	Output
5	35
6	42
60. 7	■
61. 8	■

62. Rule: _____

Input	Output
18	3
24	4
63. 30	■
64. 36	■

65. Rule: _____

Input	Output
3	27
66. 4	■
5	45
67. 6	■

▲ **Kid Connection**
Birdwatching, also called birding, is a popular hobby. Becky Florez learned how to bird while becoming a Junior Park Ranger at Saguaro National Park, Arizona.

Cactus Wren

Gambel's Quail

Roadrunner

Gila Woodpecker

Using Algebra

Developing Skills for
Problem Solving

*First read for understanding and then focus on
which operation to use to solve a problem.*

READ FOR UNDERSTANDING

Diana collects three different kinds of paperback books. She has 26 mystery books, 19 cartoon books, and 38 biographies in her collection.

1 How many kinds of books does Diana have?

2 How many of each kind of book does she have?

THINK AND DISCUSS

MATH FOCUS

Choose the Operation Addition, subtraction, and multiplication are operations you sometimes use to solve problems. When you combine items, you can add or multiply. When you want to find how many more of one thing you have than another, you subtract.

Reread the paragraph at the top of the page.

3 Suppose you want to know how many more biographies than cartoon books Diana has. Would you add or subtract to find out? Explain why.

4 Can Diana fit all her mystery and cartoon books on a shelf that holds 50 books? Explain what you need to do to solve this problem.

5 Explain how you know whether to add, subtract, or multiply.

Show What You Learned

Answer each question. Give a reason for your choice.

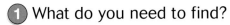Kyle has 24 space books, 33 joke books, and 18 mystery books. How many more joke books does Kyle have than space books?

1 What do you need to find?

a. The number of books altogether

b. How many more space books than joke books Kyle has

c. How many more joke books than space books Kyle has

2 Which operation could you use to solve the problem?

a. Subtraction

b. Addition

c. Multiplication

3 Which number sentence could you use to solve the problem?

a. $24 + 18 = 42$

b. $33 - 24 = 9$

c. $33 - 18 = 15$

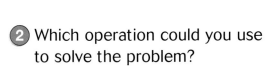Andy keeps all 20 of his biographies in one bookcase. He keeps all of his mystery books in another bookcase that has 4 shelves. He has 8 mystery books on each of the 4 shelves. How many mystery books does Andy have?

4 What do you need to find?

a. The number of mystery books

b. The number of biographies

c. The number of books on each shelf

5 Which number sentence shows how many mystery books Andy has?

a $8 + 8 + 4 + 4 = 24$

b. $32 - 4 = 28$

c. $4 \times 8 = 32$

6 **Explain** Look back at your answer for Problem 5. What is another number sentence you could use to show how many mystery books Andy has?

Checkpoint

Multiplication Facts

Complete. Use words from the Word Bank.

1. You multiply numbers to find a ___?___ .

2. The ___?___ states that the way numbers are grouped does not change the product.

3. A number you multiply is a ___?___ .

4. The ___?___ states that the product of any number multiplied by 1 is that number.

5. The ___?___ states that when you multiply any number by 0, the product is 0.

Word Bank

factor
product
Property of One
Zero Property
Associative
  Property

Using Algebra **Solve each pair.** (pages 86–87)

6. $2 \times 2 = $ ■
$4 \times 2 = $ ■

7. $2 \times 5 = $ ■
$4 \times 5 = $ ■

8. $2 \times 6 = $ ■
$4 \times 6 = $ ■

9. $2 \times 7 = $ ■
$4 \times 7 = $ ■

10. $2 \times 8 = $ ■
$4 \times 8 = $ ■

11. $2 \times 3 = $ ■
$4 \times 3 = $ ■

12. $2 \times 9 = $ ■
$4 \times 9 = $ ■

13. $2 \times 4 = $ ■
$4 \times 4 = $ ■

14. $2 \times 1 = $ ■
$4 \times 1 = $ ■

What do you think?

Why do you think multiplication and division are called opposite or inverse operations?

Using Algebra **Use properties to solve.** (pages 88–89)

15. $6 \times$ ■ $= 8 \times 6$

16. $0 \times 125 = $ ■

17. $1 \times 715 = $ ■

18. $(8 \times 0) \times 4 = $ ■

19. ■ $\times 7 = 7 \times 3$

20. $(4 \times 5) \times 2 = 4 \times (5 \times$ ■$)$

21. $9 \times$ ■ $= 7 \times 9$

22. $247 \times 0 = $ ■

23. $4 \times (8 \times 7) = (4 \times 8) \times$ ■

24. $(9 \times 0) \times 8 = $ ■

25. $7 \times$ ■ $= 6 \times 7$

26. $(3 \times 4) \times 5 = $ ■ $\times (4 \times 5)$

Multiply. (pages 90–91, 92–93, 94–97)

27. $\begin{array}{r} 1 \\ \times\, 3 \\ \hline \end{array}$

28. $\begin{array}{r} 4 \\ \times\, 3 \\ \hline \end{array}$

29. $\begin{array}{r} 2 \\ \times\, 6 \\ \hline \end{array}$

30. $\begin{array}{r} 3 \\ \times\, 3 \\ \hline \end{array}$

31. $\begin{array}{r} 5 \\ \times\, 6 \\ \hline \end{array}$

32. $\begin{array}{r} 3 \\ \times\, 7 \\ \hline \end{array}$

33.
$$\begin{array}{r} 9 \\ \times\ 6 \\ \hline \end{array}$$

34.
$$\begin{array}{r} 6 \\ \times\ 6 \\ \hline \end{array}$$

35.
$$\begin{array}{r} 6 \\ \times\ 3 \\ \hline \end{array}$$

36.
$$\begin{array}{r} 8 \\ \times\ 6 \\ \hline \end{array}$$

37.
$$\begin{array}{r} 7 \\ \times\ 3 \\ \hline \end{array}$$

38.
$$\begin{array}{r} 0 \\ \times\ 0 \\ \hline \end{array}$$

39.
$$\begin{array}{r} 9 \\ \times\ 5 \\ \hline \end{array}$$

40.
$$\begin{array}{r} 7 \\ \times\ 10 \\ \hline \end{array}$$

41.
$$\begin{array}{r} 5 \\ \times\ 5 \\ \hline \end{array}$$

42.
$$\begin{array}{r} 10 \\ \times\ 10 \\ \hline \end{array}$$

43.
$$\begin{array}{r} 0 \\ \times\ 5 \\ \hline \end{array}$$

44.
$$\begin{array}{r} 6 \\ \times\ 10 \\ \hline \end{array}$$

45. $3 \times 9 = $ ■

46. $8 \times 8 = $ ■

47. $9 \times 0 = $ ■

48. $9 \times 5 = $ ■

49. $7 \times 3 = $ ■

50. $6 \times 7 = $ ■

51. $7 \times 8 = $ ■

52. $7 \times 6 = $ ■

53. $9 \times 9 = $ ■

54. $7 \times 5 = $ ■

55. $9 \times 4 = $ ■

56. $5 \times 8 = $ ■

Problem Solving

57. Each model sailboat will have 3 sails. How many sails are needed for 5 boats?

58. **Analyze** A product is 0. One factor is 0. Why can't you tell what the other factor is?

59. A minicar carrier holds 10 cars. Robert has 6 full carriers. How many cars does he have?

60. A model airplane costs $3.50, a boat $2.75, and a car $5.00. How much will it cost to buy all three?

Journal Idea

Explain how knowing that $3 \times 8 = 24$ helps you find the product of 6×8.

Critical Thinking Corner

Logical Thinking

True or False

Write *true* or *false* for each sentence. If the answer is *false*, explain why.

1. $1 \times 9 = 9 \times 0$

2. $(8 \times 2) \times (7 \times 1) \times (0 \times 9) = 0$

3. $1 \times 1 \times 1 \times 1 = 4$

4. $(4 \times 2) \times 3 = (4 \times 3) \times 2$

5. $(5 \times 4) \times 1 = 1$

6. $6 \times 4 = (3 \times 2) \times (2 \times 2)$

Sticker Families

Using Algebra

Arrays and fact families show you how multiplication and division are related.

Learning About It

Susan discovered that she could group 12 stickers in different ways. She arranged them in rows and columns to make arrays.

4 rows with 3 stickers in a row

4 × 3 = 12

3 rows with 4 stickers in a row

3 × 4 = 12

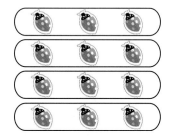

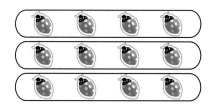

12 stickers can be divided into 4 groups of 3.

12 ÷ 4 = 3

12 stickers can be divided into 3 groups of 4.

12 ÷ 3 = 4

Fact families show how multiplication and division are related. This is the fact family for 3, 4, and 12.

$$4 \times 3 = 12 \qquad 3 \times 4 = 12$$
$$12 \div 4 = 3 \qquad 12 \div 3 = 4$$

Think and Discuss How are the arrays for 3 × 4 and 4 × 3 the same? How are they different?

Try It Out

Write the fact family for each array.

1.

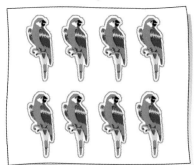 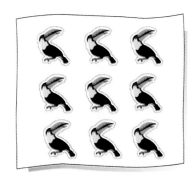

Write the fact family for each set of numbers.
Use counters or draw arrays if you wish.

3. 4, 6, 24   **4.** 2, 9, 18   **5.** 5, 3, 15   **6.** 1, 8, 8

7. Analyze Why is there only one multiplication and
one division sentence for Exercise 2?

Practice

Copy and complete each fact family.

8. $3 \times 6 = 18$
$6 \times 3 = \blacksquare$
$18 \div 3 = \blacksquare$
$18 \div 6 = \blacksquare$

9. $2 \times 8 = 16$
$8 \times 2 = \blacksquare$
$16 \div 2 = \blacksquare$
$16 \div 8 = \blacksquare$

10. $7 \times 5 = 35$
$5 \times 7 = \blacksquare$
$35 \div 7 = \blacksquare$
$35 \div 5 = \blacksquare$

11. $6 \times 9 = 54$
$9 \times 6 = \blacksquare$
$54 \div 6 = \blacksquare$
$54 \div 9 = \blacksquare$

12. $3 \times 7 = \blacksquare$
$7 \times 3 = \blacksquare$
$21 \div 3 = \blacksquare$
$21 \div 7 = \blacksquare$

13. $4 \times 2 = \blacksquare$
$2 \times 4 = \blacksquare$
$8 \div 4 = \blacksquare$
$8 \div 2 = \blacksquare$

14. $8 \times 7 = \blacksquare$
$7 \times 8 = \blacksquare$
$56 \div 8 = \blacksquare$
$56 \div 7 = \blacksquare$

15. $5 \times 9 = \blacksquare$
$9 \times 5 = \blacksquare$
$45 \div 5 = \blacksquare$
$45 \div 9 = \blacksquare$

**Write the fact family for each. Use
counters or draw arrays if you wish.**

16. 2, 7, 14   **17.** 8, 4, 32

18. 7, 4, 28   **19.** 3, 9, 27

20. 5, 4, 20   **21.** 9, 7, 63

22. 5, 5, 25   **23.** 6, 8, 48

24. 9, 8, 72   **25.** 8, 8, 64

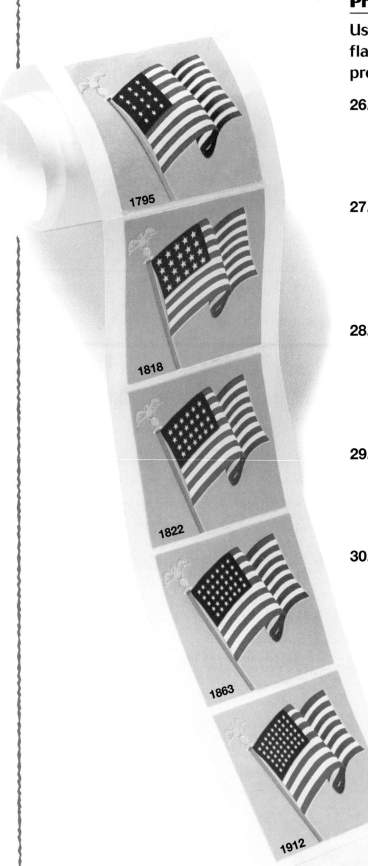

1795

1818

1822

1863

1912

Problem Solving

Use this collection of United States flag stickers to solve these problems.

26. Write two multiplication sentences that describe the array of stars in the 1795 flag. Then write the rest of the fact family.

27. How many stars did the flag have in 1818? What multiplication sentence describes this array? Write the fact family for the set of numbers shown by this array.

28. Before 1912, there were no rules about how the stars should be arrayed. Draw all the possible arrays that could be made with the stars in the 1822 flag.

29. In 1863 the Civil War flag had a star for every state in the North and the South. Draw another array for these stars.

30. Could any other arrays have been used for the stars in the flag of 1912? Write a fact family to describe each of the possible arrays for this flag.

31. Social Studies Connection Today, the U.S. flag has 50 stars. Study the arrangement of the stars on the flag in your classroom. Why do you think the stars were not placed in a rectangular array?

Review and Remember

Add, subtract, or multiply.

32. $\begin{array}{r} 25 \\ +\ 63 \\ \hline \end{array}$

33. $\begin{array}{r} 41 \\ +\ 17 \\ \hline \end{array}$

34. $\begin{array}{r} \$5.86 \\ +\ 4.77 \\ \hline \end{array}$

35. $\begin{array}{r} 95 \\ +\ 76 \\ \hline \end{array}$

36. $\begin{array}{r} 427 \\ +\ 38 \\ \hline \end{array}$

37. $\begin{array}{r} 504 \\ -\ 73 \\ \hline \end{array}$

38. $\begin{array}{r} 462 \\ -\ 385 \\ \hline \end{array}$

39. $\begin{array}{r} 306 \\ -\ 197 \\ \hline \end{array}$

40. $\begin{array}{r} \$3.05 \\ -\ 2.32 \\ \hline \end{array}$

41. $\begin{array}{r} \$6.14 \\ -\ 4.37 \\ \hline \end{array}$

42. $\begin{array}{r} 9 \\ \times\ 9 \\ \hline \end{array}$

43. $\begin{array}{r} 6 \\ \times\ 8 \\ \hline \end{array}$

44. $\begin{array}{r} 7 \\ \times\ 7 \\ \hline \end{array}$

45. $\begin{array}{r} 8 \\ \times\ 8 \\ \hline \end{array}$

46. $\begin{array}{r} 9 \\ \times\ 8 \\ \hline \end{array}$

47. $\begin{array}{r} 922 \\ +\ 59 \\ \hline \end{array}$

48. $\begin{array}{r} 7 \\ \times\ 6 \\ \hline \end{array}$

49. $\begin{array}{r} 680 \\ -\ 493 \\ \hline \end{array}$

50. $\begin{array}{r} \$7.98 \\ +\ 5.13 \\ \hline \end{array}$

51. $\begin{array}{r} 7 \\ \times\ 5 \\ \hline \end{array}$

Time for Technology

Using the MathProcessor™ on CD-ROM

Using the Large Frames

You can model fact families like 3, 6, 18.

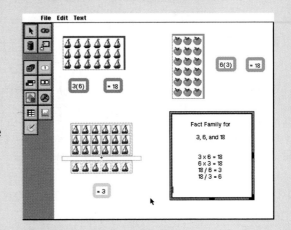

- Click large frames ▦ to make a 6 x 3 array and a 3 x 6 array. Fill the arrays. Link them to number spaces ▣. Click ▣ for each.

- Make a 3 x 6 array and a 1 x 6 row. Click on the 3 x 6 array.

- Click ÷. Click on the 1 x 6 row. Link the division to a new number space. Click ▣.

- Make a 6 x 3 array and a 1 x 3 row. Click on the 6 x 3 array.

- Click ÷. Click on the 1 x 3 row. Link the division to a fourth number space. Click ▣.

- Write the number sentences for fact family 3, 6, 18.

For Extra Practice, see Set F, page 125.

Boats and Boxes

Knowing the multiplication facts will help you to divide.

Learning About It

Karen and her dad are shipping their model boats to a craft show. They have 8 boats and 2 boxes. How many boats will they put in each box if they divide them equally?

$8 \div 2 = $

THERE'S ALWAYS A WAY!

• **One way** is to use 8 counters and put them into 2 equal groups.

• **Another way** is to divide.

$$8 \div 2 = 4$$
dividend | quotient
divisor

$$2\overline{)8}$$
4 quotient
divisor dividend

Word Bank

dividend
divisor
quotient

They can put 4 boats in each box.

If they had 4 boxes to ship 8 boats, how many could they pack in each box?

$8 \div 4 = $ Think: $\times 4 = 8$
$2 \times 4 = 8$
So, $8 \div 4 = 2$

They could put 2 boats in each box.

Think and Discuss What happens to the quotient when the divisor is doubled from 2 to 4?

Try It Out

Find each quotient.

1. $4 \div 2 = \blacksquare$
$4 \div 4 = \blacksquare$

2. $12 \div 2 = \blacksquare$
$12 \div 4 = \blacksquare$

3. $8 \div 2 = \blacksquare$
$8 \div 4 = \blacksquare$

4. $18 \div 3 = \blacksquare$
$18 \div 6 = \blacksquare$

5. $24 \div 4 = \blacksquare$

6. $18 \div 2 = \blacksquare$

7. $36 \div 4 = \blacksquare$

8. $14 \div 2 = \blacksquare$

Practice

Divide.

9. $4\overline{)12}$

10. $2\overline{)14}$

11. $4\overline{)20}$

12. $4\overline{)4}$

13. $2\overline{)12}$

14. $4\overline{)32}$

15. $2\overline{)16}$

16. $4\overline{)28}$

17. $2\overline{)10}$

18. $2\overline{)8}$

19. $2\overline{)4}$

20. $4\overline{)8}$

21. $2\overline{)6}$

22. $2\overline{)18}$

23. $4\overline{)16}$

Using Algebra Find the quotient or missing factor.

24. $16 \div 4 = n$

25. $32 \div 4 = n$

26. $4 \times n = 32$

27. $n \times 4 = 24$

28. $28 \div 4 = n$

29. $n \times 3 = 12$

30. $n \times 2 = 6$

31. $20 \div 4 = n$

32. $n \times 7 = 14$

33. $18 \div 2 = n$

34. $36 \div 4 = n$

35. $8 \div 2 = n$

Problem Solving

36. Karen's dad paid $8 in postage to ship two boxes of models. Each box weighed the same. What was the postage per box?

37. A model-ship builder has 35 sails. If each model must have 4 sails, how many ships can be built?

38. **Using Algebra** You have twice as many books about whales as about steamships. You have 1 more book about steamships than about sailboats. You have 3 books about sailboats. How many books do you have?

Review and Remember

Write the value of the 5 in each number.

39. 25

40. 4,510

41. 527,812

42. 152,089

43. 651

For Extra Practice, see Set G, page 125.

3... 2... 1... Blast Off

*Related multiplication facts help you
learn division facts.*

Learning About It

Eighteen rockets were
built for the Rocket Club
field day. If rockets were
launched 3 at a time,
how many launchings
would there be?

$$18 \div 3 = \blacksquare$$

THERE'S ALWAYS A WAY!

● **One way** is to think of a
related multiplication fact.

$$18 \div 3 = \blacksquare$$

Think: $\blacksquare \times 3 = 18$

$$6 \times 3 = 18$$

So, $18 \div 3 = 6$

● **Another way** is to subtract
3s until you get to 0.

18   15   12   9   6   3   0

−3   −3   −3   −3   −3   −3

You subtracted 6 times, so
the quotient must be 6.

There will be 6 launchings.

If 6 rockets are launched at the same time,
how many launchings will there be?

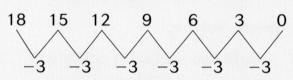

$$18 \div 6 = \blacksquare$$ Think: $\blacksquare \times 6 = 18$

$$3 \times 6 = 18$$

So, $18 \div 6 = 3$

Think and Discuss Describe another way to divide.
Use $21 \div 3$.

INTERNET ACTIVITY
www.sbgmath.com

Try It Out

Find each quotient.

1. 6 ÷ 3
6 ÷ 6

2. 12 ÷ 3
12 ÷ 6

3. 18 ÷ 3
18 ÷ 6

4. 24 ÷ 3
24 ÷ 6

5. 30 ÷ 3
30 ÷ 6

6. 27 ÷ 3

7. 15 ÷ 3

8. 42 ÷ 6

9. 54 ÷ 6

10. 36 ÷ 6

11. 3 ÷ 3

12. 60 ÷ 6

13. 48 ÷ 6

14. 45 ÷ 5

15. 81 ÷ 9

Practice

Find each quotient.

16. 3)21

17. 6)42

18. 3)27

19. 6)60

20. 3)30

21. 6)54

22. 3)24

23. 3)3

24. 6)36

25. 3)18

26. 15 ÷ 3

27. 9 ÷ 3

28. 6 ÷ 6

29. 12 ÷ 6

30. 30 ÷ 6

31. Explain How can you use 24 ÷ 3 = 8 to help you solve 24 ÷ 6?

Problem Solving

32. Katie's rocket flew 157 meters. Alex's rocket flew 27 meters farther. How far did Alex's rocket fly?

33. What If? It took Katie's rocket 6 seconds to go 54 meters. How many meters per second did her rocket fly?

34. A rocket kit comes with 12 decals. There are 3 fins on the rocket. If you put the same number of decals on each fin, how many decals will each fin get?

35. Analyze A small rocket kit costs $3. The larger rocket kit costs 6 times as much. You spent $48. How many of each did you buy?

Review and Remember

Write each number in word form.

36. 305

37. 6,280

38. 595

39. 15,098

40. 59,704

For Extra Practice, see Set H, page 126.

Play by the Rules

Using Algebra

You can use division rules to find quotients.

Learning About It

Kenny gave away some of his poster collection. He shared 4 posters equally among 4 friends. How many posters did each friend get?

4 ÷ 4 = 1

Kenny gave 1 poster to each friend.

These rules can help you divide with 0 and 1.

Division Rules

- When a number is divided by itself, the quotient is 1.

  4 ÷ 4 = 1

- When a number is divided by 1, the quotient is the same as that number.

  4 ÷ 1 = 4

- When 0 is divided by any number except 0, the quotient is 0.

  0 ÷ 4 = 0

- You cannot divide a number by 0.

  4 ÷ 0

Think and Discuss Explain why the quotient must be 0 when 0 is divided by another number.

Try It Out

Use the division rules to find the missing numbers.

1. 0 ÷ 9 = ▒ **2.** 5 ÷ 5 = ▒ **3.** 6 ÷ ▒ = 1 **4.** ▒ ÷ 1 = 6

5. ▒ ÷ 8 = 0 **6.** 3 ÷ 1 = ▒ **7.** 7 ÷ 7 = ▒ **8.** 0 ÷ 2 = ▒

Practice

Use division rules to find each missing number. If it is not possible to divide, explain why.

9. $8 \div 8 = \blacksquare$ **10.** $9 \div 1 = \blacksquare$ **11.** $1 \div 1 = \blacksquare$ **12.** $5 \div 1 = \blacksquare$

13. $\blacksquare \div 1 = 8$ **14.** $0 \div 6 = \blacksquare$ **15.** $\blacksquare \div 1 = 5$ **16.** $3 \div \blacksquare = 3$

17. $8 \div 0 = \blacksquare$ **18.** $\blacksquare \div 5 = 1$ **19.** $\blacksquare \div 4 = 0$ **20.** $0 \div 0 = \blacksquare$

Compare. Use >, <, or = for ●.

21. $3 \div 1$ ● $5 \div 1$ **22.** $6 \div 6$ ● $9 \div 9$ **23.** $0 \div 1$ ● $0 \div 2$

24. $7 \div 1$ ● $7 \div 7$ **25.** $2 \div 2$ ● $0 \div 4$ **26.** $0 \div 1$ ● $2 \div 1$

27. $0 \div 8$ ● $8 \div 8$ **28.** $3 \div 1$ ● $6 \div 1$ **29.** $9 \div 9$ ● $0 \div 9$

Problem Solving

30. Jesse had eight posters. She decided to give one to each of her friends. How many friends could receive a poster?

31. Travel posters are $1 each. How many can you buy with $8?

32. **Analyze** Sports posters sell for $1 each or 3 for $2. What is the greatest number of posters Emily can buy for $5?

Travel posters
$1 each

Sports posters
$1 each
3 for $2

Review and Remember

Use six digits from the number poster for each answer.

33. Write the greatest number possible.

34. Write the least number possible.

35. Write the greatest number possible with 5 in the ten thousands place.

Be a Sport

Related multiplication facts help you learn division facts.

Learning About It

You and four friends buy a package of 20 basketball trading cards. You want to divide the trading cards equally. How many cards will each of you get?

$$20 \div 5 = \blacksquare$$

Use the 5s facts to find the answer.

Think: $5 \times 4 = 20$
   So, $20 \div 5 =$ 4 cards each

Suppose you want to divide 20 cards equally among 10 people?

$$20 \div 10 = \blacksquare$$

Think: $10 \times 2 = 20$
   So, $20 \div 10 =$ 2 cards each

Think and Discuss How does knowing the multiples of 5 and 10 help in division?

Try It Out

Find each quotient.

1. $10\overline{)20}$ **2.** $5\overline{)0}$ **3.** $10\overline{)10}$ **4.** $5\overline{)30}$

5. $10\overline{)40}$ **6.** $10\overline{)60}$ **7.** $5\overline{)50}$ **8.** $10\overline{)90}$

9. $100 \div 10$ **10.** $15 \div 5$ **11.** $35 \div 5$ **12.** $25 \div 5$

13. $45 \div 5$ **14.** $80 \div 10$ **15.** $10 \div 5$ **16.** $70 \div 10$

Practice

Find each quotient.

17. 5)‾40 **18.** 5)‾20 **19.** 10)‾30 **20.** 10)‾40 **21.** 5)‾5

22. 5)‾35 **23.** 10)‾100 **24.** 10)‾10 **25.** 5)‾25 **26.** 5)‾45

27. 50 ÷ 10 **28.** 0 ÷ 5 **29.** 80 ÷ 10 **30.** 20 ÷ 5 **31.** 20 ÷ 10

32. 27 ÷ 3 **33.** 54 ÷ 6 **34.** 50 ÷ 5 **35.** 100 ÷ 10 **36.** 10 ÷ 10

Problem Solving

37. Basketball camp has 45 players. If there are 5 on a team, how many teams can there be?

38. A coach gave 60 basketball cards to 10 campers to share equally. How many cards did each camper get?

39. Analyze The coaches want to make 7 seven-person teams. They have 36 players. How many more players do they need?

40. Create Your Own Write a problem for a classmate to solve that includes dividing by 5 or 10.

Review and Remember

Choose a Method Use a calculator or paper and pencil to add or subtract.

41. $51.86
     + 4.77

42. 413
     + 175

43. $10.88
     − 7.90

44. 2,085
     + 9,026

45. 432
     − 146

Critical Thinking Corner

Number Sense

Puzzler!

Using Algebra Study the examples. Then tell what number each symbol stands for.

1. △
    × □
    ‾‾‾‾
    6

2. □
    × ✳
    ‾‾‾‾
    2

3. ○
    × △
    ‾‾‾‾
    12

4. ✳
    × ✳
    ‾‾‾‾
    1

Problem Solving
Act It Out

*Sometimes you can act out a problem
to help you solve it.*

Scott has 16 rocks in his collection. He
wants to arrange them so that there are
the same number of rocks in each row.
This is one way that he could display them.
How many other ways are there?

 UNDERSTAND

What do you need to find?

You need to find all the other ways to arrange
16 rocks into equal rows.

 PLAN

How can you solve the problem?

You can use counters to **act it out**. Arrange
16 counters in as many different ways as you can
with the same number of counters in each row.

 SOLVE

Look at the arrangements on
the right. They show that there
are four other ways to arrange
the rocks in equal rows.

 LOOK BACK

What other strategy could you have used
to solve the problem?

Using the Strategy

Use counters to act out each problem.

1 Kathy has 18 mineral samples. How many ways can she arrange them so that there are the same number of minerals in each row?

2 **Explain** Justin found 8 pieces of quartz. Can he use them to make an outline of a square?

3 Nichole arranges 15 minerals in a pattern. She puts one in the first row, two in the second row, and three in the third row. If she continues this pattern, how many minerals are in the last row?

4 Suppose you arrange 48 rocks into groups. The first group has 3 rocks. Each group after that has 2 more rocks than the group before. How many groups do you have?

⋀ Science Connection
Rocks are fun to collect. These rocks from Franklin, NJ, have minerals that glow under special light.

Mixed Strategy Review

Try these or other strategies to solve each problem. Tell which strategy you used.

THERE'S ALWAYS A WAY!

Problem Solving Strategies

- *Act It Out*
- *Solve a Simpler Problem*
- *Write a Number Sentence*
- *Find a Pattern*

5 Brian is collecting leap-year pennies. He has pennies from 1956, 1960, 1964, and 1968. Should he put a 1976 penny in his collection? Why or why not?

6 Jenna lines up her pennies like this: tails, heads, heads, tails, heads, heads, tails, heads. If she continues the pattern, how would she place the next 4 pennies?

7 Chris trades 45 of his pennies for their value in nickels. How many nickels does Chris get?

8 **Analyze** Show how Brian used fewer than 12 pennies to make a triangle with 4 pennies on a side.

All Dolled Up!

Related multiplication facts help you learn division facts.

Learning About It

Hina Matsuri, Japan's Doll Festival, is on March 3. You have 35 dolls and accessories to display on 7 shelves. How many items can be displayed on each shelf if you display the same number on each shelf?

35 ÷ 7 = ▨

Think: 7 × 5 = 35
So, 35 ÷ 7 = 5

There are 5 items on each shelf.

Related multiplication facts also help you learn the division facts for 8 and 9.

40 ÷ 8 = ▨

Think: 8 × 5 = 40
So, 40 ÷ 8 = 5

45 ÷ 9 = ▨

Think: 9 × 5 = 45
So, 45 ÷ 9 = 5

▲ **Social Studies Connection** Each year a festival called Hina Matsuri, a doll festival, takes place in Japan. Beautiful sets of dolls and accessories are displayed in homes in Japan and in many Japanese American homes.

Think and Discuss How does knowing 8 × 3 = 24 help you find 24 ÷ 8?

More Examples

A. 7 × 4 = 28

  28 ÷ 7 = 4

B. 8 × 4 = 32

  32 ÷ 8 = 4

C. 7 × 8 = 56

  56 ÷ 8 = 7

D. 9 × 4 = 36

  36 ÷ 9 = 4

Try It Out

Find each quotient.

1. $7\overline{)7}$ **2.** $8\overline{)16}$ **3.** $7\overline{)14}$ **4.** $9\overline{)27}$ **5.** $8\overline{)32}$

6. $7\overline{)21}$ **7.** $9\overline{)45}$ **8.** $9\overline{)36}$ **9.** $7\overline{)42}$ **10.** $8\overline{)72}$

11. Analyze If you divide this number by 7, you get 7. What is the number? How do you know?

Practice

Divide.

12. $7\overline{)7}$ **13.** $9\overline{)18}$ **14.** $7\overline{)49}$ **15.** $9\overline{)36}$ **16.** $8\overline{)16}$

17. $7\overline{)35}$ **18.** $8\overline{)24}$ **19.** $9\overline{)45}$ **20.** $8\overline{)64}$ **21.** $7\overline{)14}$

22. $8\overline{)32}$ **23.** $8\overline{)56}$ **24.** $7\overline{)28}$ **25.** $9\overline{)63}$ **26.** $7\overline{)63}$

27. $8\overline{)48}$ **28.** $7\overline{)21}$ **29.** $8\overline{)40}$ **30.** $9\overline{)54}$ **31.** $7\overline{)42}$

32. $7\overline{)56}$ **33.** $8\overline{)8}$ **34.** $9\overline{)72}$ **35.** $10\overline{)90}$ **36.** $5\overline{)35}$

Using Algebra **Find the rule. Then complete each table.**

37. Rule: _____

	Input	Output
	42	6
38.	56	■
39.	21	■
40.	63	■
	14	2

41. Rule: _____

	Input	Output
	24	3
42.	48	■
43.	72	■
44.	16	■
	56	7

45. Rule: _____

	Input	Output
	9	1
46.	54	■
47.	27	■
48.	81	■
	36	4

INTERNET ACTIVITY
www.sbgmath.com

▼ **Social Studies Connection** Traditionally, tiny "worry dolls" from Guatemala are put under pillows to make troubles go away.

Problem Solving

49. It is 42 days until the hobby fair. How many weeks is that?

Hint 7 days = 1 week

50. There are 24 students in your class. Your teacher wants to divide the class equally into 8 groups. How many students will be in each group?

51. You have 27 dolls to display on 9 shelves. You want the same number of dolls on each shelf. How many dolls will be on each shelf?

52. The product of two numbers is 63. Their sum is 16. What are the numbers?

53. Journal Idea What is the least mystery number that can be divided evenly by 3, 5, and 6?

54. Explain A rag doll weighs about 2 pounds. How can you package 48 rag dolls so that no package weighs more than 15 pounds? Explain your reasoning.

55. If you divide this number by 7, you get 6. What is the number?

56. Create Your Own Write a problem that uses division. The answer should be 9.

9 shelves

Review and Remember

Using Algebra Choose +, −, ×, or ÷ to make each sentence true.

57. 5 ● 4 = 9

58. 36 ● 6 = 6

59. 2 ● 0 = 0

60. 12 ● 2 = 10

61. 7 ● 7 = 49

62. 8 ● 4 = 2

63. 12 ● 2 = 6

64. 45 ● 9 = 5

65. 7 ● 7 = 1

66. 63 ● 9 = 72

67. 8 ● 7 = 56

68. 6 ● 6 = 12

69. 14 ● 75 = 89

70. 165 ● 45 = 210

71. 18 ● 9 = 9

72. 14 ● 7 = 2

73. 56 ● 8 = 7

74. 789 ● 249 = 540

Critical Thinking Corner

Logical Thinking

What Comes Next?

Using Algebra By studying a pattern carefully, you can figure out what will happen next. Find the next item in each pattern.

1. ★ ☆ ☆ ★ ☆ ☆ ★

2.

3. 3　6　9　12　15

4. 9　18　27　36　45

5. Solve the division exercises below and then add the digits in each dividend. What pattern do you notice?

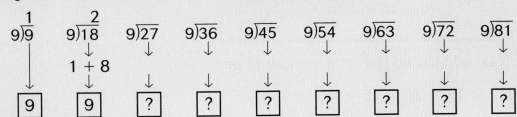

For Extra Practice, see Set K, page 126.

Problem Solving
Using a Pictograph

You can use a pictograph to solve problems.

Cindy made this pictograph of her sports pins collection. How many pins does Cindy have in her collection?

 UNDERSTAND

What do you need to find?

You need to find how many pins Cindy has altogether.

 PLAN

How can you solve the problem?

First, use the graph to find the number of pins for each sport. Then add to find the total number of pins.

 SOLVE

Find the total number of pins for each sport.

Sports Pins Collection	
Sport	**Number of Pins**
Soccer	◇ ◇ ◇ ◇ ◁
Basketball	◇ ◇ ◇ ◇ ◇ ◁
Hockey	◇ ◇ ◇ ◁
Football	◇ ◇ ◁
Each ◇ stands for 6 pins.	

Sport	◆ = 6 pins ◁ = 3 pins
Soccer	$(4 \times 6) + 3 = 24 + 3 = 27$
Basketball	$(5 \times 6) + 3 = 30 + 3 = 33$
Hockey	$(3 \times 6) + 3 = 18 + 3 = 21$
Football	$(2 \times 6) + 3 = 12 + 3 = 15$

> Always do the operation inside the parentheses first!

Now add to find the total number of pins.

$27 + 33 + 21 + 15 = 96$

Cindy has 96 pins in her collection.

 LOOK BACK

Can you think of another way to find the answer?

Show What You Learned

Suppose you have a collection of sports caps. The pictograph below shows how many caps you have for each sport. Use the pictograph to answer Problems 1–8.

Sports Cap Collection

Baseball	Basketball	Hockey	Football

Each 🧢 stands for 4 caps.

① For which sport do you have the least number of caps?

② List the types of caps you have in order from greatest to least.

③ How many baseball caps do you have?

④ Do you have more baseball caps or more football caps? how many more?

⑤ If you add 12 more football caps to your collection, how many more 🧢 will you draw? How many football caps will you have in your collection?

⑥ Is it true that you have twice as many basketball caps as hockey caps? Explain.

⑦ **Explain** How could you show 29 basketball caps on your pictograph?

⑧ **Create Your Own** Write a problem that can be solved by using the pictograph above. Ask a classmate to solve it.

Problem Solving

★ ★ ★ ★ ★ **Preparing for Tests**

Practice What You Learned

Choose the correct letter for each answer.

1 There are more than 8 boxes of candles on a shelf at a store. Each box holds 4 candles. Which of these is reasonable for the total number of candles?

A. Less than 12
B. Between 12 and 30
C. Between 30 and 32
D. More than 32

Tip

Words like *more than* can tell you that numbers are estimated, not exact. Which number in this problem is estimated?

---

2 Mrs. Anato has 44 sheets of craft paper to divide equally among 6 students. When she is finished, how many sheets of paper will be left over?

A. 1
B. 2
C. 7
D. 38

Tip

You can use the *Act It Out* strategy to help you solve this problem.

---

3 Alex has 6 empty soda cans. He needs 4 times that many cans to win a prize in the recycling program at school. How many more cans does Alex need to win a prize?

A. 18
B. 20
C. 24
D. 28

Tip

When more than one step is needed to solve a problem you must decide both *what* to do and in what *order* to do it.

4 Sheila has 7 coins. Some are quarters and some are nickels. Their total value is 95¢. Which of these is a reasonable number of nickels for Sheila to have?

A. 4 nickels

B. 5 nickels

C. 6 nickels

D. 7 nickels

5 Brendan finds some colored markers on sale. There are a total of 36 markers in 3 boxes. How many markers are there in 2 boxes?

A. 12

B. 24

C. 33

D. 39

6 Mark and 3 friends want to share 24 marbles. How can you find the number of marbles each of them will get?

A. Add 3 to 24.

B. Multiply 24 times 3.

C. Divide 24 by 3.

D. Divide 24 by 4.

7 There were 89 children and 48 adults who signed up for a trip to the science museum. Which is the best estimate of the number of people going to the museum?

A. 60   **C.** 140

B. 130   **D.** 200

8 Shawna has 8 boxes of golf balls. Each box holds 3 balls. Which number sentence could be used to show how many golf balls Shawna has?

A. $8 \times 3 = $ ▨

B. $8 \div 3 = $ ▨

C. $8 + 3 = $ ▨

D. $8 - 3 = $ ▨

9 Tim, Jake, Penny, and Nan are in line to pay for a movie. Jake is second. Penny is behind Nan. Which shows the order of the four friends from first to last?

A. Nan, Tim, Jake, Penny

B. Penny, Jake, Tim, Nan

C. Tim, Jake, Nan, Penny

D. Tim, Jake, Penny, Nan

The graph below shows the number of animals seen on a nature trip.

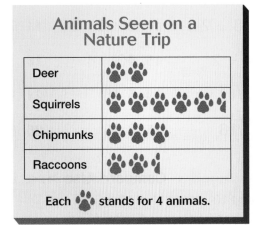

Animals Seen on a Nature Trip

Deer	
Squirrels	
Chipmunks	
Raccoons	

Each 🐾 stands for 4 animals.

10 How many more squirrels were seen than raccoons?

A. 2   **C.** 10

B. 8   **D.** 12

✔ Checkpoint

Division Facts

Vocabulary

Complete. Use the words from the Word Bank.

1. The number you divide by is called the ___?___.

2. The number that is being divided is called the ___?___.

3. The answer in division is called the ___?___.

4. Facts that use the same numbers are part of a ___?___.

Word Bank

divisor
dividend
fact family
quotient

Concepts and Skills

Complete each fact family. (pages 102–105)

5. $2 \times \blacksquare = 8$
$\blacksquare \times 2 = 8$
$8 \div 2 = \blacksquare$
$8 \div \blacksquare = 2$

6. $\blacksquare \times 9 = 9$
$9 \times \blacksquare = 9$
$9 \div \blacksquare = 9$
$9 \div 9 = \blacksquare$

7. $5 \times 6 = \blacksquare$
$6 \times 5 = \blacksquare$
$\blacksquare \div 5 = 6$
$\blacksquare \div 6 = 5$

8. $7 \times \blacksquare = 56$
$\blacksquare \times 7 = 56$
$56 \div \blacksquare = 7$
$56 \div \blacksquare = 8$

Divide. (pages 106–107, 108–109)

9. $18 \div 2$
10. $8 \div 2$
11. $2 \div 2$
12. $20 \div 2$
13. $36 \div 4$

14. $4 \div 2$
15. $40 \div 4$
16. $28 \div 4$
17. $16 \div 4$
18. $20 \div 4$

19. $2\overline{)12}$
20. $6\overline{)48}$
21. $4\overline{)32}$
22. $7\overline{)63}$
23. $3\overline{)6}$

24. $3\overline{)18}$
25. $8\overline{)56}$
26. $6\overline{)24}$
27. $4\overline{)24}$
28. $9\overline{)18}$

Using Algebra Compare. Use >, <, or = for ●.
(pages 110–111, 112–113)

29. $5 \div 1 ● 6 \div 1$

30. $40 \div 10 ● 20 \div 5$

31. $0 \div 5 ● 5 \div 5$

32. $35 \div 5 ● 70 \div 10$

33. $0 \div 6 ● 0 \div 7$

34. $2 \div 2 ● 0 \div 2$

35. $0 \div 1 ● 1 \div 1$

36. $9 \div 1 ● 9 \div 9$

Using Algebra **Find the rule. Then complete each table.**
(pages 116–119)

37. Rule: _____

Input	Output
21	3
35	5

38. | 56 | ▦ |

39. Rule: _____

Input	Output
72	9
16	2

40. | 40 | ▦ |

41. Rule: _____

Input	Output
36	4
63	7

42. | 81 | ▦ |

Problem Solving

43. Molly needs 7 boards that are each 2 feet long. She has two 9-foot boards to cut them from. Will that be enough?

44. Analyze The product of two numbers is 24. Their sum is 14. What are the numbers?

What do you think?
Can knowing multiplication facts help me with division?

Journal Idea

Explain why it is said that division "undoes" multiplication.

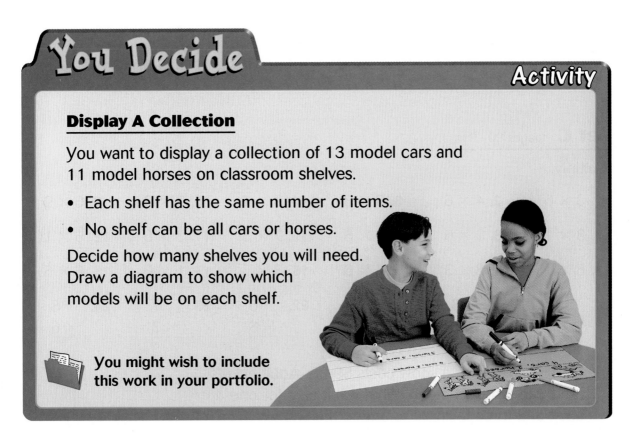

You Decide

Activity

Display A Collection

You want to display a collection of 13 model cars and 11 model horses on classroom shelves.

- Each shelf has the same number of items.

- No shelf can be all cars or horses.

Decide how many shelves you will need. Draw a diagram to show which models will be on each shelf.

You might wish to include this work in your portfolio.

Extra Practice

Multiply.

1. 8 $\times\ 2$	**2.** 6 $\times\ 2$	**3.** 9 $\times\ 4$	**4.** 5 $\times\ 2$	**5.** 4 $\times\ 4$	**6.** 3 $\times\ 4$
7. 3 $\times\ 2$	**8.** 5 $\times\ 4$	**9.** 6 $\times\ 4$	**10.** 7 $\times\ 2$	**11.** 7 $\times\ 4$	**12.** 4 $\times\ 2$

13. Your soccer coach has 6 pairs of size small soccer socks and 4 pairs of size large soccer socks. How many socks does she have? How many pairs?

Set B (pages 88–89)

Using Algebra **Use properties to solve.**

1. 0×5 **2.** 6×1 **3.** 0×967 **4.** 1×1 **5.** $1 \times 4{,}678$

6. $4 \times 6 = 6 \times \blacksquare$ **7.** $3 \times \blacksquare = 5 \times 3$ **8.** $(4 \times 2) \times 3 = 4 \times (2 \times \blacksquare)$

9. $(1 \times 6) \times 4 = \blacksquare$ **10.** $(2 \times 3) \times 6 = \blacksquare \times (3 \times 6)$ **11.** $(0 \times 3) \times 6 = \blacksquare$

Set C (pages 90–91)

Multiply.

1. 3×6 **2.** 4×6 **3.** 9×3 **4.** 3×4 **5.** 3×3 **6.** 6×9

7. 3×10 **8.** 9×6 **9.** 5×6 **10.** 7×3 **11.** 3×8 **12.** 6×10

13. 6×2 **14.** 8×3 **15.** 7×6 **16.** 3×5 **17.** 1×6 **18.** 6×5

19. 1 $\times\ 3$	**20.** 3 $\times\ 6$	**21.** 3 $\times\ 2$	**22.** 6 $\times\ 6$	**23.** 7 $\times\ 3$	**24.** 8 $\times\ 6$

25. A child's ticket for a show costs $9.00. Adult tickets are three times as much. What will it cost for one adult and three children to attend the show?

Extra Practice

Set D (pages 92–93)

Multiply.

1. 10×5 **2.** 5×6 **3.** 1×5 **4.** 10×1 **5.** 5×5 **6.** 6×9

7. 10×0 **8.** 5×7 **9.** 10×6 **10.** 9×5 **11.** 10×7 **12.** 2×5

13. Ana made 5 bracelets. Each bracelet has 8 beads. Sam made 3 bracelets. Each bracelet has 10 beads. How many more beads did Ana use than Sam?

Set E (pages 94–97)

Multiply.

1. 9×7 **2.** 8×5 **3.** 9×4 **4.** 6×8 **5.** 8×7 **6.** 9×0

7. 8×8 **8.** 9×3 **9.** 7×6 **10.** 9×9 **11.** 7×3 **12.** 8×1

13. A textbook weighs about 2 pounds. The books are packaged in boxes of 8. About how much does each box weigh?

Set F (pages 102–105)

Write the fact family for each.

1. 2, 5, 10   **2.** 6, 2, 12   **3.** 8, 3, 24   **4.** 5, 8, 40

Set G (pages 106–107)

Divide.

1. $4\overline{)36}$ **2.** $2\overline{)14}$ **3.** $4\overline{)24}$ **4.** $4\overline{)20}$ **5.** $2\overline{)8}$

6. $4\overline{)28}$ **7.** $2\overline{)18}$ **8.** $4\overline{)32}$ **9.** $2\overline{)10}$ **10.** $4\overline{)12}$

11. $2\overline{)20}$ **12.** $2\overline{)16}$ **13.** $4\overline{)16}$ **14.** $2\overline{)12}$ **15.** $4\overline{)40}$

16. Greg bought 3 sets of model cars for $12. There are 2 cars in each set. How much did he pay for each car?

Extra Practice

Set H (pages 108–109)

Divide.

1. $6\overline{)18}$
2. $3\overline{)15}$
3. $6\overline{)48}$
4. $6\overline{)12}$
5. $3\overline{)3}$

6. $3\overline{)9}$
7. $6\overline{)24}$
8. $3\overline{)12}$
9. $6\overline{)18}$
10. $3\overline{)24}$

11. At field day Ben, Josh, and Jim won 27 medals.
They each won the same number of medals.
How many medals did each boy win?

Set I (pages 110–111)

Using Algebra **Use division rules to find each missing number.**

1. $6 \div \blacksquare = 1$
2. $6 \div \blacksquare = 6$
3. $8 \div \blacksquare = 1$
4. $0 \div 6 = \blacksquare$

5. $3 \div 3 = \blacksquare$
6. $7 \div \blacksquare = 7$
7. $0 \div 9 = \blacksquare$
8. $5 \div \blacksquare = 1$

Set J (pages 112–113)

Divide.

1. $5\overline{)10}$
2. $10\overline{)50}$
3. $10\overline{)60}$
4. $5\overline{)15}$
5. $10\overline{)90}$

6. $5\overline{)30}$
7. $10\overline{)20}$
8. $5\overline{)45}$
9. $10\overline{)70}$
10. $5\overline{)25}$

11. A bag of 30 beads has an equal number of red, green,
and blue beads. If Amy uses all of the blue and red
beads, how many beads are left?

Set K (pages 116–119)

Divide.

1. $9\overline{)27}$
2. $7\overline{)56}$
3. $8\overline{)72}$
4. $9\overline{)81}$
5. $7\overline{)63}$

6. $8\overline{)48}$
7. $9\overline{)90}$
8. $7\overline{)63}$
9. $8\overline{)56}$
10. $9\overline{)9}$

11. Markers come in boxes of 8. If you need 48 markers,
how many boxes should you buy?

Chapter Test

Complete. Use words from the Word Bank.

1. In $3 \times 4 = 12$, 3 and 4 are the ___?___ .
   12 is the ___?___ .

2. The answer in division is called the ___?___ .

3. 0, 4, 8, 12 are ___?___ of 4.

4. The number you divide by is called the ___?___ .

5. In the problem $21 \div 7 = 3$, 21 is the ___?___ .

6. Related numbers form a ___?___ .

Word Bank

fact family
factors
product
dividend
divisor
quotient
multiples

Write the fact family for each set of numbers.

7. 1,5,5   8. 6,9,54   9. 4,9,36   10. 7,3,21   11. 6,8,48

Multiply.

12. $3 \times 5 = $ ■   13. $6 \times 7 = $ ■   14. $3 \times 9 = $ ■

15. $5 \times 10 = $ ■   16. $4 \times 2 = $ ■   17. $7 \times 8 = $ ■

Divide.

18. $28 \div 7 = $ ■   19. $100 \div 10 = $ ■   20. $0 \div 8 = $ ■

21. $16 \div 2 = $ ■   22. $40 \div 8 = $ ■   23. $72 \div 9 = $ ■

Solve.

24. Colored pencils cost 7 cents each. Plain pencils cost 5 cents each. Is 50 cents enough to buy 4 colored pencils and 5 plain pencils? Explain why or why not.

25. Mark has 40 old pennies to display in rows. How many different ways could he arrange the pennies in equal rows?

 Self-Check
Explain what you have learned about how multiplication and division are related.

Performance Assessment

Show What You Know About Multiplication and Division

1 Make two spinners like the ones shown.

a. Spin both pointers. Use the two numbers spun to write a family of related multiplication and division facts. Show your fact families by using counters, pictures, numbers, or words.

b. Repeat two more times.

c. Using these spinners, how many fact families can you make that have only two sentences?

Self-Check Did you use the two numbers you spun in each number sentence?

What You Need

two blank 8-part spinners
a paper clip
counters

2 The school store buys supplies in various quantities and sells them one at a time. You are to buy supplies for your class. You must spend exactly $50 and buy some of every item on the list.

School Store Price List		
Supply Item	**Quantity Cost**	**Cost for One**
Computer disks	5 for $15	
Notebooks	6 for $18	
Audio tapes	4 for $8	
Index cards	3 packs for $6	
3-ring binders	9 for $36	
Headsets	2 for $16	

a. First, fill in the last column in the Price List.

b. Then decide which combination of items you will buy and what they will cost.

Self-Check Did you check to see that you spent exactly $50?

For Your Portfolio
You might wish to include this work in your portfolio.

Extension

Prime and Composite Numbers

Copy the chart shown below. Then follow the directions to find prime and composite numbers.

1	2	3	4	5	6	7	8	9	10
11	12	13	14	15	16	17	18	19	20
21	22	23	24	25	26	27	28	29	30
31	32	33	34	35	36	37	38	39	40
41	42	43	44	45	46	47	48	49	50

Step 1 Cross off the number 1.

Step 2 Circle the number 2. It is prime. Now cross off each multiple of 2. Start with 4.

Step 3 Circle the number 3. It is prime. Now cross off each multiple of 3 that has not been crossed off already.

Step 4 Repeat the process in Step 3 for 5 and 7.

Step 5 Circle the numbers that are not crossed off. These are all the prime numbers from 1 to 50. Except for 1, the numbers you crossed off are the composite numbers up to 50.

> ◀ **Math Note**
>
> The number 1 has only one factor. Therefore it is neither prime nor composite.

Use the chart to complete Exercises 1–4.

1. Write 8 as the sum of two prime numbers.

2. Write 47 as the sum of two composite numbers.

3. Write 24 as the product of a prime number and a composite number.

4. Create a plan for finding all prime numbers from 1 to 100. Give an example of how your plan would work. Then find the prime numbers.

Using Math in Science

Measure temperature and *graph* your results to find out
how the temperature at different surfaces can vary.

Where's the Heat?

Have you ever noticed that in the summer
your bare feet feel cool when you walk on
grass but feel hot when you walk on a
sidewalk? Try this activity to find how the
surfaces of different kinds of material often
differ in temperature.

What You Need

For each group:
   thermometer
   cardboard
   timer

Explore

Step 1 Make a chart like the one below.

Type of Surface	Predicted Temperature	Actual Temperature
grass	/////////	

Step 2 Go outside with your group to a grassy surface.

Step 3 Put a thermometer on
the surface so that the bulb
of the thermometer rests
on the surface.

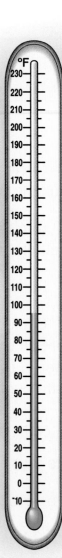

Step 4 Bend a piece of cardboard to make a tent. Place the tent over the thermometer. Wait at least three minutes. Read the temperature on the thermometer and record it in your chart.

Step 5 Choose three other materials to test. Make sure to choose some light-colored and some dark-colored materials. Predict what the temperature of the surface of each material will be. Record your predictions.

Step 6 Repeat Steps 3 and 4 for each surface you chose. Record your data.

▲ **Step 4**

Analyze

1. Make a bar graph that shows the temperatures of the four different types of surfaces. List the surfaces in order of their temperatures, from lowest to highest.

2. Compare your group's results with those of other groups. At which surfaces did you find the highest temperature? At which did you find the lowest?

 For Your Portfolio
Describe the activity you did. Include the bar graph that shows your results. Explain how two groups might get different results when measuring the temperature of the same surface.

Explore Further!

Predict How does the temperature at a surface that is wet differ from the temperature at that surface when it is dry? Repeat the activity to test your hypothesis. What did you find out?

Cumulative Review

★ ★ ★ ★ ★ **Preparing for Tests**

Choose the correct letter for each answer.

Operations	Patterns, Relationships, and Algebraic Thinking

1. 435 + 396 + 43 =

 A. 764   **C.** 874
 B. 774   **D.** 8,614

---

2. Roberto weighs 114 pounds. His older brother Carlos weighs 185 pounds. What is the best estimate of their total weight?

 A. 200 lb   **C.** 350 lb
 B. 300 lb   **D.** 400 lb

---

3. Kristina put 36 beads into 6 equal groups. Which number sentence would you use to find how many beads are in each group?

 A. $36 \times 6 = $ ▨
 B. $6 \div 36 = $ ▨
 C. $36 - 6 = $ ▨
 D. $36 \div 6 = $ ▨

---

4. Judy took 57 cookies to school to share with the class. If each student in the class gets 3 cookies, how many students are in Judy's class?

 A. 11
 B. 19
 C. 54
 D. 60

5. Which number makes this sentence true?

 $72 \div$ ▨ $= 9$

 A. 7   **C.** 9
 B. 8   **D.** 12

---

6. One pencil costs 9¢. Two pencils cost 18¢. Three pencils cost 27¢. How much would 9 pencils cost?

 A. 45¢   **C.** 81¢
 B. 54¢   **D.** 90¢

---

7. Point C best represents what number?

 A. 11
 B. 10
 C. 9
 D. 8

---

8. If 4 plus a number is 18, which expression could be used to find the number?

 A. 4 + 18
 B. 4 × 18
 C. 18 ÷ 4
 D. 18 − 4

Geometry and Spatial Reasoning	Probability and Statistics

Geometry and Spatial Reasoning

9. Which pair of shapes appear to be congruent (same size, same shape)?

A.

B.

C.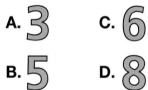

D.

10. Which numeral has two lines of symmetry?

A. 3   **C.** 6

B. 5   **D.** 8

11. How many more sides does a quadrilateral have than a triangle?

A. 1   **C.** 3
B. 2   **D.** 4

12. The hat has the shape of a _____.

A. sphere
B. cylinder
C. pyramid
D. cone

Probability and Statistics

13. Look at the spinner. How many possible outcomes are there?

A. 3
B. 4
C. 5
D. 6

Use the graph for Questions 14–16.

The bar graph shows the types of birds seen on a field trip.

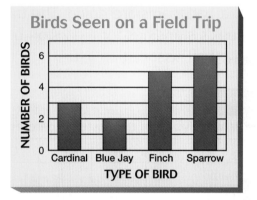

14. What bird was seen the most?

A. cardinal
B. blue jay
C. finch
D. sparrow

15. How many more sparrows were seen than finches?

A. 1   **C.** 5
B. 2   **D.** 6

16. How many birds were seen on the trip?

A. 16   **C.** 18
B. 17   **D.** 19

Chapter 4

Using Data and Probability

Chapter Theme: SPORTS AND FITNESS

·················Real Facts···················

For many people, playing basketball is both fun and good exercise. Newspapers use tables to show how basketball teams are doing. The table below shows a week's standings for a division of the National Basketball Association (NBA).

NBA Standings			
Atlantic Division of the Eastern Conference			
	W	L	GB
Miami	17	8	—
Orlando	16	10	$1\frac{1}{2}$
New York	15	10	2
New Jersey	13	11	$3\frac{1}{2}$
Washington	13	14	5
Boston	11	12	5
Philadelphia	6	18	$10\frac{1}{2}$

The "W" column shows games won.

The "L" column shows games lost.

The "GB" column shows the number of games behind the first place team.

• How can you tell how many games a team has played in all?

• How many games has the Orlando team won out of the total they have played?

······Real People···················

Meet Greg Gumbel, a TV sportscaster. He helps bring the excitement of big league sports to viewers across America. Sportscasters use data and statistics to predict which team is likely to win.

Reach to the Sky!

You can collect and organize information.

Learning About It

They scored 54 points! He finished the race in 2 minutes! She threw the ball 83 feet!

Every sport is filled with all kinds of information, or **data**. In basketball, how high a player can reach is useful data to know. The higher the reach, the easier it can be for a player to shoot or block the ball.

Step 1 Work with a partner. Find the height of *your* reach.

- Stand next to the chalkboard and reach as high as you can.

- Ask your partner to measure your reach rounded to the nearest inch, from the floor to your fingertips.

- Record the height of your reach.

Step 2 Compare your reach to others in your class.

- Ask others how high they reached. Record their answers.

- Did anyone reach as high as you did?

- Can you tell if most of the class had about the same reach?

Word Bank

data
mode
median
range

What You Need

For each pair:
  yardstick

Step 3 Organize your class data.

- Make a chart to record your data.

- Mark each classmate's reach with a tally mark (I).

- How many tally marks should there be in your chart? Explain.

Reach in Inches	Number of Students
65	
66	
67	
68	
69	
70	
71	
72	
73	

Step 4 Study the data you collected.

- Describe your reach. Is it higher, lower, or about the same as the rest of the class?

- Which reach do you think best describes the typical student in your class? Why?

Below you can see how one group in Mr. Chang's class organized the data.

One way to describe the data is to find the **mode**. The mode is the number that occurs most often. The mode is the number on this chart that has the most tally marks.

Mr. Chang's Class

Reach in Inches	Number of Students
65	I
66	IIII
67	
68	
69	I
70	I
71	
72	
73	II

- What does the mode tell you about the group?

Another way to describe the data is to find the **median.** First list the data in order as shown below. The median is the middle number of this data set.

65, 66, 66, 66, 66, 69, 70, 73, 73

- What does the median tell you about the group?

- What does the range tell you about the group?

The **range** is the difference between the greatest number and the least number.

73 − 65 = 8

The range is 8 for this data.

Think and Discuss How would you find the median if you had an even number of data? Explain.

Practice

Use your class data.

1. What is the highest reach in your class? What is the lowest reach in your class? Is your reach closer to the highest or lowest reach?

2. Name another way to organize your data. Explain why you might choose this way.

3. Would you choose the mode, the median, or the range to describe a typical student's reach? Explain.

4. In what ways did organizing the class data help you to describe the group's reach better?

5. What if the reaches of four professional basketball players were included in your class data?

   a. Do you think the median would stay the same or change? Explain why you think this would happen.

   b. Would the mode stay the same or change? Describe what you think would happen to it.

   c. Would the range stay the same or change? Describe what you think would happen.

   d. Now which would be a better way to describe the reach of a typical student in your class—the mode or the median? Explain.

◀ **Social Studies Connection**
At the Basketball Hall of Fame, in Springfield, Massachusetts, visitors test their jumping reach in the "How High" exhibit. Basketball was invented in Springfield over 100 years ago by James Naismith. He had his gym class toss soccer balls at peach baskets hung on 10-foot poles.

Use the table to answer these questions about women's basketball.

6. How many players are included in the table?

7. Who scored the most points in one season?

8. Who scored the fewest points in one season?

9. What is the median of the list of points? the mode? the range?

10. **Explain** Is the data in the table organized by name, season, or points? Why do you think it was done this way?

Most Points Scored in a Season		
Player	Season	Points
Cindy Brown, Long Beach State	1987	974
Genia Miller, Cal. State–Fullerton	1991	969
Sheryl Swoopes, Texas Tech	1993	955
Andrea Congreaves, Mercer	1992	925
Wanda Ford, Drake	1986	919
Barbara Kennedy, Clemson	1982	908
Patricia Hoskins, Mississippi Valley	1989	908
LaTaunya Pollard, Long Beach State	1983	907
Tina Hutchinson, San Diego State	1984	898

Time for Technology

Surfing the Net

Using a Search Engine

You can use keywords and a search engine to find information.

- Log on to the Internet.

- Use a search engine like AltaVista, Yahoo, Lycos, or Excite to find out about sports in your state.

- In the Search box, type in the name of your state and the word *sports*.

  For example, if you live in Texas, type "Texas and sports" or "Texas + sports."

- Your search engine will give you a hint about how to type in your keywords.

- Click Search or press Return.

- The first line of the list tells you how many matching documents there are. You will see a phrase like "Documents 1–10 of 3,209 matching Texas and sports." Click with the hand icon to link to another site.

- Explore sites for the sport that interests you. Record some of your findings in your journal.

Taking Things in Stride

You can make a bar graph to organize and display data.

stride

Learning About It

Did you know that walking is an Olympic event? Olympic walkers can walk almost as fast as some people can run. At the 1996 Olympics, the 20,000 meter walk was won by Jefferson Pérez of Ecuador in 1 hour 20 minutes!

The length of your stride helps determine how fast you can walk. Do you know how long your stride is when you walk?

The data in this table shows the stride lengths of some ten-year-olds. You could also use a **bar graph** to display and organize this data.

Follow the steps on page 139 to make a vertical bar graph.

Word Bank
bar graph

Stride Lengths of Ten-Year-Olds	
Name	**Length**
Richard	14 in.
Nora	13 in.
Tina	12 in.
Josh	16 in.
Mario	11 in.
Leah	14 in.

Step 1 Draw the side and the bottom of the graph. Label the side of the graph as shown. The numbers will be used to show the length of the strides in inches.

Step 2 Label the bottom of the graph. Write the students' names along the bottom so there is room to draw the bars.

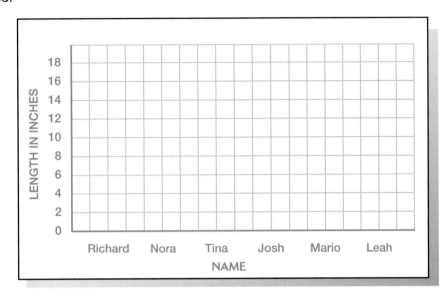

Step 3 Draw bars on the graph that show the length of each person's stride. You will find that some lengths are between two numbers.

Step 4 Choose a title for your graph. Your title should describe the subject of the graph.

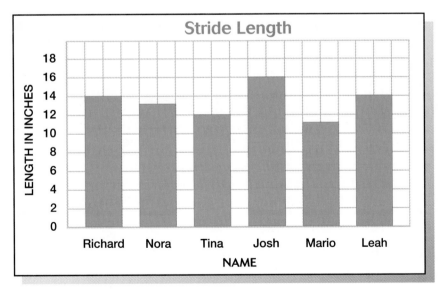

Step 5 Check your work. Be sure your title describes the data and the labels are accurate.

Think and Discuss How do you decide what numbers to use on the side of a graph?

Try It Out

Make a vertical bar graph using the data from the table on adult stride length.

Adult Stride Length	
Name	**Length**
Isabel	25 in.
Amanda	20 in.
Philip	30 in.
Andrew	30 in.
Randy	23 in.
Kenesha	20 in.

1. What are the least and greatest numbers that you must have on the side of your graph?

2. How many bars must you have on your graph?

3. What will you use for the labels of the graph?

4. Is the order of names at the bottom of the graph important? Why or why not?

5. If you had drawn a horizontal bar graph, how would it have differed from your first graph?

Practice

Make a bar graph for the data in each of these tables.

6.

Hand Span	
Name	**Length**
Richard	8 in.
Nora	8 in.
Tina	7 in.
Josh	9 in.
Mario	7 in.
Leah	8 in.

7.

Monthly Sneaker Sales	
Month	**Pairs of Sneakers**
April	900
May	750
June	250
July	475
August	600

8. In Exercise 6, who has the shortest hand span? the longest?

9. **Describe** What is the mode of the data in Exercise 6? the median?

10. In Exercise 7, which month had the least sales? How can you tell from the graph?

Problem Solving

Answer Problems 11–14 using the bar graph to the right.

11. Who has the longest arm span?

12. About how much longer is Nora's arm span than Mario's?

13. **Using Estimation** If all these students touched each other with outstretched arms, about how long a line would they make? How could you check if your answer is reasonable?

14. Measure your arm span. Whose arm span in the graph is closest to yours?

15. **Create Your Own** Write a problem about the Adult Stride Length table on page 140. Ask a classmate to solve it.

16. **Predict** Which do you think is greater, the distance between your outstretched arms or your height? Measure each and compare.

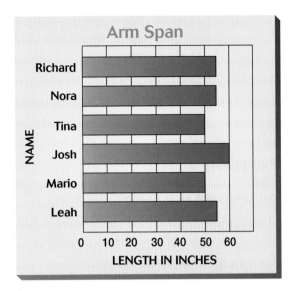

Arm Span

INTERNET ACTIVITY
www.sbgmath.com

Review and Remember

Find each answer.

17. 8×9

18. $24 \div 6$

19. $27 \div 3$

20. $295 - 15$

21. $359 + 204$

22. $32 \div 4$

23. $146 - 70$

24. $54 \div 6$

Use a calculator. Find the missing digits in each exercise.

25.
```
   3,568
 + 7,▮29
  11,197
```

26.
```
   1,936
 −   5▮7
   1,429
```

27.
```
   2,134
 − 1,▮5▮
     875
```

28.
```
    525
 + ▮▮▮
    700
```

Time Out!

A pictograph is like a bar graph that uses pictures to organize and display data.

Learning About It

A **pictograph** is a graph that uses pictures to describe data. You can make a pictograph to show the number of timeouts in a football game.

The table to the right shows the number of timeouts that were taken during 5 football games.

You can make a pictograph to show the data in the table.

Step 1 Divide the pictograph into rows—one for each game.

Step 2 Choose a symbol to represent a timeout—a football, for example. Decide how many timeouts equal 1 football. Explain the symbol on your graph.

Step 3 Draw footballs to represent the number of timeouts during each game. Write a title for your graph.

Number of Timeouts

Game	Timeouts
1	4
2	6
3	4
4	4
5	8

Number of Timeouts

Game 1	🏈 🏈
Game 2	🏈 🏈 🏈
Game 3	🏈 🏈
Game 4	🏈 🏈
Game 5	🏈 🏈 🏈 🏈

Each 🏈 stands for 2 timeouts.

Sometimes a half symbol is used.

◖ stands for 1 timeout.

Add a row to your pictograph that shows 5 timeouts in Game 6.

Think and Discuss How would the graph change if each football stood for 4 timeouts?

Try It Out

Use the pictograph below to answer Exercises 1-6.

Number of Points Scored

Jaguars	🪖🪖🪖🪖🪖🪖
Colts	🪖🪖🪖🪖🪖🪖🪖🪖🪖
Panthers	🪖🪖🪖🪖🪖🪖🪖
Bears	🪖🪖🪖🪖🪖🪖🪖🪖

Each 🪖 stands for 2 points.

▼ Steve Young of the San Francisco 49ers

1. Which team scored the most points?

2. Which team scored the fewest points?

3. How many more points did the Bears score than the Panthers?

4. **Using Mental Math**   How many points were scored by all four teams?

5. If the Jaguars scored 7 more points, how many helmets would the graph show?

6. If the Bears scored 3 fewer points, how many helmets would the graph show?

Use the data below to make two pictographs.

7.
Number of Team Penalties

Team	Penalties
Bengals	6
Dolphins	9
Seahawks	5

8.
Number of Team Touchdowns

Team	Touchdowns
Ravens	4
Broncos	6
Lions	8

Practice

Use the pictograph below to answer Exercises 9–13.

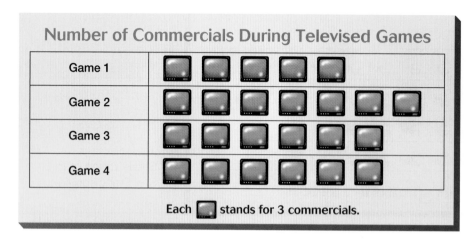

Number of Commercials During Televised Games

Game 1	🖥 🖥 🖥 🖥 🖥
Game 2	🖥 🖥 🖥 🖥 🖥 🖥 🖥
Game 3	🖥 🖥 🖥 🖥 🖥 🖥
Game 4	🖥 🖥 🖥 🖥 🖥 🖥

Each 🖥 stands for 3 commercials.

9. What does the pictograph describe?

10. How many commercials does each picture represent?

11. How many more commercials were there in Game 2 than in Game 1?

12. Which game had the most commercials? the fewest?

13. Explain Why are there no half symbols in this graph?

Problem Solving

Make a pictograph for the data at the right.

14. What picture symbol did you choose? What did each picture represent?

15. Did you need to use a half symbol?

16. What length of commercials occurred most often?

17. What is the mode? How do you know?

18. What lengths of commercials occurred least often?

19. How many commercials occurred in all?

Number of Commercials During Game 3

Length	Number
30 seconds	2
60 seconds	4
90 seconds	6
120 seconds	4
150 seconds	2

20. Explain Do you think pictographs would be more useful for showing data with greater numbers or lesser numbers? Tell why.

21. Describe After you complete a pictograph, how can you check if you have used the correct number of pictures?

22. Journal Idea Why is it easier to read data in a pictograph than in a table?

23. Why is it appropriate for a picture in a pictograph to stand for more than 1 item?

Review and Remember

Choose a Method Use paper and pencil, mental math, or a calculator to add or subtract. Tell which method you used and why.

24. 2,944 507 + 68	**25.** 721 4,535 + 18,000	**26.** 6,000 3,000 + 8,000	**27.** 51,021 5,934 + 780	**28.** 1,613 87 + 676

29. 784 632 + 51	**30.** 47 132 + 508	**31.** 555 125 + 75	**32.** 5,467 6,392 + 1,204	**33.** 240 60 + 300

34. 82,348 + 36,924	**35.** 95,000 − 15,000	**36.** 12,345 − 6,789	**37.** $234.15 − 95.88	**38.** 18,426 − 3,819

Critical Thinking Corner

Visual Thinking

Reading a Pictograph

Suppose the data set for a pictograph was 150, 225, 375, 300, 250, and 400, and each symbol used to represent the data was equal to 100. Would the pictograph be easy, or difficult, to read? Why?

Using Algebra

Developing Skills for Problem Solving

First read for understanding and then focus on getting information from line graphs that have no numbers on them.

READ FOR UNDERSTANDING

You can look at line graphs as pictures that tell a story. Even when there are no numbers on a line graph, you can still tell what the story is. The graph at the right tells the story of a soccer ball that has been kicked.

1 What is the graph about?

2 What are the two labels on the graph?

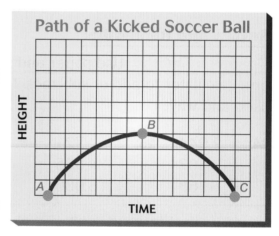

Path of a Kicked Soccer Ball

HEIGHT

TIME

THINK AND DISCUSS

MATH FOCUS

Understanding Line Graphs Line graphs tell a story by showing a relationship. For example, the line graph above shows the relationship between time and the height of the ball.

Look back at the graph.

3 Which point shows when the ball was kicked?

4 At which point was the ball the highest?

5 Tell what happened to the ball from Point *B* to Point *C*.

6 Do you think it would be easier to understand the graph if numbers were on it? Why or why not?

Show What You Learned

Use Graphs A, B, and C to answer Problems 1–5. You can use a graph more than once.

1 Which graph might tell a story about a barrel that is filling with rainwater during a rainstorm?

a. Graph A

b. Graph B

c. Graph C

2 Which graph might tell a story about a car stopped at a red light?

a. Graph A

b. Graph B

c. Graph C

3 Which graph might show what happens when a beach ball gets a leak?

a. Graph A

b. Graph B

c. Graph C

4 Which graph might tell the story of a girl who puts money into her piggy bank each week?

a. Graph A

b. Graph B

c. Graph C

5 Which graph might tell the story of a bathtub filled with water that is draining?

a. Graph A

b. Graph B

c. Graph C

6 **Explain** Look at Graph D. Use the graph to write a story of your own.

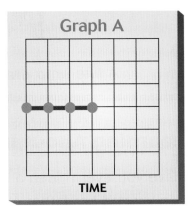
Graph A
TIME

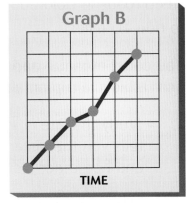
Graph B
TIME

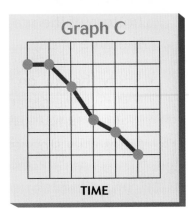
Graph C
TIME

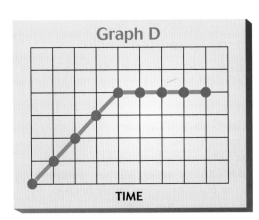
Graph D
TIME

Pedal Power

A line on a graph tells a story about the data in the graph.

Learning About It

Have you ever ridden a bicycle for 10 miles? Marcela Iniguez and her father once rode for 60 miles over steep roads in Colorado! It took them about $2\frac{1}{2}$ hours to ride 10 miles.

You could organize and display data from a bicycle trip on a **line graph.**

- Study the line graph. The graph tells you the distance Marcela and her father bicycled in miles.

- The information along the bottom of the graph tells you the time of day.

- Study the line on the graph. It shows the distance Marcela and her father pedaled and the times they stopped to rest.

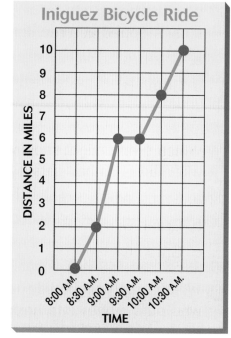

Think and Discuss

Marcela and her dad began bicycling at 8 A.M. and ended at 10:30 A.M. Did they bicycle at the same speed the whole time? How do you know?

Kid Connection ➤

A tandem bike is a bicycle built for two. Marcela enjoys riding a tandem bike with her father. Marcela pedals in the back while her father pedals and steers in the front.

Try It Out

Use the line graph on page 148 to answer the following questions.

1. Between 8:30 A.M. and 9:00 A.M. how far did they bike?

2. During which hour did Marcela and her dad bicycle the farthest?

3. How many miles did they bicycle altogether that morning?

4. Why is the line horizontal from 9:00 A.M. to 9:30 A.M.?

Practice

Use the line graph to the right to answer the following questions.

5. During which one hour period did Mike bike the farthest? How can you tell?

6. About what time of the morning did Mike stop and rest? What part of the line shows that he was resting?

7. Mike earned $1.00 for each mile he biked. How much money did he earn at the end of the Charity Bike Race?

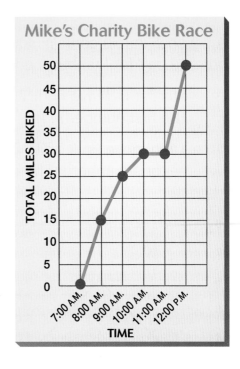

Problem Solving

8. **Predict** Mike earned $25.00 an hour riding for 2 hours. How much could he have earned in all if he had biked for 3 more hours?

9. **What If?** Suppose Mike biked for 3 more hours. He went 16 miles in the first hour. He went half as far in the next hour and half again in the next hour. How far did he go?

Review and Remember

Using Algebra Find each missing number.

10. $n \times 40 = 10 \times 80$

11. $90 - n = 140 - 50$

12. $60 \times 50 = 50 \times n$

13. $20 + 100 = n + 50$

14. $n \times 90 = 20 \times 45$

15. $180 - 30 = 200 - n$

Take Me Out to the Ballgame

Using Algebra

Reading grids is a useful skill.

Learning About It

You can think of a grid as a kind of map. To find your way around a grid, use ordered pairs. An **ordered pair** is a pair of numbers that describe the location of a point on a grid.

A baseball infield contains four bases. What is the ordered pair for first base, point *A*?

- Start at 0. Move right 7 units. This gives you the first number in the ordered pair.

- Then move up 3 units. This gives you the second number in the ordered pair.

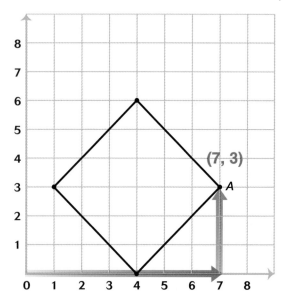

The ordered pair for point *A* is (7, 3).

The order of the numbers in an ordered pair is important. (7, 3) is not the same as (3, 7). (3, 7) is a point that is right 3 units and up 7 units.

Word Bank

ordered pair

plot

What You Need

For each pair:
  grid paper
  ruler

▲ **Social Studies Connection** In 1996, Dot Richardson helped the U.S. win the first-ever Olympic gold medal in softball.

More Examples

A. What is the ordered pair for second base, point *B*?

- Start at 0. Move right 4 units.

- Then move up 6 units.

B. What is the ordered pair for third base, point *C*?

- Start at 0. Move right 1 unit.

- Then move up 3 units.

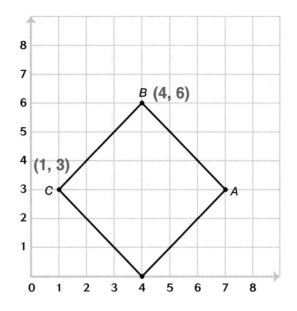

Connecting Ideas

Now that you know how to name points on a grid you can plot points using ordered pairs. To plot a point on a grid, you locate and mark the numbers in the ordered pair.

Here's how to **plot** the shortstop at point (2, 5).

- Always begin with the first number of the ordered pair. Start at 0. Move right 2 units.

- Then look at the second number in the ordered pair. Move up 5 units.

- Label the point *E*.

Another Example

Plot the catcher at point (4, 0).

- Start at 0. Move right 4 units.

- The second number in the pair is 0, so you do not move up.

- Label the point *D*.

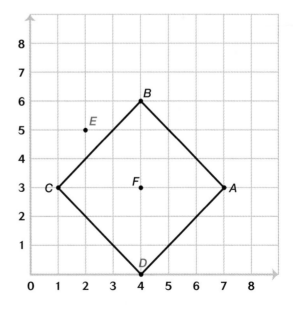

Think and Discuss Describe how you can find the ordered pair for the pitcher's mound, point *F*.

Try It Out

Use the grid at the right. Write the ordered pair for each point.

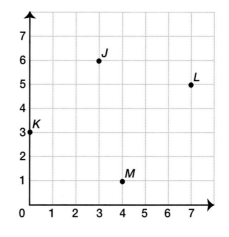

1. point *J* 2. point *K*

3. point *L* 4. point *M*

Draw a grid like the one at the right. Plot and label the following points.

5. point *W* at (1, 4) 6. point *X* at (0, 6)

7. point *Y* at (5, 4) 8. point *Z* at (2, 3)

Practice

Use the grid below. Write the ordered pair for each point.

9. point *A* 10. point *B* 11. point *C* 12. point *D*

13. point *E* 14. point *F* 15. point *G* 16. point *H*

Draw a grid like the one below. Plot and label the following points.

17. point *I* at (5, 0) 18. point *J* at (10, 6) 19. point *K* at (6, 10)

20. point *L* at (2, 0) 21. point *M* at (3, 7) 22. point *N* at (1, 8)

Now plot and label each of these points.

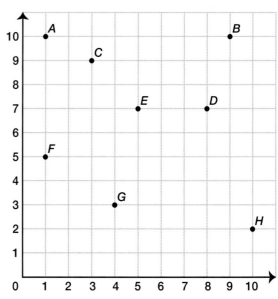

23. point *O* at (1, 1)

24. point *P* at (5, 9)

25. point *Q* at (9, 1)

26. Connect points *O*, *P*, and *Q* using line segments. What figure is formed?

27. **Explain** Whenever you plot points on a graph, which way do you move first? Then which way do you move?

Problem Solving

Use this grid to answer Problems 28–30.

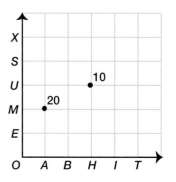

28. Describe How would you describe the location of point 10? point 20?

29. Analyze How is using letters the same as using numbers? How is it different?

30. Copy the graph and plot this sentence: (*B*, *E*) (*A*, *S*) (*H*, *E*) (*I*, *S*). Label your points 1 to 4.

31. Describe what you will see if you plot these points and connect them: (1, 1), (2, 2), (3, 3), (4, 4). You many wish to refer to the grid on page 152.

Review and Remember

Find each product or quotient.

32. 4×9	**33.** 7×3	**34.** $18 \div 3$	**35.** $27 \div 9$	**36.** 9×6
37. 7×8	**38.** 8×6	**39.** 8×4	**40.** $64 \div 8$	**41.** $16 \div 2$

 # Money $ense

Baseball Bargains

Estimate by rounding to the nearest dollar to answer the questions below.

1. About how much will it cost to buy 2 bats and 8 balls for your team?

2. About how much money will you save if you buy the Baseball Bargain Box instead of buying a glove, a bat, and a ball separately?

3. Suppose you bought two items that cost about $34.00. What did you buy?

Ball = $8.96
Glove = $22.17
Bat = $24.80

Baseball Bargain Box
$49.99

Problem Solving
Make a Graph

*Making a graph can help you see
information more easily.*

n in-line skate company made a table
to show how many skates they sold each
year for 5 years. Between which 2 years
did skate sales increase the most?

In-Line Skates Sold	
Year	**Sales (in millions)**
1994	10
1995	25
1996	50
1997	60
1998	95

UNDERSTAND

What do you need to find?

You need to find between which two
years sales increased the most.

PLAN

What could you do to solve the problem?

You could **make a bar graph** to help you see the
information more easily. Then look for the two
bars next to each other that have the greatest
difference in height.

SOLVE

Make the bar graph. Then compare
the heights of the bars.

The greatest difference is between
the bars for 1997 and 1998.

So, skate sales increased the most
between 1997 and 1998.

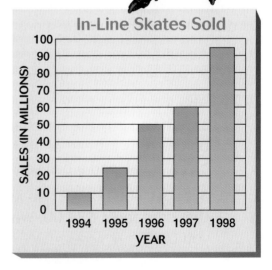

LOOK BACK

Why is it easier to answer the question by looking
at a bar graph than by looking at a table?

Using the Strategy

Use the tally chart to answer Problems 1 – 6.

Members of the Rolling-On Skate Club were asked what type of in-line skates they have used. Their answers are shown in the tally chart at the right.

Type of Skate	
Multipurpose	ℍℍ ℍℍ
Speed	ℍℍ
Hockey	IIII
Aggressive	ℍℍ

1 Make a bar graph or pictograph to show the results of the survey.

2 Which has been used more, speed skates or hockey skates?

3 Which skate has been used the most? Which skate has been used the least?

4 Can you tell how many people were interviewed by using the data given?

5 How many more people have used multipurpose skates than aggressive skates?

6 How might the graph change if 10 more people were asked and each had used all 4 types of skates?

Mixed Strategy Review

Try these or other strategies to solve each problem. Tell which strategy you used.

Problem Solving Strategies

- *Find a Pattern*
- *Logical Reasoning*
- *Make a Graph*
- *Make a List*

7 In an in-line skating tournament, each team will play every other team once. If there are 6 teams in all, how many games will there be?

8 Four friends are skating in a line. Jack is in front of Samantha. Laura is third. Nobody is in front of Bob. How are the friends lined up?

9 At Rollin' Rentals, skates can be rented for up to five hours. Skates cost $5 for the first hour, $4 for the second hour, $3 for the third hour, and so on. If you rent skates for all five hours, how much will it cost?

Checkpoint
Organizing and Displaying Data

Use the tally chart to answer Problems 1–4. (pages 134–137)

1. What information does the tally chart contain?

2. What does each tally mark represent?

3. How many players are shown on the chart?

4. What is the median of the number of minutes? the mode of the number of players? the range of minutes?

Minutes Played in Game 1	
Minutes	**Number of Players**
4	II
5	I
6	I
7	III
8	I
9	IIII

Make a bar graph. (pages 138–141)

5. Use the data in the table to make your graph.

6. What was the greatest traveling time? the least?

7. How many minutes were traveled altogether?

Time Spent Traveling to Games	
Game	**Travel Time**
3	20 min
4	30 min
6	60 min
9	20 min
10	50 min

Use the pictograph to answer Problems 8–10. (pages 142–145)

8. How many runs does each symbol represent?

9. In which game were the most runs scored? How many?

10. In which game were the fewest runs scored? How can you tell?

Runs Scored in Softball Games

Game 1	🥎
Game 2	🥎🥎🥎🥎
Game 3	🥎🥎🥎🥎
Game 4	🥎🥎🥎🥎🥎🥎
Game 5	🥎🥎🥎🥎

Each 🥎 stands for 2 runs.

Use the line graph to answer Problems 11–13.
(pages 148–149)

11. Using Algebra Tell what can be learned from the line on the graph.

12. How many gallons of water were used in 3 hours?

13. How many gallons of water were used each hour?

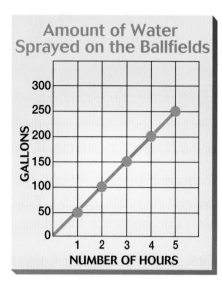

Amount of Water Sprayed on the Ballfields

Using Algebra Use the grid. Identify the ordered pairs to spell the word. (pages 150–153)

14. SEA

15. HEART

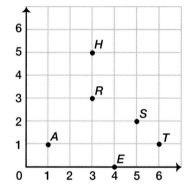

Journal Idea

What kind of graph do you find easiest to read? hardest to read? Explain your thinking.

What do you think?

How do charts and graphs help you to organize and understand data?

Critical Thinking Corner

Visual Thinking

What's Wrong?

• What's wrong with the labeling on this graph? What would you do to fix it?

• On which day was 25 minutes spent on homework?

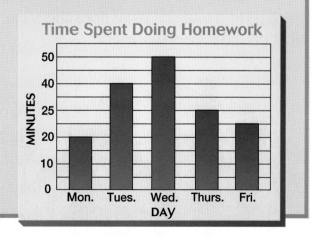

Time Spent Doing Homework

In the Swing

A stem-and-leaf plot can help you compare data.

Learning About It

The heights of 11 fourth-grade badminton players are 56, 61, 61, 60, 59, 57, 58, 58, 63, 61, and 59 inches. You can organize this data in a **stem-and-leaf plot**.

First, order your data from least to greatest: 56, 57, 58, 58, 59, 59, 60, 61, 61, 61, 63.

> ### Word Bank
> **stem-and-leaf plot**
> **stem**
> **leaf**

Each **stem** stands for the first digit of each number.

Record the tens digits in order from least to greatest.

Height in Inches	
Stem	Leaves
5	6, 7, 8, 8, 9, 9
6	0, 1, 1, 1, 3

Each **leaf** stands for the second digit of each number.

Record the ones digits in order from least to greatest.

A stem of 5 and a leaf of 6 tells you that the shortest player's height is 56 inches.

You can use a stem-and-leaf plot to find the median and mode.

> ### Median
> Find the middle number of a set of numbers. The median is 59 inches.

> ### Mode
> Find the number that occurs most often in a set of numbers. The mode is 61 inches.

Think and Discuss What does the stem represent? What do the leaves represent?

Try It Out

Use the stem-and-leaf plot on page 158.

1. How many leaves are shown on the stem-and-leaf plot?

2. What is the height shown by the second stem and its third leaf?

Practice

Use the stem-and-leaf plot at the right for Exercises 3–5.

Points Scored by Erin in Each Game	
Stem	Leaves
0	5, 8, 9
1	1, 3, 5, 5, 5, 5

3. What was the least number of points Erin scored? the greatest?

4. What is the median number of points Erin scored? the mode?

5. How many games did Erin play?

INTERNET ACTIVITY
www.sbgmath.com

Problem Solving

6. **What If?** Suppose Erin's team plays 2 more games and Erin scores 9 points in each game. How would the median number of points change? the mode?

7. **Analyze** Each time Erin scored 15 points, her team won the game. Her team lost all the other games. How many wins and how many losses did Erin's team have?

Review and Remember

Write the fact family for each set of numbers.

8. 6, 7, 42   **9.** 8, 6, 48   **10.** 9, 8, 72   **11.** 7, 9, 63   **12.** 8, 7, 56

Critical Thinking Corner

Logical Thinking

Venn Diagrams

A Venn diagram is another way to organize information.

How many students are only on the swim team? only on the soccer team? on both teams?

Swim Team   Soccer Team

Kristen
José
Sarah
Lee
Sal
Toby
Carol
Stephen
Joanne

Problem Solving
Ways to Represent Data

Often you can represent data in different ways.

The graphs at the right both show the number of people who went to a Frisbee festival. Which graph would be easier to use to find how many more people there were on Day 5 than on Day 2?

 UNDERSTAND

What do you need to know?

You need to know that each graph shows the same information.

 PLAN

How can you solve the problem?

Look at how the data has been shown in each graph. Then decide which graph is easier to use to find the difference.

 SOLVE

To use the bar graph, count up from the top of the bar for Day 2 until you get to the top of the bar for Day 5. The number you count is the difference.

To use the pictograph, find the rows of 👤 for Day 2 and Day 5. Since Day 5 has 1 more 👤 than Day 2, find the value of the 👤 to find the difference.

Some people may think it's easier to use the bar graph. Other people may think it's easier to use the pictograph. Explain which way you think is easier.

 LOOK BACK

What is another way you could show the Frisbee Festival data?

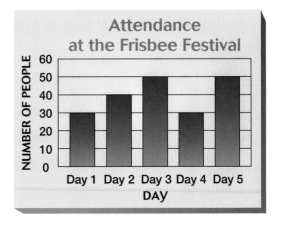

Show What You Learned

Use the table or bar graph shown below to answer Problems 1–3. Explain which you used and why.

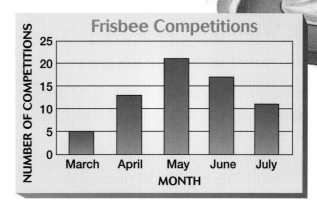

Frisbee Competitions	
Month	**Number**
March	5
April	13
May	21
June	17
July	11

1 Which months had Frisbee competitions?

2 How many months had less than 15 Frisbee competitions?

3 Exactly how many Frisbee competitions were held in June?

Use the pictograph or stem-and-leaf plot shown below to answer Problems 4–6. Explain which you used and why.

Best Frisbee Throw

Elijah	⬭⬭⬭⬭⬭⬭⬭⬭⬭
Maria	⬭⬭⬭⬭⬭⬭⬭
Dominic	⬭⬭⬭⬭⬭⬭⬭⬭⬭
Roger	⬭⬭⬭⬭⬭
Bess	⬭⬭⬭⬭⬭⬭⬭⬭⬭⬭
Olivia	⬭⬭⬭⬭⬭⬭⬭⬭

Each ⬭ stands for 4 feet.

Best Frisbee Throw in Feet

Stem	Leaf
2	0, 6
3	2, 6, 8
4	0

4 How many distances were at least 30 feet but no more than 39 feet?

5 Who threw a Frisbee twice as far as Roger did?

6 **Explain** Which graph would you use to find the mode, median, and average?

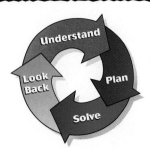

Problem Solving

★★★★★ **Preparing for Tests**

Practice What You Learned

Choose the correct letter for each answer.

1 Two players play a game using this spinner. If the spinner lands on a number less than 10, Player A wins. If not, Player B wins. Which of these numbers could be put in the empty part of the spinner to make the game fair?

A. 2
B. 4
C. 7
D. 14

Tip

Which are the winning numbers for Player A? Now choose a number so that Player B has the same number of winning numbers.

2 Three friends ran in a road race. It took Scott 24 minutes to finish. It took Marty 29 minutes to finish. Fred finished after Scott but before Marty. Which is reasonable for the amount of time it took Fred to finish the race?

A. 22 minutes
B. 27 minutes
C. 29 minutes
D. 32 minutes

Tip

You can use the *Make a List* strategy to help you solve the problem. Make a list of all the possible number of minutes it could have taken Fred to finish the race.

3 A landscaper planted 3 trees on each even-numbered street and 5 trees on each odd-numbered street. How many trees did he plant on Fourth, Fifth, Sixth, and Seventh avenues?

A. 12
B. 15
C. 16
D. 20

Tip

Try making a list to show the pattern in this problem. Then add to find the total number of trees.

4 Mike made a square using square tiles. Which could be the number of tiles he used?

A. 2
B. 5
C. 9
D. 10

5 Susie bought 3 books that cost between $6 and $14. Which of these is reasonable for the total cost of the 3 books?

A. Less than $14
B. Between $14 and $17
C. Between $18 and $42
D. More than $42

6 Which is the best estimate of the total cost of 4 toys with prices of $14.56, $21.89, $25.95, and $19.20?

A. about $50
B. about $60
C. about $70
D. about $80

7 Four friends are sharing a box of 24 cookies equally. Which number sentence could **NOT** be used to show this situation?

A. $24 \div 4 = 6$
B. $24 \div 3 = 8$
C. $6 + 6 + 6 + 6 = 24$
D. $4 \times 6 = 24$

8 A set of 60 building blocks has an equal number of blocks in red, green, blue, and yellow. Which method could be used to find the number of red blocks?

A. Add 60 and 4.
B. Multiply 60 times 4.
C. Divide 60 by 4.
D. Subtract 4 from 60.

The table below shows the number of marbles Jeff has in his collection.

Jeff's Marbles	
Color	**Number**
Green	49
Blue	38
Red	21
Yellow	32

9 **About** how many green marbles and red marbles does Jeff have?

A. 50
B. 70
C. 80
D. 90

10 One day a music store sold 28 classical music CDs and 57 country music CDs. Which number sentence shows how many classical and country music CDs the store sold that day?

A. $28 + 28$
B. $57 - 28$
C. $28 + 57$
D. $57 + 57$

Ready? Set? Go!

You can predict how likely it is that an event will happen.

Learning About It

A swim class is making teams by pulling marbles out of a bag without looking. Swimmers who pull a red marble will be on one team and swimmers who pull a blue marble will be on the other team.

Look at the bag. Is there a chance of pulling a green marble?

There are no green marbles in the bag, so there is no chance of pulling a green marble.
It would be **impossible** to pull a green marble.

Probability tells the chance that an event will happen.

What is the probability of pulling a red or a blue marble?

Since all the marbles are red or blue, the probability of pulling a red or blue marble is **certain**.

Sometimes we can predict what is more likely or less likely to happen.

Look at the bag again. Is it **more likely** or **less likely** that red will be pulled than blue?

There are more red marbles than blue marbles in the bag, so the probability of pulling red is more likely.

Think and Discuss Which bag at the right shows an **equally likely** probability of pulling a red marble as pulling a blue marble?

Word Bank

impossible
probability
certain
more likely
less likely
equally likely

Bag A

Bag B

Try It Out

For each bag, use the words below to describe how likely it is to pull a green tile.

| IMPOSSIBLE | LESS LIKELY | EQUALLY LIKELY | MORE LIKELY | CERTAIN |

1. 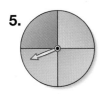 **2.**   **3.**   **4.**

Practice

For each spinner, use the words shown above to describe how likely it is to spin blue.

5. **6.** **7.** **8.**

9. **10.** **11.** **12.**

Problem Solving

13. Adam reaches into a bag that has 4 red markers and 6 yellow markers. Which color marker is he more likely to pull out? What color marker would it be impossible for Adam to pull out?

14. Create Your Own Draw a picture of a bag of colored marbles. Write a probability question about it and ask a classmate to solve it.

Review and Remember

Write each number in word form.

11. 9 **12.** 15 **13.** 263

14. 5,407 **15.** 13,090 **16.** 356,700

▲ **Fitness and Health Connection**
Swimming is an excellent form of exercise and an important safety skill. More than 10 million children in the U.S. who are 7-11 years old participate in swimming.

For Extra Practice, see Set F, page 172.

What's Happening?

Outcomes are a part of every probability experiment.

Learning About It

Probability can help you predict what the results of an experiment might be.

Step 1 Work with a partner and place your different-colored paper squares on the table.

- How many paper squares are there?

- Are all of the paper squares the same color?

Step 2 Make a chart. List the paper squares by color.

- Leave room for making tally marks.

Step 3 Place all the paper squares in the bag.

- A possible result of an experiment is called an **outcome.** Each time you reach into the bag and remove a paper square, you obtain an outcome.

- Name the possible different outcomes in this experiment. Name an impossible outcome.

- How many different outcomes are there?

- How likely is it that you will choose a red? a purple?

What You Need

For each pair:
5 different-colored
paper squares
paper bag
number cube

Color	Tallies
red	
blue	
yellow	
green	
orange	

Step 4 Without looking, reach into the bag and draw a paper square. On your chart, make a tally mark for the color drawn. Then place the square back in the bag and repeat the activity until you have drawn a square of each color at least once. Record the outcome each time.

- How many total tries did it take you to obtain every outcome on your chart?

- Compare your results with the results of your classmates. How are your results the same? How are they different?

Think and Discuss How would the results of your experiment have changed if you didn't replace the paper square each time?

Practice

A number cube is a six-sided cube. Label the sides of a number cube with the numbers 1, 2, 3, 4, 5, and 6.

1. If a number cube is tossed once, how many outcomes are possible? Name each outcome.

2. **Journal Idea** Are all of the outcomes on a number cube equally likely? Tell why or why not.

3. **Predict** Would the number of different outcomes change if the number cube were tossed two times instead of once? Toss the number cube several times to test your prediction.

4. **Predict** Would the number of outcomes change if the number cube were tossed 100 times?

EXPLORE: Evaluating Fairness

That's Not Fair!

Spinners can be fair or unfair.

Learning About It

Step 1 Work with your class. Divide a spinner into two equal parts. Label one part *Team 1* and label the other part *Team 2*.

Step 2 Use the spinner to divide your class into two teams.

Spin the pointer once for each member of your class.

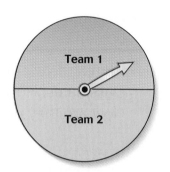

- Do you think the teams will be equal? Explain.

- How many members does Team 1 have?

- How many members does Team 2 have?

- Do you think this spinner is a fair way to divide your class in half? Explain why you think it is or is not.

Step 3 Divide another spinner into three equal parts. Label one part *Team 1* and label each of the other two parts *Team 2*.

Use this spinner to divide your class into two teams.

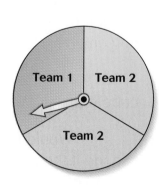

- Is it likely or unlikely that there will be an equal number of members on each team? Explain.

- How many members does Team 1 have?

- How many members does Team 2 have?

- Do you think this spinner is a fair way to divide your class in half? Tell why or why not.

Think and Discuss What makes a spinner fair? What makes it unfair?

What You Need

For each class:
   two-part spinner
   three-part spinner

Practice

Which of the spinners in Exercises 1–8 would be fair?
Which would be unfair? Tell why.

1.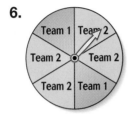
Team 1 | Team 1
Team 2

2.
Team 1 | Team 1
Team 2 | Team 2

3.
Team 1 | Team 1
Team 2 | Team 2
Team 1

4.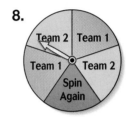
Team 1 | Team 2
Team 2 | Team 1
Team 1 | Team 2

5.
Team 1 | Team 1
Team 1 | Team 2

6.
Team 1 | Team 2
Team 2 | Team 2
Team 2 | Team 1

7.
Team 1 | Team 2
Spin Again

8.
Team 2 | Team 1
Team 1 | Team 2
Spin Again

9. Jeremy designed a mathematics game using the spinner to the right. Players begin with a score of 1 and get the same number of spins. The first player to reach a score of 50 or more wins. Is the spinner fair? Tell why or why not.

Add 2 | Add 3
Add 10 | Add 5

10. **Create Your Own** Make two spinners. One should be fair, the other unfair. Show your spinners to your classmates. Ask them to decide which one is fair.

11. **Analyze** Is the spinner to the right a fair way to choose two teams that should have about the same number of members? Tell why or why not.

Team 1 | Team 1
Team 2 | Team 2
Choose a Team

INTERNET ACTIVITY
www.sbgmath.com

Checkpoint

Comparing Data and Understanding Probability

Vocabulary

Complete. Use the words from the Word Bank.

1. The chance that something will happen is its __?__.

2. The possible results of an experiment are called __?__.

3. If an event will definitely not happen, it is __?__ for it to happen.

4. If an event will definitely happen, it is __?__ that it will happen.

Word Bank

certain
impossible
outcomes
probability

Concepts and Skills

Use the stem-and-leaf plot to answer Problems 5–8. (pages 158–159)

5. How many track meets were there?

6. What was the greatest number of volunteers at a meet? the least?

7. What is the median of the data? the mode?

8. At how many meets were there more than 16 volunteers?

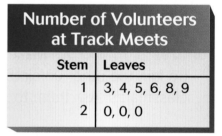

Number of Volunteers at Track Meets	
Stem	Leaves
1	3, 4, 5, 6, 8, 9
2	0, 0, 0

Describe how likely it is that each event will happen. Write *impossible, more likely, less likely,* or *certain.* (pages 162–163)

9. The spinner will land on green.

10. The spinner will land on blue.

11. The spinner will land on yellow.

12. The spinner will land on either blue or green.

Problem Solving

Use the spinners below for Problems 13–15.

(pages 166–167)

13. Which of these spinners offers the best chance of choosing teams fairly?

14. Which spinner is unfair? Explain why.

15. What could you do to the unfair spinner to make it fair?

What do you think?

How can understanding probability help you to make good everyday decisions?

A.

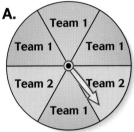

B.

Journal Idea

Tell about something in your daily life that is very likely to happen. Then tell about something that is not likely.

You Decide

Activity

Display Your Data

Take a survey of your class. Find out what sports or other outside activities everyone likes to play and do.

Name 3 different ways you can show this data. Then display the data the way you think is best. Explain why you displayed your data the way you did.

You might wish to include this work in your portfolio.

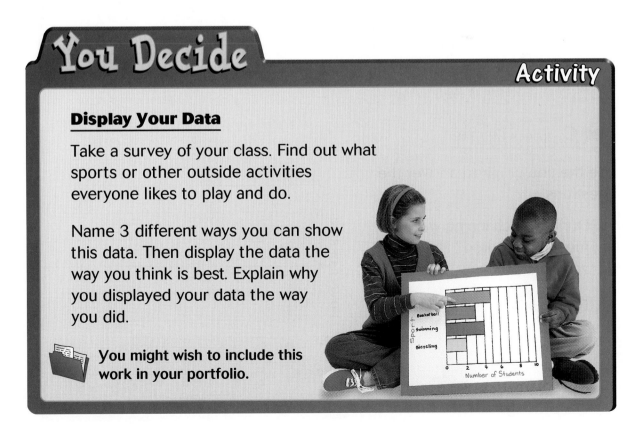

Extra Practice

Set A (pages 138–141)

Make a bar graph for this data.

1. For which games did you draw the longest or tallest bars? the shortest?

2. Which games have the same length bars?

3. Did you make a horizontal or vertical bar graph?

Number of Error-Free Innings Played

Game	Innings
1	7
2	5
3	7
4	8
5	7

Set B (pages 142–145)

Make a pictograph for this data.

1. What symbol did you use? How much does it stand for?

2. If your symbol stood for 2 players instead of 1, would you have to draw more or fewer symbols each time?

Number of Players in Each Game

Game	Players
1	10
2	12
3	16
4	10

Set C (pages 148–149)

Use the line graph to answer the questions.

1. During which inning were the most runs scored? How can you tell?

2. During which innings were no runs scored? Tell how you know.

3. How many runs were scored in the entire game?

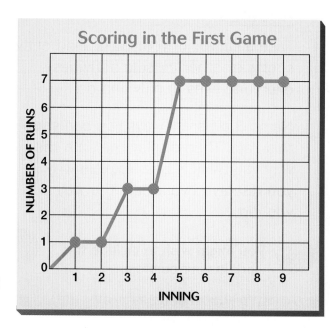

Scoring in the First Game

Extra Practice

Set D (pages 150–153)

Using Algebra **Use the grid.
Write the ordered pair for each point.**

1. point *B*

2. point *N*

3. point *Q*

4. point *T*

**Copy the grid. Plot
and label each point.**

5. point *C* (2, 4)

6. point *X* (9, 0)

7. point *Y* (4, 3)

8. point *Z* (10, 5)

9. point *J* (3, 1)

10. point *R* (7, 8)

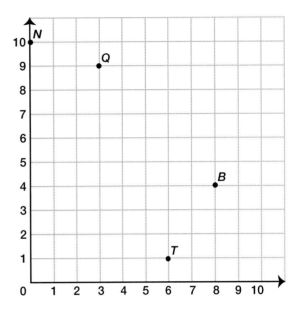

Set E (pages 158–159)

**A group of students was asked to
name all the sports teams that they
could remember. The results are
shown in the stem-and-leaf plot.**

1. What was the least number of
teams named? the greatest?

2. How many students remembered
fewer than 15 teams?

3. How many students responded
to the question?

4. What is the median number of
teams named? the mode?

5. Create Your Own Write a
problem using the data given.
Ask a friend to solve it.

Number of Teams Named	
Stem	**Leaves**
0	4, 7, 7, 8
1	2, 3, 5, 7, 7, 7
2	1, 1, 4,
3	2, 2

Extra Practice

Set F (pages 162–163)

For each bag, use the words *impossible, less likely, equally likely, more likely,* or *certain* to describe the probability of pulling a blue tile.

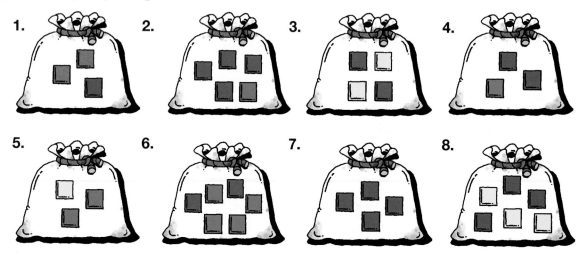

1.
2.
3.
4.

5.
6.
7.
8.

Set G (pages 164–165)

Choose one of these cards out of a bag, without looking.

1. How many outcomes are possible?

2. Name each outcome.

3. Are the outcomes equally likely? Why or why not?

4. If the letter *E* was printed on another card and added to the bag, would the number of outcomes change? Explain.

5. If the letter *E* was in the bag with *A, B, C,* and *D,* are the outcomes equally likely? Explain.

Chapter Test

Use the line graph for Exercises 1–5.

1. What does the graph show?

2. During which 30-minute period did Mary bicycle the farthest?

3. Did Mary bicycle at the same speed throughout? Explain.

4. At what time did Mary take a break?

5. How many total miles did Mary travel?

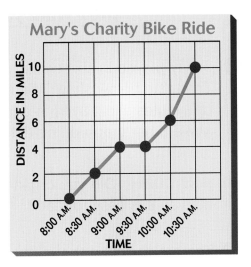

Mary's Charity Bike Ride

**Use the coordinate graph for Exercises 6–9.
Write the ordered pair for each point.**

6. point *B*

7. point *C*

8. point *A*

9. point *D*

Use the words *less likely, equally likely, more likely, certain,* or *impossible* to describe the probability of spinning green for Exercises 10–12.

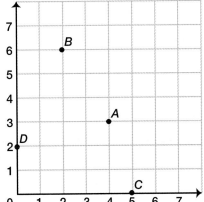

10.

11.

12.

Use the stem-and-leaf plot for Exercises 13–15.

13. How many members are on the team?

14. What is the median of the data?

15. What is the mode of the data?

 Self-Check Explain why a graph is sometimes better than a table for showing data.

Bowling Team Scores

Stem	Leaves
7	3, 8
8	
9	5, 8
10	2, 6
11	4, 7, 7, 7, 9
12	0, 5

Performance Assessment

Show What You Know About Using Data

① Jenny played in six soccer games. The table below shows the number of minutes she played in each game. Make a bar graph of the data in the table.

Self-Check Did you organize your data so it is easy to read?

② The graph below shows the number of fans who attended basketball games at Westlake School. Use the graph to answer the following questions.

  a. Which games were seen by more than 150 fans?

  b. Thirty-five of the fans at Game 4 were adults. How many of the fans were children?

  c. Did the three middle games have a total attendance of more than 500 fans? Explain how you got your answer.

  d. Find the mode for the data shown in the graph.

  e. Predict the attendance at Game 6. Explain your reasoning.

Self-Check Did you read the bars on the graph correctly?

For Your Portfolio

You might wish to include this work in your portfolio.

What You Need

grid paper

Jenny's Playing Times	
Game	Time
1	14 minutes
2	12 minutes
3	4 minutes
4	18 minutes
5	0 minutes
6	8 minutes

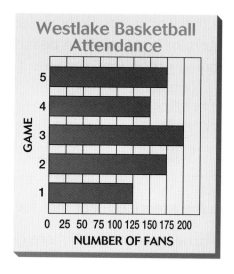

174

Extension

Graphing a Relationship

Using Algebra

Suppose you buy soccer game tickets. If one ticket costs $15, how much would 5 tickets cost?

You can make a table to show the relationship of the number of tickets to the cost of the tickets. A graph can also show the relationship.

Buying Soccer Tickets

Number of Tickets	Cost of Tickets
1	$15
2	$30
3	$45
4	■
5	■

Think of the numbers in the table as ordered pairs. Graph the pairs. Draw a line through the points and beyond.

1. Use the line graph to find the cost of 4 tickets.

2. For each additional ticket, by how much does the cost of the tickets increase?

3. How does the graph show this relationship?

4. Extend the line on the graph to find out how much 5 tickets would cost.

5. **What If?** Suppose one ticket costs $12. How much would 5 tickets cost? Make a table for 1, 2, and 3 tickets. Then graph the data to find the cost of 5 tickets.

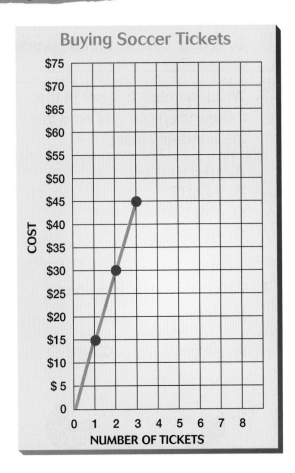

Buying Soccer Tickets

COST

$75 $70 $65 $60 $55 $50 $45 $40 $35 $30 $25 $20 $15 $10 $5 0

0 1 2 3 4 5 6 7 8
NUMBER OF TICKETS

Cumulative Review

★★★★★ Preparing for Tests

Choose the correct letter for each answer.

Number Concepts	Measurement

Number Concepts

1. What is the value of the 7 in 971,234?

   A. 7 thousand
   B. 70 thousand
   C. 700 thousand
   D. 7 million

2. Which group of numbers is in order from *least* to *greatest*?

   A. 6,808 6,088 6,008 6,880
   B. 6,880 6,808 6,088 6,008
   C. 6,008 6,088 6,808 6,880
   D. 6,808 6,008 6,088 6,880

3. Which number has a 9 in the thousands place and an 8 in the hundreds place?

   A. 49,850
   B. 94,508
   C. 459,580
   D. 495,850

4. Which circle has **less than** $\frac{1}{3}$ shaded?

   A.   **C.**

   B.   **D.**

Measurement

5. The movie started at 7:20 P.M. and ended at 9:15 P.M. How long did the movie last?

   A. 2 hours 5 minutes
   B. 1 hour 55 minutes
   C. 1 hour 50 minutes
   D. 1 hour 20 minutes

6. Jill has a banner that measures 20 in. by 55 in. She wants to put ribbon around the edges. How much ribbon does she need?

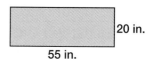
20 in.
55 in.

   A. 35 inches   **C.** 150 inches
   B. 75 inches   **D.** 1,100 inches

7. How many minutes are there in 2 hours 5 minutes? (Hint: 60 minutes equals 1 hour.)

   A. 25 min   **C.** 120 min
   B. 65 min   **D.** 125 min

8. Lisa biked 2 kilometers on Saturday and 3 kilometers on Sunday. How many *meters* did she bike? (Hint: 1 kilometer equals 1,000 meters.)

   A. 5 m   **C.** 500 m
   B. 6 m   **D.** 5,000 m

Geometry and Spatial Reasoning	Probability and Statistics

9. How many faces does this pyramid have?

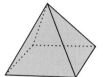

A. 6
B. 5
C. 4
D. 2

13. Look at the bag. How many possible outcomes are there?

A. 3
B. 4
C. 6
D. 10

10. How many sides does a pentagon have?

A. 4
B. 5
C. 6
D. 7

Use the graph for Questions 14–16.

The graph shows the heights of 4 fourth graders.

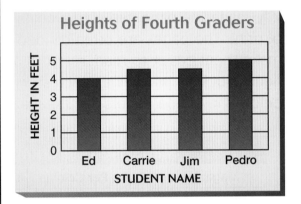

11. This soup can has the shape of a _____.

A. cone
B. sphere
C. cylinder
D. pyramid

14. Which student is the shortest?

A. Carrie   C. Jim
B. Ed   D. Pedro

12. Which figure has more than one line of symmetry?

A.

B.

C.

D.

15. Which student is closest in height to Carrie?

A. Ed   C. Carrie
B. Jim   D. Pedro

16. How much taller is Jim than Ed? (Hint: 1 foot equals 12 inches.)

A. 1 inch
B. 3 inches
C. 6 inches
D. 10 inches

Chapter 5

Multiplying by One-Digit Numbers

Chapter Theme: COMMUNICATIONS

Real-World Math

························Real Facts····················

A magazine page can hold a certain number of lines of print. The pages are often divided into columns to make them easier to read. A layout artist uses math to figure out how many lines each story needs. The chart below shows line counts for 3 magazines.

Magazine Line Counts		
Magazine	Lines Per Column	Columns Per Page
American Girl	33	2
Nickelodeon	40	2
Spider	28	1

• How many lines could you fit on 1 page of American Girl? of Nickelodeon? of Spider?

• Suppose you have a 5-page story without art in Nickelodeon. How many lines of copy is that?

·················Real People··················

Meet Nancy Leonard. She is a layout artist for *Nickelodeon*, a magazine for people your age. Ms. Leonard uses mathematics and art to decide on the best way to fit a story on the page.

Using Algebra

Yakety-Yak

Basic facts and patterns of zeros can help you multiply with multiples of 10, 100, and 1,000.

Learning About It

Talking is the most common form of communication.

How fast do you think a person can talk? Many people can say 200 words a minute.

If you say 200 words in one minute, how many words could you say in 3 minutes?

$$3 \times 200 = \blacksquare$$

THERE'S ALWAYS A WAY!

- **One way** to find the answer is to use basic facts and look for patterns with zeros.

  $3 \times 2 \quad = 3 \times 2$ ones $\quad = 6$ ones $\quad = 6$
  $3 \times 20 \; = 3 \times 2$ tens $\quad = 6$ tens $\quad = 60$
  $3 \times 200 = 3 \times 2$ hundreds $= 6$ hundreds $= 600$

  Extend the pattern. What is the product of $3 \times 2,000$?

- **Another way** to find the answer is to skip count by 200s to find 3×200.

  0   100   200   300   400   500   600

You could say 600 words in 3 minutes.

Think and Discuss What shortcut rule could you use to multiply with multiples of 10, 100, and 1,000? Give an example of how your rule works for $7 \times 3,000$.

Try It Out

Find the product. You can use *n* or any letter
instead of ▓ to show a missing number.

1. $2 \times 4 = $ ▓
$2 \times 40 = $ ▓
$2 \times 400 = $ ▓
$2 \times 4,000 = $ ▓

2. $4 \times 7 = n$
$4 \times 70 = n$
$4 \times 700 = n$
$4 \times 7,000 = n$

3. $5 \times 6 = n$
$5 \times 60 = n$
$5 \times 600 = n$
$5 \times 6,000 = n$

4. $6 \times 3 = n$
$6 \times 30 = n$
$6 \times 300 = n$
$6 \times 3,000 = n$

Practice

Use basic facts and patterns to find each product.

5. $2 \times 80 = $ ▓

6. $7 \times 20 = $ ▓

7. $3 \times 400 = $ ▓

8. $2 \times 2,000 = $ ▓

9. $5 \times 800 = $ ▓

10. $3 \times 30 = $ ▓

11. $5 \times 50 = $ ▓

12. $9 \times 200 = $ ▓

13. $8 \times 600 = $ ▓

14. $5 \times 9,000 = $ ▓

15. $4 \times 300 = $ ▓

16. $6 \times 60 = $ ▓

17. $4 \times 8,000 = n$

18. $6 \times 5,000 = n$

19. $7 \times 300 = n$

20. $4 \times 90 = n$

21. $2 \times 700 = n$

22. $8 \times 9,000 = n$

23. $9 \times 8,000 = n$

24. $6 \times 80 = n$

Problem Solving

Use the fact that John Moschitta, Jr., can read
aloud at the rate of 600 words a minute to solve
Problems 25–27.

25. How many more words could he read aloud in
9 minutes than in 7 minutes?

26. **Analyze** A book has 200 words on each page.
How many pages can he read aloud in 8 minutes?

27. **Using Mental Math** About how long will John
Moschitta, Jr., take to read aloud a 6-page story
with 300 words on each page?

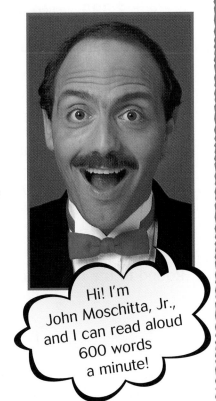

Hi! I'm
John Moschitta, Jr.,
and I can read aloud
600 words
a minute!

Review and Remember

Write the fact family for each set of numbers.

28. 3, 5, 15

29. 2, 7, 14

30. 4, 3, 12

31. 6, 8, 48

32. 9, 8, 72

33. 7, 6, 42

For Extra Practice, see Set A, page 208.

Telephone Talking

You can estimate products by rounding.

Learning About It

There are 164 apartments in this building. Each apartment has 2 phones. About how many phones are there in all?

2 phones each apartment

Round to greatest place value to estimate products.

    2 × 1<u>6</u>4   rounds to ⮕   2 × 200 = 400

There are about 400 telephones in this building.

More Examples

A. Estimate to the nearest ten.
    7 × **8<u>5</u>**   rounds to ⮕   7 × **90** = 630

B. Estimate to the nearest thousand.
    4 × **<u>2</u>,399**   rounds to ⮕   4 × **2,000** = 8,000

164 apartments

C. Estimate to the nearest dollar.
    9 × **$<u>4</u>.87**   rounds to ⮕   9 × **$5.00** = $45.00

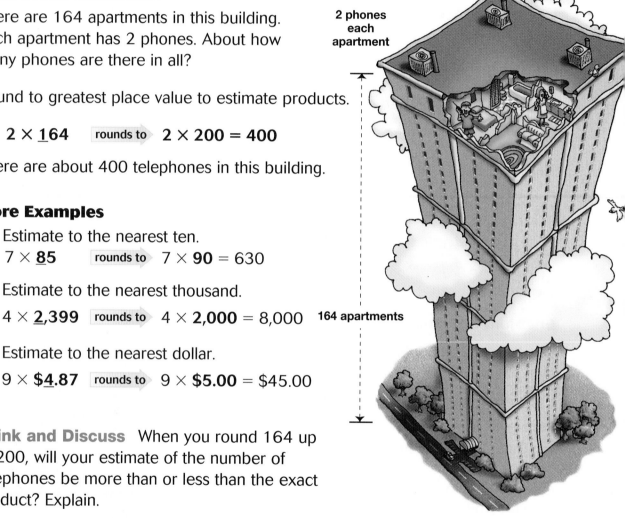

Think and Discuss When you round 164 up to 200, will your estimate of the number of telephones be more than or less than the exact product? Explain.

Try It Out

Round to the underlined place. Estimate the product.

1. 2<u>3</u> × 8	**2.** <u>4</u>06 × 7	**3.** $<u>6</u>7.95 × 5	**4.** <u>5</u>,866 × 2	**5.** <u>4</u>45 × 3

6. 9 × 2<u>4</u>   **7.** 3 × <u>3</u>41   **8.** 4 × $<u>5</u>7   **9.** 6 × <u>9</u>,802   **10.** 7 × <u>2</u>69

11. 5 × <u>7</u>6   **12.** 9 × <u>7</u>,137   **13.** 8 × <u>9</u>99   **14.** 2 × <u>4</u>78   **15.** 5 × <u>5</u>45

Practice

Round to the underlined place. Estimate the product.

16.   1<u>9</u>7
      × 5

17.   <u>3</u>9
      × 7

18. $1<u>0</u>.99
      × 9

19.   <u>7</u>39
      × 8

20.   <u>4</u>49
      × 6

21. 4 × $1<u>9</u>.72

22. 4 × <u>7</u>8

23. 9 × <u>8</u>07

24. 5 × <u>7</u>67

25. 3 × <u>2</u>,792

26. 7 × <u>8</u>9

27. 6 × <u>4</u>2

28. 8 × <u>6</u>65

29. 4 × <u>1</u>15

30. 9 × <u>6</u>06

31. 7 × <u>5</u>25

32. 3 × <u>3</u>41

33. 9 × <u>7</u>,137

34. 4 × $<u>6</u>8

35. 3 × <u>3</u>,321

36. 5 × $1<u>8</u>.52

Choose two factors from the box for
each of these estimated products.

37. 1,500

38. 900

39. 300

40. 5,000

132   313
   3
5   998

Problem Solving

Use the information in the table to estimate
the answers to Problems 41–43.

41. The Lewis family makes about the
same number of calls each month.
About how many calls will they
make in 3 months?

42. About how many calls were made by
the four families altogether?

43. Analyze Estimate how many more
calls the Chan family made than
the Rodríguez family in two months.

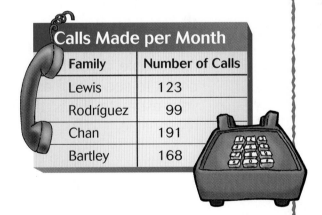

Family	Number of Calls
Lewis	123
Rodríguez	99
Chan	191
Bartley	168

Calls Made per Month

Review and Remember

Using Algebra Find the missing numbers.

44. 2, 5, 8, ▨, ▨, 17, ▨

45. 36, 30, ▨, 18, 12, ▨, ▨

46. 14, 25, 36, ▨, ▨, 69, ▨

47. 42, 36, ▨, 24, ▨, 12, ▨

Developing Skills for Problem Solving

First read for understanding and then focus on whether an answer is reasonable or not.

READ FOR UNDERSTANDING

*S*torytelling festivals are a fun place to hear stories from different cultures. Suppose one storytelling festival lasts for a week. A 3-day ticket to the festival costs $49.00, a 2-day ticket costs $38.00, and a 1-day ticket costs $21.00.

1 How much does a 1-day ticket cost?

2 How much does a 3-day ticket cost?

▲ Joyce Grear, a well-known storyteller, entertains her audience at the National Storytelling Festival in Jonesborough, Tennessee. In October of 1999, the Festival celebrated its 27th anniversary.

THINK AND DISCUSS

Reasonable Answers It is important to know whether an answer to a problem is reasonable. If you have estimated first, check to see if your answer is close to your estimate. If it is, then your answer is reasonable.

3 About how much would three 1-day tickets cost?

4 If you wanted to go to the festival for 3 days, how much money would you save by buying a 3-day ticket instead of three 1-day tickets? Would $30.00 be a reasonable answer? Explain why or why not.

5 Why is it helpful to estimate to see if an answer is reasonable or not?

Show What You Learned

Answer each question. Give a reason for your choice.

Sue Ann told the story of Anansi the Spider in American Sign Language. She signed for 4 groups on Saturday and 4 groups on Sunday. Each group had 95 people in it.

1 Which of the following is true?

   a. Sue Ann told the story to 4 groups in all.

   b. Sue Ann told the story to 8 groups in all.

   c. Sue Ann told the story to 400 groups in all.

2 Which of the following could you use to estimate the number of people who saw Sue Ann tell the story?

   a. 4×100

   b. $2 \times 4 \times 100$

   c. 2×100

3 **Explain** Would it be reasonable to say that 395 people saw Sue Ann sign? Why or why not?

Juan is going to tell a story about kites to an audience of 48 people. Then everyone in the audience will make 2 kinds of kites. One kite needs 2 straws, and the other kite needs 4 straws. Juan says he needs exactly 318 straws.

4 How many straws did Juan decide each person needs?

   a. 4 straws

   b. 6 straws

   c. 2 straws

5 How could Juan have estimated the total number of straws he needed?

   a. 4×50

   b. 6×50

   c. 6×48

6 **Explain** Is Juan's exact answer reasonable? Why or why not?

✓ Checkpoint

Understanding One-Digit Multiplication

Using Algebra Use the pattern to find each product.
(pages 178-179)

1. a. $3 \times 2 = n$
b. $3 \times n = 60$
c. $3 \times 200 = n$
d. $n \times 2,000 = 6,000$

2. a. $5 \times n = 20$
b. $5 \times 40 = n$
c. $n \times 400 = 2,000$
d. $5 \times 4,000 = n$

3. a. $7 \times 4 = n$
b. $n \times 40 = 280$
c. $7 \times 400 = n$
d. $7 \times n = 28,000$

Find the product. (pages 178-179)

4. 9×50

5. 9×80

6. 3×600

7. $4 \times 8,000$

8. 2×800

9. $4 \times 4,000$

10. 6×20

11. 2×50

12. $3 \times 8,000$

13. 8×200

14. $7 \times 6,000$

15. $2 \times 9,000$

16. 5×600

17. 7×90

18. 6×400

19. $8 \times 6,000$

20. $7 \times 3,000$

21. 9×60

22. 4×700

23. $8 \times 9,000$

Round to the underlined place.
Then estimate the product. (pages 180-181)

24. $5 \times \underline{5}9$

25. $\underline{2}9 \times 4$

26. $7 \times \underline{8}2$

27. $\underline{8}5 \times 5$

28. $2 \times \underline{6}59$

29. $5 \times \underline{1},935$

30. $\underline{1}72 \times 5$

31. $8 \times \underline{4},022$

32. $2 \times \$.\underline{9}7$

33. $\$\underline{4}.87 \times 9$

34. $5 \times \$\underline{2}.15$

35. $\$\underline{1}.25 \times 8$

36. $\underline{2}05 \times 2$

37. $9 \times \underline{8}8$

38. $\underline{3},115 \times 3$

39. $\underline{4}15 \times 5$

Mixed Practice
Multiply.

40. 8×600

41. $5,000 \times 9$

42. 60×6

43. 8×30

44. 900×2

45. $6,000 \times 5$

46. 6×400

47. 700×7

48. $5 \times 4,000$

49. 3×300

50. $8,000 \times 2$

51. 200×9

52. 4×700

53. $7 \times 7,000$

54. $3,000 \times 3$

55. $9,000 \times 2$

56. 4×300

57. 5×80

58. 7×400

59. $9,000 \times 6$

Round to the underlined place. Estimate the product.

60. 3<u>8</u>
  × 4

61. <u>2</u>48
  × 8

62. <u>2</u>,806
  × 9

63. <u>4</u>49
  × 4

64. <u>4</u>59
  × 6

65. <u>9</u>35
  × 4

66. <u>4</u>,618
  × 6

67. <u>5</u>9
  × 9

Problem Solving

68. Using Estimation If one radio costs $38.00, about how much would 4 radios cost?

69. When a mystery number is multiplied by 9, the product is 3,600. What is the number?

70. Analyze Only 10 minutes of commercials are allowed for an hour-long children's TV program. Each commercial lasts 1 minute. How many commercials would you see after 3 hours of TV?

What do you think?

How can you estimate products quickly by using rounding?

Journal Idea

Estimate how many words are on a page of your favorite book. Explain your estimate.

Critical Thinking Corner

Number Sense

Clustering to Estimate

Sometimes you can use clustering to estimate a sum. For example, in 395 + 407 + 376, all the addends cluster around 400. The sum is about 3 × 400, or 1,200.

Look at the bar graph to the right. Use clustering to estimate the total number of telephones in these four office buildings.

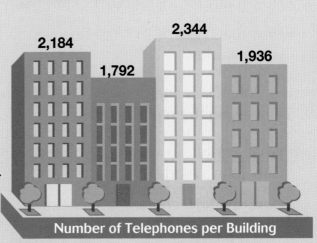

2,184

1,792

2,344

1,936

Number of Telephones per Building

Block It!

Base-ten blocks can help you explore multiplying by one-digit numbers.

Learning About It

Step 1 Work with a partner. Find 3×21.

• Use base-ten blocks to model the problem.

Each row shows
2 tens, 1 one,
or 21.

What You Need

For each pair:
base-ten blocks
  1 hundred
  12 tens
  32 ones

• How many tens altogether? How many ones?

• How much is 3×21? Tell how you found your answer.

Step 2 John used another way. He showed 3×21 by using the model to the right.

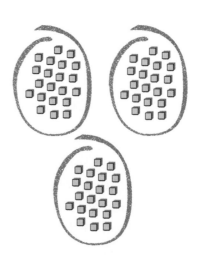

• What answer do you get if you find 3×21 with John's model?

• Describe how you find the answer.

• Which model is easier to use, the first model or John's model? Why?

Step 3 Now think about 4 × 33.

- First, make an estimate. What do you think the exact product will be?

- Use the base-ten blocks to find the product. What is 4 × 33? Think about your estimate. Does your exact product seem reasonable?

- Compare your answer with that of another group. Did you have the same answer?

Think and Discuss Did you and your partner both find your answer in the same way? Explain.

Practice

1. Estimate the products for 3 × 54 and 5 × 34. Then model the exact products with base-ten blocks.

   - How do your models differ from your estimates?

   - Were you able to regroup?

   - **Explain** Is it easier to compare the two groups of blocks after you regroup? Explain why or why not.

Estimate. Then use base-ten blocks to find each product.

2. 4 × 28   **3.** 5 × 17   **4.** 3 × 32   **5.** 6 × 21

'Toon In

You can show regrouping when you multiply.

Learning About It

Cartoon movies can tell great stories. They are made with thousands of pictures called frames. Each second uses 24 frames of film. How many frames are needed to make 3 seconds of a movie?

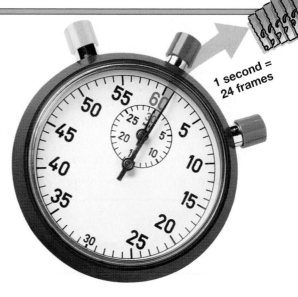

1 second = 24 frames

$$3 \times 24 = n$$

Estimate first: $3 \times 20 = 60$

Then multiply to find the exact product.

Step 1 Think about 3 groups of 24.		$\begin{array}{r} 24 \\ \times\ 3 \\ \hline \end{array}$
Step 2 Multiply the ones. 3×4 ones = 12 ones Regroup 12 ones as 1 ten 2 ones.		$\begin{array}{r} 1 \\ 24 \\ \times\ 3 \\ \hline 2 \end{array}$ 12 ones
Step 3 Multiply the tens. 3×2 tens = 6 tens Add the 1 regrouped ten. 6 tens + 1 ten = 7 tens		$\begin{array}{r} 1 \\ 24 \\ \times\ 3 \\ \hline 72 \end{array}$

For 3 seconds, 72 frames are needed.

Compare the product with your estimate. Is the product reasonable? Why or why not?

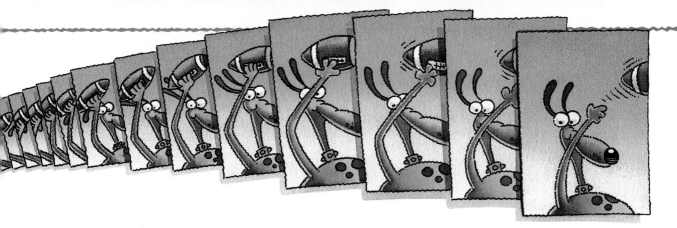

Connecting Ideas

Regrouping tens is similar to regrouping ones.

Find the product of **5 × 24.**

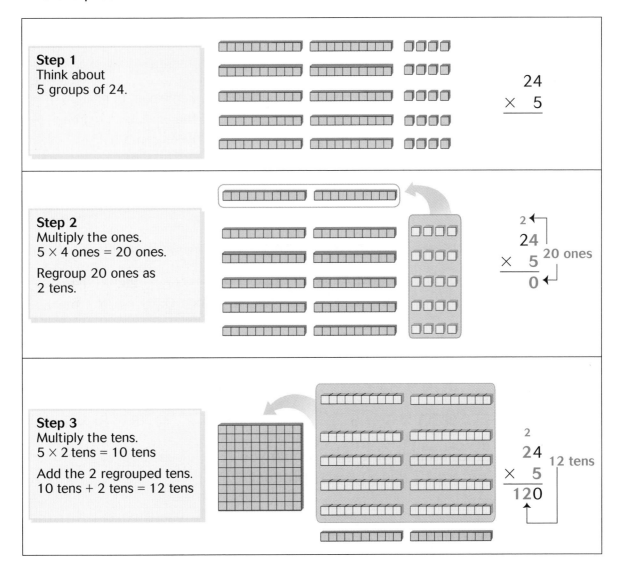

Step 1
Think about
5 groups of 24.

$$\begin{array}{r} 24 \\ \times\ 5 \end{array}$$

Step 2
Multiply the ones.
5 × 4 ones = 20 ones.

Regroup 20 ones as
2 tens.

2
24   20 ones
× 5
0

Step 3
Multiply the tens.
5 × 2 tens = 10 tens

Add the 2 regrouped tens.
10 tens + 2 tens = 12 tens

2
24   12 tens
× 5
120

The product of 5 × 24 is 120.

Think and Discuss When do you need to regroup
when multiplying?

Try It Out

Estimate. Then find the product. Use base-ten blocks if you wish.

1. $\begin{array}{r} 25 \\ \times\ 3 \\ \hline \end{array}$
2. $\begin{array}{r} 23 \\ \times\ 4 \\ \hline \end{array}$
3. $\begin{array}{r} 35 \\ \times\ 5 \\ \hline \end{array}$
4. $\begin{array}{r} 18 \\ \times\ 5 \\ \hline \end{array}$
5. $\begin{array}{r} 22 \\ \times\ 6 \\ \hline \end{array}$

6. $\begin{array}{r} 32 \\ \times\ 8 \\ \hline \end{array}$
7. $\begin{array}{r} 77 \\ \times\ 7 \\ \hline \end{array}$
8. $\begin{array}{r} 37 \\ \times\ 2 \\ \hline \end{array}$
9. $\begin{array}{r} 72 \\ \times\ 9 \\ \hline \end{array}$
10. $\begin{array}{r} 42 \\ \times\ 5 \\ \hline \end{array}$

11. 6×96
12. 4×93
13. 7×63
14. 8×92

Practice

Find the product.

15. $\begin{array}{r} 36 \\ \times\ 5 \\ \hline \end{array}$
16. $\begin{array}{r} 64 \\ \times\ 6 \\ \hline \end{array}$
17. $\begin{array}{r} 72 \\ \times\ 8 \\ \hline \end{array}$
18. $\begin{array}{r} 47 \\ \times\ 3 \\ \hline \end{array}$

19. $\begin{array}{r} 67 \\ \times\ 9 \\ \hline \end{array}$
20. $\begin{array}{r} 18 \\ \times\ 3 \\ \hline \end{array}$
21. $\begin{array}{r} 73 \\ \times\ 6 \\ \hline \end{array}$
22. $\begin{array}{r} 22 \\ \times\ 4 \\ \hline \end{array}$

23. $\begin{array}{r} 87 \\ \times\ 5 \\ \hline \end{array}$
24. $\begin{array}{r} 58 \\ \times\ 1 \\ \hline \end{array}$
25. $\begin{array}{r} 24 \\ \times\ 4 \\ \hline \end{array}$
26. $\begin{array}{r} 54 \\ \times\ 3 \\ \hline \end{array}$
27. $\begin{array}{r} 37 \\ \times\ 9 \\ \hline \end{array}$
28. $\begin{array}{r} 14 \\ \times\ 6 \\ \hline \end{array}$

29. 6×45
30. 9×39
31. 7×67
32. 3×68

33. 8×53
34. 6×84
35. $8 \times (6 \times 2)$
36. $9 \times (7 \times 9)$

37. $4 \times (9 \times 9)$
38. $(3 \times 6) \times 6$
39. $5 \times (5 \times 5)$
40. $(8 \times 8) \times 2$

> **Math Note**
>
> Remember to multiply the ones, then regroup if you can. Multiply the tens. Regroup if you can.

41. **Analyze** Without multiplying, how would you know that Exercise 17 has a greater product than Exercise 21?

Find the missing factors.

42.

X	?	?
?	25	30
?	30	36

43.

X	?	?
?	36	72
?	4	8

44.

X	?	?
?	15	35
?	0	0

45.

X	?	?
?	27	18
?	18	12

Problem Solving

Use the graph for Problems 46–48.

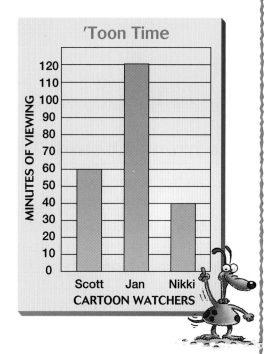

'Toon Time

46. Nikki's brother watches cartoons three times as long as Nikki. How long does he watch?

47. How many more minutes did Jan watch than Scott?

48. Create Your Own Using the data from the graph, write your own problem. Ask a classmate to solve it.

49. Six artists worked together on a cartoon movie. Each drew 75 frames a day. How many frames in all did they complete in a day?

50. Fine Arts Connection A four-second cartoon scene needs 96 photo frames. How many frames are needed for an eight-second scene? How are 4 and 8 related? How are the products related?

Review and Remember

INTERNET ACTIVITY
www.sbgmath.com

Find each answer.

51. 21 ÷ 3   **52.** 6 × 6   **53.** 45 ÷ 9   **54.** 200 − 97

55. 6 × 8   **56.** 7 × 7   **57.** 81 ÷ 9   **58.** 701 − 296

Critical Thinking Corner

Number Sense

Mystery Multiplication

Using Algebra Follow the puzzle steps. Compare your result with those of your classmates. What do you notice about the answer?

Puzzle Steps

1. Multiply your age by 5.
2. Add 25. Then, multiply by 2.
3. Add the number of your brothers and sisters.
4. Subtract 50.

Write On!

Remember the rules for regrouping when you multiply.

Learning About It

Susan has 6 pen pals from around the world. Last year, each pen pal sent Susan 12 postcards. How many postcards did she receive in all?

$$6 \times 12 = n$$

Estimate first: $6 \times 10 = 60$

Then multiply to find the exact answer.

Step 1 Multiply the ones.	**Step 2** Regroup if you can.	**Step 3** Multiply the tens. Add the regrouped tens.
$\begin{array}{r} 12 \\ \times\ 6 \\ \hline 2 \end{array}$ 6×2 ones = 12 ones	$\begin{array}{r} 1 \\ 12 \\ \times\ 6 \\ \hline 2 \end{array}$ 12 ones = 1 ten + 2 ones	$\begin{array}{r} 1 \\ 12 \\ \times\ 6 \\ \hline 72 \end{array}$ 6×1 ten = 6 tens 6 tens + 1 ten = 7 tens

Susan received 72 postcards.

Compare the product with your estimate. Is the product reasonable?

Think and Discuss How would you multiply 8×27? Describe the steps you would follow.

Try It Out

Estimate. Then find the exact product.

1. $\begin{array}{r} 63 \\ \times\ 2 \\ \hline \end{array}$
2. $\begin{array}{r} 19 \\ \times\ 4 \\ \hline \end{array}$
3. $\begin{array}{r} 26 \\ \times\ 8 \\ \hline \end{array}$
4. $\begin{array}{r} 13 \\ \times\ 7 \\ \hline \end{array}$
5. $\begin{array}{r} 39 \\ \times\ 5 \\ \hline \end{array}$
6. $\begin{array}{r} 54 \\ \times\ 3 \\ \hline \end{array}$

7. 4×21 **8.** 6×53 **9.** 3×45 **10.** 9×36 **11.** 52×8

Practice

Find each product.

12. 62 $\times$ 5	**13.** 33 $\times$ 4	**14.** 16 $\times$ 6	**15.** 18 $\times$ 5	**16.** 56 $\times$ 3	**17.** 84 $\times$ 2
18. 75 $\times$ 7	**19.** 40 $\times$ 8	**20.** 27 $\times$ 1	**21.** 17 $\times$ 2	**22.** 94 $\times$ 0	**23.** 63 $\times$ 8

24. 3×16 **25.** 86×4 **26.** 5×53 **27.** 12×8 **28.** 56×2

29. 25×3 **30.** 7×33 **31.** 84×5 **32.** 52×4

Problem Solving

33. Rosa wrote 17 postcards. Tara wrote twice as many. How many postcards did Tara write?

34. Kari is buying sheets of stamps. If she buys 8 sheets of 36 stamps and 4 sheets of 16 stamps, how many stamps will she have altogether?

35. **Explain** Jenna wants to mail a newsletter to her 24 classmates. She has 150 sheets of paper. Is that enough to make newsletters that are 8 pages long?

▲**Language Arts Connection**
Writing letters and postcards to students from other countries is a great way to make friends. Find out how to get a pen pal.

Review and Remember

Using Algebra **Find the missing number.**

36. $3 \times 1 = n$ **37.** $63 \div n = 7$ **38.** $27 \div 3 = n$ **39.** $n \times 8 = 56$

40. $n + 7 = 49$ **41.** $8 \div n = 1$ **42.** $0 \times 9 = n$ **43.** $54 - n = 9$

For Extra Practice, see Set D, page 209.

Problem Solving
Make a Table

Making and using a table can help you solve a problem.

Y̶ou are in charge of filling a column in your school newsletter. You are asked to put 72 lines in the column. You need to use the same number of articles and ads. All articles are 15 lines long, and all ads are 9 lines long. How many articles and ads should you use?

 UNDERSTAND

What do you need to find?

You need to find the same number of articles and ads that will fit exactly in a 72-line column.

 PLAN

How can you solve the problem?

You can **make a table.** Then you can find the row in your table that tells you how many ads and articles will fit on 72 lines.

 SOLVE

Make a table like the one shown at the right.

Look across the rows to see how many lines the articles and ads will fill. Find the row where the sum of the article and ad lines will be 72 lines.

$45 + 27 = 72$

So, you should use 3 articles and 3 ads to fill your column.

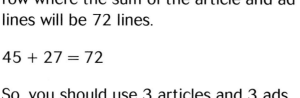

Newsletter Page

Number of Each	Number of Article Lines	Number of Ad Lines
1	15	9
2	30	18
3	45	27
4	60	36
5		

 LOOK BACK

Why is using a table helpful?

Using the Strategy

Copy the table on page 194. Continue filling it in until you have shown the number of lines there are in 10 articles and in 10 ads. Then use your table to solve Problems 1–5.

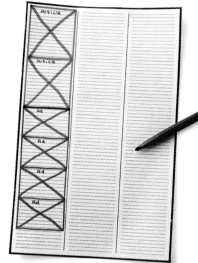

1 How many ads fill the same number of lines as 3 articles?

2 Suppose you can fit 80 lines in your column. If you only have articles, how many articles will fit?

3 **Analyze** One week you can only use 50 lines because you want to include a big picture. You have 2 articles for the column. How many ads can you fit?

4 **You Decide** What are two different combinations of articles and ads that you could fit on 75 lines?

5 **Create Your Own** Design a newsletter page of your own that has articles and ads on it. Write a problem about how many articles and ads there are on your page, and ask a classmate to solve it.

Mixed Strategy Review

Try these or other strategies to solve each problem. Tell which strategy you used.

Problem Solving Strategies

- Find a Pattern
- Guess and Check
- Draw a Picture
- Make a Graph

6 Cara spends 15 minutes more each week than the week before on her newspaper project. If she works 45 minutes the first week, how long will she work the fourth week?

7 Joe fills a section in the newsletter with ads. Each ad is 1-inch square in size. If Joe fills an area 4 inches across and 3 inches down, how many ads can he fit on the page?

8 A page of a newsletter has a total of 14 articles and ads. There are 6 more articles than ads. How many articles are there? How many ads are there?

News From the Net

Now you can multiply greater numbers.

Learning About It

The Hubble Space Telescope sends pictures of the universe back to Earth. It can send about 346 pictures every week.

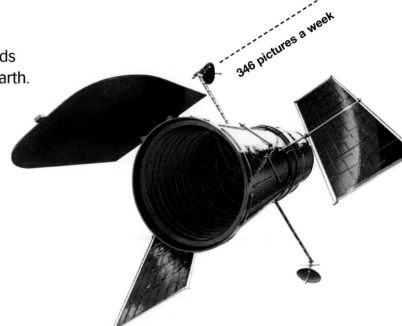

346 pictures a week

How many pictures can it send back in 4 weeks?

$$4 \times 346 = n$$

Estimate first: $4 \times 300 = 1,200$

Then multiply to find the exact product of 4×346.

THERE'S ALWAYS A WAY!

• **One way** to find the exact product is to use paper and pencil.

Step 1 Multiply the ones. Regroup if you can.	**Step 2** Multiply the tens. Add. Regroup if you can.	**Step 3** Multiply the hundreds. Add the regrouped hundreds.
2 346 × 4 ————— 4	1 2 346 × 4 ————— 84	1 2 346 × 4 ————— 1,384

• **Another way** to find the product of 4×346 is to break the number apart.

Think of 346 as $300 + 40 + 6$. Multiply each part by 4.

$$300 \times 4 \qquad 40 \times 4 \qquad 6 \times 4$$

$$1,200 \quad + \quad 160 \quad + \quad 24 \quad = \quad 1,384$$

In 4 weeks, 1,384 pictures can be sent back to Earth.

More Examples

A. $\begin{array}{r} 603 \\ \times\quad 2 \\ \hline 1{,}206 \end{array}$

B. $\begin{array}{r} {}^{1} \\ 120 \\ \times\quad 5 \\ \hline 600 \end{array}$

C. $\begin{array}{r} {}^{7\,1} \\ 192 \\ \times\quad 8 \\ \hline 1{,}536 \end{array}$

D. $\begin{array}{r} {}^{2\,2} \\ 378 \\ \times\quad 3 \\ \hline 1{,}134 \end{array}$

Connecting Ideas

Now that you know how to regroup ones and tens, you can regroup hundreds.

HST's Greatest Hits 1990–1995

A Photo Gallery of the Universe
You may access HST's Greatest Hits by visiting:
www.uni-hohenheim.de/dienste/planeten/hubble/

◄ **Science Connection**
The Hubble Space Telescope orbits Earth. It operates as a resource for astronomers worldwide. The Hubble Space Telescope's Greatest Hits home page on the Internet presents a selection of the Hubble's most spectacular images.

INTERNET ACTIVITY
www.sbgmath.com

If a computer page is visited about 1,225 times a week, how many times might it be visited in 6 weeks?

$$6 \times 1{,}225 = n$$

Estimate first: $6 \times 1{,}000 = 6{,}000$

Multiply to find the exact product of $6 \times 1{,}225$.

Step 1 Multiply the ones. Regroup if you can.	**Step 2** Multiply the tens. Add. Regroup if you can.	**Step 3** Multiply the hundreds. Add. Regroup if you can.	**Step 4** Multiply the thousands.
$\begin{array}{r} {}^{3} \\ 1{,}225 \\ \times\quad 6 \\ \hline 0 \end{array}$	$\begin{array}{r} {}^{1\,3} \\ 1{,}225 \\ \times\quad 6 \\ \hline 50 \end{array}$	$\begin{array}{r} {}^{1\,1\,3} \\ 1{,}225 \\ \times\quad 6 \\ \hline 350 \end{array}$	$\begin{array}{r} {}^{1} \\ 1{,}225 \\ \times\quad 6 \\ \hline 7{,}350 \end{array}$

It might be visited 7,350 times in 6 weeks.

Think and Discuss How is multiplying larger numbers like multiplying three-digit numbers?

Try It Out

**Estimate first. Then multiply to find the product.
Regroup whenever you need to.**

1. 502 × 7	**2.** 678 × 2	**3.** 460 × 6	**4.** 964 × 5	**5.** 525 × 9
6. 6,423 × 2	**7.** 3,530 × 3	**8.** 5,271 × 4	**9.** 1,589 × 5	**10.** 4,367 × 6

Practice

Choose a Method Multiply, using paper and pencil
or a calculator. Tell which method you used.

11. 173 × 4	**12.** 5,907 × 2	**13.** 419 × 8	**14.** 3,107 × 6	**15.** 3,784 × 7
16. 640 × 3	**17.** 8,135 × 7	**18.** 285 × 6	**19.** 6,168 × 9	**20.** 462 × 7

Solve for *n*.

21. $4 \times 875 = n$ **22.** $4 \times 908 = n$ **23.** $6 \times 671 = n$

24. $3 \times 200 = n$ **25.** $4 \times 609 = n$ **26.** $9 \times 110 = n$

27. $2 \times 4,926 = n$ **28.** $8 \times 400 = n$ **29.** $5 \times 231 = n$

30. Journal Idea The number 5 compares
to the number 500 as 10 would compare
to what number? Explain.

Problem Solving

Use the pictograph to the right to
solve Problems 31–32.

31. How many History sites
are there on the Internet?

32. How many more Games sites
are there than Science sites?

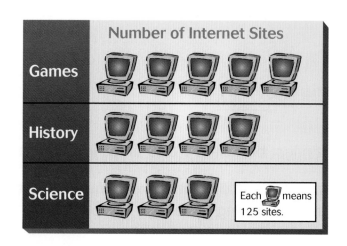

Number of Internet Sites

| Games |
| History |
| Science |

Each 🖥 means
125 sites.

Solve. Check to see if each answer is reasonable.

33. **What If?** About 57 million people in North America used the Internet by 1997. Suppose that seven times that many people use it by the year 2000. How many people will that be?

34. In three weeks, a class visited 42 Internet sites. In the fourth week, they visited 12 sites each school day. How many sites were visited in all four weeks?

35. **Analyze** Suppose the number of sites on the Internet doubles every 53 days. If you start with 385 sites, how many sites will there be in 106 days? Explain the strategy you used to solve the problem.

Review and Remember

Find the answer.

36.	37.	38.	39.	40.
7,084	401	8,007	257	908
− 5,995	− 15	+5,735	− 252	+ 107

41. 49 ÷ 7 **42.** 3 × 6 **43.** 9 ÷ 3 **44.** 9 × 7 **45.** 42 ÷ 6

Money $ense

Time Is Money!

Use the information at the right to help you figure out the best deal for using the Internet.

1. How much would you pay to use the Internet 20 minutes a month if you had Plan A? Plan B? Plan C?

2. You think you'll use the Internet about 5 hours a month. Which plan is the most economical for you? About how much money will you pay each month?

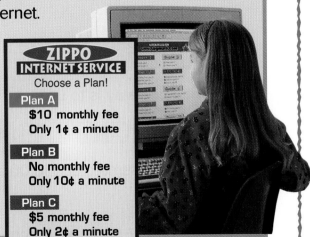

ZIPPO INTERNET SERVICE
Choose a Plan!

Plan A
$10 monthly fee
Only 1¢ a minute

Plan B
No monthly fee
Only 10¢ a minute

Plan C
$5 monthly fee
Only 2¢ a minute

For Extra Practice, see Set E, page 210.

Greetings!

Multiplying with money is like multiplying whole numbers.

Learning About It

Greeting cards are a great way to send messages. Ten-year-old Spencer Heelan realized this when he decided to make greeting cards to sell.

If you paid 3 friends $12.50 each to help you make greeting cards, how much would you pay in all?

$$3 \times \$12.50 = n$$

Estimate first: $3 \times \$10.00 = \$30.00$

Then multiply to find the exact product of $3 \times \$12.50$.

▲ **Kid Connection** Spencer Heelan pays his friends $0.25 for each card they help him make. Then he sells the cards for $1.00 each.

THERE'S ALWAYS A WAY!

● **One way** to find the exact product is to use paper and pencil.

Step 1 Multiply as with whole numbers.	**Step 2** Regroup as needed.	**Step 3** Show dollars and cents in the product.
$$\begin{array}{r} \$12.50 \\ \times \quad 3 \\ \hline \end{array}$$	$$\begin{array}{r} {}^{1}\ \ \ \\ \$12.50 \\ \times \quad 3 \\ \hline 3750 \end{array}$$	$$\begin{array}{r} \$12.50 \\ \times \quad 3 \\ \hline \$37.50 \end{array}$$

● **Another way** is to use your calculator to find the total amount.

Press: ③ ✕ ① ② ● ⑤ ⓪ ＝   Display: ⌐ 37.5 ⌐

Use the estimate of $30.00 to help you write the product $37.50.

You would pay $37.50 to your friends.

Think and Discuss What do the underlined digits in $37.<u>50</u> represent? When you multiply money, how do you know where to place the decimal point in the product?

Try It Out

Estimate. Then multiply to find each product. Check that each answer is reasonable.

1. $8.31 × 2	**2.** $12.80 × 7	**3.** $0.45 × 3	**4.** $44.65 × 9	**5.** $19.98 × 4
6. $2.71 × 8	**7.** **$63.78** × **6**	**8.** $0.67 × 4	**9.** $31.64 × 5	**10.** $20.96 × 5

 11. Journal Idea In what way is multiplying money like multiplying whole numbers? How is it different?

Practice

Find each product.

12. $14.59 × 4	**13.** $89.90 × 3	**14.** $0.79 × 9	**15.** $99.99 × 2	**16.** $7.55 × 7
17. $12.67 × 8	**18.** $76.44 × 5	**19.** $0.83 × 8	**20.** $12.75 × 2	**21.** $3.59 × 6
22. $40.03 × 9	**23.** $10.89 × 3	**24.** $7.29 × 5	**25.** $25.99 × 3	**26.** $5.55 × 2
27. $0.55 × 7	**28.** $17.50 × 9	**29.** $44.62 × 3	**30.** $1.72 × 6	**31.** $32.88 × 3

32. 4 × $33.93   **33.** 9 × $67.01

34. 6 × $51.96   **35.** 2 × $50.67

36. 4 × $0.09   **37.** 7 × $2.95

38. 8 × $1.57   **39.** 9 × $12.06

Choose a Method Use a calculator or paper
and pencil to solve. Tell which method you used.

40. 7 × $18.90   **41.** 4 × $0.85   **42.** 9 × $1.39   **43.** 8 × $122.37

44. 3 × $79.06   **45.** 8 × $1.25   **46.** 5 × $10.26   **47.** 3 × $100.02

48. 6 × $4.81   **49.** 7 × $50.06   **50.** 5 × $86.25   **51.** 9 × $1.02

Problem Solving

Use the table to answer
Problems 52–57.

52. How much does it cost to
make 9 buttons?

53. How much does it cost
to make 7 T-shirts? How
much will you collect if
you sell them?

54. How much does
Damon earn by making
and then selling 16
T-shirts?

55. What If? Dottie earned
$5.50 for making and then
selling 10 of one of the
items shown in the table.
Which item was she selling?

56. Analyze Leroy sells 5
buttons and John sells 4
hats. Who has more money
after paying to make the
items? Explain the strategy
you used to get your answer.

57. Create Your Own Use the
data from the table to write
your own problem. See if a
classmate can solve it.

Item	Cost to Make	Selling Price
Hat	$ 2.67	$ 4.25
T-Shirt	$ 7.00	$13.00
Button	$ 0.20	$ 0.75

Review and Remember

Use the graph to answer Problems 58–61.

58. During which month were sales the lowest? the highest?

59. Between which two months was the greatest increase in sales? the greatest decrease?

60. Find the total number of cards sold for all six months shown on the graph.

61. Order the months according to sales, starting with the month that had the greatest sales.

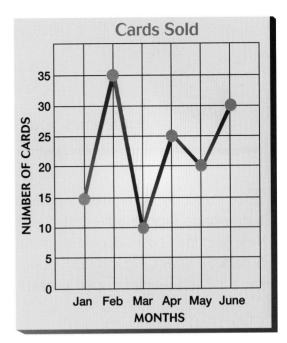

Cards Sold

NUMBER OF CARDS

Jan Feb Mar Apr May June
MONTHS

Time for Technology

Using the MathProcessor™ on CD-ROM

Using Money Manipulatives

You can model 3 x $8.15.

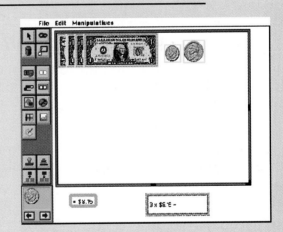

- Open a money manipulative. Link it to a number space.

- Show $8.15. Click the number space, then click $.

- To select all the money, click above the top left corner and drag to the lower right corner. You should see a box around each piece of the money.

- Click and stamp out two more sets of $8.15.

- Click and write a number sentence for 3 x $8.15.

For Extra Practice, see Set F, page 210.

Problem Solving
Using Money

Sometimes you can use money to help you solve problems.

The Publicity Committee needs to make 475 copies of a one-page flier to advertise the Rose City Festival. Yellow paper costs 8 cents a sheet. White paper costs 5 cents a sheet. How much money will the committee save if it uses white paper instead of yellow paper?

 ## UNDERSTAND

What do you need to know?

You need to know that yellow paper costs $0.08 a sheet and white paper costs $0.05 a sheet. You also need to know that the committee needs 475 sheets of paper.

 ## PLAN

How can you solve the problem?

Subtract to find the difference between the cost of yellow paper and white paper. Then multiply that difference by the number of copies.

 ## SOLVE

Step 1 $0.08 − $0.05 = $0.03

Step 2   475 × $0.03 = $14.25

The committee will save $14.25.

 ## LOOK BACK

What's another way you could solve the problem?

Show What You Learned

Use the data from the posters to solve each problem.
Estimate to be sure your answer is reasonable.

1. There are 4 children and 2 adults going to the festival. Is $10.00 enough to pay for their admissions? Why or why not?

2. If 5 children and 3 adults go to the festival together, how much will they spend on admission tickets?

3. Tickets for rides cost $0.25 each. If Keisha has $1.25, how many tickets can she buy?

COME TO THE ROSE CITY
Festival
Rides! Prizes! Refreshments!
June 23-27
Admission
Children $1.25
Adults $1.75

☆ Ride Tickets ☆
1	$0.25
2	$0.50
3	$0.75
4	$1.00
5	$1.25
6	$1.50

PUPPET SHOW
Adults $5.00
Children $2.00

REFRESHMENTS
Hot Dogs $1.25
Lemonade $0.75

4. Steven buys a child's admission ticket to the festival. He also buys 4 tickets for rides, a hot dog, and a glass of lemonade. How much money does he spend?

5. **Analyze** Jenny sold $35.00 worth of puppet show tickets. She sold some $2.00 tickets and some $5.00 tickets. How many of each type of ticket might she have sold?

6. Miguel's mom gave him $5.00 for lunch. He wants to buy 3 hot dogs and 2 lemonades. Does he have enough money? Why or why not?

7. Rebecca pays for 2 children's tickets to the festival with $10.00. How much change should she get back?

8. A book of 10 ride tickets costs $2.25. How much cheaper is it to buy a book of 10 tickets instead of 10 separate tickets?

9. **Create Your Own** Write a problem using the information in the posters. Give it to a classmate to solve.

Problem Solving

Practice What You Learned

Choose the correct letter for each answer.

1 Gina used 3 rolls of crepe paper to decorate for a party. Each roll was more than 8 feet long and less than 11 feet long. Which is reasonable for the amount of crepe paper Gina used?

A. Less than 11 ft
B. Between 20 ft and 24 ft
C. Between 24 ft and 33 ft
D. More than 33 ft

Tip

Start by finding the lowest possible sum and the highest possible sum. Use what you find to pick the correct answer.

2 Paul had $27.00. He bought a baseball for $8.95. He gave the clerk $10.00. How much change should Paul get back?

A. $1.05
B. $2.05
C. $18.05
D. $18.95

Tip

Use estimation to eliminate one or more of the answer choices in this problem.

3 A student is arranging chairs for a school play. He puts 14 chairs in the first row, 17 in the second row, 20 in the third row, and 23 in the fourth row. If he continues this pattern, how many chairs will he put in the 10th row?

A. 44
B. 41
C. 40
D. 38

Tip

Use one of these strategies to solve the problem.
• Find a Pattern
• Make a Table
• Draw a Picture

4 Kevin has 65¢. He wants to buy 8 pencils that cost 9¢ each. How much more money does he need?

A. 7¢

B. 13¢

C. 56¢

D. 72¢

5 Keesha has a CD case that holds 48 CDs. Each row in the case holds 8 CDs. Which shows how many rows there are in the case?

A. $48 - 8 = $ ▨

B. $48 \div 8 = $ ▨

C. $48 + 8 = $ ▨

D. $48 \times 8 = $ ▨

6 During the first 3 months of the year, a toy store sold the following number of games: 879, 914, 809. Which is the best estimate for the number of games sold in the 3 months?

A. 2,500

B. 2,600

C. 2,800

D. 3,000

7 Kayla lives 3 miles from school. Claire lives 7 miles from school. Maisha lives farther from school than Claire. Which is reasonable for the distance from Maisha's home to school?

A. Less than 3 miles

B. Between 3 and 5 miles

C. Between 5 and 7 miles

D. More than 7 miles

8 Jack, Angie, and 3 of their friends each checked out 4 books from the library. Angie returned her books within a week. How many books were still checked out of the library?

A. 7

B. 12

C. 14

D. 16

Use the graph for Problems 9–10.

The graph below shows the number of people in different age groups who read the newspaper each day.

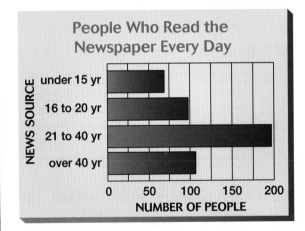

9 Which age group has the greatest number of people who read the newspaper every day?

A. Over 40 years

B. 21 to 40 years

C. 16 to 20 years

D. Under 15 years

10 **About** how many of the people who are 21 years old **or older** read the newspaper every day?

A. 150

B. 200

C. 300

D. 400

# Checkpoint

Multiplying by One-Digit Numbers

Vocabulary

Complete. Use the words from the Word Bank.

1. The numbers that are multiplied are called ___?___.

2. If you round the numbers before multiplying, your answer will be an ___?___.

3. The answer in multiplication is called the ___?___.

Word Bank

array
estimate
factors
product

Concepts and Skills

Write the multiplication sentence shown by each picture. (pages 188–191)

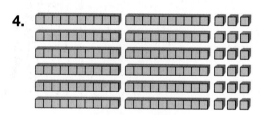

4.

5.

Find each product. (pages 192–193, 196–203)

6. 83 × 2	7. 20 × 5	8. 64 × 3	9. 72 × 8	10. 47 × 3
11. 314 × 4	12. 6,701 × 9	13. 8,350 × 2	14. 560 × 9	15. 6,402 × 3
16. $4.92 × 8	17. $9.23 × 5	18. $10.45 × 2	19. $5.19 × 7	20. $32.36 × 8

21. 3 × 43   22. 9 × 83   23. 7 × 56   24. 2 × 38

25. 413 × 5   26. 1,150 × 4   27. 321 × 8   28. 8,880 × 2

29. 6 × $62.73   30. 5 × $17.93   31. 4 × $12.31   32. 7 × $4,609

Problem Solving

33. Six libraries share books. Each library has 4,550 books. How many books have they in all?

34. **Using Estimation** You want to invite eight friends to a party. Each invitation costs $0.30 and each stamp costs $0.32. You have $5.00. Do you have enough money?

35. **Analyze** Suppose it costs $0.05 a minute to be on the Internet. If you used the Internet 1 hour every day, how much would you be charged after 30 days?

Journal Idea

Look back at your answers to the questions above. Which were the easiest for you to find? Which were the hardest? Why?

What do you think?

Do base-ten blocks display multiplication problems clearly? Explain.

You Decide

Activity

Plan a Window Display

A video store manager wants to display 400 video tapes in packs of 2, 3, and 4.

Decide how many of each kind of pack you would display. Remember, you need to display all 400 tapes.

Make a chart like the one above. Draw a picture of your display. Write how many of each kind of pack you used.

 You might wish to include this work in your portfolio.

Tapes per Pack	Number of Packs	Total Tapes
2		
3		
4		

Extra Practice

Set A (pages 178–179)

Using Algebra Use basic facts and patterns to find each product.

1. 3 × 90 **2.** 9 × 200 **3.** 6 × 50 **4.** 5 × 700

5. 8 × 700 **6.** 9 × 400 **7.** 3 × 70 **8.** 9 × 900

9. 2 × 100 **10.** 5 × 8,000 **11.** 4 × 400 **12.** 7 × 7,000

13. 2 × 300 **14.** 3 × 400 **15.** 5 × 900 **16.** 2 × 700

17. 5 × 300 **18.** 8 × 4,000 **19.** 6 × 9,000 **20.** 8 × 9,000

21. 4 × 6,000 **22.** 7 × 500 **23.** 5 × 4,000 **24.** 7 × 6,000

25. During a commercial on television, an actor spoke 700 words a minute for 3 minutes. How many words were said?

Set B (pages 180–181)

Round to the underlined place. Estimate each product.

1. 7 × <u>3</u>19 **2.** 6 × <u>3</u>6 **3.** 4 × <u>3</u>2 **4.** 5 × <u>6</u>8

5. 3 × <u>8</u>,652 **6.** 5 × <u>3</u>61 **7.** 7 × <u>2</u>66 **8.** 4 × <u>8</u>24

9. 9 × <u>7</u>4 **10.** 4 × <u>5</u>8 **11.** 2 × <u>4</u>70 **12.** 3 × <u>3</u>41

13. <u>1</u>50
    × 4

14. <u>9</u>60
    × 3

15. <u>6</u>28
    × 8

16. <u>3</u>,615
    × 2

17. <u>8</u>77
    × 2

18. <u>9</u>08
    × 4

19. <u>9</u>70
    × 9

20. <u>8</u>90
    × 6

21. <u>6</u>,009
    × 8

22. <u>6</u>,600
    × 3

23. <u>6</u>,580
    × 5

24. <u>3</u>,458
    × 4

25. About 694 phone calls are made each minute to the Pentagon, in Washington, D.C. About how many calls are received at this government building every 5 minutes?

Extra Practice

Set C (pages 188–191)

Write each multiplication sentence.

1.

2.

Use blocks or drawings to find each product.

3. 2×18 4. 4×28 5. 5×45 6. 3×28 7. 6×39

8. 2×12 9. 3×18 10. 4×22 11. 5×33 12. 8×28

13. 5×32 14. 7×24 15. 7×14 16. 8×14 17. 7×12

18. A video store sold 42 copies of a cartoon video in 1 day. At this rate, how many will they sell in 7 days?

Set D (pages 192–193)

Estimate first and then find each product.

1. 86×3 2. 47×9 3. 24×5 4. 36×4 5. 55×3 6. 42×6

7. 87×2 8. 39×7 9. 24×8 10. 67×9 11. 91×4 12. 59×6

13. 79×2 14. 54×6 15. 85×5 16. 23×4

17. 3×43 18. 2×28 19. 4×59 20. 9×83

21. 61×3 22. 76×5 23. 94×6 24. 37×4

25. 28×8 26. 64×5 27. 49×8 28. 78×3

29. Two pen pals wrote letters to each other for 75 years. They exchanged 8 letters a year. How many letters did they exchange?

Extra Practice

Set E (pages 196–199)

Estimate first and then find each product.

1. 130
× 6

2. 811
× 7

3. 328
× 3

4. 494
× 2

5. 109
× 5

6. 239
× 4

7. 980
× 8

8. 758
× 9

9. 639
× 3

10. 508
× 4

11. 5,124
× 8

12. 6,739
× 5

13. 2,009
× 9

14. 8,092
× 6

15. 3,407
× 7

16. 164 × 2   **17.** 600 × 8   **18.** 710 × 9   **19.** 164 × 2

20. 9 × 6,027   **21.** 6 × 3,648   **22.** 4 × 1,509   **23.** 2 × 9,999

24. 3 × 243   **25.** 5 × 160   **26.** 2 × 347   **27.** 5 × 482

28. On the Internet you found 128 articles on pandas. It takes 3 minutes to access and to print each article. How many minutes will it take to print them all?

Set F (pages 200–203)

Estimate and then multiply.

1. $1.36 × 8   **2.** $0.73 × 4   **3.** $2.99 × 3   **4.** $18.45 × 5

5. $42.69 × 6   **6.** $5.05 × 7   **7.** $0.18 × 9   **8.** $10.55 × 2

9. $2.15 × 7   **10.** $3.25 × 5   **11.** $1.87 × 6   **12.** $4.09 × 9

13. $30.89
× 4

14. $21.50
× 7

15. $10.99
× 3

16. $1.39
× 8

17. $11.25
× 6

18. $22.02
× 9

19. $35.47
× 3

20. $21.04
× 8

21. $43.21
× 2

22. $79.09
× 9

23. T-shirts cost $11.59 at T-Shirt Express. If Erin buys 4 T-shirts, how much will they cost her?

Chapter Test

Match the multiplication example to its drawing.

1. 3 × 23   **a.**

2. 2 × 35   **b.**

3. 2 × 22   **c.**

Find each product.

4. 20	**5.** 50	**6.** 3,000	**7.** 800	**8.** 900
× 4	× 4	× 3	× 2	× 6

Round to the underlined place. Estimate each product.

9. <u>2</u>89	**10.** <u>5</u>18	**11.** <u>8</u>,760	**12.** <u>3</u>32	**13.** <u>2</u>,899
× 2	× 3	× 5	× 4	× 6

Estimate first and then find each product.

14. 41	**15.** 23	**16.** 506	**17.** 432	**18.** 4,710
× 3	× 7	× 5	× 8	× 4

19. $2.55	**20.** $28.80	**21.** $64.52	**22.** $0.25	**23.** $20.05
× 6	× 3	× 2	× 5	× 4

Solve.

24. You are at your school's book sale and you want to buy three books. They cost $4.59, $5.35, and $4.98. About how much money will they cost in all?

25. A jet plane travels at 450 miles per hour. It takes 6 hours to fly from Boston to San Francisco. What is the distance between the cities?

 Self-Check
Did you place the dollar sign and decimal point correctly in Exercises 19–23?

Show What You Know About Multiplication

1 Work with a partner. Explain how to multiply these numbers. You can use base-ten blocks, grid paper, pictures, numbers, or words. Show your work. Then explain how you can check your answer to determine if it is reasonable.

What You Need

base-ten blocks
grid paper

a. 5 × 33

b. 4 × 48

Self-Check Did you remember to show your work?

2 Solve this problem using the chart on the right. Show your work.

One Internet service costs $11.50 a month for the first 10 hours. Each additional hour costs $2.95. Another Internet service costs $9.95 for the first 5 hours. Each additional hour costs $1.50. Use the information in the chart to decide which service would be the best for one family.

Self-Check Did you remember that the first 5 hours of service are included in the monthly costs?

Monthly Usage	
Month	**Hours**
January	10
February	6
March	17
April	22
May	5
June	20
July	13
August	35
September	19
October	14
November	32
December	29

For Your Portfolio

You might wish to include this work in your portfolio.

Extension

Napier's Bones

John Napier was a Scottish mathematician who invented an unusual method of multiplying. He used a special set of sticks or "bones" with the multiples of the numbers 1 through 9 on them.

Use the pattern you see on the 2 and 3 Bones, shown at the right, to make a set of Napier's Bones for the numbers 0 through 9. Use construction paper or tongue depressors. Label each bone.

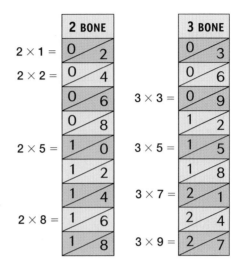

Work in a small group.

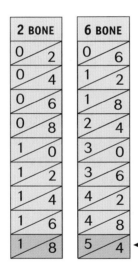

1 Use the bones to find 9×26.

2 Place the 2 Bone and the 6 Bone side by side. Look down to the ninth row.

3 Add the digits along each diagonal as shown below. Begin at the right. Regroup if necessary.

9th row →

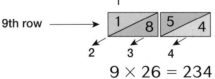

$9 \times 26 = 234$

Use Napier's method to find each product.
Exercise 1 is modeled below.

1. 2×59

2nd row →

5 BONE	9 BONE
0 / 5	0 / 9
1 / 0	1 / 8
1 / 5	2 / 7

2. 3×45

3. 5×32 **4.** 3×64 **5.** 8×89 **6.** 7×48

Cumulative Review

Choose the correct letter for each answer.

Number Concepts	Operations

Number Concepts

1. What is the value of the 6 in 6,987,457?

A. 6 thousand
B. 60 thousand
C. 600 thousand
D. 6 million

2. Which figure has more than $\frac{1}{2}$ shaded?

A.   **C.**

B.   **D.**

3. Which set of numbers is in order from *least* to *greatest*?

A. 2,311   3,022   2,331   3,113
B. 2,311   2,331   3,022   3,113
C. 3,113   3,022   2,331   2,311
D. 2,331   2,311   3,022   3,113

4. Which number has a 3 in the ten thousands place and a 9 in the tens place?

A. 291,532
B. 231,952
C. 231,529
D. 231,592

Operations

5. What is the product of 47 × 5?

A. 9   **C.** 52
B. 42   **D.** 235

6. Perry spent $18 on colored markers. He bought 2 yellow markers, 3 pink markers, and 4 blue markers. If each marker costs the same amount, how much did each marker cost?

A. $2.00   **C.** $9.00
B. $3.00   **D.** $22.00

7. At Computer World you can get 4 computer games for $36. How much would 20 computer games cost?

A. $80
B. $144
C. $180
D. $720

8. Tia bought a CD for $13.99 and a tape on sale for $5.49. The tape originally cost $7.89. How much money did Tia save?

A. $2.40
B. $6.10
C. $13.38
D. $19.48

Patterns, Relationships, and Algebraic Thinking	**Measurement**

9. Which expression could help you solve $6 \times \blacksquare = 42$?

A. 6×42
B. $42 \div 6$
C. 42×6
D. $42 - 6$

10. Which number sentence is **NOT** in the same family of facts as $63 \div 7 = 9$?

A. $63 \div 9 = 7$
B. $9 \times 7 = 63$
C. $9 \times 3 = 27$
D. $7 \times 9 = 63$

11. The fourth-grade class had a read-a-thon. Ed read 2 chapters of a book in the first week. Each week after that, he read 2 more chapters than the week before. How many chapters did he read in the *sixth* week?

A. 6
B. 8
C. 12
D. 14

12. What is the missing number in the number pattern?

36, 32, 28, $\blacksquare$, 20, 16

A. 18
B. 22
C. 24
D. 26

13. A rectangle is 14 feet wide by 16 feet long. What is the *perimeter* of the rectangle?

A. 30 ft
B. 60 ft
C. 120 ft
D. 224 ft

14. The *perimeter* of a table is 14 feet. If the width is 3 feet, what is the length?

A. 3 ft
B. 4 ft
C. 11 ft
D. 17 ft

15. A car weighs 1,780 pounds. The driver weighs 210 pounds. There are ten 16-ounce bottles in the back seat. What is the total weight of the car and the bottles? (Hint: 16 ounces equals 1 pound.)

A. 1,790 lb
B. 1,940 lb
C. 2,000 lb
D. 2,150 lb

16. Chip started a 3-mile race at 3:30 P.M. He crossed the finish line at 4:05 P.M. How long did it take him to run the race?

A. 25 minutes
B. 35 minutes
C. 45 minutes
D. 75 minutes

Chapter 6

Multiplying by Two-Digit Numbers

Chapter Theme: ANIMALS

Real Facts

Some young people are business owners. The two boys pictured at the right sell animal trading cards. They use mathematics to help them figure out quantities and to fill out order forms. The chart below shows the prices of some of their card sets.

Animal Trading Cards	
Number of Cards per Set	Price in Dollars
100	$10.00
15	$2.20
7	$1.00

- What is the greatest number of cards you can get for $2? for $10? for $20?

- If an order is placed for 128 cards, what sets can you use to fill the order exactly?

Real People

Meet Matt and Trevor Kent. They own M & T Cards, an animal trading card company. Their dad takes most of the pictures, and the boys take care of business! They even have their own web site! As business owners, they work hard to keep their customers satisfied.

Elephant Chow

Use facts you already know to multiply two-digit numbers by multiples of 10, 100, and 1,000.

Learning About It

Would you like an elephant as a pet? You'd better think twice. They eat a lot each year, and a female elephant lives about 70 years! About how many pounds of carrots will she eat over her lifetime?

70 × 800 = ▨

You can use a basic fact and a pattern with zeros to multiply 70 × 800 mentally.

7 × 8 = 56
7 × 80 = 560
70 × 80 = 5,600
70 × 800 = 56,000 pounds of carrots

> The number of zeros in both factors equals the number of zeros in the product.

Hay	40,000 pounds
Elephant Pellets	2,000 pounds
Apples	900 pounds
Carrots	800 pounds

More Examples

A. 30 × 30 = ▨
  3 × 3 = 9
  3 × 30 = 90
  30 × 30 = 900

B. 50 × 800 = ▨
  5 × 8 = 40
  5 × 80 = 400
  50 × 80 = 4,000
  50 × 800 = 40,000

> When the product of a basic fact includes a zero, that zero is not part of the pattern.

 Science Connection
Average amount of zoo food for one female elephant each year

Think and Discuss Use patterns with zeros to explain why 30 × 500, 300 × 50, and 3 × 5,000 have the same product.

Try It Out

Using Mental Math Use patterns with zeros to solve mentally.

1. 8 × 40
   80 × 40
   80 × 400

2. 6 × 70
   60 × 70
   60 × 700

3. 9 × 30
   90 × 30
   90 × 300

4. 5 × 40
   50 × 40
   50 × 400

5. 20 × 30

6. 70 × 900

7. 40 × 50

8. 20 × 200

Practice

Use patterns with zeros to solve.

9.   20
   × 20

10.   40
   × 70

11.   800
   × 30

12.   700
   × 700

13.   3,000
   ×   50

14. 300 × 300

15. 80 × 5,000

16. 50 × 50

17. 90 × 400

18. 6,000 × 70

19. 400 × 200

20. 90 × 8,000

21. 300 × 8,000

Problem Solving

Use the data on page 216 to solve Problems 22–24.

22. About how many pounds of apples would 20 zoo elephants eat every year? About how many pounds of elephant pellets would they eat?

23. A male elephant eats about twice as much as a female elephant. About how many pounds of food will he eat every year? Explain the strategy you used to find the answer.

24. Science Connection A newborn elephant weighs 200 pounds and gains an average of 500 pounds a year for 20 years. How much does the elephant weigh after 20 years?

▲ Social Studies
Connection In Zambia, where wild elephants live, young people are encouraged to join Changologo Clubs, which stress animal conservation.

Review and Remember

Find each answer.

25. 8 x 9

26. 56 ÷ 8

27. 247 + 349

28. 603 − 234

29. 8 x 6

Moving Along

Rounding factors can help you estimate products.

Learning About It

A blue whale is larger than any dinosaur ever was. Even though the whale is large, it can swim fast. Suppose a blue whale can swim about 20 miles an hour. At that rate, about how far could a blue whale swim in 24 hours?

Round to estimate the product.

$$
\begin{array}{r} 20 \\ \times\ 24 \end{array} \quad \text{rounds to} \quad \begin{array}{r} 20 \\ \times\ 20 \\ \hline 400 \end{array}
$$

A blue whale could travel about 400 miles in 24 hours.

San Francisco

CALIFORNIA

Los Angeles

Blue whales can swim about 20 miles in 1 hour.

More Examples

A. 45 × 48

50 × 50 = 2,500

B. 59 × 401

60 × 400 = 24,000

Think and Discuss How can you predict if your estimate will be higher or lower than the exact product?

INTERNET ACTIVITY
www.sbgmath.com

Try It Out

Round each factor to the underlined place.
Then estimate each product.

1. 6̲2 × 1̲2   **2.** 8̲9 × 1̲8   **3.** 4̲2 × 5̲3   **4.** 6̲1 × 1̲45   **5.** 1̲04 × 1̲0

Practice

Round each factor to the underlined place.
Then estimate each product.

6. 4̲8 × 2̲5   **7.** 6̲1 × 8̲6   **8.** 2̲31 × 6̲5   **9.** 1̲36 × 7̲8

10. $\underline{6}6 \times \underline{1}66$ **11.** $\underline{8}4 \times \underline{1}42$ **12.** $\underline{4}32 \times \underline{5}9$ **13.** $\underline{1}28 \times \underline{1}9$

14. $\underline{1}58 \times \underline{2}5$ **15.** $\underline{3}9 \times \underline{2}89$ **16.** $\underline{4}49 \times \underline{2}1$ **17.** $\underline{8}82 \times \underline{3}3$

18. $\underline{7}8 \times \underline{1}95$ **19.** $\underline{4}9 \times \underline{6}12$ **20.** $\underline{7}32 \times \underline{6}9$ **21.** $\underline{5}23 \times \underline{4}98$

22. $\underline{2}09 \times \underline{9}02$ **23.** $\underline{2},019 \times \underline{2}3$ **24.** $\underline{8}44 \times \underline{3}6$ **25.** $\underline{4}08 \times \underline{4}9$

Problem Solving

Use the table to solve Problems 26–28.

26. Estimate how many feet a cheetah can run in 12 seconds.

27. **What If?** Suppose the kangaroo and the jack rabbit are in a race. Estimate how far each will go in 18 seconds. Will an estimate tell you the winner? Explain.

28. **Create Your Own** Use the data to write your own problem. Give it to a classmate to solve.

Top Animal Speeds	
Animal	**Feet per Second**
Blue whale	34
Kangaroo	63
Cheetah	104
Jack rabbit	61
Human	31

Review and Remember

Find each answer.

29.
$$\begin{array}{r} \$438.75 \\ -29.40 \\ \hline \end{array}$$

30.
$$\begin{array}{r} 44{,}293 \\ +17{,}842 \\ \hline \end{array}$$

31.
$$\begin{array}{r} 47 \\ \times9 \\ \hline \end{array}$$

32. $6\overline{)36}$

Money $ense

Math Riddles

Solve each math riddle.

1. You spend $2.00 on lunch. If you have $1.40 left over, how much money did you start with?

2. Matt has between $5 and $8 in quarters. If he writes the amount, the number will have 3 digits. The sum of the digits will be 11. How much money does Matt have?

Developing Skills for Problem Solving

Read for understanding and then focus on whether there is too much or too little information to solve a problem.

READ FOR UNDERSTANDING

Sarah volunteers at the Raptor Trust. One of her jobs is to copy a newsletter. Last month she made 80 copies of the newsletter. This month she needs to make 100 copies. She has $5.00 to spend.

1. How many copies of her newsletter does Sarah need to make this month?

2. How much money does Sarah have to spend?

THINK AND DISCUSS

Too Much or Too Little Information
Sometimes word problems contain too much or too little information. If there is too much, you need to choose what you need to solve the problem. If there is too little information, you cannot solve the problem.

▲ Science Connection
The Raptor Trust is an organization that provides care for injured or orphaned wild birds. The group was founded in 1968 to care for raptors. Raptors are birds of prey, such as hawks and vultures.

Reread the paragraph at the top of the page.

3. Do you have enough information to find out how many more copies Sarah needs to make this month than she made last month? Why or why not?

4. Does Sarah have enough money to make 100 copies of her newsletter? Does the paragraph give too much or too little information?

5. Find the information in the paragraph that is needed to solve Problem 4. Then identify any information that is not needed or any that is missing.

Show What You Learned

Answer each question. Give a reason for your choice.

Leslie wants to sell bags of peanuts to earn money for "Friends of African Elephants." She will fill 25 bags and sell them for $1.00 a bag. She wants to put 50 peanuts in each bag. She spent $10 for 1,000 peanuts. Does Leslie have enough peanuts to fill the 25 bags?

1 What information do you need to solve the problem?

a. Leslie will charge $1.00 for each bag of peanuts.

b. Leslie wants to put 50 peanuts in each bag.

c. Leslie spent $10 on peanuts.

2 What other information do you need to solve the problem?

a. Each bag will sell for $1.00.

b. Leslie paid $10 for the peanuts.

c. Leslie has 1,000 peanuts.

3 Which number sentence tells how many peanuts she needs for 25 bags?

a. $25 \times 2 = 50$

b. $25 \times 50 = 1,250$

c. $25 \times 1,000 = 25,000$

More than 2,000 of the world's plants and animals are endangered. In the U.S. alone, nearly 850 plants and animals are endangered. A group of concerned students posted photos of some endangered animals on their school's web page. Each student posted 4 photos. How many photos did they post on the school's Web site?

4 What information is not needed to solve the problem?

a. Each student in the group posted 4 photos on the Web site.

b. Over 2,000 plants and animals in the world are endangered.

c. Both of the above

5 What information do you need to solve the problem?

a. Nearly 850 plants and animals in the U.S. are endangered.

b. Each student posted 4 photos.

c. Both of the above

6 Explain Is there enough information to find the total number of photos posted by the students? Explain your answer.

✔ Checkpoint

Multiplication by Two-Digit Numbers

Using Algebra Use patterns with zeros to solve.
(pages 216–217)

1.	2.	3.	4.	5.
20 × 60	40 × 40	300 × 50	600 × 600	2,000 × 40

6.	7.	8.	9.	10.
50 × 40	300 × 90	700 × 20	6,000 × 50	400 × 60

11.	12.	13.	14.	15.
5,000 × 200	400 × 80	8,000 × 70	900 × 90	800 × 300

16. 30 × 70   17. 80 × 1,000   18. 70 × 600   19. 500 × 400

20. 400 × 800   21. 300 × 7,000   22. 200 × 9,000   23. 80 × 8,000

Round each factor to the underlined place. Then estimate each product. (pages 218–219)

24. 4̲6 × 2̲9   25. 7̲2 × 3̲8   26. 6̲4 × 1̲31   27. 8̲6 × 2̲08

28. 5̲1 × 2̲86   29. 7̲7 × 1̲95   30. 2̲62 × 3̲7   31. 9̲5 × 1̲79

32. 3̲,018 × 1̲3   33. 4̲06 × 8̲42   34. 7̲,989 × 2̲5   35. 3̲98 × 2̲65

36. 5̲2 × 7̲81   37. 8̲75 × 6̲18   38. 1̲,850 × 3̲8   39. 8̲,125 × 6̲,980

Mixed Practice

Using Algebra Complete each table. Use patterns with zeros and rounding to estimate each product.

Rule: Multiply by 30

	Input	Output
40.	30	▣
41.	34	▣
42.	175	▣
43.	600	▣

Rule: Multiply by 400

	Input	Output
44.	14	▣
45.	72	▣
46.	208	▣
47.	419	▣

Rule: Multiply by 6,000

	Input	Output
48.	23	▣
49.	65	▣
50.	127	▣
51.	600	▣

Problem Solving

Use the table to solve Problems 52–55.

52. Using Estimation If a pig was able to run at a steady pace for 3 days, about how many miles would it run?

53. Suppose a wild turkey and a chicken could run at their fastest speed for 12 hours. Estimate how far each would go.

54. Predict Estimate how many miles the chicken, pig, and squirrel could each go in 3 hours. Why won't an estimate help you predict which will go the farthest?

55. Create Your Own Use the data from the table to write your own problem. See if a classmate can solve it.

Animal Speeds	
Animal	**Miles per Hour**
Chicken	9
Pig	11
Squirrel	12
Wild turkey	15

What do you think?

How can estimating help you with multiplying?

Journal Idea

Estimate how many words you can write in 10 seconds, in 60 seconds, and in 5 minutes. Then try it. Write about how close you were.

Critical Thinking Corner

Logical Thinking

What's Wrong?

Janet sorted these numbers so that the numbers in each box were related through addition, subtraction, multiplication, and division. But one number in each box doesn't belong. Which one doesn't belong? Explain.

1.	2.	3.	4.
2,400	30	80	10,000
60	40	30	70
240	120	4,000	50
100	1,200	400	20
40	70	50	1,000

Grid Lock

A drawing can help you find the product when multiplying by two-digit numbers.

Learning About It

Work with a partner.

Step 1 You can use a model to find 12×23.

- Use grid paper to draw a rectangle that is 23 squares by 12 squares.

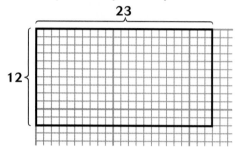

- How many squares are inside the rectangle? Record your answer on your drawing.

Step 2 Here is another way to show 12×23.

- Redraw your rectangle and divide it as shown in the drawing below.

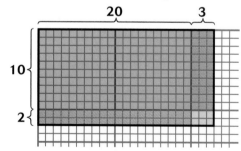

- Find the number of squares in each of the shaded rectangles. Record your answers on your drawing.

- What is the sum of the squares in the four rectangles?

- What does this sum represent?

What You Need

For each pair:
  grid paper
  ruler
  colored pencils

Step 3 You can also use multiplication to find the answer.

- What multiplication sentences could you use to find the number of squares in each shaded section on page 224?

- Add the answers from the multiplication sentences to find the answer to 12 × 23.

Step 4 Use the rectangle below to find the product of 14 × 27.

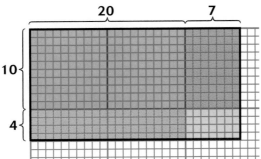

Practice

1. Write a multiplication sentence for each rectangle in the grid below. Then add the numbers to find the total product.

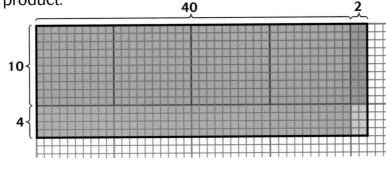

2. Analyze How are each of the numbers written on the pad at right related to the colored parts of the grid above?

3. Use a grid to find each product. Divide your grid paper into smaller rectangles.

  a. 11 × 14   **b.** 23 × 45

```
    42
  × 14
     8
   160
    20
 + 400
   588
```

Danger! Endangered!

Use a grid or regrouping to multiply two-and three-digit numbers by multiples of 10.

Learning About It

The endangered woolly spider monkeys in Brazil's rain forests live in groups of at least 20. They live in 23 protected reserves. What is the least number of woolly spider monkeys living on reserves?

$$20 \times 23 = \blacksquare$$

SOUTH AMERICA

Brazil

23 reserves

THERE'S ALWAYS A WAY!

• **One way** is to use a grid and add the parts.

20   3

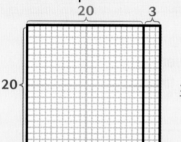

20

$$\begin{array}{cc} 20 & 3 \\ \times\ 20 & \times\ 20 \end{array}$$

Think of 23 as 20 + 3. Multiply each part by 20.

20×20 20×3

400   +   **60**   =   **460**

• **Another way** is to use paper and pencil.

Step 1 Multiply by the ones. Place a zero in the ones place.	**Step 2** Multiply by the tens.
$\begin{array}{r} 23 \\ \times\ 20 \\ \hline 0 \end{array}$ ←0 ones × 23	$\begin{array}{r} 23 \\ \times\ 20 \\ \hline 460 \end{array}$ ←2 tens × 23

▲ **Science Connection**
The woolly spider monkey is the most endangered monkey in South America. Many of the forests in Brazil in which they live have been cut down. Today, most of the woolly spider monkeys live in protected reserves.

There are at least 460 woolly spider monkeys in Brazil.

More Examples

A.
$$\begin{array}{r} \overset{1}{85} \\ \times\ 20 \\ \hline 1{,}700 \end{array}$$

B.
$$\begin{array}{r} \overset{1\ 2}{147} \\ \times\ 40 \\ \hline 5{,}880 \end{array}$$

C.
$$\begin{array}{r} \overset{3\ 1}{7{,}052} \\ \times\ 60 \\ \hline 423{,}120 \end{array}$$

Think and Discuss Write a rule for multiplying two numbers by a multiple of 10.

Try It Out

Estimate first. Then multiply to find each product. Check that each answer is reasonable.

1. $\begin{array}{r} 20 \\ \times\ 20 \end{array}$
2. $\begin{array}{r} 72 \\ \times\ 50 \end{array}$
3. $\begin{array}{r} 4{,}230 \\ \times\ 20 \end{array}$
4. $\begin{array}{r} 82 \\ \times\ 30 \end{array}$
5. $\begin{array}{r} 236 \\ \times\ 70 \end{array}$

Practice

Find each product.

6. $\begin{array}{r} 18 \\ \times\ 20 \end{array}$
7. $\begin{array}{r} 22 \\ \times\ 50 \end{array}$
8. $\begin{array}{r} 34 \\ \times\ 90 \end{array}$
9. $\begin{array}{r} 72 \\ \times\ 60 \end{array}$
10. $\begin{array}{r} 93 \\ \times\ 30 \end{array}$

11. 95×50
12. 72×60
13. $1{,}180 \times 80$
14. 440×20
15. 239×70

16. 45×40
17. 20×65
18. 30×223
19. 80×221
20. $30 \times 2{,}402$

Problem Solving

21. **Science Connection** About 20 inches of rain falls monthly in a coastal rain forest. About how many inches is that yearly?

22. **Analyze** Tropical rain forests are being destroyed at a rate of 22 acres a minute. Estimate how many acres are destroyed each day.

▲ Twenty-two acres is about the size of 16 football fields!

Review and Remember

Using Algebra Find each missing number.

23. $805 + n = 904$
24. $n \times 9 = 63$
25. $n - 8 = 27$
26. $\$4.75 - n = \$3.76$

For Extra Practice, see Set C, page 241.

Herd It All

Use what you learned about grids to multiply 2 two-digit numbers.

Learning About It

Would you like to care for a newborn lamb? Many Navajo families raise sheep on their lands. If 12 families each had a flock of 26 sheep, how many sheep would there be altogether?

$$12 \times 26 = \blacksquare$$

Estimate first: $10 \times 30 = 300$

▲ **Kid Connection**
Alicia Bahe, a Navajo girl, cares for a newborn lamb until it is old enough to join the flock. Here, Alicia wears a dress made of wool produced from her family's sheep.

THERE'S ALWAYS A WAY!

● **One way** is to use a grid and add the parts.

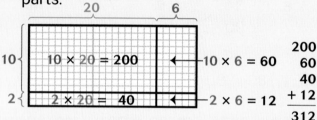

```
            20              6
      ┌─────────────┬──────────┐
   10 │10 × 20 = 200│ ←──10 × 6 = 60      200
      │             │                      60
      │             │                      40
    2 │ 2 × 20 = 40 │ ←── 2 × 6 = 12    + 12
      └─────────────┴──────────┘          ───
                                          312
```

● **Another way** is with paper and pencil.

Step 1 Multiply by the ones. Regroup if you can. Add the regrouped ten.

$$\begin{array}{r} \overset{1}{}26 \\ \times\ 12 \\ \hline 52 \end{array} \leftarrow 2 \times 26$$

Step 2 Place a zero in the ones place. Multiply by the tens. Regroup if you can.

$$\begin{array}{r} \overset{1}{}26 \\ \times\ 12 \\ \hline 52 \\ 260 \end{array} \leftarrow 10 \times 26$$

Step 3 Add the products.

$$\begin{array}{r} \overset{1}{}26 \\ \times\ 12 \\ \hline 52 \\ +\ 260 \\ \hline 312 \end{array}$$

There are 312 sheep in all twelve flocks. The answer is reasonable, since it is close to the estimate of 300.

More Examples

A.

$$
\begin{array}{r}
63 \\
\times\ 47 \\
\hline
441 \\
2\,520 \\
\hline
2{,}961
\end{array}
$$

Think:

$$
\begin{array}{r}
63 \\
\times\ 7 \\
\hline
441
\end{array}
\qquad
\begin{array}{r}
63 \\
\times\ 40 \\
\hline
2{,}520
\end{array}
$$

B.

$$
\begin{array}{r}
\$0.49 \\
\times\ 68 \\
\hline
392 \\
2940 \\
\hline
\$33.32
\end{array}
$$

Think:

$$
\begin{array}{r}
49 \\
\times\ 8 \\
\hline
392
\end{array}
\qquad
\begin{array}{r}
49 \\
\times\ 60 \\
\hline
2{,}940
\end{array}
$$

Remember to show dollars and cents in the product.

Think and Discuss When you multiply a two-digit number by a two-digit number, what is the greatest number of digits that can be in the product?

Try It Out

Estimate first. Then multiply to find each product.

1. $\begin{array}{r} 73 \\ \times\ 11 \end{array}$

2. $\begin{array}{r} 32 \\ \times\ 23 \end{array}$

3. $\begin{array}{r} 59 \\ \times\ 51 \end{array}$

4. $\begin{array}{r} 70 \\ \times\ 64 \end{array}$

5. $\begin{array}{r} 42 \\ \times\ 25 \end{array}$

6. 17×34

7. 32×31

8. 68×12

9. 52×21

Practice

Find each product.

10. $\begin{array}{r} 45 \\ \times\ 16 \end{array}$

11. $\begin{array}{r} 36 \\ \times\ 52 \end{array}$

12. $\begin{array}{r} 87 \\ \times\ 28 \end{array}$

13. $\begin{array}{r} 63 \\ \times\ 49 \end{array}$

14. $\begin{array}{r} 85 \\ \times\ 33 \end{array}$

15. $\begin{array}{r} 24 \\ \times\ 35 \end{array}$

16. $\begin{array}{r} 48 \\ \times\ 18 \end{array}$

17. $\begin{array}{r} 36 \\ \times\ 94 \end{array}$

18. $\begin{array}{r} 52 \\ \times\ 76 \end{array}$

19. $\begin{array}{r} 67 \\ \times\ 43 \end{array}$

20. $\begin{array}{r} 80 \\ \times\ 55 \end{array}$

21. $\begin{array}{r} 39 \\ \times\ 87 \end{array}$

22. $\begin{array}{r} 86 \\ \times\ 25 \end{array}$

23. $\begin{array}{r} 41 \\ \times\ 69 \end{array}$

24. $\begin{array}{r} 98 \\ \times\ 33 \end{array}$

Find each product.

25. 75 × 68	**26.** 27 × 59	**27.** 48 × 57	**28.** 63 × 28	**29.** 59 × 32
30. 76 × 41	**31.** 39 × 22	**32.** 47 × 53	**33.** 57 × 25	**34.** 34 × 49

 Use a calculator. Find the missing digits in each factor.

35. 6■ × ■6 = 5,848   **36.** ■4 × ■3 = 5,312   **37.** 6■ × 4■ = 2,970

38. 2■ × 3■ = 1,102   **39.** 2■ × 4■ = 1,075   **40.** ■5 × 7■ = 5,400

Problem Solving

41. One sheep can produce enough wool in one year to make 18 yards of fabric. If you had 58 sheep in your flock, how many yards of wool could they produce?

42. Social Studies Connection Hernando de Soto brought 13 hogs to Florida in 1539. If his herd increased by 229 each year for 3 years, how many hogs did he have in 1542?

43. Create Your Own Using the data from the table below, write your own problem. Give it to a classmate to solve.

44. Analyze Suppose there are 56 penguins in a colony and each penguin eats 12 pounds of fish, 2 pounds of krill, and 18 pounds of squid each day. How much food does the colony eat each day?

Animal Groups	
Name	**Number in Group**
Pod of whales	20
Kindle of kittens	6
Mob of kangaroos	25
Band of gorillas	8
Colony of penguins	300
Pride of lions	15

Language Arts Connection ➤
During the breeding season, colonies of penguins form a large rookery. The names for animal groups are often unusual. How many of the animal group names in the table have you heard before?

45. What If? Suppose 10 chicks join the penguin colony. Each eats half as much as an adult. How much food is now needed each day?

46. A zoo gives 32 large apples to a band of 8 gorillas. How many apples would 48 gorillas get? What strategy did you use?

Review and Remember

Choose a Method Use paper and pencil or a calculator to add or subtract.

47.
$$4,012 + 6,846$$

48.
$$57,519 - 36,297$$

49.
$$\$798.30 - 1.95$$

50.
$$5,349 + 9,021$$

51.
$$19,605 - 11,872$$

52.
$$\$238.74 \\ 788.10 \\ + 102.25$$

53.
$$58,091 \\ 20,904 \\ + 1,005$$

54.
$$40,592 \\ 35,267 \\ + 47,908$$

55.
$$28,835 \\ 43,926 \\ + 25,013$$

56.
$$\$721.38 \\ 447.16 \\ + 6.50$$

Time for Technology

Using the MathProcessor™ on CD-ROM

Using the Small Frames

You can use frames to find 12×15.

- Open two small frames.

- Click-drag the right bar of one frame to show one row of 15.

- Click-drag the top bar of the other frame to show a column of 12.

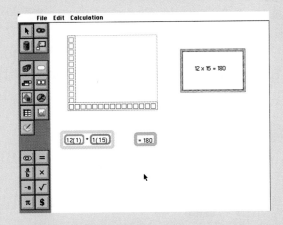

- Drag the 15 frame to overlap the first frame of the 12 frame with the first frame of the 15 frame.

- Click to open two number spaces. Click in the overlapped frames. Link it to the number spaces.

- Click one number space, then click = to display the answer to 12×15.

- Open a writing space and write a number sentence for the multiplication.

Problem Solving
Make a List

You can use a tree diagram to make a list to solve a problem.

A school group is doing volunteer work at a zoo. The volunteers wear special shirts and hats. The shirts are red or blue. The hats are either purple, orange, or green. What are the different ways a volunteer could choose one shirt and one hat?

 UNDERSTAND

What do you need to find?

You need to find all the ways you can pick one shirt and one hat from a choice of two shirts and three hats.

 PLAN

How can you solve the problem?

You can **make a list** of all the choices by drawing a tree diagram. The branches farthest to the right list all the possible choices of shirts and hats.

 SOLVE

Shirts	Hats	Possible Choices

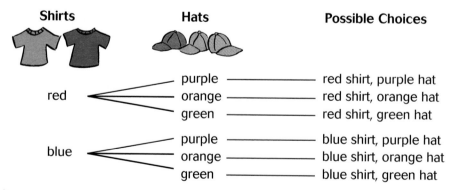

	purple	red shirt, purple hat
red	orange	red shirt, orange hat
	green	red shirt, green hat
	purple	blue shirt, purple hat
blue	orange	blue shirt, orange hat
	green	blue shirt, green hat

 LOOK BACK

Explain how you know that you have found all the choices.

Using the Strategy

Use a tree diagram to make a list to solve each problem.

1. Each volunteer gets a free lunch. The lunch choices are tacos and hamburgers. The dessert choices are ice cream, fruit, or yogurt. List all the possible choices for picking one lunch and one dessert.

Menu
- 🌮 – $1⁵⁰
- 🍔 – $2⁵⁰
- 🍨 – $1⁰⁰
- 🍎 – $0.50
- 🥤 – $1⁰⁰

2. The volunteers can wear either jeans or black pants. They also can choose one of four different-colored pins: yellow, green, blue, or red. List all of the combinations of pants and pins.

3. Angela can volunteer either Friday, Saturday, or Sunday. She can also pick either mornings or afternoons. Make a list of the days and times Angela can volunteer.

4. Josh is mixing animal food to feed the monkeys. He uses either cereal, pasta, or popcorn. He mixes one of those with either raisins, apples, or dried bananas. What are the different combinations he can make?

Mixed Strategy Review

Try these or other strategies to solve each problem.
Tell which strategy you used.

THERE'S ALWAYS A WAY!

Problem Solving Strategies

- *Write a Number Sentence*
- *Work Backwards*
- *Use Logical Reasoning*
- *Solve a Simpler Problem*

5. On Sunday 124 volunteers were at the zoo. This was 31 more than on Saturday. How many volunteers were there on Saturday?

6. At the zoo gift shop, Tina bought 2 pins for $1.75 each and a book for $3.60. How much change does she get back from a $20 bill?

7. Sarah watches three seals play with a red ring, a blue ring, and a green ring. Each seal plays with a different-colored ring. The first seal does not play with a blue ring. The third seal plays with the red ring. Which seal plays with which ring?

Pet Pals

*You can multiply a three- or four-digit number
the same way you multiply a two-digit number.*

Learning About It

Would you like to have a dog as a pet?
Before you decide, you should find out how
much dogs eat. A medium-sized dog can eat
24 ounces of dry dog food each day! How
many ounces would the dog eat in a year?

$$24 \times 365 = \blacksquare$$

THERE'S ALWAYS A WAY!

● **One way** to find the answer is to
use paper and pencil.

Step 1 Multiply by the ones. Regroup if you can.	**Step 2** Multiply by the tens. Use one zero as a placeholder. Regroup if you can.	**Step 3** Add the products.
2 2 365 × 24 1460	1 1 2 2 365 × 24 1460 7300	365 × 24 1460 + 7300 8,760

● **Another way** is to use a calculator.

Press: ③ ⑥ ⑤ × ② ④ = Display:  8760

Place a comma in your answer: 8,760

The dog eats 8,760 ounces of dog food each year.

INTERNET ACTIVITY
www.sbgmath.com

Think and Discuss How does estimating first
help you to multiply a three-digit number?

Try It Out

Estimate first. Then multiply to find each product.

1. 145	**2.** 3,111	**3.** 645	**4.** 786	**5.** 504
× 15	× 87	× 13	× 23	× 41

Practice

Find each product.

6. 716	**7.** 398	**8.** 113	**9.** 875	**10.** 922
× 19	× 11	× 23	× 17	× 70

11. 215	**12.** 483	**13.** 560	**14.** 608	**15.** 647
× 63	× 82	× 35	× 28	× 91

Using Algebra Compare. Write >, < , or = for each ⬤.
Use a calculator or paper and pencil to solve.

16. $58 \times 2{,}340$ ⬤ $58 \times 1{,}340$ **17.** $37 \times 1{,}234$ ⬤ $38 \times 2{,}345$

Problem Solving

18. Your dog eats 27 bags of dry dog food a year. If each bag of dog food costs $10.99, how much do you spend each year for dog food?

19. Using Estimation Your cat eats 2 cans of cat food a day. Each can costs $0.35. Will $325 be enough to pay for cat food for the year? Explain.

20. Analyze It cost $290.69 last year to care for your chickens. They laid 2 dozen eggs a day, which you sold for $1.00 a dozen. How much money did you make last year after expenses?

▲ **Kid Connection**
Katie Beste of Indiana has two pet silkies. Silkies are white, fluffy chickens. Katie also raises other chickens for their eggs. She sells the eggs for $1.00 a dozen.

Review and Remember

Using Mental Math Use mental math to solve.

21. $425 + 10$ **22.** $602 + 18$ **23.** $85 - 15$ **24.** 3×400 **25.** 6×70

26. 5×20 **27.** $733 + 112$ **28.** $852 - 541$ **29.** 4×11 **30.** $97 - 72$

For Extra Practice, see Set E, page 242.

Understand · Plan · Solve · Look Back

Problem Solving
Choose a Computation Method

You can use paper and pencil, a calculator, or mental math to solve problems.

A newborn manatee and his mother are shown below at the right. The newborn weighs 30 kilograms. His mother weighs 30 times this amount. How much does the mother manatee weigh?

 UNDERSTAND

What do you need to find?

You need to find the weight of the mother manatee.

 PLAN

How can you solve the problem?

You can **write a number sentence** to find the weight of the mother. Then you can use paper and pencil, mental math, or a calculator to find the product. Since you can use basic facts and patterns of zeros to find 30 × 30, using mental math is an easy way to find the product.

 SOLVE

Think: 3 × 3 = 9

So, 30 × 30 = 900

The mother manatee weighs 900 kilograms.

▲ **Science Connection**
The manatee is an endangered sea mammal. Most manatees can be found living along the Florida coasts.

 LOOK BACK

What if the father of this newborn manatee weighed 46 times the newborn's weight? How could you find the father's weight? What method of computation would you use? Explain.

Show What You Learned

Solve each problem using paper and pencil, mental math, or a calculator. Tell the method you chose.

1. The newborn manatee pictured on page 236 is 124 centimeters long. The mother is 3 times as long as her baby. How long is the mother manatee?

2. Manatees have been known to grow to be 55 times as heavy as a 30-kg newborn. How much would a manatee this size weigh?

3. One year, there were 87 manatees at a Florida refuge. The next year, 77 of them returned. How many manatees did not return?

▲**Science Connection**
Manatees often float just under the water's surface. Boaters are warned to drive slowly to avoid hitting them. In Florida, a total of 66 manatees were killed in 1998 by watercrafts.

Use the chart at the right to solve Problems 4 and 5. Tell which computation method you chose.

4. How many manatees were seen in Florida in 1991?

5. In which year, 1991 or 1992, were more manatees seen on the east coast? How many more were seen?

Manatees Seen in Florida

Date	East Coast	West Coast
1991	697	589
1992	907	949

Use the chart at the right to solve Problems 6 and 7. Tell which computation method you chose.

6. In which year were there 3 times as many manatees as in 1968?

7. How many more manatees were seen in King's Bay in 1992 than in 1968?

Manatees in King's Bay, Florida

1968	38
1982	114
1992	292

8. An adult manatee can eat 100 pounds of plants in one day. How many pounds can one adult eat in one week?

9. **Create Your Own** Write a problem about manatees that can be solved using paper and pencil, mental math, or a calculator. Give it to a classmate to solve.

Problem Solving

Practice What You Learned

Choose the correct letter for each answer.

1 Sally went to the store to buy supplies for school. She spent $3.50 on pencils, $4.25 on pens, and $2.15 on notepaper. How much money did Sally spend on pencils and pens?

A. $9.90
B. $7.75
C. $6.40
D. $5.75

Tip

Sometimes a problem gives information you don't need. Start by deciding what information in this problem you *do* need.

2 Kelley took a ride on a train that traveled 63 miles per hour. The train trip took exactly 11 hours. How can you find the distance Kelley traveled?

A. Add 63 and 11.
B. Subtract 11 from 63.
C. Multiply 11 times 63.
D. Divide 63 by 11.

Tip

Think about the action in the problem and then see which operation matches that action.

3 Patrick bought 16 tickets for a play. Each ticket cost $18. Which number sentence could be used to find the change he got from $300?

A. $16 \times \$18 - \$300$
B. $\$300 - 16$
C. $\$300 - (16 \times \$18)$
D. $\$300 - 16 - \$18$

Tip

When more than one step is needed to solve a problem, you must decide both *what* to do and in what *order* you should do it.

4 Terry is making a mural that is 15 feet wide. She uses a 1-foot strip of paper to divide the mural into 2 equal sections. How wide is each section of mural?

A. 4 ft
B. 7 ft
C. 12 ft
D. 16 ft

5 The cook at a restaurant bought 22 lb of spaghetti, 78 lb of oranges, 48 lb of grapes, and 34 lb of meat. **About** how many pounds of fruit did the cook buy?

A. 30 pounds
B. 130 pounds
C. 150 ponds
D. 180 pounds

6 Shari earns $5.80 an hour for baby-sitting. Which shows how much money Shari will make if she baby-sits for 3 hours?

A. $5.80 + $5.80 = ▨
B. $5.80 × 3 = ▨
C. $5.80 − $3.00 = ▨
D. $5.80 ÷ 3 = ▨

7 Small cans of soup cost $1.08. Large cans of soup cost $2.99. **About** how much more does a large can cost than a small can?

A. $4
B. $3
C. $2
D. $1

8 A store has more puzzles than games, but fewer puzzles than books. There are 65 books. Which of the following is a reasonable conclusion?

A. There are more books than puzzles.
B. There are more games than books.
C. There are more than 65 games.
D. There are more games than puzzles.

9 Today Luanne has 45 magazines, 12 newspapers, and more than 85 books for sale in her shop. Which is reasonable for the number of items Luanne has in her shop today?

A. Fewer than 120
B. Between 120 and 130
C. Between 130 and 140
D. More than 140

10 Look at the graph below. How many more people picked soccer than swimming as their favorite sport?

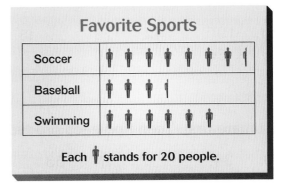

Favorite Sports

Soccer	👤 👤 👤 👤 👤 👤 👤 ᛁ
Baseball	👤 👤 👤 ᛁ
Swimming	👤 👤 👤 👤 👤 👤

Each 👤 stands for 20 people.

A. 20
B. 30
C. 60
D. 150

 **Checkpoint**

Multiplying by Two-Digit Numbers

Vocabulary

Complete. Use the words from the Word Bank.

1. The numbers you multiply are called ___?___.

2. An ___?___ shows objects in rows and columns.

3. The answer in multiplication is called the ___?___.

Word Bank

array

factors

product

Concepts and Skills

Use the grids to find each product. Write each multiplication sentence. (pages 224-225)

4. 15 × 36

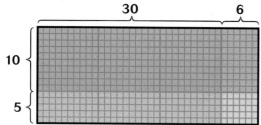

5. 11 × 29

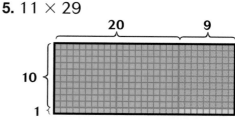

Estimate first. Then find each product. (pages 218–219, 226–227)

6.	7.	8.	9.	10.
25	31	74	59	83
× 10	× 60	× 20	× 50	× 30

11.	12.	13.	14.	15.
190	723	268	336	795
× 30	× 40	× 70	× 20	× 60

Estimate first. Then find each product. (pages 218–219, 228–231)

16.	17.	18.	19.
34	53	29	76
× 12	× 24	× 44	× 38

20. 326 × 72   21. 39 × 670   22. 875 × 42

Problem Solving

23. **Social Studies Connection** The Seeing Eye is the first and oldest dog guide school in the United States. If it can train 29 dogs each month, how many dogs will it train in 12 months?

24. If 348 dogs are trained each year, how many dogs have been trained in the last 25 years?

25. **Analyze** Students are asked to pay $150.00 for the first visit to the dog guide school and $50.00 for each visit after that. Is $400.00 enough for 8 visits? Explain.

Journal Idea

Suppose you are explaining how to solve a problem to a friend. Write the steps you used to solve one of the problems above.

What do you think?

How can you check your answers to see if they are reasonable?

You Decide
Activity

Make an Exercise Plan

Write an exercise plan that would help someone burn an extra 2,000 calories in a week.

Activity	Calories Burned per Minute
Bicycling	11
Running	19
Handball	13

- Choose at least 2 different activities. Decide how many minutes to spend doing each activity.
- Then decide on which days to do the activities and make a chart to show a weekly schedule.

 You might wish to include this work in your portfolio.

Extra Practice

Set A (pages 216–217)

Using Algebra Use patterns to find each product.

1. 6 × 60	**2.** 60 × 10	**3.** 9 × 20	**4.** 90 × 20	**5.** 900 × 20
6. 80 × 50	**7.** 800 × 50	**8.** 800 × 500	**9.** 30 × 70	**10.** 300 × 70
11. 5 × 40	**12.** 50 × 40	**13.** 500 × 40	**14.** 7 × 90	**15.** 700 × 90
16. 700 × 70	**17.** 8,000 × 90	**18.** 200 × 80	**19.** 300 × 50	**20.** 5,000 × 80

21. 70 × 800 **22.** 6,000 × 90 **23.** 400 × 700 **24.** 800 × 900

25. At the nature center, 39 students gathered 10 bags of acorns each. Each bag had 10 acorns. How many acorns did they find?

Set B (pages 218–219)

Round to the underlined place. Estimate the product.

1. 9 × 85   **2.** 36 × 72   **3.** 41 × 17   **4.** 63 × 43

5. 37 × 109   **6.** 29 × 362   **7.** 158 × 34   **8.** 822 × 476

9. 2,799 × 45   **10.** 36 × 6,220   **11.** 2,431 × 66   **12.** 591 × 538

13. 7,001 × 15   **14.** 3,010 × 325   **15.** 192 × 887   **16.** 1,345 × 604

17. 18 × 2,868   **18.** 429 × 575   **19.** 8,999 × 49   **20.** 88 × 2,009

21. 555 × 8,280   **22.** 882 × 8,082   **23.** 3,900 × 85   **24.** 710 × 910

25. The Science Club held a science fair. Each grade displayed 135 projects. There were 6 grades. How many projects were displayed?

Extra Practice

Set C (pages 226–227)

Estimate first. Then find each product.

1. 40 × 10	**2.** 72 × 10	**3.** 29 × 20	**4.** 87 × 80	**5.** 38 × 60
6. 30 × 70	**7.** 156 × 40	**8.** 99 × 30	**9.** 362 × 20	**10.** 577 × 40
11. 171 × 20	**12.** 360 × 40	**13.** 298 × 50	**14.** 754 × 90	**15.** 922 × 30

16. 30×65 **17.** 54×10 **18.** 147×40 **19.** $\$326 \times 70$

20. 30×53 **21.** 81×50 **22.** 60×352 **23.** 90×122

24. Each of the 87 fourth graders earned $25.00 to donate to a wildlife organization. Estimate how much was earned altogether.

Set D (pages 228–231)

Estimate first. Then find each product.

1. 76 × 32	**2.** 41 × 18	**3.** 92 × 23	**4.** 65 × 62	**5.** 37 × 43
6. 49 × 92	**7.** 83 × 25	**8.** 56 × 74	**9.** 44 × 97	**10.** 26 × 89
11. 17 × 54	**12.** 30 × 67	**13.** 32 × 36	**14.** 58 × 68	**15.** 94 × 35

16. 36×18 **17.** 52×39 **18.** 55×75 **19.** 27×37

20. The pet store chain sold 48 pets a day for one 30-day month. Did they sell more or less than 1,500 pets that month?

Extra Practice

Set E (pages 234–235)

Estimate first. Then find each product.

1. 17
    × 15

2. 29
    × 65

3. 143
    × 6

4. 30
    × 30

5. 386
    × 50

6. 192
    × 27

7. 3,005
    × 6

8. 400
    × 9

9. 725
    × 60

10. 51
    × 51

11. 26
    × 93

12. 348
    × 19

13. 55
    × 80

14. 964
    × 38

15. 409
    × 70

16. 370
    × 64

17. 2,138
    × 6

18. 188
    × 73

19. 847
    × 32

20. 636
    × 89

21. 40 × 753

22. 561 × 18

23. 892 × 42

24. 47 × 209

25. 745 × 39

26. 640 × 30

27. 1,063 × 9

28. 655 × 70

29. 132 × 13

30. 390 × 41

31. 870 × 30

32. 215 × 63

Using Algebra **Find the missing number. Explain how you found it.**

33. $35 \times \blacksquare = 70$

36. $\blacksquare \times 9{,}000 = 360{,}000$

34. $93 \times 12 = \blacksquare \times 93$

37. $68 \times 30 = 15 \times \blacksquare$

35. $86 \times 10 = 20 \times \blacksquare$

38. $741 \times 83 = \blacksquare \times 741$

Solve.

39. The teacher gave each of his 35 students 30 pieces of writing paper. How many sheets of writing paper did he give out?

40. The fourth-grade class sold 550 animal booklets at the book fair. They charged 5 cents a booklet. Their goal was to make $25.00. Did they make their goal?

Chapter Test

Round each factor to the underlined place.
Then estimate each product.

1. $\underline{7}2 \times \underline{3}5$

2. $\underline{4}9 \times \underline{1}28$

3. $\underline{5}06 \times \underline{6}4$

4. $\underline{7},422 \times \underline{8}8$

5. $\underline{3}67 \times \underline{9}9$

6. $\underline{2},076 \times \underline{4}03$

Write the multiplication sentences to find each product.

7. 13×25

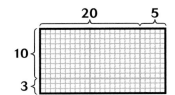

8. 11×32

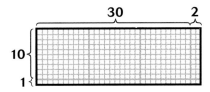

Estimate first. Then find each product.

| **9.** 24 $\times$ 20 | **10.** 165 $\times$ 40 | **11.** 88 $\times$ 60 | **12.** 352 $\times$ 70 | **13.** 709 $\times$ 30 |

| **14.** 47 $\times$ 23 | **15.** 200 $\times$ 65 | **16.** 72 $\times$ 47 | **17.** 65 $\times$ 82 | **18.** 240 $\times$ 35 |

| **19.** 621 $\times$ 37 | **20.** 596 $\times$ 42 | **21.** 377 $\times$ 86 | **22.** 199 $\times$ 58 | **23.** 634 $\times$ 97 |

Solve.

24. To ensure they survive, prairie dogs can be adopted, in name only, for $10 each. Your school collected $4,500. Can your school adopt 500 prairie dogs?

25. You board your dog in a kennel for $13 a day. Estimate the costs for 1 week and for 1 month.

 Self-Check Explain why your answers to Exercises 19–23 are reasonable.

Performance Assessment

Show What You Know About Multiplication

1 Make a spinner like the one shown. To show your multiplication, you can use base-ten blocks, pictures, numbers, or words.

What You Need

two 1–6 number cubes

blank 5-part spinner

paper clips

base-ten blocks

a. Roll the two number cubes. Write a two-digit number with the two numbers that turn up.

b. Spin the spinner. Use the number on the spinner and your two-digit number from the cubes to write a multiplication problem.

c. Estimate first. Will your product be greater than 10,000? Explain why or why not.

d. Multiply. Show your work.

Self-Check Did you use the numbers on the number cubes to write a two-digit number?

2 An average of 214 people visited an animal exhibit every hour. The exhibit was open 14 hours a day.

a. About how many people visited the exhibit each day?

b. If each ticket to the exhibit cost $1.50, how much money was collected each day?

Self-Check Did you estimate your answer before you computed?

For Your Portfolio

You might wish to include this work in your portfolio.

Extension

The Factor Game

Play the Factor Game with a group. Whoever has the highest score wins.

What You Need

For each group:

0–9 number cards

calculators

paper

① Make a set of number cards like the ones shown for the numbers 0–9. Turn the cards face down.

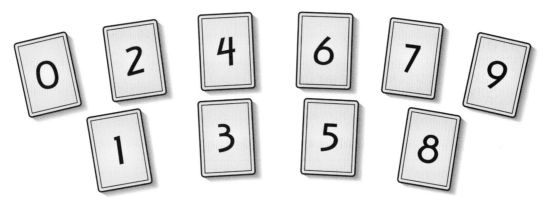

② Group members should copy Exercises 1–4 below on their own papers.

1. ▦ ▦
    × ▦ ▦

2. ▦ ▦ ▦
    × ▦

3. ▦ ▦ ▦
    × ▦ ▦

4. ▦ ▦
    × ▦

③ One person turns over 4 number cards. The numbers on these cards are then written by each group member in the boxes for Exercise 1. Use each number only once. At the end of this first turn, each member should have 4 boxes filled. Return the 4 cards to the pile and shuffle.

④ Take turns turning over cards until group members have filled up all the boxes for Exercises 1–4.

⑤ Use paper and pencil or a calculator to find the products. Then add all 4 products together. The winner is the person whose sum is the greatest.

Using Math in Science

Collect and *organize data* to investigate how the color of an animal may help it survive.

Color Matters

Animals come in many different colors. How might an insect's color affect its ability to survive? Try this activity to find out.

Explore

Step 1 Make a chart like the one below. Leave room for making tally marks.

What You Need

For each group:
pipe cleaners (50 red, 50 blue, 50 green, and 50 yellow)
timer, with second hand
large white cloth or paper
large green cloth

Number of Pipe Cleaners				
Trial	Red	Blue	Green	Yellow
Trial 1 (On a white cloth)				
Trial 2 (On a green cloth)				

Step 2 Spread a white cloth or paper on the floor. Mix up the pipe cleaners and scatter them over the white surface.

Step 3 While a group member times you, pick up as many pipe cleaners, one at a time, as you can in 15 seconds. Use tally marks to record each color drawn in the row for Trial 1.

The green color of the ➤ praying mantis helps to hide it from its enemies.

Step 4 Think about a bird looking for insects in a grassy field. Use a green cloth to represent grass. Use pipe cleaners to represent insects of different colors. Predict which color insect will be the hardest to see. Record your prediction.

Step 5 Spread a green cloth out on the floor. Mix up the pipe cleaners and scatter them over the cloth.

Step 6 Repeat Step 3, recording the results in the row for Trial 2 in your chart.

Analyze

◄ Step 6

1. Look at your data from Trial 1 and that of your classmates. How many possible colors of pipe cleaners can be chosen? Were any colors picked more or less often than the others?

2. Look at your data from Trial 2 and that of your classmates. How did it differ from that of Trial 1?

3. Compare your predictions in Step 4 with the results of Trial 2. What can you infer about an insect's color and its ability to survive?

 For Your Portfolio

Explain what you discovered about how the color of an animal may help it survive. Include the chart of your data along with your explanation.

Explore Further!

Predict Suppose the field is yellow. Which color insect do you think would have a better chance of surviving? Why? Set up an experiment to test your hypothesis.

Cumulative Review

★ ★ ★ ★ ★ **Preparing for Tests**

Choose the correct letter for each answer.

Number Concepts	Operations

Number Concepts

1. What is 3,458 rounded to the nearest thousand?

    A. 3,000
    B. 3,400
    C. 3,500
    D. 4,000

2. Lauren wrote a number with a 2 in the ten thousands place and a 1 in the hundreds place. Which number did Lauren write?

    A. 4,231,334
    B. 4,233,134
    C. 4,323,134
    D. 4,324,314

3. Which is a set of odd numbers?

    A. 6 7 8 9
    B. 3 7 9 15
    C. 3 4 7 9
    D. 5 7 9 12

4. Which set of numbers is in order from *greatest* to *least*?

    A. 3,201 4,003 3,932 3,699
    B. 3,932 3,699 3,201 4,003
    C. 3,201 3,699 3,932 4,003
    D. 4,003 3,932 3,699 3,201

Operations

5. What is the quotient of 63 ÷ 7?

    A. 9
    B. 56
    C. 70
    D. 441

6. Annie read a 324-page book in one week. The next week she read a book about twice as long. **About** how many pages did she read in the 2 weeks?

    A. 600
    B. 800
    C. 900
    D. 1,200

7. Tina makes $11 a week on her paper route and $5 a week for babysitting. How much will Tina make in a year? (Hint: There are 52 weeks in a year.)

    A. $68.00   **C.** $572.00
    B. $312.00   **D.** $832.00

8. There are 27 girls and 18 boys camping at Camp Sunrise. Nine people can sleep in each cabin. How many cabins are needed for all the girls?

    A. 3   **C.** 7
    B. 5   **D.** 9

Patterns, Relationships, and Algebraic Thinking	Probability and Statistics

9. What is the missing number in the number pattern?

2, 6, 18, 54, ■, 486

A. 152   **C.** 162
B. 156   **D.** 262

10. Which number line shows the graph of all whole numbers less than 9 **and** greater than 4?

A. 0 1 2 3 4 5 6 7 8 9

B. 0 1 2 3 4 5 6 7 8 9

C. 0 1 2 3 4 5 6 7 8 9

D. 0 1 2 3 4 5 6 7 8 9

Use the table for Questions 11 – 12.

Number of Kites	Number of Sticks
1	2
2	4
3	6

11. How many sticks would you need to make 8 kites?

A. 8   **C.** 12
B. 10   **D.** 16

12. How many kites could you make with 20 sticks?

A. 5   **C.** 20
B. 10   **D.** 40

13. In a total of 25 spins, which color will the spinner probably point to the greatest number of times?

A. green
B. blue
C. red
D. yellow

Use the graph for Questions 14-16.

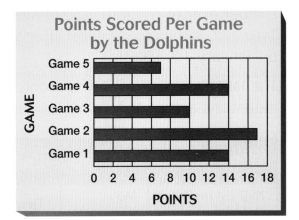

14. In which game did the Dolphins score the fewest points?

A. Game 2   **C.** Game 4
B. Game 3   **D.** Game 5

15. In which games did the Dolphins score the same number of points?

A. 1 and 2   **C.** 3 and 4
B. 2 and 5   **D.** 1 and 4

16. How many more points did the Dolphins score in Game 4 than in Game 5?

A. 3   **C.** 7
B. 6   **D.** 8

Chapter 7

Time and Measurement

Chapter Theme: WORLD RECORDS

REAL-WORLD Math

............Real Facts..................

Joshua Stewart, shown at the right, is the youngest climber ever to reach the top of Mount Kilimanjaro in Tanzania. Joshua made it just after his 11th birthday on January 10, 1994!

The table below shows some record heights of mountains around the world.

Record	Mountain	Location	Height in Feet
Highest mountain in Africa	Mount Kilimanjaro	Tanzania	19,340
Highest mountain in the world	Mount Everest	Nepal-Tibet border	29,028
Highest mountain in North America	Mount McKinley	Alaska	20,320

- Joshua Stewart plans to climb Mount McKinley next. How much higher is Mount McKinley than Mount Kilimanjaro?

- How can you estimate to find out how much taller Mount Everest is than Mount Kilimanjaro?

..............Real People....................

Meet Ashrita Furman, the world-record holder for holding the most world records! He has set more than 30 different world records, including the record for the number of consecutive jumps on a pogo stick.

Time After Time

You can use some clocks to tell time to the nearest second.

Learning About It

Clocks and watches come in many sizes, but even the smallest watch in the world can help you tell time!

Look at the analog clock below. What time is it?

World's Smallest Wristwatch

This is the actual size of the world's smallest wristwatch.

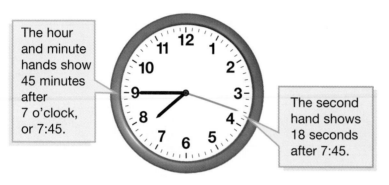

The hour and minute hands show 45 minutes after 7 o'clock, or 7:45.

The second hand shows 18 seconds after 7:45.

The time is seven forty-five and eighteen seconds.

Now look at the digital clock below. What time is it?

- 8:30
- eight-thirty
- half past eight
- thirty minutes past eight

Connecting Ideas

You can multiply to change from a larger unit of time to a smaller unit of time.

3 minutes = ▇ seconds

Think: 1 minute = 60 seconds

3 minutes = 180 seconds

Units of Time
1 minute (min) = 60 seconds (s)
1 hour (h) = 60 minutes (min)
1 day = 24 hours (h)

Think and Discuss How many minutes does it take for the second hand to go around the analog clock once?

Try It Out

Write each time two ways using words and numbers.

1. 

2. 

3. 

4. 

Write each missing number.

5. 2 min = ▒ s
6. 10 min = ▒ s
7. 48 h = ▒ days
8. 3 h = ▒ min
9. 3 days = ▒ h
10. 2 h 17 min = ▒ min

Practice

Write each time two ways using words and numbers.

11. 

12. 

13. 

14. 

15. eight thirty-five
16. 1:20
17. two-fifty
18. 8:25

Write each missing number.

19. 3 min = ▒ s
20. 7 h = ▒ min
21. 4 days = ▒ h
22. 1 min 30 s = ▒ s
23. 1 h 15 min = ▒ min
24. 4 h = ▒ min
25. 3 h 55 min = ▒ min
26. 1 day 22 h = ▒ h
27. 1 day = ▒ min

Problem Solving

28. **Analyze** Your watch loses 2 minutes a day. If your watch shows 9 A.M. on Monday, what time will your watch show in exactly 30 days?

29. **Journal Idea** What time is it now? Write the time shown on your clock in as many different ways as you can.

Review and Remember

Find each answer.

30. 36×535
31. $408 - 205$
32. $5{,}965 + 2{,}819$
33. 35×208

For Extra Practice, see Set A, page 290.

From Time to Time

You can find out how much time has elapsed,
or how long it takes to do something.

Start

Finish

Word Bank

elapsed time

World's Fastest Female Marathon Runner

In 1985, Ingrid Kristiansen of Norway set a new world-record time for the women's marathon.

Learning About It

Suppose Ingrid Kristiansen began her record-setting marathon at 9:10 A.M. and finished the race at 11:31 A.M. How long did it take her to run the marathon?

To find out, you can count on from 9:10.

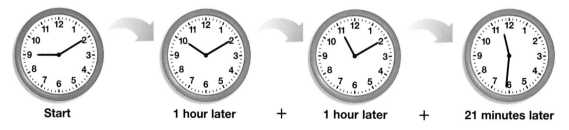

| Start | 1 hour later | + | 1 hour later | + | 21 minutes later |

It took Ingrid 2 hours 21 minutes to run the marathon. This was the **elapsed time**.

Another Example

A race began at 10:00 A.M., and the winner crossed the finish line at 11:48 A.M.. What was the winning time?

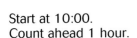

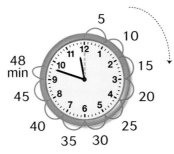

Start at 10:00.
Count ahead 1 hour.

Now count by 5s for 45 minutes.
Then count 3 minutes more.

The winning time was 1 hour 48 minutes.

◀ **Math Note**

The hour hand goes around an analog clock twice each day.

• It goes around once for the morning, or A.M. hours, which are before noon.

• It goes around a second time for the P.M. hours, which are after noon.

Connecting Ideas

You can use elapsed time with addition and subtraction to find starting and ending times.

It is now 5:25 P.M. What time will it be in 1 hour 35 minutes?

```
    5 hours  25 minutes
 +  1 hour   35 minutes
 _____
    6 hours  60 minutes = 7 hours
```

It will be 7:00 P.M.

Now

5:25 P.M.

Later

7:00 P.M.

Another Example

It is now 10:40 P.M. What time was it 3 hours 30 minutes ago?

```
   10 hours  40 minutes
 −  3 hours  30 minutes
 _____
    7 hours  10 minutes
```

It was 7:10 P.M.

Now

10:40 P.M.

Earlier

7:10 P.M.

Think and Discuss When might you need to use elapsed time during a school day?

Try It Out

Find each elapsed time.

1. Start: 2:30 A.M.
   Finish: 4:15 A.M.

2. Start: 7:10 P.M.
   Finish: 1:15 A.M.

3. Start: 8:15 A.M.
   Finish: 12:45 P.M.

4. Start: 2:45 P.M.
   Finish: 7:45 P.M.

5. Start: 6:45 P.M.
   Finish: 8:15 P.M.

6. Start: 10:35 A.M.
   Finish: 1:55 P.M.

Practice

Find each missing time.

	Start	Elapsed Time	Finish
7.	8:00 A.M.	2 hours	
8.	4:00 P.M.	3 hours 30 minutes	
9.	1:00 P.M.		6:15 P.M.
10.	2:30 P.M.		8:45 P.M.
11.		5 hours	7:30 P.M.
12.		4 hours 10 minutes	8:10 P.M.
13.	4:25 P.M.	1 hour 40 minutes	
14.	7:40 A.M.	2 hours 5 minutes	

▲ Belayneh Dinsamo of Ethiopia became the men's world-record holder for the marathon in 1988. His winning time was 2 h 6 min 50 s.

Give the ending time for Exercises 15–16.

15. The race started at 2:15 P.M. It lasts 4 hours 30 minutes.

16. The practice started at 10:30 A.M. It lasts 2 hours 30 minutes.

Give the starting time for Exercises 17–18.

17. The marathon ended at 4:35 P.M. It lasted 3 hours 27 minutes.

18. The victory parade ended at 1:30 P.M. It lasted 3 hours.

Problem Solving

19. The men's world record for running the marathon is about 2 hours 7 minutes. If the record-setting marathon started at 10:05 A.M., what time did the winner cross the finish line?

20. A 10-kilometer race started at 11:30 A.M. The winner crossed the finish line at 12:04 P.M. What was the winning time?

21. A 10-kilometer walk started at 8:00 A.M. The winner crossed the finish line at 9:32 A.M. What was the winning time?

22. The Tevis Cup is a 100-mile endurance race for horses and riders. It takes about 18 hours to finish the race. If a team started the race at 7:00 A.M., about what time would it finish?

23. **Analyze** To break a world record, 14 students played leapfrog nonstop. They began May 16 at 9 A.M. and they stopped May 26 at 1:43 P.M. What was the new world-record time for leapfrogging?

▲ Kid Connection
Andréa Moore, age 10, of Maryland, ran a 100-meter race in a record-breaking time of 12.83 seconds. She also won five gold medals in the Regional Junior Olympics in 1996.

Review and Remember

Using Algebra Solve for *n*.

24. $n \times 3 = 12$	**25.** $24 \div n = 8$	**26.** $n + 39 = 121$	**27.** $100 + n = 123$
28. $n - 40 = 41$	**29.** $n \times 8 = 64$	**30.** $55 - n = 50$	**31.** $n \div 7 = 3$
32. $90 - n = 55$	**33.** $9 \times n = 27$	**34.** $n \div 9 = 4$	**35.** $n + 25 = 30$
36. $10 \div n = 10$	**37.** $27 + n = 30$	**38.** $7 \times n = 42$	**39.** $n + 87 = 98$

Critical Thinking Corner

Number Sense

Estimating Time

1. Estimate how many times you can count to 25 in 1 minute. Try it. How close was your estimate?

2. Estimate how many times you can blink your eyes in 5 seconds. Try it. How close was your estimate?

For Extra Practice, see Set B, page 290.

Developing Skills for Problem Solving

First read for understanding and then focus on whether the numbers are exact numbers or estimates.

READ FOR UNDERSTANDING

THE TIMES

It's a Record!

About 8,600,000 tickets were sold for the 1996 Olympic Games in Atlanta, Georgia. That is the most tickets sold for any sports event in history.

Softball Gold

At Golden Park, more than 8,700 people saw the contest for the 1st gold medal ever awarded for women's softball. The U.S. team scored 3 runs over China's 1 run to win the gold medal. Tickets to the game cost $33.00.

1 How many tickets were sold for the 1996 Olympic Games?

2 How many people saw the U.S. women's softball game?

THINK AND DISCUSS

MATH FOCUS

Exact Numbers or Estimates Exact numbers represent amounts that can be counted or measured. Estimates represent amounts that have been rounded or that cannot be counted or measured.

Reread the newspaper articles above.

3 Is it possible that only 8,679 people saw the softball game?

4 What was the total number of runs scored in the game? Is your answer an exact number or an estimate? Explain how you know.

5 What words or phrases in the newspaper articles help you know when numbers are estimates?

Show What You Learned

Answer each question. Give a reason for your choice.

> In the 84 days before the 1996 Olympic Games, the Olympic torch was carried more than 15,000 miles from Los Angeles to Atlanta. It traveled about 150 miles a day, passing through 42 states and the District of Columbia.

1 Which statement is true?

   a. The torch traveled exactly 150 miles each day.

   b. The torch traveled exactly 15,000 miles in all.

   c. The torch was carried for exactly 84 days.

2 Which word in the paragraph tells you that the number after it will be an estimate?

   a. *about*

   b. *from*

   c. *through*

3 Which number is used in the paragraph as an estimate?

   a. 84 days

   b. 42 states

   c. 15,000 miles

> On August 4, 1996, over 80,000 people jammed into Olympic Stadium for the close of the 100th-anniversary celebration of the Olympic Games. A 3-hour program was presented by more than 3,500 performers, including about 600 Atlanta children who sang "Power of the Dream."

4 Which of the numbers is used as an exact number?

   a. 3,500 performers

   b. 100th-anniversary

   c. 600 children

5 Which number might represent the attendance at Olympic Stadium?

   a. 81,234

   b. 79,500

   c. 80,000

6 **Explain** What words from the paragraph above help you know when a number is an estimate?

A Time for All Ages

You can use a calendar to keep track of days, weeks, months, and years.

Learning About It

In 1995 the oldest living person was Jeanne Louise Calment of France. She was 1 century 2 decades old. How many years old was she?

World's Oldest Living Person

1 century 2 decades = ▦ years

You can multiply to change from a larger unit of time to a smaller unit of time.

Think: 1 century = 100 years
1 decade = 10 years

$$1 \times 100 \text{ years} = 100 \text{ years}$$
$$2 \times 10 \text{ years} = \underline{+ 20 \text{ years}}$$
$$120 \text{ years}$$

In 1995 Jeane Louise Calment was 120 years old.

You can divide to change from a smaller unit of time to a larger unit of time.

35 days = ▦ weeks

Think: 7 days = 1 week

$$35 \div 7 = 5$$

35 days = 5 weeks

Think and Discuss Why are the 1900s called the 20th century?

Calendar Units
1 week = 7 days
1 year = 52 weeks
1 year = 12 months
1 year = 365 days
1 leap year = 366 days (adds one day to February)
1 decade = 10 years
1 century = 100 years
1 millennium = 1,000 years

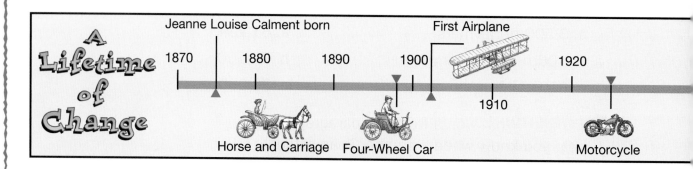

A Lifetime of Change

Jeanne Louise Calment born

First Airplane

1870   1880   1890   1900   1920

1910

Horse and Carriage   Four-Wheel Car   Motorcycle

Try It Out

Find each missing number.

1. 3 weeks = ■ days   **2.** 56 days = ■ weeks   **3.** 4 decades = ■ years

Practice

Find each missing number.

4. 4 weeks = ■ days   **5.** 3 years = ■ months   **6.** 63 days = ■ weeks

7. 3 decades 52 weeks = ■ years   **8.** 4 years 3 weeks = ■ weeks

Problem Solving

Use this calendar to answer Problems 9–10.

9. If today is January 16, what day of the week is 1 week 3 days from now?

10. **Analyze** Look at the dates in any of the columns of the calendar. What is the pattern?

11. **Social Studies Connection** In 1863, Lincoln began the Gettysburg Address with the words "Four score and seven years ago…" A score is 20 years. What year was Lincoln referring to?

January

Sun.	Mon.	Tues.	Wed.	Thurs.	Fri.	Sat.
				1	2	3
4	5	6	7	8	9	10
11	12	13	14	15	16	17
18	19	20	21	22	23	24
25	26	27	28	29	30	31

Review and Remember

Using Algebra Find the missing numbers.

12. 1, 3, 9, ■, ■, 243   **13.** 1, 2, 4, 8, ■, 32, ■   **14.** 72, 60, 48, ■, ■, ■, 0

15. 90, 75, ■, 45, ■, ■   **16.** ■, 9, 18, 27, ■, ■   **17.** 5, 10, 20, ■, 55, ■, ■

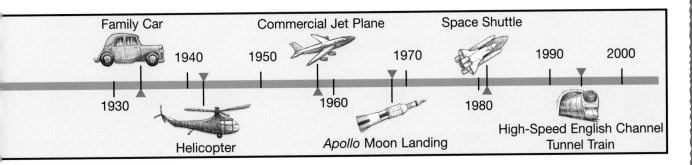

Family Car — 1940   Commercial Jet Plane — 1950   Space Shuttle   1970   1990   2000

1930   Helicopter   1960 *Apollo* Moon Landing   1980   High-Speed English Channel Tunnel Train

For Extra Practice, see Set C, page 290.

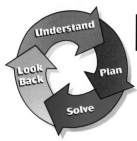

Problem Solving
Work Backwards

Sometimes you can solve a problem by working backwards from what you know.

In 1996, Gary Hall, Jr., and his team set a world swimming record. His dad had set a world swimming record 21 years earlier. Five years before that, Gary's dad had set his first world swimming record. In what year did Gary's dad set his first world swimming record?

UNDERSTAND

What do you need to know?

You need to know how many years have passed from the year that Gary's dad set his first world swimming record to the year 1996.

▲ Gary Hall, Jr.

PLAN

How can you solve the problem?

Start in 1996. **Work backwards** to find the year that Gary's dad set his first world swimming record.

▲ Gary Hall, Sr.

SOLVE

Start in 1996. Subtract 21 years: $1996 - 21 = 1975$

Then subtract 5 years more: $1975 - 5 = 1970$

So, Gary's dad set his first world swimming record in 1970.

LOOK BACK

How can you use addition to check your work?

Using the Strategy

Work backwards to help you solve Problems 1–3.

1 Gary Hall, Jr.'s team set their world record in August, 1996, five months after Gary joined the team. Seven months before he joined the team, Gary won a 50-meter freestyle race. In what month and year did Gary win the race?

2 Austin has a class at 9:00 A.M. He wants to swim for an hour and a half before class. He needs 45 minutes to get dressed and get to class after he swims. What time should Austin plan to start swimming?

▲ The 1996 U.S. men's Olympic 400-meter medley team

3 Calla's family heads to swim practice. On the way they pick up 3 people. They drop off 4 people, then pick up 2 people. When the group finally arrives at swim practice, 6 people get out of the car. How many people were in the car in the first place?

Mixed Strategy Review

**Try these or other strategies to solve each problem.
Tell which strategy you used.**

THERE'S ALWAYS A WAY!

Problem Solving Strategies

- Use a Pattern
- Make a List
- Work Backwards
- Guess and Check
- Make a Table
- Act It Out

4 Bruce wants to get to the pool 45 minutes before the meet. It takes 25 minutes to get there. At what time should he leave if the meet starts at 7:30 P.M.?

5 Meg has 3 bathing suits: red, blue, and green. She has 2 swim caps: yellow and white. Name all the different combinations of bathing suits and caps that she can wear.

6 The summer Olympics are held every 4 years. Suppose a swimmer was in three Summer Olympics in a row. If her first Olympics were in 1984, in what years were her other two Olympics?

7 The lanes in a pool are separated by plastic floats that are arranged in this order: green, white, blue, white, green, white, blue, white, and so on. If there are 26 floats, how many of the floats are white?

Do You Measure Up?

You can use nonstandard measurements to find lengths.

Learning About It

Work in a group. You can measure the length of objects by using ancient Egyptian units of measure.

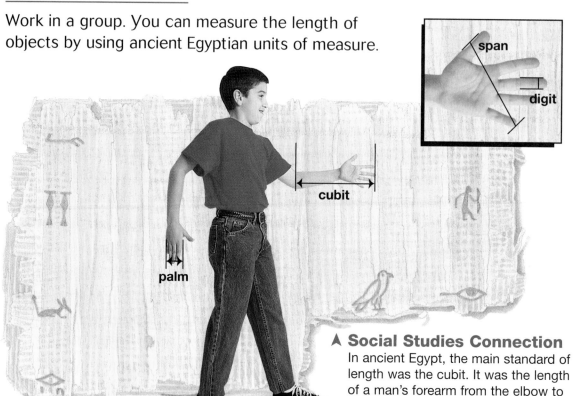

▲ **Social Studies Connection**

In ancient Egypt, the main standard of length was the cubit. It was the length of a man's forearm from the elbow to the tip of the middle finger.

Step 1 Choose five objects in your classroom to measure. To measure each object, decide on three units of measure from those pictured above.

- Each group member should measure each object, using the three units decided on by the group.

- Record your data in tables like the ones started below.

Frank

Object	Cubit	Palm
desk	2	11
rug	8	39

Josie

Object	Cubit	Palm	Digit	Foot	Span
desk	2	10	—	—	5
rug	7	35	—	10	—
book			—		—

Step 2 Compare your results with the results of the other members of your group.

- Are the measurements the same?

- Why do you think the measurements of an object are sometimes different?

Step 3 Invent your own unit of measure and name it.

- Measure the distance around your desk, using your own unit of measure.

- Would the measurement be the same using another person's invented unit of measure? Why or why not?

Think and Discuss If each person in your group used his or her own hand to draw a line segment 10 hands long, would all the line segments be the same length? Why or why not?

Practice

1. A student measures a cabinet and finds that it is 7 cubits high. Another cabinet is 7 spans high. Which cabinet is higher? Explain how you know.

2. Estimate the length of your cubit in palm units. Check by measuring.

3. **Explain** Suppose your friend said she needed some ribbon that was 3 spans long. Would you be able to buy the correct amount of ribbon for your friend? Explain why or why not.

4. **Journal Idea** Why do you think ancient Egyptian units are not often used in everyday life?

Big and Little Gadgets

You can use customary units to measure length.

Learning About It

When the telephone below was made, it was the smallest telephone built in the United States! You can use an inch ruler to measure it to the nearest $\frac{1}{8}$ inch.

What You Need

inch ruler

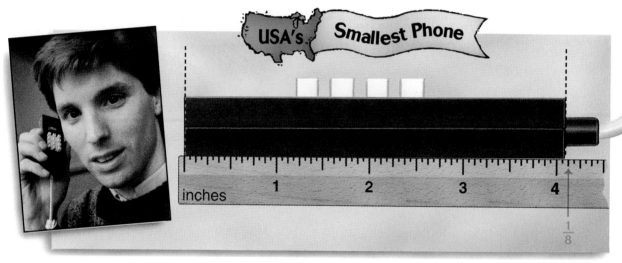

USA's **Smallest Phone**

inches
1 2 3 4

$\frac{1}{8}$

To the nearest $\frac{1}{8}$ inch, the telephone is $4\frac{1}{8}$ inches long.

You can use customary units of length to measure objects of many different sizes.

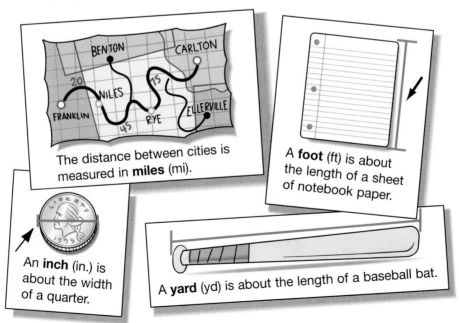

The distance between cities is measured in **miles** (mi).

A **foot** (ft) is about the length of a sheet of notebook paper.

An **inch** (in.) is about the width of a quarter.

A **yard** (yd) is about the length of a baseball bat.

The chart to the right shows the relationships between the units of length. You can use the chart to change a measurement from one unit to another unit.

To change from a larger unit of length to a smaller unit of length, multiply.

8 feet = ▧ inches

Think: 1 ft = 12 in.

$8 \times 12 = 96$
8 feet = 96 inches

To change from a smaller unit of length to a larger unit of length, divide.

21 feet = ▧ yards

Think: 3 ft = 1 yd

$21 \div 3 = 7$
21 feet = 7 yards

Think and Discuss How many inches are in 5 feet 3 inches? Explain how you know.

Try It Out

Find each length to the nearest $\frac{1}{8}$ inch.

1. ⊢————⊣

2. ⊢——————————————⊣

3. ⊢————⊣

4. ⊢————————————⊣

Write each missing number.

5. 4 yd = ▧ ft

6. 3 mi = ▧ ft

7. 13 ft 7 in. = ▧ in.

8. 2 yd 1 ft = ▧ ft

9. 18 ft = ▧ yd

10. 3 mi = ▧ yd

Choose the most appropriate unit of measure for the length of each. Write *in.*, *ft*, or *yd*.

11. pencil   **12.** child   **13.** ball field   **14.** bed

Practice

Find each length to the nearest $\frac{1}{8}$ inch.

15. ├─────────────────────┤

16. ├─────────────────┤

Using Estimation Without using a ruler, find objects that are about the following lengths. Then use a ruler to measure the length of each object.

17. 1 in.   **18.** 3 in.   **19.** $\frac{1}{2}$ in.   **20.** 36 in.

21. 2 yd   **22.** 6 in.   **23.** 12 in.   **24.** 24 in.

Write each missing number.

25. 2 mi = ▮ ft   **26.** 2 yd = ▮ ft   **27.** 15 ft = ▮ yd

28. 5 mi = ▮ ft   **29.** 2 ft = ▮ in.   **30.** 24 ft = ▮ yd

31. 3 ft = ▮ in.   **32.** 8 ft = ▮ in.   **33.** 5 yd = ▮ ft

34. 2 yd 4 in. = ▮ in.   **35.** 3 yd 2 ft = ▮ ft   **36.** 1 yd 2 ft = ▮ ft

Choose the most appropriate unit of measure for the length of each. Write *in., ft, yd,* or *mi.*

37. belt   **38.** candle   **39.** bus trip   **40.** car

41. eraser   **42.** river   **43.** room   **44.** necktie

World's Largest Tricycle

Problem Solving

45. The rear wheels on the world's largest tricycle are 11 feet high. Is that more or less than 3 yards?

46. The tricycle has a front wheel that is 70 in. high. Is that taller or shorter than you are? by how many feet or inches?

◄ Riding the Dillon Colossal Tricycle is its designer, Arthur Dillon, and his son, Christopher.

Use the drawing to solve Problems 47–49.

47. How many inches taller was the Austrian snowman than the one built in the U.S.A.?

48. **Using Estimation** Which snowman is about half as tall as the one built in Switzerland?

49. **Create Your Own** Make up a problem using the data about the snowmen.

90 ft 1 in.   69 ft 2 in.   47 ft 6 in.

Review and Remember

Choose a Method Use mental math or paper and pencil.

50. $500 + 800$

51. $2,500 - 400$

52. $800 + 8,000$

53. $430 - 370$

54. 600×200

55. $80 \times 5,000$

56. $40 \times 8,000$

57. 90×500

Time for Technology

Using the MathProcessor™ on CD-ROM

Changing Units

Use frames and number spaces to change 8 yards into inches.

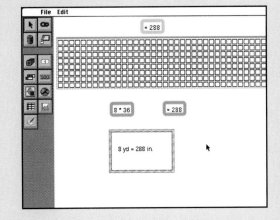

- Click ▦ to open a small-frames workspace. Click-drag the right bar to show 36. Click-drag the top bar to show 8.

- Link ⬛ the array to a number space ▢. Click =.

- Open and link together two more number spaces. Do not link them to the array. In one, type 8*36. [* means "multiply."]

- In the other, click =. So, 8 yd = 288 in.

Use the CD-ROM to solve.

1. 2 ft = ▨ in.

2. 12 yd = ▨ ft

3. 2 mi = ▨ ft

For Extra Practice, see Set D, page 291.

That's Heavy, Man

You can use customary units to measure weight.

Learning About It

Himmy, the world's heaviest cat, weighed 46 pounds 15 ounces. That's about the size of four average-sized cats. How much did he weigh in ounces?

46 lb 15 oz   46 lb 15 oz

Customary Units of Weight

1 pound (lb) = 16 ounces (oz)
1 ton (T) = 2,000 pounds (lb)

46 pounds 15 ounces = ▓ ounces

> Think: 1 lb = 16 oz

$46 \times 16 = 736$

$736 + 15 = 751$

Himmy weighed 751 ounces.

Another Example

6 tons = ▓ pounds

> Think: 1 T = 2,000 lb

$6 \times 2,000 = 12,000$

There are 12,000 pounds in 6 tons.

World's Heaviest Cat

Himmy lived in Australia. He measured 33 inches around his waist!

Think and Discuss How can you estimate the weight of a pet cat if you have no scale?

Try It Out

Find each missing number.

1. 3 T = ▓ lb

2. 4 lb = ▓ oz

3. 10 lb = ▓ oz

4. ▓ lb = 4 T

5. 2 T = ▓ lb

6. 3 lb = ▓ oz

7. 10 T = ▓ lb

8. ▓ oz = 4 lb

Practice

Find each missing number.

9. 8 lb = ▦ oz

10. 5 T = ▦ lb

11. 16 oz = ▦ lb

12. 7 lb = ▦ oz

13. 7 T = ▦ lb

14. 5 lb = ▦ oz

15. 2 T = ▦ lb

16. 2 lb = ▦ oz

17. 6 lb = ▦ oz

18. 3 lb = ▦ oz

19. 4 T = ▦ lb

20. 5 lb 8 oz = ▦ oz

Choose the most appropriate unit to measure the weight of the following. Write *oz, lb,* or *T*.

21. an elephant

22. a wheelbarrow

23. a shoe

24. a book

25. a pencil

26. a truck

27. a calculator

28. a computer

29. a bird

Problem Solving

30. One great white shark weighed 1,587 lb. How many pounds less than 1 ton is this?

31. Name three things whose weight would usually be measured in pounds.

32. **Using Estimation** The heaviest dog in the world weighs 343 pounds. About how many 343-pound dogs would make a ton?

33. You have 2 weights that weigh 5 ounces each and 3 weights that weigh 4 ounces each. What total weights can you make with 2 to 5 weights? Explain your strategy.

Review and Remember

Using Estimation Round to the underlined place and then estimate each answer.

34. $\underline{2}2 \div 2$

35. $6 \times \underline{4}8$

36. $\underline{4}04 - \underline{1}88$

37. $\underline{6}21 + \underline{4}92$

38. $\underline{9}7 - \underline{4}7$

39. $\underline{4}9 \div 5$

40. $8 \times \underline{1}9$

41. $4 \times \underline{6}2$

Fill It Up!

The capacity of a container tells you how much it can hold.

Learning About It

You have a 2-gallon goldfish bowl. You want to use a quart-sized pitcher to fill it. How many quarts are in 2 gallons?

2 gallons = ▨ quarts

Customary Units of Capacity

1 tbsp	**1 c**	**1 c**
1 tablespoon (tbsp) = 3 teaspoons (tsp)	1 cup (c), dry = 16 tablespoons (tbsp)	1 cup (c), fluid = 8 fluid ounces (fl oz)

1 pt	**1 qt**	**$\frac{1}{2}$ gal**	**1 gal**
1 pint (pt) = 2 cups (c)	1 quart (qt) = 2 pints (pt)	1 half gallon ($\frac{1}{2}$ gal) = 2 quarts (qt)	1 gallon (gal) = 4 quarts (qt)

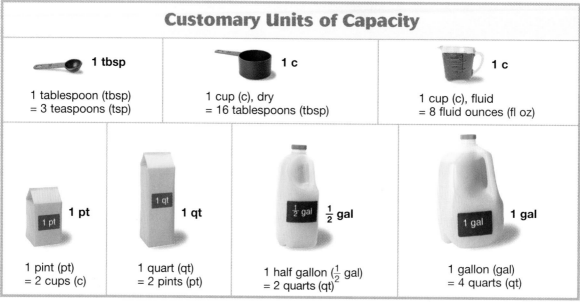

To change larger units to smaller units, multiply.

2 gallons = ▨ quarts

> Think: 1 gal = 4 qt

$2 \times 4 = 8$

2 gallons = 8 quarts

To change smaller units to larger units, divide.

32 fluid ounces = ▨ cups

> Think: 8 fl oz = 1 c

$32 \div 8 = 4$

32 fluid ounces = 4 cups

Think and Discuss How could you find out how many pints are in 1 gallon?

Try It Out

Write each missing number.

1. 4 qt = ▩ pt

2. 2 tbsp = ▩ tsp

3. 2 c = ▩ fl oz

4. 8 qt = ▩ gal

5. 5 qt = ▩ pt

6. 6 c = ▩ pt

Practice

Write each missing number.

7. 5 c = ▩ tbsp

8. 5 c = ▩ fl oz

9. 4 gal = ▩ qt

10. 32 fl oz = ▩ c

11. 12 tbsp = ▩ tsp

12. 2 gal = ▩ qt

13. 6 qt = ▩ half gallons

14. 2 c = ▩ tbsp

15. 5 qt = ▩ pt

16. 12 qt = ▩ gal

17. 2 qt = ▩ pt

18. 16 pt = ▩ qt

Choose the most appropriate unit of capacity. Write *gal*, *qt*, *pt*, *c*, or *tbsp*.

19. washing the car

20. brushing your teeth

21. making lemonade

22. taking medicine

23. making a tray of ice cubes

24. drinking a glass of juice

Problem Solving

25. The Living Seas aquarium filters water at 600 gallons a second. How many quarts are filtered each second?

26. **Science Connection** Each fish in a fishbowl needs about one gallon of water to live. How many fish can you put in a fishbowl that holds thirty-two cups of water?

▲ The Living Seas aquarium in Orlando, Florida, is the world's largest aquarium. It is 203 feet wide and 27 feet deep!

Review and Remember

Estimate first. Find each answer. Check that each answer is reasonable.

27.
```
  308
+ 964
```

28.
```
  1,930
-   577
```

29.
```
   232
×   57
```

30.
```
   2,418
-  1,641
```

31.
```
   3,971
+    655
```

You're Getting Warmer!

In the customary system, temperature is measured in degrees Fahrenheit.

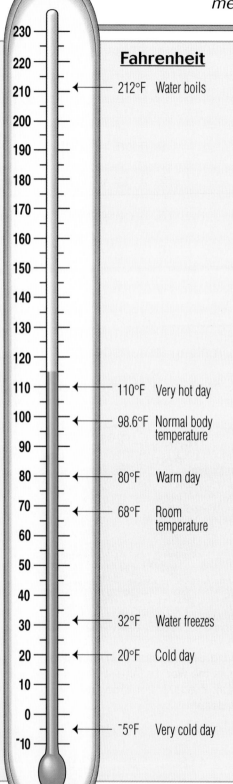

Fahrenheit

212°F   Water boils

110°F   Very hot day

98.6°F Normal body temperature

80°F   Warm day

68°F   Room temperature

32°F   Water freezes

20°F   Cold day

⁻5°F   Very cold day

Learning About It

What is the outside temperature today? Is it hot, cold, or just right? You can measure temperature in **degrees Fahrenheit** (°F).

Look at this Fahrenheit thermometer.

What is room temperature on this thermometer?

Write: 68°F
Say: Sixty-eight degrees Fahrenheit

What is the temperature on a very cold day?

Write: ⁻5°F
Say: Five degrees Fahrenheit below zero, or minus five degrees Fahrenheit

Think and Discuss It was 10°F on Saturday. On Sunday, it was ⁻8°F. What was the difference in temperatures between Saturday and Sunday? Explain your answer.

Word Bank

degrees Fahrenheit

Try It Out

Use each thermometer to find the temperature.

1.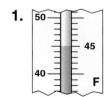

2.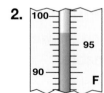

3.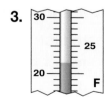

Find the difference between the two temperatures.

4. 0°F and 52°F **5.** 48°F and 223°F **6.** 25°F and 79°F **7.** 117°F and 3°F

Practice

Use each thermometer to find the temperature.

8. 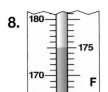 **9.** 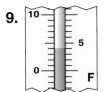 **10.** 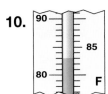 **11.**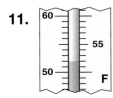

Find the difference between the two temperatures.

12. 68°F and 198°F **13.** 45°F and 32°F **14.** 215°F and 58°F

Choose the most appropriate temperature.

15. making snowballs **a.** 75°F **b.** 22°F **c.** 105°F

16. going swimming **a.** 32°F **b.** 44°F **c.** 81°F

17. wearing a light jacket **a.** 59°F **b.** 96°F **c.** 18°F

Problem Solving

18. If the temperature is 38°F and it rises 17 degrees, what is the new temperature?

19. Suppose the temperature at 6 A.M. was ⁻5°F. If the temperature rose 2 degrees every hour, what would the temperature be at 2 P.M.? What strategy would you use to solve this problem?

20. **Analyze** If the temperature is ⁻16°F and it rises 7 degrees, what is the new temperature?

▲ **Science Connection**
Your body sweats to maintain a normal temperature. When the sweat evaporates, you feel cooler.

Review and Remember

Find each answer.

21. 7,291 + 1,468 **22.** 47 × 623 **23.** 490 − 152 **24.** 94 × 89

25. 8 × 135 **26.** 2,364 + 985 **27.** 3,452 − 1,826 **28.** 86 × 646

For Extra Practice, see Set G, page 291.

✔ Checkpoint

Time and Customary Measurement

Write each time two ways using words and numbers. (pages 250–251)

1.

2.

3.

4. 6:30

Complete each table. (pages 252–255)

	Start	Elapsed Time	Finish
5.	8:00 P.M.	3 hours 10 minutes	
6.	5:00 A.M.		9:15 A.M.
7.		2 hours 15 minutes	1:15 A.M.

	Start	Elapsed Time	Finish
8.	11:00 A.M.	2 hours 5 minutes	
9.	4:45 A.M.		7:30 A.M.
10.		9 hours 30 minutes	6:00 A.M.

Find each length to the nearest $\frac{1}{8}$ in. for Exercises 11–12.
Use each thermometer to find the temperature for
Exercises 13–14. (pages 264–267; 272–273)

11. ├─────────────┤   12. ├─────────┤   13.   14.

Write each missing number.
(pages 258–259; 264–271)

15. 3 weeks 3 days = ▨ days

16. 2 years 3 weeks = ▨ weeks

17. 1 century 3 years = ▨ years

18. 5 decades = ▨ years

19. 2 gal = ▨ qt

20. 27 ft = ▨ yd

21. 2 mi = ▨ ft

22. 2 lb = ▨ oz

23. 3 T = ▨ lb

24. 5 tbsp = ▨ tsp

Mixed Practice

Write the units you would use to measure each of the following.

25. spoonful of medicine

26. weight of your cat

27. glass of water

28. weight of a dump truck

29. distance to school

30. water in a bathtub

31. length of a subway car

32. age of an adult

33. length of a hand

Write each missing number.

34. 4 years = ▇ months

35. 7 cups = ▇ ounces

36. 3 decades = ▇ years

37. 16 qt = ▇ gal

Problem Solving

38. **Explain** A sign before a bridge says "Weight Limit 2 Tons." The pickup truck weighs 1,675 lb, and has a bag of sand that weighs 400 lb in the back. The driver weighs 175 lb. Should she drive the truck across the bridge?

39. **Analyze** As a warm-up for soccer practice, you run around the field. The distance is 380 yards. How many feet did you run? About how many times around would you have to run if you wanted to run a mile?

40. Your friend told you that he will be 520 weeks old on his next birthday. What age is that in years?

Journal Idea

Make a list of all the things you do in one day and how long each thing lasts. Examples may include sleep 10 hours, school 5 hours 45 minutes, basketball practice 1 hour. Add it all up and see if your total equals 24 hours.

What do you think?

Why is it better to use a standard unit rather than a nonstandard unit to measure length?

Critical Thinking Corner

Logical Thinking

Measure for Measure

You need exactly 4 qt of water. You have two pitchers, one that holds 5 qt and another that holds 3 qt. What could you do to measure out exactly 4 qt? This first step is shown.

Hint You can pour from pitcher to pitcher, throw away water, or get more water.

5-quart pitcher

3-quart pitcher

Going to Great Lengths

You can use metric units to measure length.

Learning About It

That's not a bug, it's a bird! The male bee hummingbird is the smallest bird in the world. You can use a metric ruler to measure the length of its wingspan to the nearest centimeter (cm).

What You Need

metric ruler

World's Smallest Bird

This is the actual size of the male bee hummingbird of Cuba.

The wingspan of the male bee hummingbird is between 6 cm and 7 cm long. It is closer to 6 cm.

So, to the nearest centimeter, the wingspan of the male bee hummingbird is 6 cm long.

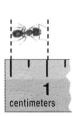

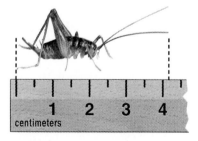

The ant is about 1 cm long, to the nearest centimeter.

The butterfly is about 3 cm wide, to the nearest centimeter.

The cricket is about 4 cm long, to the nearest centimeter.

The drawings below show metric units of length.

A **millimeter** (mm) is about the width of a pin.

A **centimeter** (cm) is about the width of a crayon.

A **decimeter** (dm) is about the width of an adult's hand.

A **meter** (m) is about the width of a door.

A **kilometer** (km) is about the length of 100 school buses lined up end to end.

You can use the chart to the right to change a measurement from one unit to another unit.

4 centimeters = ■ millimeters

Think: 1 cm = 10 mm

$4 \times 10 = 40$

4 centimeters = 40 millimeters

Metric Units of Length
1 cm = 10 mm
1 dm = 10 cm
1 m = 100 cm
1 km = 1,000 m

More Examples

A. 8 kilometers = ■ meters

Think: 1 km = 1,000 m

$8 \times 1,000 = 8,000$

8 kilometers = 8,000 meters

B. 3 meters = ■ centimeters

Think: 1 m = 100 cm

$3 \times 100 = 300$

3 meters = 300 centimeters

Think and Discuss What metric units would you use to measure your height? Explain.

Try It Out

Find each length to the nearest centimeter.

1.

2.

3. Measure the length of your shoe to the nearest cm.

4. Measure the width of your desk or table to the nearest cm.

Write each missing number.

5. 3 m = ▨ cm

6. 4 cm = ▨ mm

7. 2 dm = ▨ cm

8. 2 km = ▨ m

9. 5 dm = ▨ cm

10. 30 cm = ▨ mm

Practice

Compare. Write >, <, or = for each ⬤.

11. 10 cm ⬤ 1 dm

12. 30 dm ⬤ 3 cm

13. 7 dm ⬤ 1 m

14. 300 m ⬤ 1 km

15. 9 cm ⬤ 1 dm

16. 8,000 m ⬤ 8 km

Write each missing number.

17. 2 m = ▨ cm

18. 9 dm = ▨ cm

19. 11 km = ▨ m

20. 100 m = ▨ cm

21. 6 dm = ▨ cm

22. 25 cm = ▨ mm

23. 10 km = ▨ m

24. 50 cm = ▨ mm

25. 8 m = ▨ cm

Choose the most appropriate unit of measure for the length of each. Write *cm*, *dm*, *m*, or *km*.

26. My shoelace is 5 ▨ long.

27. The river is 75 ▨ long.

28. My in-line skate is 3 ▨ long.

29. My jump rope is 3 ▨ long.

30. My computer is 3 ▨ wide.

31. My thumb is 1 ▨ wide.

Using Mental Math Order the lengths from shortest to longest.

32. 26 cm, 2 cm, 9 mm, 3 m

33. 3 cm, 2 dm, 25 mm, 1 km, 17 m

Problem Solving

Use the bar graph below to answer Problems 34–36.

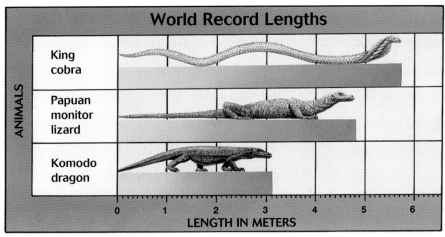

World Record Lengths

ANIMALS

King cobra

Papuan monitor lizard

Komodo dragon

0 1 2 3 4 5 6
LENGTH IN METERS

◀ **Science Connection**
The King cobra is the longest poisonous snake in the world.

34. Which animal is closest to 300 cm in length?

35. Which two animals have the greatest difference in length?

36. **Create Your Own** Using the data from the bar graph above, write your own problem. Ask a classmate to solve it.

37. **Using Estimation** The world's largest spider, a Goliath spider, measured 2 dm 7 cm 9 mm long. Is this length closer to the width of a book or the width of a door?

Review and Remember

Find each answer.

38. $\begin{array}{r} 251 \\ \times\ 18 \\ \hline \end{array}$

39. $\begin{array}{r} 5,479 \\ +\ 393 \\ \hline \end{array}$

40. $\begin{array}{r} 463 \\ \times\ 50 \\ \hline \end{array}$

41. $\begin{array}{r} 7,062 \\ -\ 429 \\ \hline \end{array}$

42. $7\overline{)49}$

Money $ense

Buying Butterflies

Nathan bought some butterfly posters that cost $5.15 each. He gave the cashier two bills. Each bill was worth less than $50. If the cashier gave him 40¢ back in change, what two bills did Nathan give the cashier? How many posters did he buy?

For Extra Practice, see Set H, page 292.

A Humongous Idea

You can use metric units to measure mass.

World's Largest Pumpkin

Learning About It

The world record for the largest pumpkin is 482 kilograms. A kilogram (kg) is a metric unit used to measure the mass of objects. Mass is the amount of matter in an object. The pumpkin held by the girl in the photo above has a mass of about 1 kilogram.

A gram (g) is a metric unit used to measure the mass of lighter objects.

482 kilograms = ■ grams

Think: 1 kg = 1,000 g

$482 \times 1,000 = 482,000$
482 kilograms = 482,000 grams

The mass of each object to the right can be measured by using metric units.

Think and Discuss Do larger objects always have more mass than smaller objects? Explain your reasoning.

Metric Units of Mass

1 kilogram (kg) = 1,000 grams (g)

large paper clip   **1 g**

penny   **3 g**

medium dog   **20 kg**

apple   **160 g**

Try It Out

Write each missing number.

1. 7 kg = ■ g

2. 4 kg = ■ g

3. 50 kg = ■ g

4. 9,000 g = ■ kg

5. 10,000 g = ■ kg

6. 92 kg = ■ g

Practice

Write each missing number.

7. 6 kg = ■ g

8. 4,000 g = ■ kg

9. 3 kg = ■ g

10. 5 kg = ■ g

11. 2 kg = ■ g

12. 12 kg = ■ g

13. 9 kg = ■ g

14. 8 kg = ■ g

15. 2,000 g = ■ kg

**Choose the most appropriate unit of measure.
Write *g* or *kg*.**

16. a watermelon

17. a ladder

18. an envelope

19. a half dollar

20. a baseball

21. a truck

22. in-line skates

23. a marker

24. a person

Problem Solving

25. The mass of the world's largest flower is 7,000 g. How many kilograms is that?

26. An average-sized watermelon is 6 kg. The world's largest watermelon was grown in Tennessee. It was 119 kg. How many kilograms more was it than the average-sized watermelon?

 27. Analyze The mass of an apple is 160 g. About how many apples are needed altogether to equal the mass of a kilogram?

▲ **Social Studies Connection**
Children in Indonesia can find the largest flower in the world, the rafflesia, in the rain forest.

Review and Remember

Find each answer.

28. 81 × 3   **29.** 205 + 105   **30.** 12 × 183   **31.** 702 − 99   **32.** $537.00 × 27

Up to the Brim

You can use metric units to measure capacity.

Learning About It

If you were thirsty, would you rather have a milliliter or a liter of water to drink?

The milliliter (mL) is a metric unit used to measure the capacities of small containers.

The liter (L) is equal to 1,000 mL, so it is used to measure the capacities of larger containers.

How many milliliters are in a 2-liter bottle?

2 liters = ■ milliliters

Think: 1 L = 1,000 mL

$2 \times 1,000 = 2,000$

There are 2,000 milliliters in a 2-liter bottle.

Think and Discuss There are about 5 milliliters in a teaspoon. There are 3 teaspoons in a tablespoon. About how many milliliters are there in a tablespoon?

> **Metric Units of Capacity**
>
> 1 liter (L) = 1,000 milliliters (mL)

1 milliliter →

1 liter

Try It Out

Write each missing number.

1. 4 L = ■ mL

2. 9 L = ■ mL

3. 12,000 mL = ■ L

4. 8 L= ■ mL

5. 2 L = ■ mL

6. 5,000 mL = ■ L

Practice

Choose the most appropriate unit of measure for the capacity of each. Write *L* or *mL*.

7. water in a bathtub

8. water in a bucket

9. water used for watercolors

10. a sip of cocoa

11. soda in a can

12. medicine on a spoon

Write each missing number.

13. 3 L = ▩ mL   **14.** 15 L = ▩ mL   **15.** 7 L = ▩ mL

16. 6 L = ▩ mL   **17.** 10 L = ▩ mL   **18.** 11 L = ▩ mL

19. 25 L = ▩ mL   **20.** 32 L = ▩ mL   **21.** 4,000 mL = ▩ L

Mexican Corn Bread
150 g yellow cornmeal
50 g all-purpose flour
360 mL buttermilk
2 large eggs
60 mL oil
4 g salt
4 g sugar
8 g baking powder
2 g baking soda

▲ **Social Studies Connection** In Mexico and in many other countries, ingredients in recipes are often measured by using milliliters and grams.

Problem Solving

Use the recipe above to answer Problems 22–24.

22. If you wanted to double the recipe for corn bread, how much buttermilk would you need?

23. What If? Suppose you and a friend both want to double the recipe for corn bread. How much buttermilk will you need?

24. The corn bread recipe makes 8 servings. How many servings would there be if 25 people each made the recipe? How many liters of buttermilk would be needed?

Review and Remember

Using Algebra Find each missing number.

25. $40 + 60 = 30 + n$ **26.** $50 - n = 100 - 90$ **27.** $35 + 100 = 100 + n$

28. $30 \div n = 36 \div 6$ **29.** $8 \times n = 20 \times 2$ **30.** $9 \times n = 2 \times 27$

Going to Extremes

In the metric system, temperature is measured in degrees Celsius.

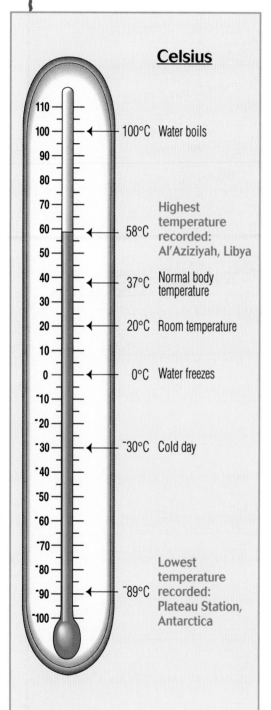

Celsius

- 100°C Water boils
- 58°C Highest temperature recorded: Al'Aziziyah, Libya
- 37°C Normal body temperature
- 20°C Room temperature
- 0°C Water freezes
- ⁻30°C Cold day
- ⁻89°C Lowest temperature recorded: Plateau Station, Antarctica

Learning About It

What's the outside temperature today? You can measure temperature in **degrees Celsius** (°C) by using a Celsius thermometer.

Look at this Celsius thermometer. It shows the world records for the highest and lowest air temperatures ever recorded on Earth.

What is the highest air temperature recorded on Earth?

> **Write:** 58°C
> **Say:** Fifty-eight degrees Celsius

What is the lowest air temperature recorded on Earth?

> **Write:** ⁻89°C
> **Say:** Eighty-nine degrees Celsius below zero

Think and Discuss Do you think the air temperature on Earth could be 100°C? Explain why or why not.

Try It Out

Use each thermometer to find the temperature.

1.

2.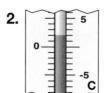

3.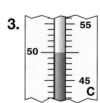

Practice

INTERNET ACTIVITY
www.sbgmath.com

Use each thermometer to find the temperature.

4.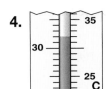

5.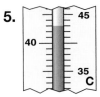

6.

7.

8.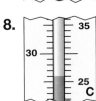

9.

10.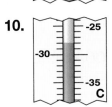

11.

Choose the most appropriate temperature.

12. wearing a sweater
   a. ⁻25°C   **b.** 14°C   **c.** 63°C

13. building a snowman
   a. ⁻3°C   **b.** 13°C   **c.** 25°C

14. going to the beach
   a. 0°C   **b.** 24°C   **c.** 74°C

15. planting a garden
   a. 75°C   **b.** 23°C   **c.** 40°C

Problem Solving

16. If you have a fever 3°C above normal, what is your temperature in degrees Celsius?

17. **Science Connection** The highest air temperature recorded in the U.S. is 57°C. The lowest air temperature recorded in the U.S. is ⁻62°C. Is the difference between the two temperatures more than 57°C? Explain.

USA's Most Extreme Temperatures

- 62°C
Prospect Creek, Alaska

57°C
Death Valley, California

18. **Journal Idea** If the temperature is 12°C, how would you describe the day? What would you wear outside?

Review and Remember

Find each answer.

19. 104×12
   20. 318×42
   21. $532 - 57$
   22. 624×60

23. $315 + 96$
   24. $629 - 85$
   25. $744 + 47$
   26. $806 - 73$

For Extra Practice, see set K, page 292.

Problem Solving
Using Measurement

Sometimes you can use measurement to help you solve problems.

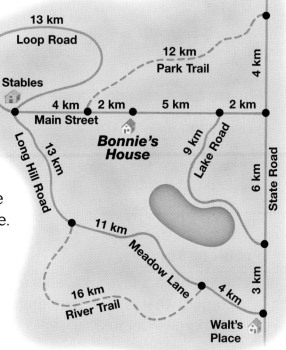

Bonnie is training for a 100-kilometer bike race. One day she wanted to ride a total of 25 kilometers, starting and ending at her house. What is a route Bonnie could take?

 UNDERSTAND

What do you need to find?

You need to find a 25-kilometer route that starts and ends at Bonnie's house.

 PLAN

How can you solve the problem?

Find a path. Add the distances of each part of it to see if they add up to 25 kilometers. Keep trying until you find a path that is 25 kilometers.

 SOLVE

Try this route.

Bonnie's house to Lake Road: 5 km
Take Lake Road to State Road: 9 km
Take State Road to Main Street: 6 km
Take Main Street to Bonnie's house: 7 km

$5 + 9 + 6 + 7 = 27$ km

This route is too long.

So try this route.

Bonnie's house to Loop Road: 6 km
Around Loop Road to Main Street: 13 km
Take Main Street to Bonnie's House: 6 km

$6 + 13 + 6 = 25$ km

This is a route Bonnie could take.

 LOOK BACK

Write a number sentence to show another route Bonnie could take.

Show What You Learned

Use the map on page 286 to solve Problems 1–4.

1 One day Bonnie rode her bike from her home to Park Trail. Then halfway up Park Trail she realized she had forgotten her water bottle, so she biked home to get it. About how many kilometers did Bonnie ride?

2 Bonnie wants to bike from one end of Main Street to the other. What is the shortest distance she can bike if she starts and ends at her house?

3 **Analyze** Suppose Bonnie starts a bike ride at the stables. What is the longest route she can take home without crossing any intersection more than once? How long is the route?

4 **You Decide** You want to bike from Bonnie's house to Walt's Place. What route could you take that is about 20 km?

The chart at the right shows the air distances between U.S. cities. To find the distance between any 2 cities, start at the row for one of the cities and move across until you reach the column for the other city.

Use the chart to solve Problems 5–8.

Distance in Kilometers Between U.S. Cities				
Cities	Atlanta	Chicago	Houston	New York
Atlanta	✕	975	1,120	1,223
Chicago	975	✕	1,504	1,140
Houston	1,120	1,504	✕	2,272
New York	1,223	1,140	2,272	✕

▲ This chart shows air distances. For example, Atlanta to Chicago is 975 kilometers.

5 How far is it from New York to Houston?

6 How far is it from Houston to Chicago?

7 A pilot flies from Houston to Chicago and then to New York. How far does she fly?

8 How much farther is it from Atlanta to New York than from Atlanta to Chicago?

Problem Solving

★ ★ ★ ★ ★ **Preparing for Tests**

Practice What You Learned

Choose the correct letter for each answer.

1 On Thursday, January 11, Rachel had 17 days left to complete her project on volcanoes. When did Rachel have to be done with her project?

A. Saturday, January 29
B. Sunday, January 29
C. Saturday, January 28
D. Sunday, January 28

Tip

Try making a drawing to solve this problem. Sketch a calendar with the 11th day on a Thursday. Then count ahead 17 days.

2 Olivia had $45 in the bank. Then she earned $27.25 for each of the next 2 weeks. Which is the best estimate for the total amount of money Olivia has?

A. $75
B. $100
C. $150
D. More than $175

Tip

Use estimation to eliminate one or more of the answer choices in this problem.

3 Brian is choosing some computer games from a catalog. Video Rangers costs $42, Mighty Meteors costs $65, Warp Out costs $13, and Time Blaster costs $36. Which 2 games can Brian buy for $70?

A. Video Rangers and Warp Out
B. Warp Out and Mighty Meteors
C. Time Blaster and Video Rangers
D. Mighty Meteors and Time Blaster

Tip

Sometimes a good way to solve a multiple-choice question is by trying each answer choice to see which one is correct.

287

4 Rebecca has a collection of 215 glass beads, 387 wooden beads, and 293 plastic beads. **About** how many glass and wooden beads does Rebecca have?

A. 200
B. 600
C. 800
D. 900

5 Choose the method Lee Ann could use to change 3 ft 8 in. to inches. (Hint: There are 12 inches in 1 foot.)

A. Add 3 to 8, then multiply by 12.
B. Multiply 8 times 12, then add 3.
C. Multiply 3 times 8, then add 12.
D. Multiply 3 times 12, then add 8.

6 Sam has more pets than Pat but fewer pets than Marta. Pat has 3 pets. Which is a reasonable answer?

A. Sam has fewer than 3 pets.
B. Sam has more pets than Marta.
C. Marta has more than 3 pets.
D. Pat has more pets than Marta.

7 If 8 tickets to a ball game cost $64.64, which is a reasonable estimate for the cost of 5 tickets?

A. $8
B. $40
C. $50
D. $56

8 This graph shows what happened when Justin rode his bike to his friend's house. Which shows a time when Justin stopped riding his bike?

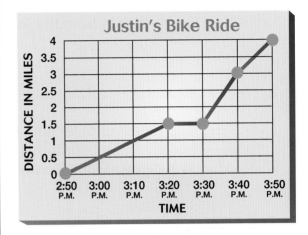

Justin's Bike Ride

A. 3:00 P.M.   C. 3:20 P.M.
B. 3:10 P.M.   D. 3:40 P.M.

9 The Garcias filled their pool with water. On the first day they put 218 gallons of water in the pool. On the second day they added 295 more gallons of water. **About** how many gallons of water were in the pool then?

A. 300 gallons   C. 500 gallons
B. 350 gallons   D. 600 gallons

10 Bill is following a recipe to make punch. He wants to know how many quarts there are in 18 pints. Which could Bill use to solve this problem? (Hint: There are 2 pints in a quart.)

A. $18 \div 2 = $ ▇
B. $18 \times 2 = $ ▇
C. $18 + 2 = $ ▇
D. $18 - 2 = $ ▇

 # Checkpoint

Metric Measurement

Vocabulary

Complete. Use the words from the Word Bank.

1. Water freezes at 32° __?__ .

2. Water boils at 100° __?__ .

3. A __?__ is a measure of length.

4. A __?__ is a measure of capacity.

Word Bank

Celsius
Fahrenheit
milliliter
yard

Skills and Concepts

Find each length to the nearest cm. (pages 276–279)

5. ├─────────────┤

6. ├──────────┤

7. ├────┤

Write each missing number. (pages 276–283)

8. 3 cm = ■ mm

9. 4 L = ■ mL

10. 4 m = ■ cm

11. 2 km = ■ m

12. 3 kg = ■ g

13. 60 dm = ■ cm

14. 1,000 cm = ■ m

15. 5 dm = ■ cm

16. 6 L = ■ mL

Use each thermometer to find the temperature. (pages 284–285)

17.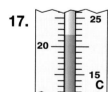

18.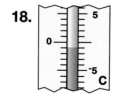

19.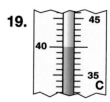

Mixed Practice

Compare. Write >, <, or = for each ●.

20. 1 kg ● 100 g

21. 2,000 mL ● 2 L

22. 5,000 g ● 5 kg

23. 5 m ● 5 cm

24. 10 mm ● 1 cm

25. 2 cm ● 2,000 mm

Problem Solving

26. You ran 2 km during a school competition. Your friend ran 2,800 m. Who ran farther? how much farther?

27. How would you dress to go outdoors if the temperature was 15°C? 35°C? ⁻10°C?

28. One mL is about 5 drops of water. About how many drops would fill a 1-liter bottle?

29. A carat is 5 grams. The world's largest diamond weighs nearly 124 carats. How many grams is it?

30. Explain You have a space in your room 5 dm 9 cm wide. You want to put a bookshelf there. The bookshelf is 50 cm wide. Will it fit?

Journal Idea

Many people think that the metric system is easier to use than the customary system of measure. Write an explanation about why they may think this way. Include examples.

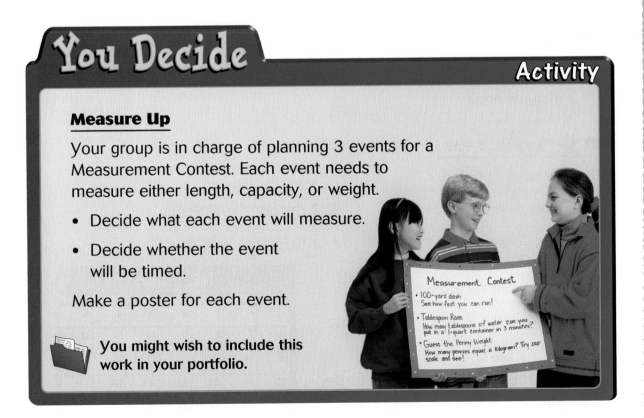

You Decide

Activity

Measure Up

Your group is in charge of planning 3 events for a Measurement Contest. Each event needs to measure either length, capacity, or weight.

- Decide what each event will measure.

- Decide whether the event will be timed.

Make a poster for each event.

You might wish to include this work in your portfolio.

Extra Practice

Set A (pages 250–251)

Write each time two ways using words and numbers.

1.

2.

3.

4.

5. The winning time for a race was 51 minutes 29 seconds. Is the winning time closer to 51 minutes or 52 minutes?

Set B (pages 252–255)

Complete the table.

	Start	Elapsed Time	Finish
1.	3:00 P.M.	4 hours	
2.		4 hours 45 minutes	11:45 A.M.
3.	7:20 P.M.		9:35 P.M.
4.	10:40 A.M.	7 hours 38 minutes	

5. It is now 9:52 P.M. What time was it 3 hours 19 minutes ago?

Set C (pages 258–259)

Find each missing number.

1. 49 days = ■ weeks

2. 2 decades = ■ years

3. 3 years = ■ weeks

4. 1 leap year = ■ days

Use this calendar for Exercises 5–6.

5. Today is March 2. What will the date be in 3 weeks?

6. What is the date of the third Saturday in March?

March

Sun.	Mon.	Tues.	Wed.	Thurs.	Fri.	Sat.
		1	2	3	4	5
6	7	8	9	10	11	12
13	14	15	16	17	18	19
20	21	22	23	24	25	26
27	28	29	30	31		

Extra Practice

Set D (pages 264–267)

Find each length to the nearest $\frac{1}{8}$ inch.

1. ├─────────────┤   **2.** ├──────────────────────┤

Write each missing number.

3. 6 yd = ▦ ft   **4.** 3 mi = ▦ ft   **5.** 5 ft = ▦ in.

6. 27 ft = ▦ yd   **7.** 14 yd = ▦ ft   **8.** 2 mi = ▦ ft

9. The park is 1,760 yd from Shawn's apartment. How
many feet is this? How many miles is this?

Set E (pages 268–269)

Write each missing number.

1. 4 T = ▦ lb   **2.** 2 lb = ▦ oz   **3.** 8 lb = ▦ oz   **4.** 3 T = ▦ lb

5. The oldest elephant in the zoo weighs 3,048 lb.
How much less is this than 2 tons?

Set F (pages 270–271)

Write each missing number.

1. 2 pt = ▦ c   **2.** 4 c = ▦ qt   **3.** 16 qt = ▦ gal   **4.** 9 tsp = ▦ tbsp

5. List as many different ways as you can to describe the
capacity of a 2-gallon bucket, using other units of measure.

Set G (pages 272–273)

Use each thermometer to find the temperature.

1. 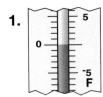   **2.** 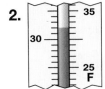   **3.** 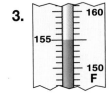   **4.**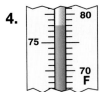

5. Which of the above temperatures is the freezing
point of water?

Extra Practice

Set H (pages 276–279)

Find each length to the nearest centimeter.

1. ├──────────────────────────────┤   **2.** ├────┤

Write each missing number.

3. 6 dm = ■ cm   **4.** 5 m = ■ cm   **5.** 2 km = ■ m

6. 2 cm = ■ mm   **7.** 4 dm = ■ cm   **8.** 6 m = ■ cm

9. The library is 856 m from school. How much less than 1 km is this?

Set I (pages 280–281)

Write each missing number.

1. 4 kg = ■ g   **2.** 2 kg = ■ g   **3.** 7 kg = ■ g   **4.** 5 kg = ■ g

5. A large koi fish has a mass of 7,000 g. Is this greater than, less than, or equal to 7 kg?

Set J (pages 282–283)

Write each missing number.

1. 5 L = ■ mL   **2.** 9 L = ■ mL   **3.** 3 L = ■ mL   **4.** 2 L = ■ mL

5. Write 13L 462 mL as mL.

Set K (pages 284–285)

Use each thermometer to find the temperature.

1. 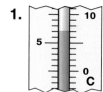   **2.** 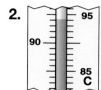   **3.** 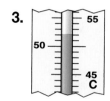   **4.**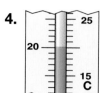

5. Which temperature reading above might be room temperature?

Chapter Test

Write each time two ways using words.

1. 12:15   **2.** 7:46   **3.** 4:20   **4.** 11:55

Choose the most appropriate unit of measure. Write
_m_, _km_, _cm_, _pt_, _lb_, _kg_, _in._, or _tsp_.

5. length of a train   **6.** soap in a bottle

7. weight of a TV   **8.** mass of a watermelon

9. height of a mountain   **10.** length of a pencil

Use each thermometer to find the temperature.

Fahrenheit   Celsius   Fahrenheit   Celsius

11. 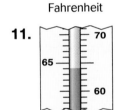   **12.** 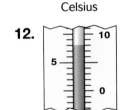   **13.** 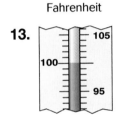   **14.**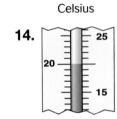

Write each missing number.

15. 3 lb = ▨ oz   **16.** 2 qt = ▨ c   **17.** 2 mi = ▨ ft   **18.** 2 m = ▨ cm

19. 5 ft = ▨ in.   **20.** 2 T = ▨ lb   **21.** 12 ft = ▨ yd   **22.** 8 L = ▨ mL

Use this calendar for Exercises 23–24.

23. Find the date 4 weeks from May 2.

24. If today is May 10, what day of the week is 2 weeks 4 days from now?

25. A meteorite weighs 31 tons. How many pounds is this?

May						
SUN.	MON.	TUES.	WED.	THURS.	FRI.	SAT.
	1	2	3	4	5	6
7	8	9	10	11	12	13
14	15	16	17	18	19	20
21	22	23	24	25	26	27
28	29	30	31			

 Self-Check

Explain why your answers to Exercises 5–10 are reasonable.

Performance Assessment

Show What You Know About Time and Measurement

1 Measure and describe a book and a sheet of paper in as many ways as you can.

a. How are the two objects alike?

b. How are the two objects different?

Self-Check Did you measure the height, length, and width of each object?

2 In a 6-mile race, Yoshi ran the first 3 miles of the race at 7 minutes per mile. During the second 3 miles of the race, she ran at 10 minutes per mile. The race began at 11:30 A.M.

a. For how many minutes did Yoshi run?

b. When did Yoshi cross the finish line?

Self-Check Why did you need to answer 2a before you answered 2b?

For Your Portfolio

You might wish to include this work in your portfolio.

Extension

Schedules

Schedules tell when events will happen, such as what time airplanes and buses will arrive, or when a television program will be on the air. A schedule can be written for a day, a week, a month, or even a year.

Below is a schedule for the field days at school.

School Field Days Schedule

Time	Day 1	Day 2	Day 3	Day 4	Day 5
9:00 A.M.	Opening ceremony	Rides and games	Bake sale	Book sale	Breakfast
10:05 A.M.	Grade 1 relay	Grade 3 soccer	Grade 4 soccer	Grade 2 sack race	Parent ball-throw
10:55 A.M.	Grade 3 kick ball	Grade 1 egg race	Grade 2 jump-rope	Grade 4 Ball Shoot	100-yd teacher run
11:30 A.M.	Grade 4 line dance	Grade 2 backwards race	Grade 3 step race	Grade 1 costume parade	Closing ceremony

rows

columns

There is more than one way to read a schedule.

- Read across a row to find all the events at a certain time.

- Read down a column to find all the events on a certain day.

Use the schedule above to answer these problems.

1. At what time does Grade 4 have an event on Day 1?

2. On Day 3, how much time is there between the start of the Grade 4 soccer game and the start of the Grade 3 step race?

3. When does Grade 4 have a ball shoot?

4. **Create Your Own** Write a problem that uses the information on this schedule. Ask a classmate to solve it.

Cumulative Review

Choose the correct letter for each answer.

Operations	Geometry and Spatial Reasoning

Operations

1. $81 \div 9 = \blacksquare$

A. 9
B. 72
C. 90
D. 729

2. Connie can invite 9 girls to her sleepover. She made a list of 5 girls. Which number sentence shows how many more girls she can invite?

A. $5 + 9 = \blacksquare$
B. $5 - 9 = \blacksquare$
C. $9 + 5 = \blacksquare$
D. $9 - 5 = \blacksquare$

3. The school library has 485 novels, 396 adventure books, and 284 biographies. How many more adventure books are there than biographies?

A. 112   C. 342
B. 201   D. 680

4. Mateo has 24 packages of trading cards. Each package has 11 cards in it. How many cards does Mateo have?

A. 13   C. 48
B. 35   D. 264

Geometry and Spatial Reasoning

5. Which figure appears to be congruent (same size, same shape) to the figure below?

A.   C.

B.   D.

6. How many faces does a cube have?

A. 4
B. 5
C. 6
D. 7

7. Which letter does **NOT** have a line of symmetry?

A. B   C. H

B. I   D. J

8. Which figure has 8 sides?

A. pentagon
B. square
C. octagon
D. hexagon

Measurement	**Probability and Statistics**

9. Peg boiled an egg for 4 minutes. How many seconds is that? (Hint: 60 seconds equal 1 minute.)

   A. 56 s   **C.** 100 s
   B. 64 s   **D.** 240 s

10. What is the *area* of the shaded region?

   A. 6 square units
   B. 9 square units
   C. 15 square units
   D. 16 square units

11. Jordan's dog, Rex, weighs 25 pounds 5 ounces. Ray's dog, Lady, weighs 42 pounds 10 ounces. How much more does Lady weigh than Rex?

   A. 7 lb   **C.** 17 lb 5 oz
   B. 7 lb 15 oz   **D.** 23 lb 5 oz

12. Which is the best estimate of the *area* of the shaded region?

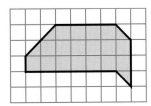

   A. 17 square units
   B. 19 square units
   C. 21 square units
   D. 28 square units

13. If you choose one of the cards below from a bag without looking, how many outcomes are possible?

   A. 2   **C.** 4
   B. 3   **D.** 5

Use the graph for Questions 14–16.

14. When did Vickie's plant grow the most?

   A. March to April
   B. April to May
   C. May to June
   D. June to July

15. How many inches did the plant grow between June and July?

   A. 1 in.   **C.** 3 in.
   B. 2 in.   **D.** 4 in.

16. How much did the plant grow from April to July?

   A. 3 in.   **C.** 6 in.
   B. 4 in.   **D.** 7 in.

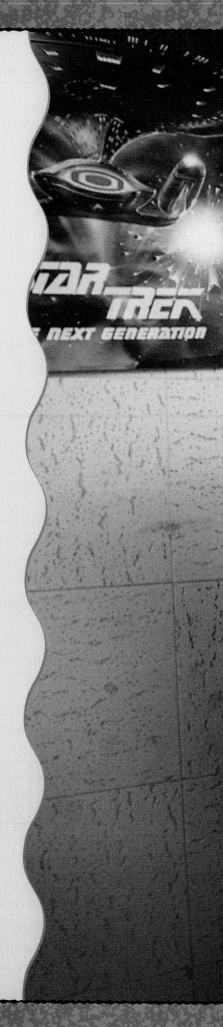

Dividing by One-Digit Divisors

Chapter Theme: PERFORMING ARTS

REAL-WORLD Math

·················· Real Facts ··················

Brian Bonsall, shown at the right, plays one of the Klingons (Worf's son, Alexander) on *Star Trek: The Next Generation*. His make-up takes two hours to apply!

The graph below shows the number of episodes broadcast in the first four seasons of *Star Trek*.

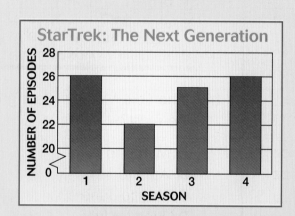

StarTrek: The Next Generation

NUMBER OF EPISODES / SEASON

• What is the total number of episodes televised for the first four seasons?

• How could you use division to estimate about how many episodes were televised each season?

········· Real People ·················

Meet Michael Westmore, make-up designer. He and his crew make all the masks for *Star Trek: The Next Generation*. They turn thousands of earthlings into androids and aliens!

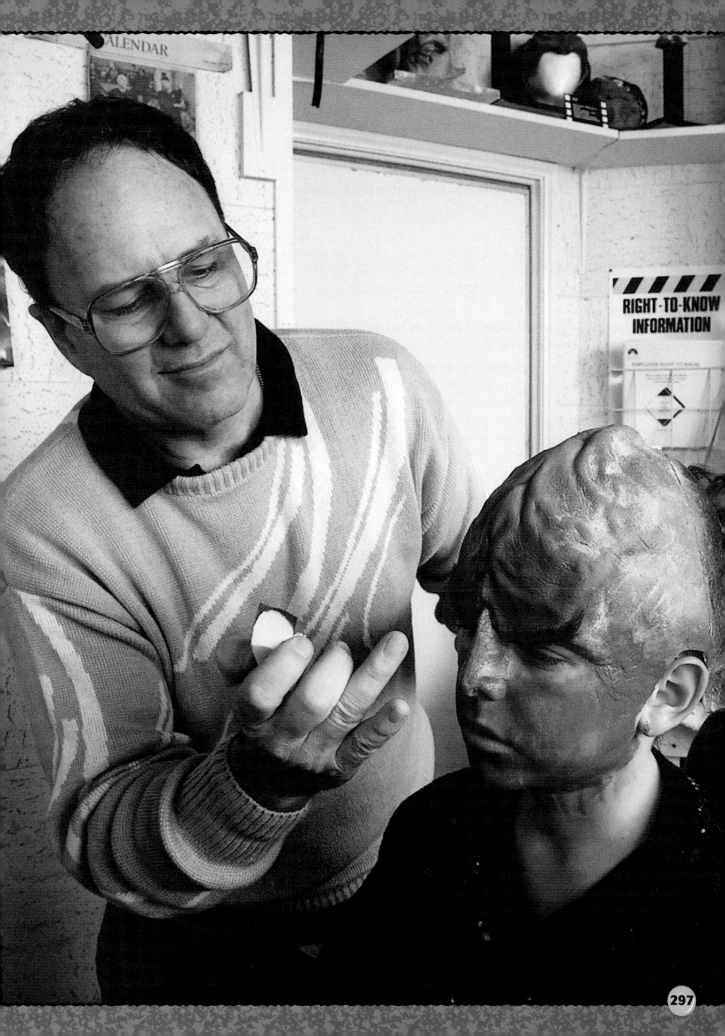

A Cast of Thousands

Basic facts, patterns of zeros, and multiplication can help you divide multiples of 10, 100, and 1,000.

Learning About It

Sometimes a director needs hundreds or even thousands of actors to make a movie just right.

Suppose a director uses 1,800 actors for a movie. If the director wants to divide the actors into 6 equal groups, how many actors will there be in each group?

$$1,800 \div 6 = \blacksquare \leftarrow \text{quotient}$$

↑ dividend   ↑ divisor

THERE'S ALWAYS A WAY!

• **One way** to find the answer is to use basic facts and look for patterns with zeros.

$$18 \div 6 = 3$$
$$180 \div 6 = 30$$
$$1,800 \div 6 = 300$$

Extend the pattern. What is $18,000 \div 6$?

• **Another way** to find the answer is to think of a related multiplication sentence.

$3 \times 6 = 18$	So:	$18 \div 6 = 3$
$30 \times 6 = 180$	So:	$180 \div 6 = 30$
$300 \times 6 = 1,800$	So:	$1,800 \div 6 = 300$

There will be 300 actors in each group.

Think and Discuss How can you use multiplication to check the answer to a division problem like $300 \div 5$?

Try It Out

Divide.

1. 24 ÷ 4
  240 ÷ 4
  2,400 ÷ 4

2. 40 ÷ 8
  400 ÷ 8
  4,000 ÷ 8

3. 9 ÷ 3
  90 ÷ 3
  900 ÷ 3
  9,000 ÷ 3

Practice

Use basic facts and patterns to divide.

4. 80 ÷ 2

5. 60 ÷ 3

6. 120 ÷ 6

7. 280 ÷ 7

8. 240 ÷ 8

9. 180 ÷ 9

10. 320 ÷ 4

11. 200 ÷ 5

12. 8,000 ÷ 4

13. 6,000 ÷ 2

14. 1,200 ÷ 6

15. 3,200 ÷ 8

16. 560 ÷ 8

17. 1,800 ÷ 9

18. 320 ÷ 8

19. 7,200 ÷ 9

20. 2,000 ÷ 5

21. 3,500 ÷ 7

22. 3,600 ÷ 6

23. 6,300 ÷ 7

Problem Solving

Use the information in the table to answer Problems 24–29.

A movie studio stores its old costumes in boxes, five costumes per box. How many boxes are needed to pack the costumes worn in each type of movie?

Old Costumes	
Type of Movie	**Number**
Western	450
Science fiction	400
Musical	1,000
Historical (U.S.)	300
Historical (Mexico)	250

24. Westerns

25. Science fiction

26. Musicals

27. Historical movies

28. Analyze Suppose the studio used boxes that held 8 costumes each. How many boxes would be needed for all the costumes in the chart?

29. Create Your Own Write a problem using the data in the table. Ask a friend to solve it.

Review and Remember

Measure each line to the nearest inch and centimeter.

30. |————————————|

31. |————————————————————|

Free Tickets

Base-ten blocks can help you explore dividing by one-digit numbers.

Learning About It

A theater is giving away 26 tickets. If the tickets are divided equally among 4 winners, how many tickets will each winner get? How many tickets will be left over?

Work with a partner.

What You Need

For each pair:
  base-ten blocks

Step 1 Use base-ten blocks to show 26. Then try to divide the blocks into 4 equal groups.

- Are there enough tens to divide among 4 equal groups?

- Regroup the tens as ones. Describe the blocks you have now.

- Do you have enough ones to divide among 4 groups?

Step 2 Now use the blocks to divide.

- How many groups did you make?

- How many blocks are in each group?

- How many blocks are left over?

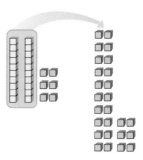

Step 3 Model each of the examples below with base-ten blocks. Then record your work in a chart like the one shown.

- Divide 33 into 2 equal groups.

- Divide 24 into 5 equal groups.

Number in All	Number of Groups	Number in Each Group	Number Left Over
33	2		

Think and Discuss Explain when you needed to regroup in each of the examples above.

Practice

Use base-ten blocks for Exercises 1–6.
Record your work in a chart like the one above.

1. Divide 22 into 4 equal groups.
2. Divide 30 into 5 equal groups.

3. Divide 34 into 3 equal groups.
4. Divide 41 into 3 equal groups.

5. Divide 35 into 7 equal groups.
6. Divide 28 into 5 equal groups.

7. Caitlin divided 29 into 4 equal groups. She said that the answer was 4 groups of 6 ones with 5 ones left over. What's wrong with Caitlin's answer?

Critical Thinking Corner

Number Sense

Math Sense and Algebra

Using Algebra Find a number for n to make each sentence true.

1. $n \div 4 = 7$
2. $n \div 2 = 34$
3. $n \div 5 = 49$

Developing Skills for
Problem Solving

*First read for understanding and then focus on how to
use a remainder when solving problems.*

READ FOR UNDERSTANDING

Forty children are in the New Star Theater production
of Peter Pan. Twenty-three green felt hats are needed
for the play. The hats are sold in boxes of 4 hats
each, and no hats can be bought individually.

1 How many green felt hats are needed?

2 How many hats are sold in each box?

3 Would it be possible to buy just 3 hats?
Explain why or why not.

THINK AND DISCUSS

Interpreting Remainders   When you
divide to solve a problem, a remainder
can affect the answer. Sometimes a
remainder means the quotient should
be rounded up to the next number.
Sometimes a remainder is the
solution. Sometimes a remainder
should be ignored.

4 If you buy 5 boxes of hats, will there be enough
hats for the show? Why or why not?

5 What is the least number of boxes of hats you could
order and still have enough hats for the show? Write
a division sentence to help you find the answer.

6 Look back at your solution to Problem 5. Explain
what you did with the remainder.

Show What You Learned

Answer each question. Give a reason for your choice.

Costume designers want to buy striped shirts for some of the actors in the play. They have $40 to spend, and each shirt costs $7. They want to buy as many shirts as possible.

1 Which of the following statements is true?

   a. The shirt costs $40.

   b. There is enough money to buy more than one shirt.

   c. There is not enough money to buy any shirts.

2 Which of these sentences could you use to find how many shirts can be bought?

   a. $40 \div $4 = \blacksquare$

   b. $40 \div $7 = \blacksquare$

   c. $7 \div $40 = \blacksquare$

3 How can the remainder from Problem 2 help you know how many shirts can be bought?

   a. Use it to round the quotient up.

   b. Add it to the quotient.

   c. Ignore it.

Three yards of cloth are needed for each sail on Captain Hook's ship. The director of the play wants to make as many sails as possible from 14 yards of cloth. The leftover cloth will be used to make flags.

4 Which helps you find out how many sails can be made?

   a. $14 \div 6 = 2$ R2

   b. $14 \div 5 = 2$ R4

   c. $14 \div 3 = 4$ R2

5 How many sails can be made?

   a. 3 sails

   b. 4 sails

   c. 5 sails

6 **Explain** What does the remainder stand for?

...

A Dance Number

You can record what you do as you divide with blocks.

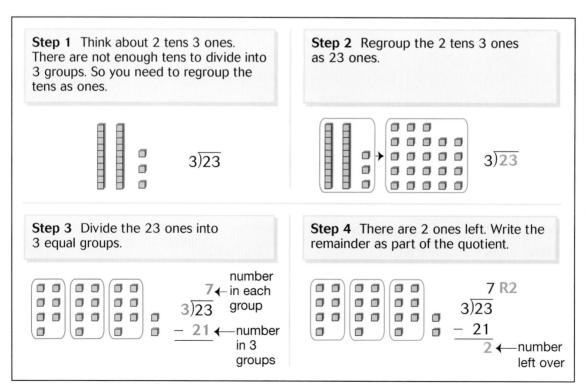

Learning About It

There are 23 dancers in a performance. If they make 3 equal groups, how many will be in each group? Will there be any dancers left over?

$$23 \div 3 = \blacksquare$$

Step 1 Think about 2 tens 3 ones. There are not enough tens to divide into 3 groups. So you need to regroup the tens as ones.

$$3\overline{)23}$$

Step 2 Regroup the 2 tens 3 ones as 23 ones.

$$3\overline{)23}$$

Step 3 Divide the 23 ones into 3 equal groups.

$$\begin{array}{r} 7 \leftarrow \text{number in each group} \\ 3\overline{)23} \\ -21 \leftarrow \text{number in 3 groups} \end{array}$$

Step 4 There are 2 ones left. Write the remainder as part of the quotient.

$$\begin{array}{r} 7\ R2 \\ 3\overline{)23} \\ -21 \\ \hline 2 \leftarrow \text{number left over} \end{array}$$

There will be 7 dancers in each group, with 2 dancers left over.

Check your answer by multiplying and adding.

A. $75 \div 8 = $ ■   Think: $8 \times 9 = 72$ **B.** $60 \div 9 = $ ■   Think: $9 \times 6 = 54$

```
      9 R3        Check.
   8)75              8    ←─── divisor
   − 72            × 9    ←─── quotient
      3             72
                  + 3
                   75    ←─
```

If this matches the dividend, you divided correctly.

```
      6 R6        Check.
   9)60              9
   − 54            × 6
      6             54
                  + 6
                   60
```

Connecting Ideas

In the example on page 304, the quotient had only one digit. However, when there are enough tens to divide, the quotient will have two digits. Look at the example below.

$$42 \div 3 = ■$$

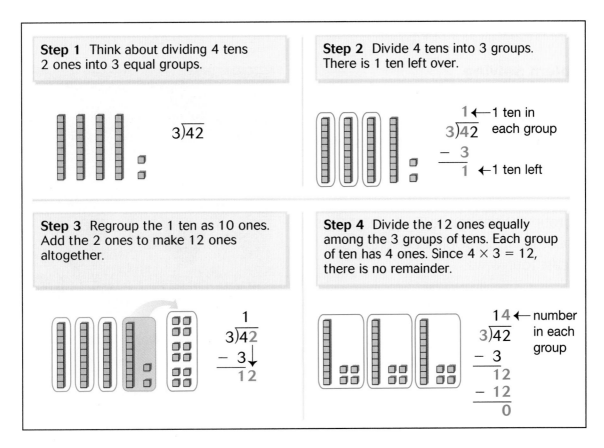

Step 1 Think about dividing 4 tens 2 ones into 3 equal groups.

$3)\overline{42}$

Step 2 Divide 4 tens into 3 groups. There is 1 ten left over.

```
      1  ←─ 1 ten in
   3)42      each group
   − 3
      1  ←─ 1 ten left
```

Step 3 Regroup the 1 ten as 10 ones. Add the 2 ones to make 12 ones altogether.

```
      1
   3)42
   − 3↓
     12
```

Step 4 Divide the 12 ones equally among the 3 groups of tens. Each group of ten has 4 ones. Since $4 \times 3 = 12$, there is no remainder.

```
     14  ←─ number
   3)42      in each
   − 3       group
     12
   − 12
      0
```

Think and Discuss Without dividing, can you tell if the quotient of $4)\overline{67}$ is greater than 9?

Try It Out

Divide by using base-ten blocks. Check by multiplying.

1. 5)48   **2.** 9)67   **3.** 4)36   **4.** 8)98   **5.** 2)72

6. Explain Tell the steps you followed to check the answer to Exercise 1.

Practice

Use base-ten blocks to divide. Check your answer.

7. 6)50   **8.** 2)19   **9.** 9)54   **10.** 5)33   **11.** 7)38

12. 4)91   **13.** 7)84   **14.** 6)64   **15.** 3)79   **16.** 5)93

17. 59 ÷ 8   **18.** 17 ÷ 3   **19.** 40 ÷ 7   **20.** 30 ÷ 4   **21.** 41 ÷ 6

22. 75 ÷ 5   **23.** 91 ÷ 7   **24.** 58 ÷ 2   **25.** 92 ÷ 6   **26.** 88 ÷ 3

27. 59 ÷ 4   **28.** 52 ÷ 7   **29.** 87 ÷ 6   **30.** 93 ÷ 4   **31.** 48 ÷ 7

Problem Solving

32. A choreographer tried out a dance routine using 65 dancers. She had them dance in 5 equal groups. How many dancers were in each group?

33. You Decide How could you group 60 dancers equally in groups of at least 3 people? Describe at least four ways.

34. A dance number in a movie musical used 36 people in red costumes and 5 people in white costumes. How many dancers were in the dance number?

35. One dance routine lasts 11 minutes. At one show, the routine finished at 2:06 P.M. What time did the routine begin?

▲ Fine Arts Connection
The Cleveland Ballet Dancing Wheels includes dancers with disabilities and those without.

36. The Dance Theatre of Harlem started in 1968. How many years ago was that? In what year did it celebrate its 25th anniversary?

37. Analyze One week the ballet sold out all 750 seats for every performance. The dancers performed once on Monday, Wednesday, and Friday, and twice on Saturday. How many people saw the show?

▲ Fine Arts Connection
Arthur Mitchell was the first African American male to dance with a major ballet company. In 1968 he founded the Dance Theatre of Harlem, the first black classical dance company.

Review and Remember

Find each answer.

38. 54 × 58

39. 1,289 − 64

40. 250 + 137

41. 42 ÷ 7

42. 731 + 182

43. 700 ÷ 10

44. 5,426 − 978

45. 2,420 × 6

46. 9)56

47. 219 + 507

48. 2,342 × 5

49. 436 − 387

Time for Technology

Using a Calculator

Check It

This is how you can use a calculator to check a division exercise like the one to the right.

14 R1
2)29

Press: 1 4 × 2 =   Display: 28

Multiply the quotient and the divisor.

Press: + 1 =   Display: 29

Add the remainder.

Use a calculator to check. Is the answer correct?

1. 6)72 → 12

2. 7)85 → 12 R3

3. 3)59 → 19 R2

4. 9)87 → 8 R4

5. 7)79 → 11 R2

Cool Ice!

Now you can divide without base-ten blocks.

Learning About It

During an ice show, skaters form 3 circles. Each circle has the same number of skaters. If there are 72 skaters, how many skaters are in each circle?

$$72 \div 3 = n$$

Divide 72 skaters into 3 equal groups.

Step 1 There are enough tens to divide into 3 groups. So, place the first digit of the quotient over the 7. $3\overline{)72}$	**Step 2** Divide the tens. Then multiply to find how many tens you used. $\begin{array}{r} 2 \\ 3\overline{)72} \\ -\ 6 \end{array}$ ← 2 tens × 3

Step 3 Subtract. Compare the difference to the divisor. The difference must be less than the divisor. $\begin{array}{r} 2 \\ 3\overline{)72} \\ -\ 6 \\ \hline 1 \end{array}$ ← 1 < 3	**Step 4** Bring down the ones. Divide. Then multiply to find how many ones you used. $\begin{array}{r} 24 \\ 3\overline{)72} \\ -\ 6\downarrow \\ \hline 12 \\ -\ 12 \end{array}$ ← 4 ones × 3 = 12	**Step 5** Subtract. The remainder is 0. $\begin{array}{r} 24 \\ 3\overline{)72} \\ -\ 6 \\ \hline 12 \\ -\ 12 \\ \hline 0 \end{array}$

There are 24 skaters in each circle.

Think and Discuss Look back at Step 3. What should you do if the difference is not less than the divisor?

Try It Out

Divide.

1. 6)82 **2.** 2)59 **3.** 9)78

4. 5)90 **5.** 4)39 **6.** 7)91

7. 8)82 **8.** 7)88 **9.** 6)49

Practice

Divide. Check by multiplying.

10. 3)72 **11.** 5)48 **12.** 2)74 **13.** 4)69 **14.** 8)51

15. 8)92 **16.** 7)59 **17.** 9)93 **18.** 5)77 **19.** 6)51

20. 72 ÷ 6 **21.** 37 ÷ 4 **22.** 83 ÷ 7 **23.** 29 ÷ 3 **24.** 81 ÷ 6

Problem Solving

25. How many skaters will be in each group if 85 skaters are placed in 5 equal groups?

26. In one routine, the skaters form 6 lines of 14 each. How many skaters are there in all?

27. **Analyze** If each car holds 4 students, how many cars will be needed to take 93 students to the ice show? Explain your reasoning.

28. **What If?** Suppose the 93 students want to sit together. How many rows of 10 seats would they need? Explain why your answer is reasonable.

Review and Remember

Choose a Method Solve, using paper and pencil or mental math. Tell why you chose the method you did.

29. 240 ÷ 6 **30.** 3,074 × 6 **31.** 6,530 − 430 **32.** 5)22

33. 734 − 127 **34.** 541 + 735 **35.** 621 + 355 **36.** 65 ÷ 7

For Extra Practice, see Set C, page 330.

✓ Checkpoint

Understanding Dividing by One-Digit Numbers

Using Algebra Use basic facts and patterns to divide.
(pages 298–299)

1. $18 \div 3$
2. $21 \div 7$
3. $30 \div 6$
4. $45 \div 9$

5. $80 \div 4$
6. $90 \div 3$
7. $350 \div 7$
8. $200 \div 5$

9. $640 \div 8$
10. $1,800 \div 6$
11. $4,500 \div 5$
12. $1,200 \div 2$

13. $7,200 \div 9$
14. $4,200 \div 6$
15. $4,000 \div 8$
16. $540 \div 9$

17. $1,800 \div 2$
18. $6,300 \div 7$
19. $6,400 \div 8$
20. $49,000 \div 7$

Divide. Use base-ten blocks if you wish. Check by multiplying.
(pages 304–307)

21. $5\overline{)37}$
22. $8\overline{)93}$
23. $2\overline{)71}$
24. $9\overline{)58}$

25. $4\overline{)76}$
26. $3\overline{)57}$
27. $5\overline{)70}$
28. $4\overline{)63}$

29. $3\overline{)41}$
30. $8\overline{)67}$
31. $64 \div 3$
32. $81 \div 7$

33. $84 \div 6$
34. $97 \div 4$
35. $73 \div 8$
36. $55 \div 9$

37. $45 \div 2$
38. $68 \div 3$
39. $78 \div 5$
40. $76 \div 6$

41. $38 \div 3$
42. $59 \div 6$
43. $60 \div 6$
44. $94 \div 3$

Divide. Check by multiplying. (pages 308–309)

45. $28 \div 5$
46. $87 \div 3$
47. $33 \div 4$
48. $89 \div 8$

49. $6\overline{)47}$
50. $8\overline{)58}$
51. $7\overline{)84}$
52. $3\overline{)65}$

Mixed Practice
Divide. Check by multiplying.

53. $30 \div 3$
54. $4\overline{)36}$
55. $82 \div 9$
56. $64 \div 4$
57. $71 \div 6$

58. $9\overline{)84}$
59. $8\overline{)59}$
60. $68 \div 4$
61. $3\overline{)97}$
62. $80 \div 8$

63. $700 \div 7$
64. $5\overline{)72}$
65. $4\overline{)39}$
66. $9\overline{)44}$
67. $7\overline{)83}$

Problem Solving

68. You can record 4 movies on a long-playing videotape. How many tapes will you need to record 58 movies? Explain.

69. A small theater holds 75 people. Every ticket is sold out for 3 performances at the theater. How much money is collected if tickets cost $30 each?

70. Analyze A band with five musicians earns $800 one weekend. The bandleader earns $300. How much do each of the other musicians earn if the remaining money is split equally?

What do you think?

What is the pattern in the quotient when 6, 60, 600, and 6,000 are each divided by 3?

Journal Idea

Write a problem in which 64 ÷ 4 represents "fair shares." Make a drawing to illustrate your problem.

Critical Thinking Corner

Logical Thinking

Finding a Number

In 1990, Miranda had more than one thousand photos. She divided the photos in 3 equal groups and put them into 3 boxes.

During the next 3 years, Miranda collected another 216 photos. She added these to the photos in one of the boxes. Then she took all the photos out of this box and put them into an album.

She put 8 photos on a page and filled 77 album pages. How many photos did Miranda have in 1990?

For Kids, by Kids

You can use compatible numbers to estimate quotients.

Learning About It

Suppose *The Kidsongs Television Show* has 331 minutes of videos to share equally among 8 shows. About how many minutes of videos will each show have?

▼ **Kid Connection**
Twelve children, ages 8 to 12, produce and direct *The Kidsongs Television Show*. Their motto is "Made for kids, by kids, and starring kids."

Estimate: **331 ÷ 8 =** ■

One way to estimate is to use **compatible numbers**. Compatible numbers are numbers that are easy to divide mentally.

Word Bank

compatible numbers

Change the dividend to the nearest number that can be divided evenly by 8. Use basic facts to help you.

Think: 32 ÷ 8 = 4   8)331 ⟶ 8)320 (40)

Change 331 to 320, because 320 and 8 are compatible numbers and 320 is close to 331.

Each show will have about 40 minutes of videos.

Think and Discuss How can you tell if your estimate is greater than or less than the exact quotient?

Try It Out

Rewrite each exercise, using compatible numbers.

1. 6)23   **2.** 9)55   **3.** 3)281   **4.** 5)389   **5.** 7)293

Practice

Estimate each quotient. Tell the numbers you used.

6. $5\overline{)37}$ **7.** $9\overline{)53}$ **8.** $6\overline{)49}$ **9.** $2\overline{)17}$ **10.** $4\overline{)31}$

11. $7\overline{)41}$ **12.** $3\overline{)23}$ **13.** $5\overline{)44}$ **14.** $8\overline{)46}$ **15.** $7\overline{)58}$

16. $2\overline{)119}$ **17.** $5\overline{)299}$ **18.** $8\overline{)636}$ **19.** $3\overline{)119}$ **20.** $9\overline{)718}$

21. $8\overline{)395}$ **22.** $9\overline{)809}$ **23.** $7\overline{)361}$ **24.** $4\overline{)370}$ **25.** $7\overline{)423}$

26. $7\overline{)634}$ **27.** $4\overline{)198}$ **28.** $3\overline{)178}$ **29.** $6\overline{)532}$ **30.** $6\overline{)487}$

31. $6\overline{)358}$ **32.** $9\overline{)452}$ **33.** $7\overline{)495}$ **34.** $6\overline{)238}$ **35.** $5\overline{)243}$

Problem Solving

Use this bar graph to estimate the number of hours per month that each type of program is viewed.

36. News   **37.** Movies

38. Sports   **39.** Comedies

40. Nature   **41.** Cartoons

42. Predict If a survey for a year was taken, which type of program do you think would be watched the most? the least? Explain your reasoning.

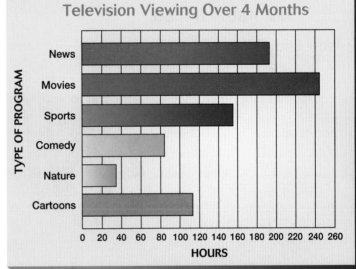

Television Viewing Over 4 Months

43. Create Your Own Write a problem using the data in the graph. Ask a classmate to solve it.

INTERNET ACTIVITY
www.sbgmath.com

Review and Remember

Find each answer.

44. $1{,}074 - 296$ **45.** 7×40

46. $19 + 389$ **47.** $4\overline{)36}$

48. $81 \div 9$ **49.** 182×5

▲ **Science Connection** The tape inside a videocassette is made of a plastic that is slightly magnetic. Placing a strong magnet next to the tape can destroy the stored recording.

Keep That Beat!

Now you can divide greater numbers.

Learning About It

Each of the 6 bands at the music festival sold the same number of tickets. Altogether they sold 474 tickets. How many tickets did each band sell?

$$474 \div 6 = \blacksquare$$

Estimate first: Use compatible numbers.

Think: $480 \div 6 = 80$

Now find the exact answer.

Step 1 There are not enough hundreds to divide into 6 groups. So regroup 4 hundreds 7 tens as 47 tens.	**Step 2** Divide the tens. Then multiply and subtract. Compare the difference to the divisor. The difference must be less than the divisor.	**Step 3** Bring down the ones. Divide. Then multiply and subtract. The remainder is 0.
$6\overline{)474}$	$\begin{array}{r} 7 \\ 6\overline{)474} \\ -42 \quad \leftarrow 7\ tens \times 6 \\ \hline 5 \quad \leftarrow 5 < 6 \end{array}$	$\begin{array}{r} 79 \\ 6\overline{)474} \\ -42\downarrow \\ \hline 54 \\ -54 \quad \leftarrow 9\ ones \times 6 \\ \hline 0 \end{array}$

Each band sold 79 tickets. Compare the answer with the estimate. Is the answer reasonable?

More Examples

A.
```
      132 R2
  6)794
  − 6
    19
  − 18
    14
  − 12
     2
```

B.
```
       74
  8)592
  − 56
    32
  − 32
     0
```

C.
```
      47 R5
  7)334
  − 28
    54
  − 49
     5
```

Think and Discuss Without dividing, how can you tell that 600 ÷ 5 is not 15 R6?

Try It Out

Estimate first. Then find the exact answer. Use your estimate to check that your answer is reasonable.

1. 7)702   **2.** 4)187   **3.** 5)374   **4.** 6)184   **5.** 9)471

6. 3)275   **7.** 6)823   **8.** 7)385   **9.** 4)576   **10.** 8)678

11. 2)149   **12.** 9)486   **13.** 6)720   **14.** 8)373   **15.** 7)378

Practice

Using Mental Math Without finding the quotient, tell how many digits each quotient would have.

16. 2)507   **17.** 7)483   **18.** 4)31   **19.** 6)73

Estimate first. Then divide. Check by multiplying.

20. 7)816   **21.** 3)551   **22.** 2)715   **23.** 3)779

24. 5)733   **25.** 4)607   **26.** 8)154   **27.** 6)288

28. 5)825   **29.** 6)914   **30.** 7)784   **31.** 9)992

32. 367 ÷ 9   **33.** 295 ÷ 7   **34.** 291 ÷ 4   **35.** 468 ÷ 8

36. 725 ÷ 4   **37.** 292 ÷ 6   **38.** 352 ÷ 9   **39.** 562 ÷ 6

Follow the rule.

Rule: Divide by 3

Input	Output
40. 123	▨
41. 204	▨
42. 381	▨

Rule: Divide by 6

Input	Output
43. 216	▨
44. 84	▨
45. 672	▨

Rule: Divide by 9

Input	Output
46. 54	▨
47. 270	▨
48. 621	▨

Rule: Divide by 5

Input	Output
49. 125	▨
50. 250	▨
51. 500	▨

Rule: Divide by 8

Input	Output
52. 200	▨
53. 144	▨
54. 648	▨

Rule: Divide by 7

Input	Output
55. 161	▨
56. 294	▨
57. 581	▨

58. Using Estimation The estimated quotient is 50. What could the actual division example be? Explain your reasoning.

59. Using Mental Math Tell how you know that the actual quotient of $371 \div 7$ is greater or less than 50. Explain your reasoning.

Problem Solving

60. A rap group with 5 members needs new instruments. The cost will be $875. If the band members share the cost equally, how much will each person pay?

61. A jazz band got a job playing for a party. There were 38 tables with 8 people sitting at each table. Estimate the number of people at the party.

62. What If? Look back at Problem 61. Suppose each table seats 10 people. How many more people can attend?

Fine Arts Connection ➤
Stomp, a musical and tap-dance group from England, uses brooms and trash cans to make musical sounds and entertain audiences.

Social Studies Connection Mariachi music began in Mexico. It was the music played during weddings. ➤

63. **Using Estimation** A mariachi musician keeps music in 4 notebooks. There is music for 330 songs. Estimate the number of songs in each notebook.

64. **Analyze** Phil started a mariachi band. He gets half of the money for each job. The other two band members divide the rest of the money equally. How should the band divide $944? Explain how you find the answer.

65. At the music festival, Daria spent $14 for food, $4.50 for a program, and $4 each for three maracas. If she had $3.75 left, how much money did she start with? Explain the strategy you used.

66. Juan visited a music festival 24 miles from his home. He drove to and from the festival 3 days in a row. How many miles did he drive altogether those three days?

Review and Remember

Estimate, then find each answer. Check that your answer is reasonable.

67.	68.	69.	70.	71.
376	8,974	3,987	1,027	8,643
× 44	+ 2,097	− 2,896	× 4	+ 709

Money $ense

That's the Ticket!
Use the concert poster to solve.

1. Suppose you plan to go to 7 concerts. How much do you save by buying a book of tickets rather than buying each ticket separately?

2. Suppose you plan to see only 5 concerts. How should you pay to get the best deal? Explain your reasoning.

Spring Concert Series
Ticket Prices
One Ticket - $5
Book of Tickets - $24
(good for 8 concerts)

My Favorite Stars

You can use place value to understand when to use zeros in the quotient.

Learning About It

The Movie Fan Club has collected 619 pictures of its favorite stars. If 6 pictures fit on each page of the club's photo album, how many pages of the album are filled?

Estimate first: **619 ÷ 6 = ▨**
                  600 ÷ 6 = 100

Then divide to find the exact quotient.

 THERE'S ALWAYS A WAY!

○ **One way** to divide is to use paper and pencil.

Step 1 There are enough hundreds to divide into 6 groups. Divide. Then multiply and subtract. Compare.	**Step 2** Bring down the tens. There are not enough tens to divide into 6 groups. Write a 0 in the quotient.	**Step 3** Bring down the ones. Divide. Multiply and subtract. Write the remainder.

$$
\begin{array}{r}
1 \\
6\overline{)619} \\
-\,6 \\
\hline
0
\end{array}
$$
←—1 hundred × 6
←—0 < 6

$$
\begin{array}{r}
10 \\
6\overline{)619} \\
-\,6 \\
\hline
01
\end{array}
$$

> 1 ten cannot be divided into 6 groups.

$$
\begin{array}{r}
103 \;\text{R1} \\
6\overline{)619} \\
-\,6 \\
\hline
019 \\
-\,18 \\
\hline
1
\end{array}
$$
←— 3 ones × 6
←— remainder

○ **Another way** to divide is to use a calculator. Some calculators display a quotient and remainder.

Press: (6) (1) (9) (INT÷) (6) (=)   Display: [*103* *1*]
                                                                Q   R

There are 103 filled pages and 1 picture left over.

Compare the answer with the estimate. Is the answer reasonable?

Think and Discuss A student divided 713 by 7 and got 11 R6. Use estimation to explain why this quotient must be wrong.

Try It Out

Estimate. Then divide and check by multiplying.

1. 8)870   **2.** 2)416   **3.** 7)842   **4.** 4)824   **5.** 9)902

Practice

Divide. Check by multiplying.

6. 5)535   **7.** 7)760   **8.** 2)215   **9.** 9)997   **10.** 4)427

11. 6)639   **12.** 3)917   **13.** 8)880   **14.** 6)614   **15.** 8)852

16. 8)859   **17.** 3)618   **18.** 7)742   **19.** 5)548   **20.** 5)330

21. 6)243   **22.** 4)821   **23.** 9)728   **24.** 2)406   **25.** 3)216

26. 480 ÷ 7   **27.** 908 ÷ 6   **28.** 855 ÷ 5   **29.** 715 ÷ 3

30. Using Mental Math Tell how you can use mental math to divide 183 by 3.

Problem Solving

31. A child star signed 424 autographs on pictures in four hours. If she signed the same number each hour, how many did she sign in one hour?

32. Create Your Own Write a problem that you solve by dividing. The answer must be 21.

▲ Fine Arts Connection Director Ron Howard began his career as a child actor at the age of four. He starred in television commercials, situation comedies, and movies.

Review and Remember

Choose a Method Use paper and pencil, mental math, or a calculator to solve. Tell the method you chose and why you chose it.

33. 56 ÷ 7   **34.** 1,468 × 88   **35.** 180 + 4,360   **36.** 3)41   **37.** 702 − 84

Problem Solving
Write a Number Sentence

*Sometimes you can solve a problem
by writing a number sentence.*

Ha Si Phu spends 5 hours 20 minutes painting 4 water puppets. He spends the same amount of time painting each puppet. How many minutes does he spend painting one puppet?

UNDERSTAND

What do you need to find?

You need to find the number of minutes it takes Ha Si Phu to paint one puppet.

PLAN

How can you solve the problem?

First **write a number sentence** to find the total number of minutes Ha Si Phu spends painting the puppets. Then write another number sentence to find how many minutes it takes him to paint one puppet.

▲ **Social Studies Connection**
Water puppetry was created by farmers in the flooded rice fields of Vietnam. The puppets are usually made out of wood.

SOLVE

First change 5 hours 20 minutes to minutes.

> 5 × 60 minutes = 300 minutes
> 300 minutes + 20 minutes = 320 minutes

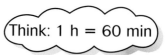

Think: 1 h = 60 min

Then divide the total number of minutes by the number of puppets painted.

> 320 ÷ 4 = 80

It takes Ha Si Phu 80 minutes to paint 1 puppet.

LOOK BACK

What is another way you can write the answer?

Using the Strategy

Write a number sentence to help you solve each problem. Show your work.

▲ Water puppets like these are often 2–3 feet tall. Water acts as a stage and the puppets float on the surface. They are controlled by a puppeteer who stands in the water and uses underwater wires and poles.

1 A water puppet theater group is made up of 12 musicians and 14 puppeteers. There are also half as many assistants as musicians. How many people work in the theater group?

2 Tickets for a water puppet show cost $15 for adults and $8 for children. How much do tickets cost for 2 adults and 3 children?

3 One puppet show lasts 75 minutes, including a 10-minute intermission. There are 5 scenes in the show and each scene lasts the same length of time. How long is each scene?

Mixed Strategy Review

Try these or other strategies to solve each problem. Tell which strategy you used.

THERE'S ALWAYS A WAY!

Problem Solving Strategies

- Guess and Check
- Use Logical Reasoning
- Draw a Picture
- Find a Pattern
- Work Backwards
- Act It Out

4 A puppeteer wants you to guess the order in which he uses 4 puppets. The lion goes right after the cat. The bird goes just before the turtle. The lion is not last. What is the order of the puppets?

5 A puppet theater put on 2 shows each day. One day 26 people in all went to the shows. If 4 more people went to the second show than to the first show, how many people went to each show?

6 Lin is making a bird puppet. He glues feathers on in this order: red, blue, yellow, green, red, blue, yellow, green, and so on. He stops after 18 feathers are on. How many yellow feathers are on the puppet?

7 Theater helpers are arranging 14 mats for an audience of children to sit on. How could they arrange the mats in rows so that each row has one more mat than the row in front of it?

Better Than Average

Paper squares can help you understand the idea of average.

Learning About It

An **average** or **mean** is a way to describe a group of numbers.

Step 1 Work with a partner. Use different-colored squares to model the numbers 18, 14, 20, and 12.

What You Need

For each pair:
  small paper squares
    18 red   14 blue
    20 yellow   12 orange

• Place all the squares of the same color in the same row.

• How many rows do you have?

Step 2 To find the average number of squares, you must have the same number of squares in each row.

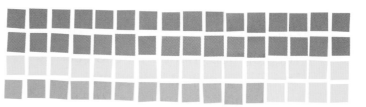

• Move squares from one row to another until the number of squares in each row is the same.

• How many squares are in each row now? How many squares are there in all?

16 is the average of 18, 14, 20, and 12.

Step 3 Can you think of another way to find the average number of squares?

- First, gather all the squares into one pile. Why does this remind you of addition?

- Then put the squares into 4 equal rows by placing 1 square in each row until you use all your squares. Why does this remind you of division?

- What is the average number of squares?

Think and Discuss Describe a different way to find the average of a group of numbers.

Practice

Find the mean of each set of numbers. Use any method you like. Show your work.

1. 5, 7, 4, 9, 5

2. 8, 6, 7, 2, 5, 8

3. 5, 2, 4, 2, 4, 3, 3, 1

4. 7, 6, 10, 8, 9

5. 12, 15, 11, 10

6. 11, 6, 7, 9, 2

7. 9, 11, 6, 15, 14

8. 13, 13, 18, 16

9. 3, 10, 13, 18, 6

Find the missing number in each set. Use paper squares to help you.

Mean = 4

Mean = 5

Mean = 6

10. 8, 4, 2, ▨

12. 4, 5, 8, ▨

14. 5, 7, 3, 8, 5, ▨

11. 4, 7, 1, ▨

13. 11, 1, 3, 7, ▨

15. 10, 8, 6, 4, 2, ▨

16. Explain Can the average or mean of a list of numbers be greater than the greatest number in the list?

Hint Look back at Step 2.

Practice Makes Perfect

To find an average, first add and then divide.

Learning About It

A musician has 6 weeks to practice for a concert. She practices 9, 12, 15, 19, 22, and 25 hours a week over the 6 weeks. What is the average number of hours per week that she practices?

MUSIC
Week 1: 9 hours
Week 2: 12 hours
Week 3: 15 hours

JOURNAL
Week 4: 19 hours
Week 5: 22 hours
Week 6: 25 hours

THERE'S ALWAYS A WAY!

● **One way** to find the average is to use paper and pencil.

Step 1 Add the numbers in the list.	**Step 2** Divide the sum by the number of addends.
9 12 15 19 22 + 25 ————— 102	$$\begin{array}{r} 17 \\ 6\overline{)102} \\ -\ 6 \\ \hline 42 \\ -\ 42 \\ \hline 0 \end{array}$$

● **Another way** to find the average is to use your calculator.

Press: ⑨ ⊕ ① ② ⊕ ① ⑤ ⊕ ① ⑨ ⊕
② ② ⊕ ② ⑤ ⊜ Display: 102

Press: ⊘ ⑥ ⊜ Display: 17

She practices an average of 17 hours per week.

Think and Discuss What is the average or mean of 36, 36, and 36? What do you notice?

◀ **Kid Connection** Christine Kwak, who has performed at
Carnegie Hall in New York City, practices violin 2 hours a day.

INTERNET ACTIVITY
www.sbgmath.com

Try It Out

Find the average time per practice session.
Copy and complete this chart.

	Practice Sessions in Minutes	Total Minutes	Number of Sessions	Average Time per Session
1.	6, 11, 13			
2.	4, 7, 7			
3.	18, 21, 27			
4.	3, 4, 5, 8			

Practice

Find each mean.

5. 4, 5, 1, 3, 2   **6.** 9, 15, 12   **7.** 21, 22, 15, 14, 18

8. 8, 5, 7, 8   **9.** 12, 21, 32, 47   **10.** 13, 31, 27, 18, 56

11. 104, 98, 257   **12.** 8, 6, 4, 6, 5 7, 6   **13.** 4, 6, 3, 4, 3, 4, 5, 3

Problem Solving

14. This is how many minutes Tricia practiced the violin each day last week: 20, 45, 30, 35, 20, 25, 35. Find the average number of minutes she practiced per day.

15. This is how many minutes Darek practiced the drums each day last week: 35, 45, 40, 30, 35, 60, 37. How much time was this in hours and minutes?

16. **Journal Idea** Two groups of numbers have the same average. Are these groups of numbers the same? Explain your reasoning.

17. **Analyze** The mean of a group of 3 different numbers is 35. One of the numbers is 46. Another is 21. What could the other number be?

Review and Remember

Find each answer.

18. 84 + 107   **19.** 74 × 79   **20.** 8)‾103   **21.** 9,245 − 254   **22.** 476 ÷ 9

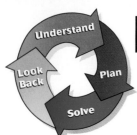

Problem Solving
Using Data

You can use what you know about mean, median, and mode to solve problems.

The bar graph shows how many hours the Carlton Children's Choir practiced each week. What is the average or mean number of hours practiced each week?

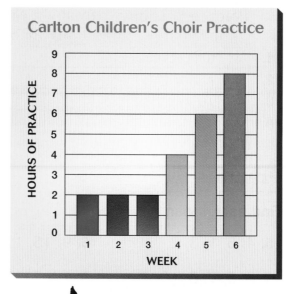

Carlton Children's Choir Practice

 UNDERSTAND

What do you need to find?

You need to find the average number of hours the choir practiced each week.

 PLAN

How can you solve the problem?

First find the number of hours each bar stands for. Next add the hours together to find the total number of hours practiced. Then divide that number by the number of weeks.

 SOLVE

Find the sum of the hours practiced.

$2 + 2 + 2 + 4 + 6 + 8 = 24$ hours

Then divide by the number of weeks of practice.

$24 \div 6 = 4$

The average or mean number of hours practiced each week is 4 hours.

 LOOK BACK

Why would it be easier to find the mode of the number of hours practiced than to find the mean?

Show What You Learned

Use the data in the graph below to solve
Problems 1–6.

Ages of Chorus Members	
9	🙂🙂🙂🙂
10	🙂🙂
11	🙂🙂
12	🙂

Each 🙂 stands for 1 member.

1 What is the average or mean age of the chorus members?

2 Suppose a new singer has joined the chorus, but the mean age of the chorus members has not changed. How old must the new singer be? Explain.

3 What is the mode of the ages of the chorus members?

4 What if two more 12-year-olds join the chorus? Will the mode change? Explain why or why not.

5 What is the median age of the chorus members?

6 If two 12-year-olds join the chorus, will the median change? If so, what will the new median be?

Use the table to solve Problems 7 and 8.

7 What is the average or mean length of a concert? What is the mode?

8 What if a Winter Concert is added that lasts 65 minutes? How would the new concert affect the mean? the mode?

9 **Create Your Own** Write a problem that can be solved using the table or graphs on these pages.

Concert Schedule	
Concert	Length in Minutes
Spring	50
Summer	60
Harvest	65
Holiday	65

Problem Solving

Practice What You Learned

Choose the correct letter for each answer.

1 Paul has 2 strips of colored paper that are each 3 in. wide and 9 in. long. He puts one strip on top of the other to make a figure like a plus sign. What shape is formed where the strips overlap?

A. a square 2 in. by 2 in.
B. a square 3 in. by 3 in.
C. a rectangle 2 in. by 3 in.
D. a rectangle 3 in. by 9 in.

Tip

Use what you know about the length and width of the strips to figure out the length and width of the area where they overlap.

2 In 1998, Saryu and her family took a trip to the Grand Canyon. Fifteen years earlier, Saryu's grandmother had visited the Grand Canyon. Five years before that, Saryu's aunt visited the Grand Canyon. Which shows the year that Saryu's grandmother visited the Grand Canyon?

A. 1998 − 15
B. 1998 − 20
C. 1998 − 30
D. 1998 + 15

Tip

Use one of these strategies to solve this problem.
- *Make a Table*
- *Draw a Picture*
- *Work Backwards*

3 T-shirts on sale are 2 for $15. How much would you pay for 8 T-shirts at this price?

A. $30
B. $60
C. $120
D. $150

Tip

Try making a table to help you solve this problem. Write down the prices of 2, 4, 6, and 8 T-shirts.

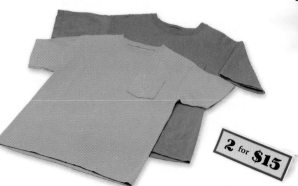

4 Philip bought a game for $29 and a stuffed toy for $12. He gave the clerk $50. **About** how much change should Philip get back from the clerk?

A. $5 **C.** $15

B. $10 **D.** $20

5 Rick is older than Mary but younger than Jerome. Sarah is younger than Rick. Which of the following is a reasonable conclusion?

A. Jerome is younger than Sarah.

B. Jerome is older than Sarah.

C. Sarah is older than Mary.

D. Mary is older than Sarah.

6 There are 74 students and 10 adults going on a school trip. Each bus holds 35 people. How many buses are needed?

A. 1 **C.** 3

B. 2 **D.** 4

7 In a swim race, Megan finished with a time of 45 seconds and Ana finished with a time of 48 seconds. Jen was the winner of the race. Which is a reasonable conclusion?

A. Jen's time was more than 48 seconds.

B. Jen's time was less than 45 seconds.

C. Megan finished last.

D. Ana finished before Megan.

8 Kate is buying 240 inches of ribbon for a project. Which number sentence shows how many feet of ribbon Kate needs? (Hint: There are 12 inches in 1 foot.)

A. 240 + 12 = ▨

B. 240 − 12 = ▨

C. 240 × 12 = ▨

D. 240 ÷ 12 = ▨

9 Tessa skated in an in-line skating race. It took her 19 minutes to skate the first half of the race and 32 minutes to skate the second half of the race. **About** how long did Tessa skate in all?

A. 60 min

B. 50 min

C. 30 min

D. 20 min

10 Look at the graph below. How many people like dogs better than birds?

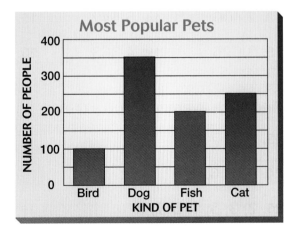

A. 100 **C.** 200

B. 150 **D.** 250

✔ Checkpoint

Dividing Numbers and Finding Averages

Vocabulary

Complete. Use the words from the Word Bank.

1. When data is arranged in order, the middle number is called the ___?___.

2. The ___?___ of 8, 12, 4, and 16 is 10.

3. The number that occurs most often in a set of data is called the ___?___.

4. Numbers that are easy to divide mentally are called ___?___.

Word Bank

average
compatible
numbers
median
mode

Skills and Concepts

Estimate each quotient. Tell the numbers you used. (pages 312–313)

5. 9)83   **6.** 6)39   **7.** 7)50   **8.** 5)29

Estimate first. Then divide. Check by multiplying. (pages 314–317)

9. 4)532   **10.** 6)366   **11.** 7)400   **12.** 9)852

Divide. Check by multiplying. (pages 318–319)

13. 2)406   **14.** 6)542   **15.** 3)911   **16.** 4)920   **17.** 7)562

18. 3)626   **19.** 4)363   **20.** 6)543   **21.** 2)614   **22.** 4)827

Find each average. (pages 324–325)

23. 3, 6, 7, 8

24. 9, 7, 6, 4, 9

25. 2, 3, 5, 1, 5, 2, 3

26. 11, 12, 16, 17

27. 384, 196, 287

What do you think?

How do you know where to place the first digit of the quotient? Use an example to explain.

Problem Solving

Use the graph to solve
Problems 28–30.

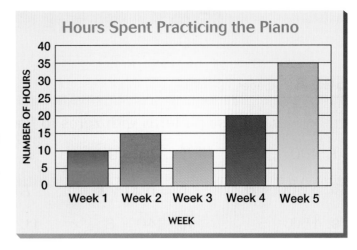

Hours Spent Practicing the Piano

28. **Describe** In general, did the number of hours per week increase or decrease?

29. Find the average number of hours per week that the pianist practiced.

30. **Analyze** If the pianist practices 5 more hours during Week 3, how will the average change?

Journal Idea

Decide on a price for a movie ticket. Estimate the number of times you could go to the movies if you had $75 to spend. Explain what you did to find your answer.

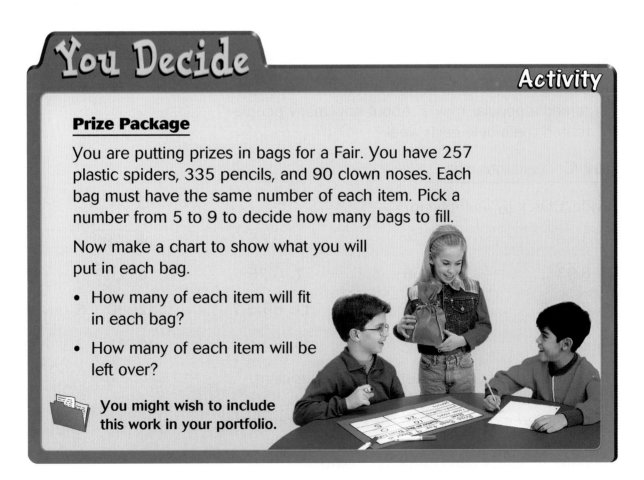

You Decide

Activity

Prize Package

You are putting prizes in bags for a Fair. You have 257 plastic spiders, 335 pencils, and 90 clown noses. Each bag must have the same number of each item. Pick a number from 5 to 9 to decide how many bags to fill.

Now make a chart to show what you will put in each bag.

- How many of each item will fit in each bag?

- How many of each item will be left over?

You might wish to include this work in your portfolio.

Extra Practice

Set A (pages 298–299)

Using Algebra **Use patterns with zeros to find each quotient.**

1. $400 \div 5$ 2. $270 \div 9$ 3. $350 \div 7$ 4. $180 \div 3$

5. $5,600 \div 8$ 6. $3,600 \div 6$ 7. $1,600 \div 2$ 8. $2,800 \div 4$

9. $150 \div 5$ 10. $240 \div 8$ 11. $3,000 \div 6$ 12. $4,900 \div 7$

13. For a dance number in a musical, costumes for 8 dancers cost $2,400. How much will the costumes cost if the number of dancers is increased to 10?

Set B (pages 304–307)

Divide. Check by multiplying.

1. $7\overline{)91}$ 2. $2\overline{)45}$ 3. $8\overline{)83}$ 4. $5\overline{)78}$

5. $3\overline{)48}$ 6. $6\overline{)77}$ 7. $4\overline{)62}$ 8. $9\overline{)60}$

9. $71 \div 3$ 10. $51 \div 6$ 11. $72 \div 4$ 12. $70 \div 5$

13. During a three-week period, a total of 78 people rented a popular movie. About how many people rented the movie each week?

Set C (pages 308–309)

Divide. Check by multiplying.

1. $3\overline{)68}$ 2. $5\overline{)74}$ 3. $9\overline{)85}$ 4. $7\overline{)96}$

5. $8\overline{)93}$ 6. $4\overline{)68}$ 7. $6\overline{)78}$ 8. $2\overline{)39}$

9. $86 \div 8$ 10. $39 \div 4$ 11. $66 \div 7$ 12. $80 \div 6$

13. $72 \div 9$ 14. $65 \div 5$ 15. $80 \div 7$ 16. $41 \div 2$

17. A small symphony orchestra has 87 musicians. There are 45 people in the string section. Each of the three other sections has an equal number of musicians. How many musicians are in the other three sections of the orchestra?

Extra Practice

Set D   (pages 312–313)

Estimate each quotient by using compatible numbers.

1. 238 ÷ 6   **2.** 212 ÷ 3   **3.** 254 ÷ 5   **4.** 416 ÷ 7

5. 159 ÷ 2   **6.** 638 ÷ 8   **7.** 239 ÷ 4   **8.** 808 ÷ 9

9. 627 ÷ 9   **10.** 359 ÷ 4   **11.** 361 ÷ 6   **12.** 317 ÷ 8

13. 152 ÷ 3   **14.** 277 ÷ 7   **15.** 397 ÷ 2   **16.** 396 ÷ 5

17. Tomo estimates that 20 people will be able to buy tickets to a movie every minute. If there are 156 people waiting, about how long will it take for them all to buy tickets?

18. A set of 8 CDs has a collection of 150 songs. Estimate the number of songs on each CD. Write a division sentence to show your estimate.

Set E   (pages 314–317)

Estimate first. Then divide. Check by multiplying.

1. 3)193   **2.** 8)914   **3.** 5)745   **4.** 9)604

5. 4)573   **6.** 7)244   **7.** 2)473   **8.** 6)516

9. 734 ÷ 6   **10.** 319 ÷ 2   **11.** 943 ÷ 7   **12.** 388 ÷ 4

13. 482 ÷ 5   **14.** 675 ÷ 9   **15.** 739 ÷ 3   **16.** 516 ÷ 8

17. 142 ÷ 7   **18.** 375 ÷ 4   **19.** 674 ÷ 3   **20.** 586 ÷ 4

21. For a parade, 350 band members line up in rows of 6. How many rows of 6 are there? How many musicians are in the last row?

22. **Explain** A small theater has 58 rows, with 8 seats in each row. Can 500 people watch a play in this theater? Explain your answer.

Extra Practice

Set F   (pages 318–319)

Divide. Check by multiplying.

1. 5)546   **2.** 7)845   **3.** 3)619   **4.** 8)823

5. 9)927   **6.** 2)616   **7.** 6)723   **8.** 4)436

9. 763 ÷ 4   **10.** 940 ÷ 9   **11.** 813 ÷ 2   **12.** 638 ÷ 6

13. 730 ÷ 7   **14.** 925 ÷ 3   **15.** 851 ÷ 8   **16.** 854 ÷ 5

17. In one section of a video rental store, 690 videos are displayed on 7 shelves. There are 108 videos on each of the first 6 shelves and 42 videos on the seventh shelf. Use subtraction and division to show that there are 690 videos in all.

18. A movie theater sells 628 tickets for one show. There are 3 sections of seats in the theater, and the number of people in each section is about the same. Estimate the number of people in each section.

Set G   (pages 324–325)

Find each average.

1. 23, 46, 87   **2.** 8, 6, 7, 2, 5, 8   **3.** 12, 15, 10, 11

4. 10, 9, 16, 7, 13   **5.** 384, 476   **6.** 236, 75, 187, 134

7. 109, 132, 125   **8.** 7, 12, 13, 8, 6, 9, 8   **9.** 91, 122, 116, 97, 124

10. 3, 1, 5, 3, 4, 3, 2 **11.** 7, 5, 4, 4, 2, 2   **12.** 33, 35, 31, 36, 32, 31

13. 62, 71, 65, 74   **14.** 176, 204, 184   **15.** 8, 6, 6, 7, 6, 8, 7, 8

16. The ages of the musicians in a polka band are 36, 42, 25, 56, 73, 39, 64, 49. What is the average age of the musicians in the band?

17. Predict The mean age of a group of 6 dancers is 24. An 18-year-old dancer joins the group. Will the mean age of the group increase or decrease? Explain your answer.

Chapter Test

Estimate each quotient by using compatible numbers.

1. 6)537   **2.** 4)278   **3.** 7)491   **4.** 8)475

Estimate first. Then divide. Check by multiplying.

5. 5)450   **6.** 7)280   **7.** 3)1,800   **8.** 9)5,400

9. 6)91   **10.** 2)78   **11.** 4)83   **12.** 8)58

13. 3)72   **14.** 6)87   **15.** 8)926   **16.** 5)385

17. 7)417   **18.** 3)582   **19.** 9)941   **20.** 4)857

Find each average.

21. 15, 20, 25, 18, 22, 26   **22.** 143, 150, 142, 157

Solve.

23. Write a number sentence to show how you would arrange 68 dancers in 4 equal groups.

24. A group of students is going to an outdoor concert in 7 buses. About how many students will be on each bus if there are 240 students in the group?

25. During the last 6 months, Paul's family spent these amounts going to the movies: $84, $114, $97, $151, $124, $90. What is the average amount they spent on movies per month?

 Self-Check Look back at Exercises 21 and 22. Compare each average to the greatest number and the least number. Tell why your answers are reasonable.

Performance Assessment

Show What You Know About Division

1 Use the numbers 84, 256, 5, and 8 to write division examples. You can use base-ten blocks, pictures, numbers, or words to show your work.

What You Need

base-ten blocks

   a. Divide the greatest number by the least number.

   b. Divide the greater of the two middle numbers by the lesser middle number.

   c. Which quotient is greater?

Self-Check Use an estimate to check whether your answer is reasonable.

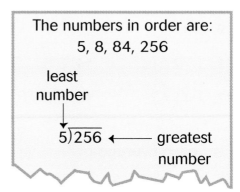

The numbers in order are:
5, 8, 84, 256

least number →

5)256 ← greatest number

2 Suppose a video store collected $41, $67, $45, and $27 in 4 hours.

   a. Use compatible numbers to estimate the average amount collected each hour. Tell the numbers you used.

   b. What was the average amount collected per hour?

   c. If it costs $3 to rent a video, about how many videos were rented each hour? Show how you solve the problem.

Self-Check Did you remember to add first and then divide when finding the average?

 For Your Portfolio

You might wish to include this work in your portfolio.

Extension

Rules for Divisibility

You can learn rules for dividing numbers by 2, 3, 5, and 10.

Step 1 Work with a partner to make one- and two-digit numbers by using these number cards.

Step 2 Write a list of the numbers you made. Then use your list to answer the questions below.

A number is **divisible** by another number when the remainder is zero.

- Which numbers are divisible by 2?

- Which numbers are divisible by 5? by 10?

- Which numbers are divisible by 3?

Step 3 Create rules for divisibility. Copy and complete this chart.

Rule	Example
1. A number is divisible by 2 if it ends in _____.	82, 64
2. A number is divisible by 5 if it ends in _____.	25, 80
3. A number is divisible by 10 if it ends in _____.	30, 60
4. A number is divisible by 3 if _____.	45

$4 + 5 = 9$
$9 ÷ 3 = 3$
So, 45 is divisible by 3.

Step 4 Add 3, 7, and 9 to your number cards. Show that your rules work with the new numbers you make.

What You Need

For each pair:
  number cards

Did You Know?

For a number to be divisible by 3, the sum of its digits must be divisible by 3.

Cumulative Review

★★★★★ **Preparing for Tests**

Choose the correct letter for each answer.

Number Concepts	**Operations**

Number Concepts

1. What is the value of the 3 in 4,321,078?

   A. 3 thousand
   B. 30 thousand
   C. 300 thousand
   D. 3 million

2. Which set of numbers is in order from *least* to *greatest*?

   A. 4,401 4,312 4,276 4,295
   B. 4,312 4,401 4,295 4,276
   C. 4,312 4,295 4,401 4,276
   D. 4,276 4,295 4,312 4,401

3. The models are shaded to show 2 equivalent fractions.

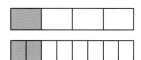

Which of the fractions below is equal to $\frac{1}{4}$?

   A. $\frac{2}{8}$ **C.** $\frac{2}{4}$

   B. $\frac{1}{3}$ **D.** $\frac{4}{1}$

4. What is 3,627 rounded to the nearest thousand?

   A. 2,000   **C.** 3,500
   B. 3,000   **D.** 4,000

Operations

5. Carmen has 19 free passes to a concert. If she keeps one for herself and divides the rest equally among three friends, how many will each friend have?

   A. 3   **C.** 8
   B. 6   **D.** 18

6. It's Peter's turn to bring in the fourth-grade snack. Peter has 23 other students in his class. How many graham crackers should Peter bring so that he and his classmates each get 4 crackers?

   A. 96   **C.** 200
   B. 108   **D.** 204

7. A benefit raffle raised $382. **About** how many tickets were sold if each ticket cost $5?

   A. 40   **C.** 80
   B. 60   **D.** 100

8. An ad says, "Buy 3 pencils, get 1 pencil free." If you decide to buy 12 pencils, how many will you get free?

   A. 3   **C.** 6
   B. 4   **D.** 12

Patterns, Relationships, and Algebraic Thinking	Geometry and Spatial Reasoning

9. Which number sentence completes the chart?

6 × 3 = 18
6 × 30 = 180
6 × 300 = 1,800
■ × ■ = ■

A. 3 × 300 = 900
B. 6 × 300 = 1,800
C. 6 × 3,000 = 18,000
D. 6 × 30,000 = 180,000

10. Which number line shows the graph of all whole numbers less than 6 **and** greater than 2?

A.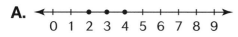
0 1 2 3 4 5 6 7 8 9

B.
0 1 2 3 4 5 6 7 8 9

C.
0 1 2 3 4 5 6 7 8 9

D.
0 1 2 3 4 5 6 7 8 9

11. If 28 divided by a number is 4, which number sentence could be used to find the number?

A. 4 × ■ = 28   **C.** 28 − ■ = 4
B. 28 + 4 = ■   **D.** 28 × 4 = ■

12. What is the missing number in the number pattern?

12, 24, 36, 48, ■, 72

A. 54   **C.** 66
B. 60   **D.** 68

13. Which space figure would you use to draw the plane figure in the box?

A.   **C.**

B.   **D.**

14. How many faces does a triangular prism have?

A. 4
B. 5
C. 6
D. 8

15. Which number has 2 lines of symmetry?

A. 8   **C.** 2

B. 3   **D.** 7

16. Which figure represents a pyramid?

A.   **C.**

B.   **D.**

9 Fractions

Chapter Theme: HOBBIES

Real Facts

Toys come in all shapes and sizes. Before they make a new toy, toymakers often use fractions to decide how long or wide to make a toy. The graph below shows the lengths of some toy animals.

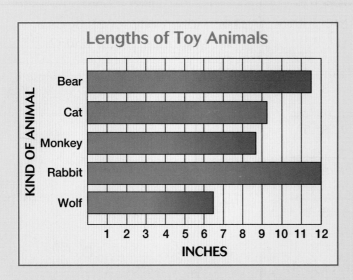

Lengths of Toy Animals

- Which toy animal is about half as long as the rabbit?

- To the nearest half-inch, about how long is the bear?

- How much longer is the rabbit than the bear?

Real People

Meet Mary Rodas. When she was 4 years old, she began helping a toy inventor decide which toys would be the most fun for kids. At the age of 13, she became vice president of the inventor's toy company!

Made in the Shade

You can use fractions to describe regions that are divided into equal parts.

Learning About It

Jocelyn and Spence decided to paint their treehouse floor four different colors. Which fraction names the part of the floor they have painted so far?

There are four equal parts, so the painted part is one fourth of the total region.

One fourth can be written as a fraction.

number of equal parts painted → $\dfrac{1}{4}$ ← **numerator**
total number of equal parts → ← **denominator**

Another Example

Write the fraction for the shaded region.

number of equal parts shaded → $\dfrac{3}{4}$
total number of equal parts →

Think and Discuss Can the fraction $\dfrac{2}{5}$ be used to describe the shaded parts of the drawing? Explain why or why not.

Try It Out

Write the fraction for the shaded parts of each region.

1.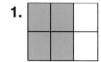

2.

3.

Draw a picture to show each fraction.

4. $\dfrac{1}{4}$ 5. $\dfrac{3}{5}$ 6. $\dfrac{2}{3}$ 7. $\dfrac{7}{8}$ 8. $\dfrac{1}{6}$ 9. $\dfrac{3}{9}$

Practice

Write the fraction for the red parts of each region.

10.

11.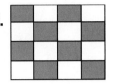

12.

13.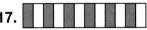

14.

15.

16.

17.

Draw a picture to show each fraction.

18. $\frac{2}{6}$ **19.** $\frac{1}{2}$ **20.** $\frac{2}{4}$ **21.** $\frac{3}{8}$ **22.** $\frac{1}{3}$ **23.** $\frac{1}{5}$

24. $\frac{6}{6}$ **25.** $\frac{2}{5}$ **26.** $\frac{5}{6}$ **27.** $\frac{3}{10}$ **28.** $\frac{7}{12}$ **29.** $\frac{1}{7}$

30. $\frac{2}{3}$ **31.** $\frac{3}{4}$ **32.** $\frac{8}{8}$ **33.** $\frac{4}{6}$ **34.** $\frac{5}{8}$ **35.** $\frac{7}{14}$

Problem Solving

36. Diane and her friend Carrie painted the floor of their treehouse as shown at the right. They wanted to paint $\frac{1}{2}$ of the floor green and $\frac{1}{2}$ white. Do you think their plan worked? Why or why not?

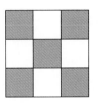

37. **Analyze** Four eighths of the circle at the right is shaded. Three sixths of the rectangle at the right is shaded. How are the figures alike? How are they different?

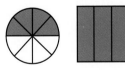

Review and Remember

Using Mental Math Is the answer more than, less than, or equal to 100? Explain your reasoning.

38. $808 \div 8$ **39.** 2×48 **40.** $739 - 692$ **41.** $25 + 25 + 26 + 27$

42. $39 + 60$ **43.** $450 \div 5$ **44.** 5×20 **45.** $563 - 472$

For Extra Practice, see Set A, page 380.

On Track

You can use fractions to describe parts of a set.

BUILD IT

| 2 flatcars | 3 boxcars | 1 engine |

Learning About It

Putting together a train set can be lots of fun. Susan's train has 2 flatcars, 3 boxcars, and 1 engine. What fraction of the train is made up of boxcars?

There are six parts in this train set and three of the parts are boxcars. Three out of six, or three sixths, can be written as a fraction.

number of boxcars ⟶ $\dfrac{3}{6}$ ⟵ numerator

total parts of train ⟶ ⟵ denominator

$\frac{3}{6}$ of the train is made up of boxcars.

More Examples

A. What fraction of the train is made up of flatcars?

number of flatcars ⟶ $\dfrac{2}{6}$

total parts of the train ⟶

$\frac{2}{6}$ of the train is flatcars.

B. What fraction of the train is the engine?

number of engines ⟶ $\dfrac{1}{6}$

total parts of the train ⟶

$\frac{1}{6}$ of the train is the engine.

C.

$\frac{3}{4}$ is shaded.

$\frac{1}{6}$ is shaded.

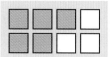

$\frac{5}{8}$ is shaded.

Connecting Ideas

Use what you know about fractions as parts of a set to find a fractional part of a number.

Suppose a train set has 20 cars, and $\frac{1}{4}$ of the cars are tanker cars. How many tanker cars are in the set?

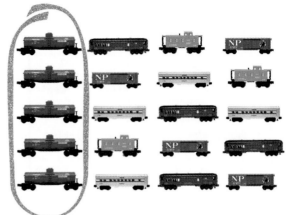

What is $\frac{1}{4}$ of 20?

Think of dividing 20 into 4 equal parts.

$$4\overline{)20} \;\; 5$$

5 of the cars are tanker cars.

Think and Discuss How do you know that three quarters of an hour and 45 minutes are the same?

Try It Out

Write the fractions that represent the following parts of this 12-piece train set.

1. tracks
2. blue and yellow cars
3. yellow cars
4. red car

5. engine
6. engine and red car
7. flatcars
8. blue cars

Write a number to complete each sentence.

9. To find $\frac{1}{2}$ of 18, divide 18 into ■ equal parts.

10. To find $\frac{1}{5}$ of 45, divide 45 into ■ equal parts.

Practice

11. What fraction of these train cars are brown? What fraction of these train cars are blue?

12. What fraction of these train accessories are tunnels? What fraction are signal bridges?

13. What fraction of the train tracks are curved? What fraction are straight?

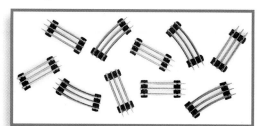

14. What fraction of the train accessories are trees? What fraction are lampposts?

Find the fractional part of each number.

15. $\frac{1}{8}$ of 48

16. $\frac{1}{3}$ of 15

17. $\frac{1}{5}$ of 30

18. $\frac{1}{2}$ of 14

19. $\frac{1}{4}$ of 16

20. $\frac{1}{10}$ of 100

21. $\frac{1}{8}$ of 32

22. $\frac{1}{4}$ of 100

Problem Solving

Use the table to the right for Problems 23–25.

23. Which fraction of the train accessories are stoplights? Which fraction are bridges, trestles, and tunnels altogether?

24. Which fraction would represent all the items in the set?

25. **Create Your Own** Use the data from the table to write your own problem. See if a classmate can solve it.

Train Set Accessories	
Number	**Accessories**
2	Trestles
2	Bridges
7	Trees
4	Stoplights
4	Warning lights
1	Train station
1	Tunnel

26. Analyze You put 24 apples in a basket. Half of the apples are red. Six of the apples are green. The rest are yellow. What fraction of the apples are yellow? Explain the strategy you used.

27. Explain You and a friend share 24 grapes. You eat $\frac{1}{4}$ and your friend eats $\frac{1}{2}$ of the grapes. How many grapes are left over? Explain your reasoning.

Review and Remember

Using Algebra Follow the rule to complete each table.

Rule: Subtract 109

	Input	Output
28.	708	■
29.	240	■
30.	157	■

Rule: Multiply by 9

	Input	Output
31.	309	■
32.	270	■
33.	195	■

Rule: Divide by 8

	Input	Output
34.	872	■
35.	560	■
36.	912	■

Find each answer.

37. $5,004 - 889$ **38.** 373×4 **39.** $4,379 + 7,637$ **40.** 8×354

41. $266 \div 7$ **42.** 26×492 **43.** $9,502 - 7,303$ **44.** $4,275 + 1,277$

Critical Thinking Corner

Visual Thinking

Fractured Fractions

Answer each question. Explain your reasoning.

Is the shaded part more or less than $\frac{1}{2}$?	Is the shaded part more or less than $\frac{1}{3}$?	Is the shaded part more or less than $\frac{1}{5}$?	Is the shaded part more or less than $\frac{1}{4}$?
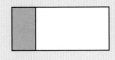			

Pieces and Parts

You can use fraction pieces to learn about equivalent fractions.

Learning About It

Work with a partner. Explore finding fractions that name the same amount. Fractions that name the same amount are called **equivalent fractions**.

> **Word Bank**
>
> **equivalent fractions**

Step 1 Collect fraction pieces labeled 1, $\frac{1}{2}$, and $\frac{1}{4}$.

- Place the 1 whole fraction strip on your desk.

- Place the $\frac{1}{2}$ fraction piece under the 1 whole strip.

- Place $\frac{1}{4}$ fraction pieces end to end under the $\frac{1}{2}$ fraction piece.

- How many $\frac{1}{4}$ fraction pieces fit exactly under the $\frac{1}{2}$ fraction piece? Does $\frac{1}{2} = \frac{2}{4}$?

What You Need

For each pair:
  fraction pieces

Step 2 Now find a fraction equivalent to $\frac{2}{3}$.

- Place two $\frac{1}{3}$ fraction pieces end to end to show $\frac{2}{3}$.

- Place $\frac{1}{6}$ fraction pieces end to end under the $\frac{2}{3}$ fraction pieces.

- Find a fraction equivalent to $\frac{2}{3}$.

Step 3 Use fraction pieces to decide if $\frac{2}{5}$ and $\frac{5}{10}$ are equivalent fractions. Tell why or why not.

Step 4 Use fraction pieces to find some other fractions that name the same amount as $\frac{1}{2}$. Compare each numerator and denominator. What patterns do you see in the fractions that are equivalent to $\frac{1}{2}$?

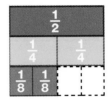

Step 5 Use fraction pieces to find equivalent fractions for 1 whole. What pattern do you notice?

Think and Discuss $\frac{1}{3}, \frac{2}{6}, \frac{3}{9}, \frac{4}{12}$ are equivalent fractions. Look at the numerators and denominators. What pattern do you see?

Practice

Use your fraction pieces to decide if the fractions are equivalent. Write *yes* or *no*.

1. $\frac{3}{4}, \frac{4}{5}$
2. $\frac{2}{8}, \frac{1}{4}$
3. $\frac{1}{3}, \frac{2}{5}$
4. $\frac{1}{4}, \frac{3}{12}$
5. $\frac{2}{6}, \frac{1}{3}$

6. $\frac{1}{2}, \frac{4}{8}$
7. $\frac{4}{6}, \frac{3}{4}$
8. $\frac{5}{6}, \frac{2}{3}$
9. $\frac{4}{12}, \frac{1}{3}$
10. $\frac{3}{8}, \frac{1}{4}$

11. $\frac{3}{3}, \frac{5}{6}$
12. $\frac{6}{8}, \frac{3}{4}$
13. $\frac{2}{8}, \frac{1}{2}$
14. $\frac{5}{8}, \frac{4}{6}$
15. $\frac{4}{5}, \frac{8}{10}$

Use your fraction pieces to write at least one equivalent fraction for each fraction. Write more than one if you can.

16. $\frac{3}{4}$
17. $\frac{2}{3}$
18. $\frac{3}{5}$
19. $\frac{1}{2}$
20. $\frac{1}{5}$

21. $\frac{1}{6}$
22. $\frac{3}{8}$
23. $\frac{1}{7}$
24. $\frac{3}{9}$
25. $\frac{4}{10}$

26. **Analyze** If the numerator of one fraction is 4 and the numerator of another fraction is 4, what else has to be true for the fractions to be equivalent?

27. **Journal Idea** Can you tell by looking at the denominators whether two fractions are equivalent? Explain.

Around the Blocks

Using Algebra

You can use fraction pieces or paper and pencil to find equivalent fractions.

Learning About It

You can build some amazing things with Legos!
Look at how some of the blocks are related.

Each black block is $\frac{1}{3}$ of the yellow block.

Each red block is $\frac{1}{6}$ of the yellow block.

Each blue block is $\frac{1}{12}$ of the yellow block.

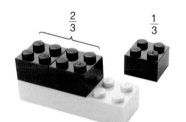

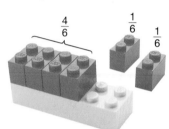

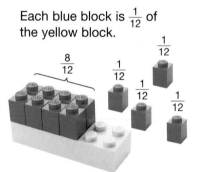

$$\frac{2}{3} = \frac{4}{6} = \frac{8}{12}$$

These fractions are equivalent fractions.
They name the same amount.

Write a fraction equivalent to $\frac{3}{4}$.

THERE'S ALWAYS A WAY!

● **One way** to find equivalent fractions is to use fraction pieces.

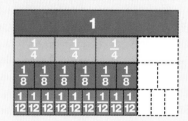

$$\frac{3}{4} = \frac{6}{8} \text{ or } \frac{3}{4} = \frac{9}{12}$$

● **Another way** is to use paper and pencil.

Multiply the numerator and denominator by the same number.

$$\overset{\times 2}{\frac{3}{4}} = \underset{\times 2}{\frac{6}{8}} \quad \text{or} \quad \overset{\times 3}{\frac{3}{4}} = \underset{\times 3}{\frac{9}{12}}$$

The fractions $\frac{6}{8}$ and $\frac{9}{12}$ are equivalent to $\frac{3}{4}$.

More Examples

Find each equivalent fraction.

A.

$\dfrac{3}{4} = \dfrac{\blacksquare}{8}$ > Think: $\overset{\times 2}{\dfrac{3}{4}} \underset{\times 2}{=} \dfrac{\blacksquare}{8}$ > $\dfrac{3}{4} = \dfrac{6}{8}$

B.

$\dfrac{1}{2} = \dfrac{\blacksquare}{12}$ > Think: $\overset{\times 6}{\dfrac{1}{2}} \underset{\times 6}{=} \dfrac{\blacksquare}{12}$ > $\dfrac{1}{2} = \dfrac{6}{12}$

Connecting Ideas

You can always use multiplication to find equivalent fractions. Sometimes you can also find equivalent fractions by dividing.

Use division to write a fraction that is equivalent to $\dfrac{12}{18}$.

$\dfrac{12}{18} = \dfrac{\blacksquare}{\blacksquare}$ > What number will divide evenly into the numerator <u>and</u> the denominator? > Think: $\overset{\div 2}{\dfrac{12}{18}} \underset{\div 2}{=} \dfrac{\blacksquare}{\blacksquare}$ > $\dfrac{12}{18} = \dfrac{6}{9}$

If you continue to divide until 1 is the only number that will divide the numerator <u>and</u> denominator evenly, you find the fraction in **simplest form**.

Write $\dfrac{12}{18}$ in simplest form.

$\dfrac{12}{18} = \dfrac{\blacksquare}{\blacksquare}$ > $\overset{\div 2}{\dfrac{12}{18}} \underset{\div 2}{=} \overset{\div 3}{\dfrac{6}{9}} \underset{\div 3}{=} \dfrac{2}{3}$ or $\overset{\div 6}{\dfrac{12}{18}} \underset{\div 6}{=} \dfrac{2}{3}$ > $\dfrac{12}{18} = \dfrac{2}{3}$

Another Example

Write $\dfrac{8}{16}$ in simplest form.

$\dfrac{8}{16} = \dfrac{\blacksquare}{\blacksquare}$ $\overset{\div 2}{\dfrac{8}{16}} \underset{\div 2}{=} \overset{\div 4}{\dfrac{4}{8}} \underset{\div 4}{=} \dfrac{1}{2}$ or $\overset{\div 8}{\dfrac{8}{16}} \underset{\div 8}{=} \dfrac{1}{2}$ $\dfrac{8}{16} = \dfrac{1}{2}$

Think and Discuss You are asked to write $\dfrac{5}{8}$ in its simplest form. What is your answer?

Try It Out

Write a pair of equivalent fractions for each picture.

1.

2.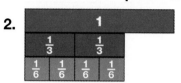

3.

Fill in the missing numbers. Then write the equivalent fraction.

4. $\dfrac{1 \times \blacksquare}{2 \times \blacksquare}$

5. $\dfrac{2 \times \blacksquare}{3 \times \blacksquare}$

6. $\dfrac{9 \div \blacksquare}{12 \div \blacksquare}$

7. $\dfrac{4 \div \blacksquare}{8 \div \blacksquare}$

8. $\dfrac{1 \times \blacksquare}{5 \times \blacksquare}$

9. $\dfrac{8 \div \blacksquare}{10 \div \blacksquare}$

10. $\dfrac{1 \times \blacksquare}{3 \times \blacksquare}$

11. $\dfrac{4 \times \blacksquare}{6 \times \blacksquare}$

12. $\dfrac{5 \div \blacksquare}{10 \div \blacksquare}$

13. $\dfrac{3 \div \blacksquare}{9 \div \blacksquare}$

Practice

Write a pair of equivalent fractions for each picture.

14.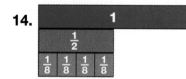

15.

16.

Use fraction pieces to write an equivalent fraction.

17. $\dfrac{1}{3}$
18. $\dfrac{6}{10}$
19. $\dfrac{4}{8}$
20. $\dfrac{3}{6}$
21. $\dfrac{1}{4}$
22. $\dfrac{2}{4}$

23. $\dfrac{1}{2}$
24. $\dfrac{4}{5}$
25. $\dfrac{6}{9}$
26. $\dfrac{1}{5}$
27. $\dfrac{4}{12}$
28. $\dfrac{3}{4}$

29. $\dfrac{1}{6}$
30. $\dfrac{2}{8}$
31. $\dfrac{3}{9}$
32. $\dfrac{5}{10}$
33. $\dfrac{6}{8}$
34. $\dfrac{8}{10}$

Write each fraction in simplest form.

35. $\dfrac{5}{10}$
36. $\dfrac{3}{9}$
37. $\dfrac{6}{9}$
38. $\dfrac{10}{12}$
39. $\dfrac{8}{12}$
40. $\dfrac{2}{8}$

41. $\dfrac{4}{8}$
42. $\dfrac{6}{12}$
43. $\dfrac{7}{8}$
44. $\dfrac{6}{8}$
45. $\dfrac{9}{12}$
46. $\dfrac{6}{10}$

47. $\dfrac{5}{15}$
48. $\dfrac{2}{6}$
49. $\dfrac{8}{16}$
50. $\dfrac{7}{21}$
51. $\dfrac{10}{20}$
52. $\dfrac{5}{25}$

53. **Explain** Do you think there are equivalent fractions for every fraction?

Problem Solving

54. Josh has 24 blocks. Three are red, seven are blue, and the rest are white. What fraction of his blocks are white? Write the fraction in simplest form.

55. **What If?** Suppose Josh has 30 blocks instead of 24. If he still has 3 red blocks and 7 blue blocks, what fraction of his blocks are now white?

56. Terry and Gail are each making the same kind of building from blocks. Terry's building is $\frac{1}{3}$ finished. Gail's building is $\frac{2}{5}$ finished. Is the same fraction of each building completed? Tell how you know.

57. **Explain** Jody used to have a set of 100 blocks. Now she has only 90. Fran used to have a set of 50 blocks. Now she has only 40. Is each of them missing the same fraction of their set? Explain.

Review and Remember

Use the table at the right for Exercises 58–59.

58. Choose a graph to display the data in the table. Then graph the data.

59. Explain why you chose the graph you did.

Number of Blocks Used	
Name	Number
Evan	250
Kathleen	175
Chan	350
Rose	100

Estimate first. Then find each answer.
Check that your answers are reasonable.

60. 68×7 **61.** $1,764 + 589$ **62.** $80 \div 7$ **63.** $8,002 - 3,986$

Critical Thinking Corner

Logical Thinking

What Comes Next?

Using Algebra Study the pattern and write what comes next. Explain your reasoning.

1. $\frac{1}{5}, \frac{2}{10}, \frac{3}{15}, \blacksquare$

2. $\frac{2}{3}, \frac{4}{6}, \frac{6}{9}, \blacksquare$

3. $\frac{8}{24}, \frac{6}{18}, \frac{4}{12}, \blacksquare$

4. $\frac{5}{10}, \frac{4}{8}, \frac{3}{6}, \blacksquare$

5. $\frac{1}{4}, \frac{3}{12}, \frac{5}{20}, \blacksquare$

6. $\frac{1}{2}, \frac{3}{6}, \frac{5}{10}, \blacksquare$

For Extra Practice, see Set C, page 380.

Developing Skills for Problem Solving

First read for understanding and then focus on whether an answer to a problem is reasonable.

READ FOR UNDERSTANDING

Julian is making a model hotel out of construction paper. His floor plan for the first floor is divided into 6 different sections. He colors the floor plan like the drawing below.

1 How many different sections is the floor plan divided into?

2 Which section uses the most space on the first floor?

3 Which sections use the same amount of space?

THINK AND DISCUSS

 MATH FOCUS

Reasonable Answers Whenever you solve a problem, you should check that your answer is reasonable. Look at the facts that are given. Then make sure your answer makes sense when compared to those facts.

Reread the paragraph at the top of the page. Look at the floor plan. How much of the first floor is the lobby?

4 Julian says that $\frac{1}{4}$ of the first floor will be the lobby. Is this reasonable?

5 Julian's friend says that $\frac{1}{2}$ of the first floor will be the lobby. Is this reasonable?

6 Look back at Problems 4 and 5. How did looking at the drawing help you decide if the answers were reasonable?

Show What You Learned

Answer each question. Give a reason for your choice.

Rich bought a pack of construction paper that had 16 sheets of paper in it. He used the paper to make model buildings. He used $\frac{8}{16}$ of the sheets to make a bank and $\frac{5}{16}$ of the sheets to make a store. He used the rest of the paper to make an office building.

1 How many sheets of paper did Rich use to make a bank?

a. 16 sheets

b. 8 sheets

c. 5 sheets

2 How many sheets of paper did Rich use to make the store?

a. 16 sheets

b. 8 sheets

c. 5 sheets

3 Explain Is it reasonable to say that most of the paper was used to make the office building? Why or why not?

4 Explain Is it reasonable to say that Rich used 15 sheets of paper to make the office building? Why or why not?

Carrie bought a package of 8 markers to help make a model city. She used $\frac{1}{4}$ of the markers and she gave another $\frac{1}{4}$ of them to a friend to use.

5 How many markers did Carrie and her friend use?

a. 1 marker

b. 2 markers

c. 4 markers

6 Which number sentence shows how many markers weren't used?

a. $8 - 4 = $ ▓

b. $8 + 4 = $ ▓

c. $8 - 8 = $ ▓

7 Explain Would it be reasonable to say that there are no markers left? Why or why not?

8 Explain Would it be reasonable to say that 7 of the markers weren't used? Why or why not?

Spice It Up

Fraction pieces can help you compare and order fractions.

Learning About It

Lisa and Jon used an authentic African recipe to make pumpkin soup for their school's International Food Fair. Does the recipe use more cilantro or salt?

You can use fraction pieces to compare the fractions $\frac{1}{2}$ and $\frac{1}{4}$.

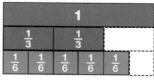

Pumpkin Soup

$4\frac{1}{2}$ oz black-eyed peas $\frac{3}{8}$ tsp black pepper

8 oz diced pumpkin $\frac{3}{4}$ tsp turmeric

2 green bananas $\frac{1}{2}$ tsp thyme

1 carrot $\frac{1}{2}$ tsp cilantro

1 green chili $\frac{1}{4}$ tsp salt

2 bay leaves

COOK IT

$\frac{1}{2}$ teaspoon cilantro ⟶

$\frac{1}{4}$ teaspoon salt ⟶

⋏ Fitness and Health Connection
Pumpkins and carrots have lots of vitamin A. Vitamin A is very important for normal growth of bones, skin, and teeth.

The fraction pieces show that the $\frac{1}{2}$ piece is greater than the $\frac{1}{4}$ piece, so $\frac{1}{2} > \frac{1}{4}$.

The recipe uses more cilantro than salt.

More Examples

A. Compare $\frac{2}{3}$ and $\frac{1}{3}$.

$$\frac{2}{3} > \frac{1}{3}$$

B. Compare $\frac{2}{3}$ and $\frac{5}{6}$.

$$\frac{2}{3} < \frac{5}{6}$$

C. Compare $\frac{2}{4}$ and $\frac{4}{8}$.

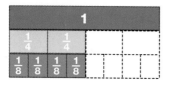

$$\frac{2}{4} = \frac{4}{8}$$

D. Compare $\frac{3}{5}$ and $\frac{4}{10}$.

$$\frac{3}{5} > \frac{4}{10}$$

Connecting Ideas

If you can compare two fractions, then you can order three or more fractions and list them from least to greatest or greatest to least.

Order the spice amounts shown to the right from least to greatest.

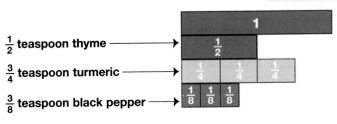

$\frac{1}{2}$ teaspoon thyme

$\frac{3}{4}$ teaspoon turmeric

$\frac{3}{8}$ teaspoon black pepper

Spices

$\frac{1}{2}$ teaspoon thyme

$\frac{3}{4}$ teaspoon turmeric

$\frac{3}{8}$ teaspoon black pepper

In order from least to greatest, the fractions are $\frac{3}{8}, \frac{1}{2}, \frac{3}{4}$.

Think and Discuss Use fraction pieces to make five fractions greater than $\frac{1}{2}$ but less than 1. What is true about all these fractions?

Try It Out

Compare. Write >, <, or = for each ●.
Use the pictures to help you.

1.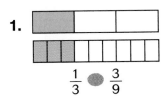

$\frac{1}{3}$ ● $\frac{3}{9}$

2.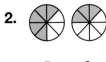

$\frac{5}{8}$ ● $\frac{3}{8}$

3.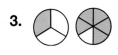

$\frac{1}{3}$ ● $\frac{5}{6}$

Draw pictures or use fraction pieces to order each set of fractions from least to greatest.

4. $\frac{1}{6}, \frac{1}{3}, \frac{1}{8}$

5. $\frac{5}{8}, \frac{1}{2}, \frac{2}{8}$

6. $\frac{1}{6}, \frac{3}{4}, \frac{3}{8}$

7. $\frac{1}{3}, \frac{1}{2}, \frac{1}{6}$

8. $\frac{3}{8}, \frac{1}{8}, \frac{7}{8}$

9. $\frac{1}{4}, \frac{5}{8}, \frac{1}{8}$

10. $\frac{1}{6}, \frac{4}{6}, \frac{2}{6}$

11. $\frac{4}{5}, \frac{3}{10}, \frac{1}{2}$

Practice

Compare. Write >, <, or = for each ●.
Use the pictures to help you.

12.

$\dfrac{2}{3}$ ● $\dfrac{3}{4}$

13.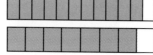

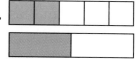

$\dfrac{11}{12}$ ● $\dfrac{7}{8}$

14.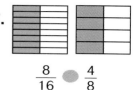

$\dfrac{2}{5}$ ● $\dfrac{1}{2}$

15.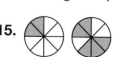

$\dfrac{2}{8}$ ● $\dfrac{5}{8}$

16.

$\dfrac{2}{4}$ ● $\dfrac{1}{4}$

17.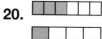

$\dfrac{8}{16}$ ● $\dfrac{4}{8}$

18.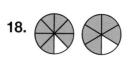

$\dfrac{7}{8}$ ● $\dfrac{5}{6}$

19.

$\dfrac{1}{3}$ ● $\dfrac{5}{6}$

20.

$\dfrac{3}{6}$ ● $\dfrac{1}{4}$

Order each set from least to greatest.

21. $\dfrac{5}{6}, \dfrac{1}{4}, \dfrac{2}{3}$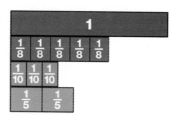

22. $\dfrac{2}{3}, \dfrac{1}{2}, \dfrac{1}{8}$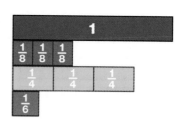

Order each set from greatest to least.

23. $\dfrac{5}{8}, \dfrac{3}{10}, \dfrac{2}{5}$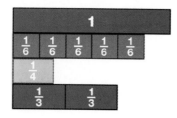

24. $\dfrac{3}{8}, \dfrac{3}{4}, \dfrac{1}{6}$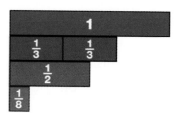

Draw pictures or use fraction pieces to order
each set of fractions from least to greatest.

25. $\dfrac{1}{2}, \dfrac{3}{8}, \dfrac{4}{6}$

26. $\dfrac{1}{3}, \dfrac{1}{4}, \dfrac{1}{5}$

27. $\dfrac{5}{6}, \dfrac{3}{4}, \dfrac{3}{5}$

28. $\dfrac{1}{8}, \dfrac{1}{3}, \dfrac{1}{4}$

29. Analyze How are all of these fractions alike?
$\dfrac{7}{8}, \dfrac{5}{6}, \dfrac{2}{3}, \dfrac{4}{5}, \dfrac{6}{7}$

Problem Solving

30. Jackie used $\frac{2}{3}$ tsp cumin for one recipe and $\frac{3}{4}$ tsp cumin for another recipe. In which recipe did she use more cumin?

31. Explain A cake recipe calls for $\frac{1}{2}$ cup of sugar. A cookie recipe calls for $\frac{3}{5}$ cup of sugar. Which recipe calls for more sugar?

32. Look at the graph to the right. If turmeric costs $0.65 an ounce and sage costs $0.45 an ounce, which jar costs more?

33. Analyze Jasper's family has a total of 24 cookbooks. Some of the cookbooks are soup cookbooks and the rest are dessert cookbooks. For every 1 soup cookbook, they have 3 dessert cookbooks. How many of each kind of cookbook does the family have? Tell which strategy you used to solve the problem.

Social Studies Connection
The earliest record of the spice, turmeric, came from the Middle East in about 600 B.C. It was used for flavoring food and as a dye because of its brilliant yellow color. ▼

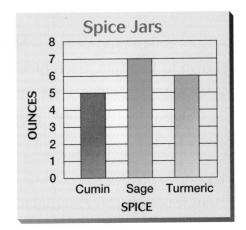

Review and Remember

Choose the most appropriate unit of measure. Write *km, m,* or *cm.*

34. the height of a doorknob from the floor

35. the distance from your home to school

36. the width of the state in which you live

37. the distance around your wrist

Using Algebra Find each missing number.

38. $n \times 3 = 12$

39. $7 \times n = 42$

40. $5 \times n = 0$

41. $27 \div n = 3$

42. $n \div 7 = 7$

43. $80 \div n = 8$

44. $72 \div n = 9$

45. $8 \times n = 64$

46. $n \times 9 = 27$

47. $n \times 9 = 54$

48. $n \div 4 = 0$

49. $28 \div n = 28$

For Extra Practice, see Set D, page 381.

Patchwork Party

Fractions can be greater than one or equal to one.

SEW IT

Learning About It

A quilt is made up of many blocks like the one shown to the right. Each block in the quilt uses 6 small triangle pieces. How many quilt blocks can be made with 13 triangle pieces?

Each triangle is $\frac{1}{6}$ of a whole block. You have 13 one-sixth pieces or $\frac{13}{6}$. By placing them together you can make $2\frac{1}{6}$ quilt blocks.

Word Bank

improper fraction

mixed number

  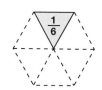

$$\frac{13}{6} = 2\frac{1}{6}$$

A fraction greater than or equal to 1 whole is an **improper fraction**.

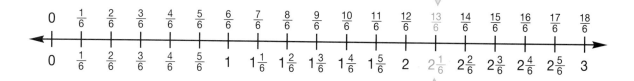

A number containing a whole number part and a fraction part is a **mixed number**.

More Examples

A.

$$\frac{5}{3} = 1\frac{2}{3}$$

B. $\frac{10}{5} = \frac{2}{1} = 2$

Think and Discuss Can the denominator of an improper fraction be greater than the numerator? Explain your answer.

Try It Out

Write an improper fraction and a mixed number for each picture.

1.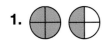

2.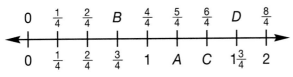

3.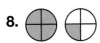

For Exercises 4-7, write the letter that locates each fraction or mixed number on the number line shown below.

4. $1\frac{1}{4}$

5. $1\frac{1}{2}$

6. $\frac{7}{4}$

7. $\frac{3}{4}$

Practice

Write an improper fraction and a mixed number for each picture.

8.

9.

10.

Find the missing numbers. Draw pictures if needed.

11. $\frac{5}{4} = \blacksquare\frac{1}{4}$

12. $\frac{11}{3} = 3\frac{\blacksquare}{3}$

13. $\frac{\blacksquare}{4} = 2\frac{1}{4}$

14. $\frac{3}{\blacksquare} = 1$

15. Draw a number line to show that $\frac{13}{4}$ is equal to $3\frac{1}{4}$.

Problem Solving

16. It takes two quilt blocks to make a pillow. You have 11 quilt blocks. How many pillows can you make? What fraction of a pillow is left over?

17. Analyze Bob needed to make 17 half circles for his decorations. He had 4 whole circles and 10 half circles. Could he make all the circles he needed? Explain.

Review and Remember

Choose a Method Use paper and pencil or a calculator to solve. Tell the method you chose.

18. $968 \div 2$

19. 392×4

20. $3,809 + 4,598$

21. $7,324 - 4,888$

For Extra Practice, see Set E, page 381.

Checkpoint

Understanding Fractions

Write the fraction for the shaded parts of each region.
(pages 338–339)

1. 　2. 　3. 　4. 　5.

Write the fractional part of each number. (pages 340–343)

6. $\frac{1}{2}$ of 20　　7. $\frac{1}{3}$ of 12　　8. $\frac{1}{6}$ of 36　　9. $\frac{1}{5}$ of 25

Write each fraction in simplest form. Use fraction pieces if needed. (pages 346–349)

10. $\frac{6}{9}$　　11. $\frac{8}{16}$　　12. $\frac{9}{36}$　　13. $\frac{6}{10}$　　14. $\frac{10}{24}$

Order each set from least to greatest. (pages 352–355)

15. $\frac{1}{3}, \frac{1}{2}, \frac{1}{4}$ 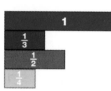　　16. $\frac{3}{8}, \frac{3}{4}, \frac{1}{2}$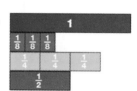

Write an improper fraction and a mixed number for each picture. (pages 356–357)

17. 　18. 　19. 　20.

Mixed Practice

Write an equivalent fraction for each. Use fraction pieces if needed.

21. $\frac{1}{2}$　22. $\frac{3}{4}$　23. $\frac{1}{8}$　24. $\frac{2}{5}$　25. $\frac{10}{4}$

Write an improper fraction and a mixed number for each picture.

26. 　27. 　28. 　29.

What do you think?
How do you know that $\frac{2}{2}, \frac{8}{8}, \frac{25}{25}$, and $\frac{100}{100}$ each equal 1?

Order each set from greatest to least.

30. $\frac{2}{5}, \frac{3}{4}, \frac{3}{5}$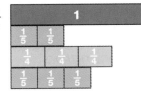

31. $\frac{1}{4}, \frac{1}{3}, \frac{1}{6}$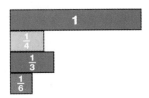

Problem Solving

32. A train is made up of 64 cars. Of those, $\frac{1}{8}$ are refrigerator cars and $\frac{1}{4}$ are boxcars. How many cars are refrigerator cars? boxcars?

33. Mario needs 12 triangles to make a design. If he has 28 triangles, how many designs can he make? What fraction of a design is left?

34. A fruit punch has $\frac{2}{3}$ cup orange juice and $\frac{3}{4}$ cup cranberry juice. Is there more cranberry juice or orange juice? How can you tell?

35. **Explain** A shape has 12 equal parts. Nine parts are shaded. Can the fraction $\frac{3}{4}$ be used to describe the shaded part? Explain.

Journal Idea

Count the words in this first sentence. Then count the total number of words in this paragraph. Write a fraction to represent the number of words in the sentence compared to the total number of words in the paragraph. Explain your answer.

Critical Thinking Corner

Visual Thinking

Estimating Fractions

Use the picture of the fraction pieces to tell if a fraction is closer to 0, $\frac{1}{2}$, or 1.

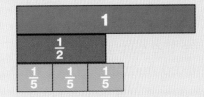

• Is $\frac{3}{5}$ about 0, $\frac{1}{2}$, or 1?

Compare $\frac{3}{5}$ with $\frac{1}{2}$ and 1.

• Is $\frac{3}{5}$ closer to $\frac{1}{2}$ or 1?

Piece It Together

*Fraction pieces can help you understand how to add
and subtract fractions with like denominators.*

Learning About It

You planted seeds from these 6 packets. What fraction
of the seed packets are flower seeds?

What You Need

For each pair:
fraction pieces

Zinnia

Petunia

Petunia

Peas

Squash

Radish

$\frac{1}{6}$ + $\frac{2}{6}$

PLANT IT

You can find out by adding $\frac{1}{6}$ and $\frac{2}{6}$. These are fractions
with like denominators. Work with a partner.

Step 1 Use fraction pieces to add $\frac{1}{6} + \frac{2}{6}$.

- Use one $\frac{1}{6}$ piece to show the zinnia
  seed packet and two $\frac{1}{6}$ pieces to
  show the petunia seed packets.

- What fraction of the seed packets are
  flower seeds?

$$\frac{1}{6} + \frac{2}{6} = \frac{3}{6}$$

Step 2 Use fraction pieces to add $\frac{3}{4}$ and $\frac{2}{4}$.

- How many fourths do you have altogether?

- Is the sum greater or less than 1? How do
  you know?

- Write the sum as an improper fraction and
  a mixed number.

Step 3 Make a chart like the one shown to
the right. Use fraction pieces to find each sum.
Complete the chart.

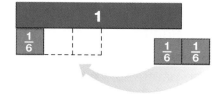

Addition Sentence	Sum
$\frac{1}{6} + \frac{2}{6}$	$\frac{3}{6}$
$\frac{3}{4} + \frac{2}{4}$	$\frac{5}{4} = 1\frac{1}{4}$
$\frac{1}{3} + \frac{1}{3}$	
$\frac{7}{8} + \frac{4}{8}$	
$\frac{1}{2} + \frac{1}{2}$	

Step 4 Use fraction pieces to subtract $\frac{4}{5} - \frac{3}{5}$.

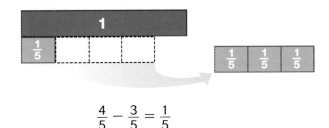

- Place four $\frac{1}{5}$ pieces under 1 whole strip.

- Take three $\frac{1}{5}$ pieces away.

- How many fifths are left?

$$\frac{4}{5} - \frac{3}{5} = \frac{1}{5}$$

Step 5 Make a chart like the one shown to the right. Use fraction pieces to find each difference and complete the chart.

Think and Discuss How is adding fractions with like denominators similar to subtracting fractions with like denominators?

Subtraction Sentence	Difference
$\frac{4}{5} - \frac{3}{5}$	$\frac{1}{5}$
$\frac{2}{3} - \frac{1}{3}$	
$\frac{5}{6} - \frac{2}{6}$	
$\frac{1}{2} - \frac{1}{2}$	

Practice

Use fraction pieces to add or subtract in Exercises 1–15. Write each answer as a mixed number or a whole number when possible.

1. $\frac{1}{3} + \frac{2}{3}$ **2.** $\frac{3}{8} + \frac{4}{8}$ **3.** $\frac{1}{5} + \frac{3}{5}$ **4.** $\frac{6}{8} + \frac{6}{8}$ **5.** $\frac{1}{2} + \frac{3}{2}$

6. $\frac{7}{8} - \frac{3}{8}$ **7.** $\frac{2}{5} - \frac{1}{5}$ **8.** $\frac{5}{6} - \frac{1}{6}$ **9.** $\frac{5}{6} - \frac{5}{6}$ **10.** $\frac{8}{6} - \frac{2}{6}$

11. $\frac{1}{4} + \frac{2}{4}$ **12.** $\frac{5}{6} - \frac{3}{6}$ **13.** $\frac{4}{8} + \frac{4}{8}$ **14.** $\frac{4}{6} - \frac{1}{6}$ **15.** $\frac{5}{10} + \frac{5}{10}$

16. Look back at Exercises 2 and 3. Compare the denominators in each exercise to the denominator of each sum. What do you notice?

17. Look back at Exercise 7. Compare the denominator of each fraction to the denominator of the difference. What do you notice?

18. Generalize Write a rule for adding and subtracting fractions when the denominators are the same. Compare adding and subtracting like fractions with adding and subtracting whole numbers.

Addition of Fractions and Mixed Numbers

Chalk It Up

Fraction pieces can help you add fractions and mixed numbers.

Learning About It

Have you ever made chalk drawings on a sidewalk? The chalk drawing to the right is $\frac{1}{8}$ pink and $\frac{3}{8}$ blue. How much of this chalk drawing is completed so far? To find out, add.

$$\frac{1}{8} + \frac{3}{8} = \blacksquare$$

DRAW IT

THERE'S ALWAYS A WAY!

• **One way** is to use fraction pieces.

Step 1 Add one $\frac{1}{8}$ piece and three $\frac{1}{8}$ pieces.

Step 2 Look for other pieces to help you write the sum in simplest form.

• **Another way** is to use paper and pencil. You can add fractions with like denominators by adding the numerators.

Step 1 The denominators are the same, so you can add the numerators.

Step 2 Check to see if you can write the sum in simplest form.

$$\frac{1}{8} + \frac{3}{8} = \frac{1 + 3}{8} = \frac{4}{8}$$

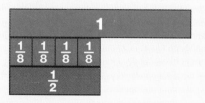

$\frac{1}{2}$ of the chalk drawing is completed so far.

More Examples

A.

$$\begin{array}{r} \frac{2}{4} \\ + \frac{3}{4} \\ \hline \frac{5}{4} \end{array}$$

Think: $\frac{5}{4}$ is an improper fraction, so change it to a mixed number.

$\frac{5}{4}$ = ⊕ ⊕ = $1\frac{1}{4}$

B.

$$\begin{array}{r} \frac{3}{8} \\ + \frac{3}{8} \\ \hline \frac{6}{8} \end{array} = \frac{3}{4}$$

$\div 2$

$\div 2$

Think: Write the answer in simplest form.

Connecting Ideas

When you add mixed numbers, you can use what you know about adding whole numbers and what you just learned about adding fractions.

Add $3\frac{1}{8} + 1\frac{3}{8}$.

Step 1 Add the fractions. The denominators are the same so add the numerators. Write the denominator.

$$\begin{array}{r} 3\frac{1}{8} \\ + 1\frac{3}{8} \\ \hline \frac{4}{8} \end{array}$$

Step 2 Add the whole numbers.

$$\begin{array}{r} 3\frac{1}{8} \\ + 1\frac{3}{8} \\ \hline 4\frac{4}{8} \end{array}$$

Step 3 Check to see if you can write the fraction in simplest form.

$$\begin{array}{r} 3\frac{1}{8} \\ + 1\frac{3}{8} \\ \hline 4\frac{4}{8} = 4\frac{1}{2} \end{array}$$

$\div 4$

$\div 4$

More Examples

A.

$$\begin{array}{r} 3\frac{2}{10} \\ + 2\frac{5}{10} \\ \hline 5\frac{7}{10} \end{array}$$

B.

$$\begin{array}{r} 1\frac{1}{4} \\ + 2\frac{2}{4} \\ \hline 3\frac{3}{4} \end{array}$$

C.

$$\begin{array}{r} 4\frac{1}{6} \\ + 2\frac{3}{6} \\ \hline 6\frac{4}{6} = 6\frac{2}{3} \end{array}$$

$\div 2$

$\div 2$

Think and Discuss Why does $6\frac{7}{6} = 7\frac{1}{6}$?

Try It Out

Add. Write each sum in simplest form.
Use fraction pieces to help you.

1.
$$\begin{array}{r} \frac{1}{3} \\ + \frac{1}{3} \\ \hline \end{array}$$

2.
$$\begin{array}{r} \frac{1}{8} \\ + \frac{5}{8} \\ \hline \end{array}$$

3.
$$\begin{array}{r} \frac{3}{10} \\ + \frac{1}{10} \\ \hline \end{array}$$

4.
$$\begin{array}{r} 4\frac{1}{4} \\ + 3\frac{1}{4} \\ \hline \end{array}$$

5.
$$\begin{array}{r} 12\frac{1}{6} \\ + 4\frac{3}{6} \\ \hline \end{array}$$

Practice

**Add. Write each sum in simplest form.
Use fraction pieces to help you.**

6. $\dfrac{2}{12}$ **7.** $\dfrac{4}{5}$ **8.** $\dfrac{4}{12}$ **9.** $\dfrac{5}{10}$ **10.** $\dfrac{5}{8}$ **11.** $\dfrac{4}{12}$

   $+\dfrac{5}{12}$ $+\dfrac{1}{5}$ $+\dfrac{3}{12}$ $+\dfrac{8}{10}$ $+\dfrac{3}{8}$ $+\dfrac{1}{12}$

12. $\dfrac{3}{10}$ **13.** $\dfrac{6}{10}$ **14.** $\dfrac{1}{6}$ **15.** $1\dfrac{3}{5}$ **16.** $5\dfrac{1}{4}$ **17.** $4\dfrac{1}{3}$

   $+\dfrac{6}{10}$ $+\dfrac{7}{10}$ $+\dfrac{1}{6}$ $+\,2\dfrac{2}{5}$ $+\,8\dfrac{1}{4}$ $+\,3\dfrac{1}{3}$

18. $3\dfrac{4}{6}$ **19.** $9\dfrac{3}{8}$ **20.** $3\dfrac{1}{4}$ **21.** $4\dfrac{6}{10}$ **22.** $2\dfrac{5}{12}$ **23.** $5\dfrac{1}{15}$

   $+\,6\dfrac{1}{6}$ $+\,1\dfrac{2}{8}$ $+\,6\dfrac{2}{4}$ $+\,10\dfrac{3}{10}$ $+\,2\dfrac{5}{12}$ $+\,8\dfrac{2}{15}$

Using Mental Math   **Find each sum.**

24. $\dfrac{2}{7}+\dfrac{3}{7}$ **25.** $\dfrac{5}{8}+\dfrac{3}{8}$ **26.** $\dfrac{7}{10}+\dfrac{2}{10}$ **27.** $\dfrac{5}{6}+\dfrac{1}{6}$

28. $\dfrac{4}{6}+\dfrac{1}{6}$ **29.** $\dfrac{2}{9}+\dfrac{5}{9}$ **30.** $\dfrac{1}{5}+\dfrac{2}{5}$ **31.** $\dfrac{9}{10}+\dfrac{4}{10}$

32. Journal Idea Without finding the exact sum,
how can you tell that $\dfrac{2}{3}+\dfrac{2}{3}$ will be greater than 1?

Problem Solving

**Use the picture to the right for Problems 33–38.
Write each answer in simplest form.**

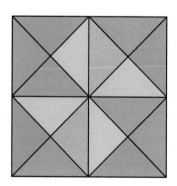

33. What fraction of the picture is orange?

34. What fraction of the picture is green?

35. What fraction of the picture is either orange
or green?

36. What fraction of the picture is neither orange nor green?

37. What fraction of the picture is colored?

38. Create Your Own Write a problem about the
picture. Challenge a classmate to solve it.

39. You spent $\frac{2}{4}$ of an hour reading the directions for making a sand art picture. Then you spent $2\frac{1}{4}$ hours making a sand art picture. How much time did you spend altogether?

40. **Explain** Your little sister knows that 4 pies are more than 3 pies. But she also thinks that $\frac{1}{4}$ of a pie is greater than $\frac{1}{3}$ of the same pie. Draw a picture to show her why she is wrong.

INTERNET ACTIVITY
www.sbgmath.com

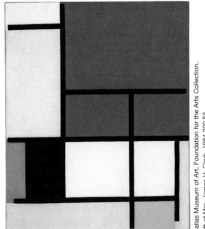

Dallas Museum of Art, Foundation for the Arts Collection, gift of Mrs. James H. Clark 1984.200.FA

▲ **Fine Arts Connection**
Piet Mondrian (1872-1944) was a Dutch geometric artist who painted unequal rectangles in primary colors. He believed that the use of right angles provided a sense of balance to the finished piece. Estimate the fraction of this painting that is blue.

Review and Remember

Using Mental Math Find each answer.

41. $400 + 700$ **42.** $70 \times 8,000$

43. $5,000 - 300$ **44.** $6,400 \div 8$

45. $5,700 - 800$ **46.** $420 \div 6$ **47.** $6,900 + 600$ **48.** 70×600

49. 40×70 **50.** $410 + 390$ **51.** $360 \div 6$ **52.** $440 - 41$

53. $250 \div 5$ **54.** $3,000 - 1,500$ **55.** $10 \times 10,000$ **56.** $2,501 + 2,499$

Money $ense

Shopping for Art Supplies
Will Anne or Bob spend more money at the art supply store? Explain how you found your answer.

Paint	$1.25
Marker	50¢
Pencil	25¢

I need 5 tubes of paint, 6 markers, and 8 colored pencils.

I need 3 tubes of paint, 10 markers, and 9 colored pencils.

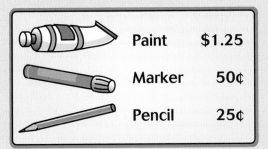

For Extra Practice, see Set F, page 381.

Weaving Wonders

Fraction pieces can help you subtract fractions and mixed numbers.

Learning About It

Daniel and Eleazar Martinez were taught to weave using traditional patterns and techniques. They want to weave a cloth that is $\frac{5}{8}$ of a yard long, and they have finished $\frac{3}{8}$ of a yard. How much more do they need to weave? You can find how much more by subtracting fractions.

$$\frac{5}{8} - \frac{3}{8} = \blacksquare$$

WEAVE IT

THERE'S ALWAYS A WAY!

● **One way** is to use fraction pieces.

Step 1 Subtract three $\frac{1}{8}$ fraction pieces from five $\frac{1}{8}$ pieces.

Step 2 Look for other pieces that help you write the difference in simplest form.

● **Another way** is to use paper and pencil.

Step 1 The denominators are the same, so you can subtract the numerators.

$$\frac{5}{8} - \frac{3}{8} = \frac{5-3}{8} = \frac{2}{8}$$

Step 2 Check to see if you can write the difference in simplest form.

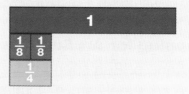

They need to weave $\frac{2}{8}$ or $\frac{1}{4}$ yard more.

Connecting Ideas

When you subtract mixed numbers, you can use what you know about whole numbers and what you just learned about subtracting fractions to help you.

INTERNET ACTIVITY
www.sbgmath.com

Subtract $2\frac{3}{4} - 1\frac{1}{4}$.

Step 1 Subtract the fractions. The denominators are the same, so subtract the numerators and write the denominator.

$$\begin{array}{r} 2\frac{3}{4} \\ -\ 1\frac{1}{4} \\ \hline \frac{2}{4} \end{array}$$

Step 2 Subtract the whole numbers.

$$\begin{array}{r} 2\frac{3}{4} \\ -\ 1\frac{1}{4} \\ \hline 1\frac{2}{4} \end{array}$$

Step 3 Check to see if you can write the fraction in simplest form.

$$\begin{array}{r} 2\frac{3}{4} \\ -\ 1\frac{1}{4} \\ \hline 1\frac{2}{4} = 1\frac{1}{2} \end{array}$$
$\div 2$

Think and Discuss How is subtracting mixed numbers like subtracting fractions?

Try It Out

Subtract. Write each answer in simplest form when possible. Use fraction pieces to help you.

1. $\begin{array}{r} \frac{3}{5} \\ -\ \frac{2}{5} \\ \hline \end{array}$

2. $\begin{array}{r} \frac{5}{8} \\ -\ \frac{3}{8} \\ \hline \end{array}$

3. $\begin{array}{r} \frac{7}{12} \\ -\ \frac{1}{12} \\ \hline \end{array}$

4. $\begin{array}{r} 2\frac{5}{6} \\ -\ 1\frac{4}{6} \\ \hline \end{array}$

5. $\begin{array}{r} 4\frac{9}{10} \\ -\ \frac{6}{10} \\ \hline \end{array}$

6. $\begin{array}{r} 6\frac{2}{3} \\ -\ 3\frac{1}{3} \\ \hline \end{array}$

7. $\begin{array}{r} 4\frac{7}{9} \\ -\ 1\frac{3}{9} \\ \hline \end{array}$

8. $\begin{array}{r} 10\frac{3}{4} \\ -\ 5\frac{1}{4} \\ \hline \end{array}$

9. $\begin{array}{r} 25\frac{7}{8} \\ -\ 23\frac{4}{8} \\ \hline \end{array}$

Kid Connection
Eleazar and Daniel use standing looms like those used by their ancestors. The boys go to the Spanish Market in Santa Fe, New Mexico, to exhibit and sell their artwork. ▼

367

Practice

Subtract. Write each answer in simplest form. Use fraction pieces if you like.

10. $\dfrac{7}{8}$ $-\dfrac{5}{8}$

11. $\dfrac{11}{12}$ $-\dfrac{4}{12}$

12. $\dfrac{8}{10}$ $-\dfrac{1}{10}$

13. $\dfrac{4}{5}$ $-\dfrac{1}{5}$

14. $\dfrac{5}{10}$ $-\dfrac{2}{10}$

15. $\dfrac{3}{4}$ $-\dfrac{1}{4}$

16. $\dfrac{3}{8}$ $-\dfrac{1}{8}$

17. $\dfrac{7}{6}$ $-\dfrac{2}{6}$

18. $\dfrac{2}{5}$ $-\dfrac{1}{5}$

19. $2\dfrac{9}{10}$ $-2\dfrac{2}{10}$

20. $9\dfrac{7}{5}$ $-8\dfrac{6}{5}$

21. $6\dfrac{1}{12}$ $-3\dfrac{1}{12}$

22. $8\dfrac{7}{8}$ $-8\dfrac{4}{8}$

23. $9\dfrac{4}{5}$ $-3\dfrac{1}{5}$

24. $2\dfrac{5}{12}$ $-\dfrac{4}{12}$

25. $7\dfrac{1}{2}$ $-3\dfrac{1}{2}$

26. $7\dfrac{3}{5}$ $-4\dfrac{3}{5}$

27. $18\dfrac{2}{3}$ $-15\dfrac{1}{3}$

28. $6\dfrac{7}{10}$ $-1\dfrac{3}{10}$

29. $9\dfrac{3}{4}$ $-\dfrac{2}{4}$

Using Mental Math Find each difference.

30. $7\dfrac{1}{2}$ $-3\dfrac{1}{2}$

31. $4\dfrac{3}{4}$ $-\dfrac{3}{4}$

32. $5\dfrac{1}{5}$ $-2\dfrac{1}{5}$

33. $4\dfrac{1}{2}$ $-\dfrac{1}{2}$

34. $4\dfrac{2}{4}$ $-2\dfrac{1}{4}$

Problem Solving

35. This serape (suh RAH pay), shown at right was made using the traditional Saltillo pattern of diamonds. If $\dfrac{3}{10}$ of the diamonds are orange and $\dfrac{4}{10}$ of the diamonds are red, what fraction tells how many more of the diamonds are red than are orange?

36. Daniel wove $1\dfrac{3}{4}$ yards of cloth. Eleazar wove $\dfrac{2}{4}$ yards of cloth. How much more cloth did Daniel weave?

Language Arts Connection
A serape is a colorful woolen poncho worn over the shoulders. ▼

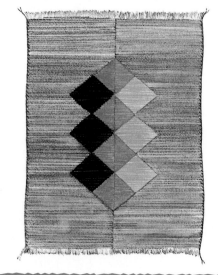

37. Analyze Yellow and gold dyes for wool are made from rabbitbrush leaves. If $2\frac{1}{2}$ pounds of leaves make enough dye to color 25 pounds of wool, how many pounds of leaves are needed to color 50 pounds of wool?

38. You Decide You have blue, green, yellow, and red yarn for weaving a striped rug $6\frac{1}{2}$ feet long. There is enough yarn to weave $2\frac{1}{2}$ feet of each color. Decide what colors you will use and how long each stripe will be. Draw a picture of your rug.

▲ **Science Connection**
Rabbitbrush is a bad-tasting plant that few animals eat. But jackrabbits often use it for shelter.

Review and Remember

Using Estimation Estimate each answer.

39. 4 × $51.97 **40.** $35.73 ÷ 9 **41.** 7,510 + 3,485 **42.** $42.10 − $33.08

43. 8 × $3.79 **44.** $586 ÷ 3 **45.** 7,570 − 2,595 **46.** $16.14 + $73.90

Time for Technology
Surfing the Net

Using Hypertext

The Internet uses **hypertext** to connect related sites. Hypertext can include underlined words and pictures.

- Explore this site on the Internet: www.sbgschool.com

- When you're in this site click on one of the pictures or <u>underlined words</u>. This will take you to another site on the Internet.

- Continue to click on pictures or underlined words to find out more about a topic.

- Print a picture or information you want to save.

- In your notebook record some of the information you find.

- Share your finding with the class.

For Extra Practice, see Set G, page 382.

Problem Solving
Guess and Check

You can use guess and check to solve some problems.

Jason used these animal pieces to make a silly animal $3\frac{3}{4}$ inches long. Which head, body, and tail might Jason have used?

1 in.   **$1\frac{3}{4}$ in.**   **$2\frac{2}{4}$ in.**

 UNDERSTAND

What do you need to find?

You need to find a head, body, and tail that total $3\frac{3}{4}$ inches in length.

$1\frac{3}{4}$ in.   **$2\frac{1}{4}$ in.**   **$\frac{3}{4}$ in.**

 PLAN

How can you solve the problem?

You can **guess and check**. Choose 3 parts and add their lengths. Keep trying until you find a head, body, and tail that total $3\frac{3}{4}$ inches.

$1\frac{1}{4}$ in.   **$2\frac{2}{4}$ in.**   **$\frac{2}{4}$ in.**

 SOLVE

First guess: iguana head, iguana body, goose tail
Check: $1 + 1\frac{3}{4} + \frac{3}{4} = 3\frac{2}{4}$ *This is too short. Try a longer head.*

Second guess: goose head, iguana body, goose tail
Check: $1\frac{3}{4} + 1\frac{3}{4} + \frac{3}{4} = 4\frac{1}{4}$ *This is too long. Try a shorter head.*

Third guess: bear head, iguana body, goose tail
Check: $1\frac{1}{4} + 1\frac{3}{4} + \frac{3}{4} = 3\frac{3}{4}$ *This works!*

Jason might have used a bear head, iguana body, and goose tail.

 LOOK BACK

What if you made a silly animal 4 inches long? What would it be?

Using the Strategy

Use guess and check to solve Problems 1–4.

1 One small and one large animal puzzle kit cost $16 altogether. If the large kit costs three times as much as the small kit, how much does each kit cost?

2 Each kit contains 20 pictures of birds, reptiles, and mammals. There are half as many birds as mammals or reptiles. How many of each kind of animal are in the kit?

3 The rabbit and turtle pictures are $16\frac{1}{2}$ inches long altogether. The rabbit picture is twice as long as the turtle picture. How long is each animal picture?

4 Marta drew 30 cats, dogs, and chickens. She drew twice as many dogs as cats. She drew 3 times as many cats as chickens. How many cats did Marta draw?

5 **Create Your Own** Write a problem that uses the animal-piece lengths shown on page 370. Ask a classmate to use guess and check to solve your problem.

Mixed Strategy Review

Try these or other strategies to solve each problem. Tell which strategy you used. Use the animal pieces on page 370 for Problems 6–7.

THERE'S ALWAYS A WAY!

Problem Solving Strategies

- Work Backwards
- Make a List
- Write a Number Sentence
- Guess and Check
- Act It Out
- Use Logical Reasoning

6 How many different animals can you make that have a goose head?

7 How much longer is the longest silly animal you can make than the shortest?

8 Max bought 6 cards for his wildlife collection. He gave 3 cards to Josh and got 4 cards from Carl. He then had 27 cards. How many cards did he start with?

9 Sara has 4 pets—a dog, a cat, a rabbit, and a duck. The duck is not gray. The cat is white. Two of the pets are gray. One pet is black. What color is each pet?

Trailing Away

Fraction pieces can help you add fractions with unlike denominators.

Trail Mix
$\frac{1}{2}$ cup peanuts
$\frac{1}{2}$ cup carob chips
1 cup cereal squares
$\frac{1}{4}$ cup raisins

Raisin Muffins

1 cup milk	3 tsp baking powder
$\frac{1}{4}$ cup oil	1 tsp salt
1 egg	$\frac{2}{3}$ cup raisins
2 cups flour	

MAKE IT

Learning About It

What's the perfect snack for a long hike—muffins or trail mix? How about both! The trail mix recipe calls for $\frac{1}{4}$ cup of raisins. The muffin recipe calls for $\frac{2}{3}$ cup of raisins. How many cups of raisins do you need in all?

$$\frac{1}{4} + \frac{2}{3} = \blacksquare$$

Step 1 Work with a partner to add $\frac{1}{4}$ and $\frac{2}{3}$.

Place one $\frac{1}{4}$ piece and two $\frac{1}{3}$ pieces end to end under a 1 whole fraction strip.

Step 2 To add these fractions with unlike denominators, find a **common denominator**. Find equal size fraction pieces that fit exactly under $\frac{1}{4}$ and $\frac{2}{3}$.

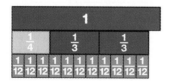

- How many $\frac{1}{12}$ pieces fit exactly under $\frac{1}{4}$?
- How many $\frac{1}{12}$ pieces fit exactly under $\frac{2}{3}$?
- How many $\frac{1}{12}$ pieces fit exactly under $\frac{1}{4}$ and $\frac{2}{3}$?
- What is the sum of $\frac{1}{4} + \frac{2}{3}$?

Word Bank

common denominator

What You Need

For each pair:
fraction pieces

Step 3 Make a chart like the one shown at the right. Use fraction pieces to complete the chart.

Think and Discuss How is adding fractions with unlike denominators different from adding fractions with like denominators?

Addition Sentence	Sum
$\frac{2}{3} + \frac{1}{4}$	$\frac{11}{12}$
$\frac{1}{2} + \frac{1}{3}$	
$\frac{2}{8} + \frac{1}{4}$	
$\frac{2}{4} + \frac{3}{6}$	
$\frac{2}{4} + \frac{3}{8}$	

Practice

Use the pictures to find each sum.

1. $\frac{1}{2} + \frac{1}{3}$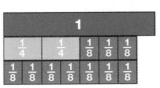

2. $\frac{1}{2} + \frac{2}{5}$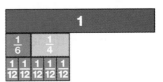

3. $\frac{2}{4} + \frac{3}{8}$

4. $\frac{1}{6} + \frac{1}{4}$

Use fraction pieces to find each sum in simplest form.

5. $\frac{1}{6} + \frac{1}{2}$ **6.** $\frac{5}{12} + \frac{1}{3}$ **7.** $\frac{2}{5} + \frac{1}{10}$ **8.** $\frac{1}{4} + \frac{3}{8}$ **9.** $\frac{1}{4} + \frac{3}{6}$

10. $\frac{1}{3} + \frac{1}{12}$ **11.** $\frac{5}{8} + \frac{1}{4}$ **12.** $\frac{1}{2} + \frac{3}{8}$ **13.** $\frac{1}{2} + \frac{1}{5}$ **14.** $\frac{2}{3} + \frac{1}{6}$

15. $\frac{1}{6} + \frac{5}{12}$ **16.** $\frac{3}{4} + \frac{1}{8}$ **17.** $\frac{4}{5} + \frac{1}{10}$ **18.** $\frac{1}{8} + \frac{1}{4}$ **19.** $\frac{1}{5} + \frac{3}{10}$

Problem Solving

20. Sandy has 2 cups of nuts, and Ling has $\frac{3}{4}$ cup of nuts. How many cups of nuts do they have altogether? Use fraction pieces to decide.

21. **Analyze** A recipe calls for $\frac{1}{4}$ tsp cinnamon, $\frac{1}{8}$ tsp nutmeg, and $\frac{1}{2}$ tsp ginger. How much spice is used in the recipe? Use fraction pieces to decide.

For Extra Practice, see Set H, page 382.

Book Nook

Fraction pieces can help you subtract fractions with unlike denominators.

Learning About It

Julie and her grandmother are making wooden bookshelves that are $\frac{3}{6}$ of a yard wide. The board is $\frac{2}{3}$ of a yard wide. How much wood should be cut off the board?

$$\frac{2}{3} - \frac{3}{6} = \blacksquare$$

Step 1 Work with a partner to subtract $\frac{2}{3} - \frac{3}{6}$.

Place two $\frac{1}{3}$ pieces under a 1 whole fraction strip. Then place three $\frac{1}{6}$ pieces under the two $\frac{1}{3}$ pieces.

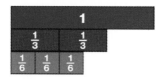

What You Need

For each pair:
  fraction pieces

Step 2 Find fraction pieces that will fill the space next to the three $\frac{1}{6}$ pieces and fit exactly under the two $\frac{1}{3}$ pieces.

 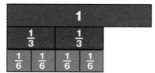

- What size fraction piece did you find to fill the space?

- How many pieces did you use to fill the space?

- What is $\frac{2}{3} - \frac{3}{6}$?

$\frac{1}{6}$ yard should be cut off the board.

Step 3 Make a chart like the one shown at the right and then use fraction pieces to complete it.

Think and Discuss How is subtracting fractions with unlike denominators different from subtracting fractions with like denominators?

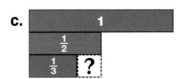

Subtraction Sentence	Difference
$\frac{2}{3} - \frac{3}{6}$	$\frac{1}{6}$
$\frac{5}{8} - \frac{1}{4}$	
$\frac{2}{4} - \frac{1}{8}$	
$\frac{3}{4} - \frac{1}{2}$	
$\frac{2}{8} - \frac{1}{4}$	

Practice

Choose the letter of the fraction pieces that model each subtraction sentence in Exercises 1–3.

1. $\frac{1}{2} - \frac{1}{3} = \frac{1}{6}$

2. $\frac{2}{3} - \frac{1}{6} = \frac{3}{6}$

3. $\frac{1}{2} - \frac{2}{6} = \frac{1}{6}$

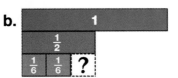

Use fraction pieces to find each difference.

4. $\frac{1}{2} - \frac{1}{4}$

5. $\frac{2}{3} - \frac{1}{6}$

6. $\frac{7}{8} - \frac{3}{4}$

7. $\frac{3}{5} - \frac{3}{10}$

8. $\frac{7}{12} - \frac{1}{6}$

9. $\frac{3}{4} - \frac{3}{8}$

10. $\frac{5}{12} - \frac{1}{6}$

11. $\frac{8}{10} - \frac{5}{10}$

12. $\frac{5}{8} - \frac{1}{2}$

13. $\frac{7}{8} - \frac{1}{4}$

Problem Solving

14. Explain Gillian and Cheryl used fraction pieces to find $\frac{1}{2} - \frac{1}{3}$. Gillian's difference was $\frac{1}{6}$ and Cheryl's difference was $\frac{2}{12}$. They are both correct. Explain why.

15. Analyze A 3-shelf bookshelf contains a total of 245 books. The top shelf contains the least number of books, the bottom shelf the greatest. Each shelf contains twice as many books as the one above it. If the top shelf has 35 books, how many do the other shelves have?

For Extra Practice, see Set I page 382.

Problem Solving
Using Circle Graphs

You can use a circle graph to solve problems.

*E*lliot spent $12.00 on materials to make a kite. He made a circle graph to show what part of the money was spent on each item. How much more did the nylon cost than the frame?

Costs of Materials

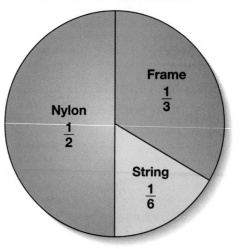

 ## UNDERSTAND

What do you need to know?

You need to know the cost of the nylon and the cost of the frame.

 ## PLAN

How can you solve the problem?

You can use the fractions on the circle graph to find the cost of each item. Then you can subtract to find the difference between the costs.

 ## SOLVE

- The nylon cost $\frac{1}{2}$ of the $12.00. So, the nylon cost $6.00.

- The frame cost $\frac{1}{3}$ of the $12.00. So, the frame cost $4.00.

$6.00 − $4.00 = $2.00

The nylon cost $2.00 more than the frame.

 ## LOOK BACK

What if the fractions were not on the circle graph? How could you know which item cost the least?

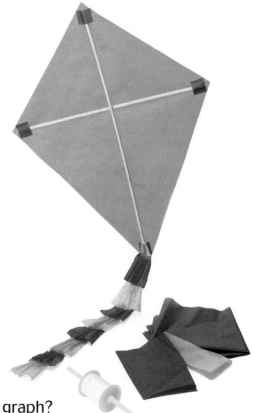

Show What You Learned

Use the information on page 376 to solve Problems 1–4.

1. Write a number sentence to show the cost of each of the three items that Elliot bought to make his kite.

2. **Explain** For which item did Elliot spend twice as much as he did for the string? How can you tell from the graph? How can you tell from the fractions?

3. **Explain** Which number must the fractions in the circle graph always add up to? Explain why.

4. **Analyze** If each item costs twice as much, would the fractions in the circle graph change? Why or why not?

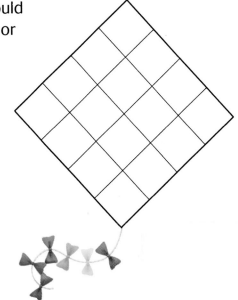

The circle graph below shows what fraction of the kite at the right will be red, blue, green, and yellow. Use the circle graph to solve Problems 5–10.

5. Which color will be used the most? the least? How can you tell from the graph? How can you tell from the fractions?

6. **Explain** Will more squares be blue or green? Explain how you know.

7. Which colors will have twice as many squares as green? How can you tell from the graph? How can you tell from the fractions?

8. How many red squares will there be? Explain how you know.

9. **Analyze** Which color has three times the number of squares as green? Tell how you know.

10. **Analyze** Which two colors make up $\frac{5}{8}$ of the kite? How many squares do these colors use?

Kite Colors

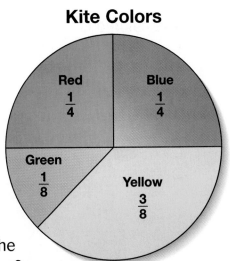

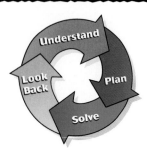

Problem Solving

★★★★★ **Preparing for Tests**

Practice What You Learned

Choose the correct letter for each answer.

1 Ruth bought a rug for $19.87 and a lamp for $32.56. Which is the best estimate of how much money Ruth spent?

A. $10
B. $30
C. $50
D. $60

$19.87 $32.56

Tip

Start by rounding each price to the nearest dollar. Then decide whether to add or subtract the rounded amounts.

---

2 Li bought $\frac{3}{8}$ yard of red fabric, $\frac{7}{8}$ yard of white fabric, and $\frac{5}{8}$ yard of blue fabric. Which is a reasonable conclusion?

A. Li bought more red fabric than blue fabric.
B. Li bought less blue fabric than red fabric.
C. Li bought less red fabric than white fabric.
D. Li bought more blue fabric than white fabric.

Tip

When you need to read the answer choices given in order to solve a problem, be sure to read all of them.

---

3 Four friends wrote letters to each other. Each friend wrote 1 letter to each of the other 3 friends. How many letters did they write altogether?

A. 7
B. 12
C. 15
D. 16

Tip

Try one of these strategies to solve the problem.
• *Draw a Picture*
• *Act It Out*
• *Make a List*

4 In a survey of 2,000 people, 887 people wanted a new library and 423 people did not. Everyone else was undecided. Which number sentence could be used to find out how many people were undecided?

A. 2,000 − 1,310 = ▒
B. 887 − 423 = ▒
C. 2,000 + 1,310 = ▒
D. 887 + 423 = ▒

5 Sarah has 82 cookies to divide equally among 7 people. When she is finished, how many of the cookies will be left over?

A. 1
B. 5
C. 12
D. 13

6 Irma has 16 records, 23 tapes, and 25 CDs. How many tapes and CDs does Irma have in all?

A. 2   **C.** 48
B. 39   **D.** 64

7 On Monday a pet store sold 13 boxes of hamster food, 16 boxes of dog food, and more than 20 boxes of cat food. Which is reasonable for the number of boxes of pet food the store sold?

A. Less than 13 boxes
B. Between 13 and 20 boxes
C. Between 20 and 49 boxes
D. More than 49 boxes

8 Dimitri has $51.50 to spend. He buys a computer game that costs $19.95. Which is the best estimate of how much money Dimitri has left?

A. $20
B. $30
C. $50
D. $60

9 Natalie is collecting recyclable items. She finds 68 plastic bottles and 31 glass bottles. Which number sentence could be used to find the total number of bottles Natalie found?

A. 31 + 31 = ▒
B. 68 + 31 = ▒
C. 68 − 31 = ▒
D. 61 × 31 = ▒

10 Look at the graph below. Four students worked at the library. How many more hours did Julia work than the person who worked the least?

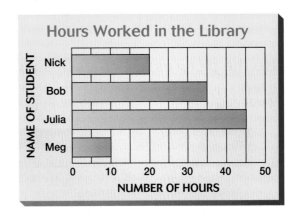

A. 10 hours   **C.** 35 hours
B. 20 hours   **D.** 55 hours

377A

Checkpoint

Adding and Subtracting Fractions

Vocabulary

Complete. Use the words from the Word Bank.

Word Bank

denominator
equivalent
   fractions
improper
   fractions
numerator

1. The number above the fraction bar is called the ___?___.

2. The number below the fraction bar is called the ___?___.

3. $\frac{2}{6}$ and $\frac{3}{9}$ are ___?___.

4. $\frac{11}{4}$ and $\frac{10}{5}$ are ___?___.

Skills and Concepts

Add or subtract. Write each sum or difference in simplest form. (pages 362–369)

5. $\frac{2}{8}$
   $+ \ \frac{3}{8}$
  —————

6. $\frac{2}{9}$
   $+ \ \frac{7}{9}$
  —————

7. $\frac{3}{12}$
   $+ \ \frac{8}{12}$
  —————

8. $\frac{5}{12}$
   $+ \ \frac{2}{12}$
  —————

9. $4\frac{3}{10}$
   $+ \ 3\frac{2}{10}$
  —————

10. $2\frac{1}{4}$
   $+ \ 3\frac{3}{4}$
  —————

11. $\frac{7}{8}$
   $- \ \frac{3}{8}$
  —————

12. $\frac{5}{6}$
   $- \ \frac{1}{6}$
  —————

13. $\frac{8}{9}$
   $- \ \frac{7}{9}$
  —————

14. $\frac{7}{10}$
   $- \ \frac{3}{10}$
  —————

15. $6\frac{4}{5}$
   $- \ 3\frac{1}{5}$
  —————

16. $7\frac{7}{9}$
   $- \ 5\frac{1}{9}$
  —————

Use the pictures to find each sum. (pages 372–373)

17. $\frac{1}{2} + \frac{1}{4}$

18. $\frac{1}{2} + \frac{2}{6}$

19. $\frac{2}{5} + \frac{3}{10}$

Use fraction pieces to find each difference. (pages 374–375)

20. $\frac{1}{2} - \frac{1}{6} =$

21. $\frac{4}{5} - \frac{1}{10} =$

22. $\frac{1}{2} - \frac{1}{4} =$

Problem Solving

23. Terry bought $3\frac{1}{4}$ pounds of red sand and $1\frac{1}{4}$ pounds of yellow sand. How many pounds of sand did Terry buy in all?

24. A bread recipe calls for $3\frac{1}{2}$ cups of wheat flour and $2\frac{1}{4}$ cups of rye flour. How much flour is in the recipe?

25. **Analyze** The sum of two fractions is $\frac{5}{6}$. Their difference is $\frac{1}{6}$. They have the same denominator. What are the two fractions?

What do you think?

When might you need to add or subtract fractions?

Journal Idea

Using the digits 1, 2, 3, and 4, write two fractions. Add these fractions. Subtract the lesser fraction from the greater one.

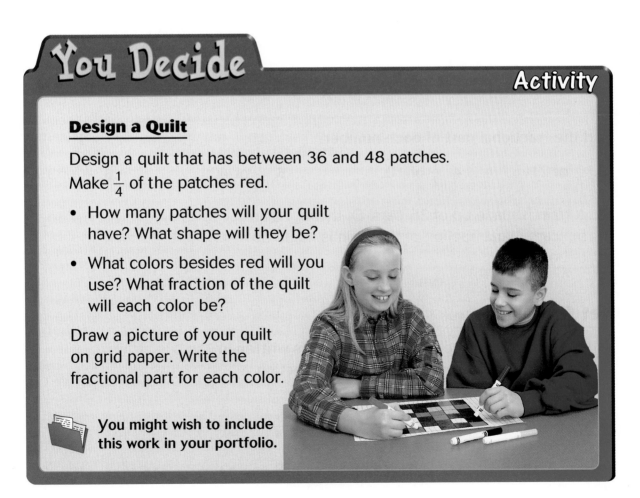

You Decide

Activity

Design a Quilt

Design a quilt that has between 36 and 48 patches. Make $\frac{1}{4}$ of the patches red.

- How many patches will your quilt have? What shape will they be?

- What colors besides red will you use? What fraction of the quilt will each color be?

Draw a picture of your quilt on grid paper. Write the fractional part for each color.

You might wish to include this work in your portfolio.

Extra Practice

Set A (pages 338–339)

Write a fraction for the shaded parts of each region.

1.

2.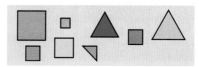

3.

Draw a picture to show each fraction.

4. $\frac{4}{6}$

5. $\frac{3}{8}$

6. $\frac{2}{3}$

7. $\frac{3}{4}$

8. $\frac{8}{9}$

9. $\frac{3}{12}$

10. Five eighths of a figure is shaded. How much of the figure is unshaded?

Set B (pages 340–343)

1. What fraction of the shapes are triangles? What fraction are circles?

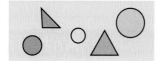

2. What fraction of the shapes are triangles? What fraction are squares?

Find the fractional part of each number.

3. $\frac{1}{3}$ of 21

4. $\frac{1}{2}$ of 10

5. $\frac{1}{8}$ of 40

6. $\frac{1}{5}$ of 35

7. A train is made up of 36 cars. Of these, 12 are boxcars. What fraction of the train is made up of boxcars?

Set C (pages 346–349)

Using Algebra Tell whether each fraction is written in simplest form. Write *yes* or *no*. Then use fraction pieces to write an equivalent fraction.

1. $\frac{2}{10}$

2. $\frac{3}{4}$

3. $\frac{2}{12}$

4. $\frac{8}{12}$

5. $\frac{1}{4}$

6. $\frac{2}{7}$

7. $\frac{6}{10}$

8. $\frac{5}{8}$

9. $\frac{1}{4}$

10. $\frac{6}{9}$

11. $\frac{1}{4}$

12. $\frac{2}{8}$

13. $\frac{6}{8}$

14. $\frac{2}{5}$

15. $\frac{2}{3}$

16. $\frac{5}{10}$

Extra Practice

Set D (pages 352–355)

Compare. Write >, <, or = for each ⬤.

1.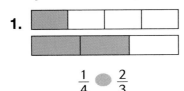

$$\frac{1}{4} \bullet \frac{2}{3}$$

2.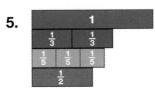

$$\frac{7}{8} \bullet \frac{3}{4}$$

3.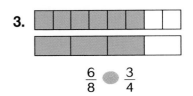

$$\frac{6}{8} \bullet \frac{3}{4}$$

Order the fractions from greatest to least.

4.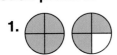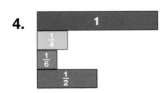

5.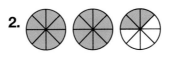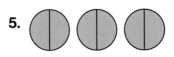

6.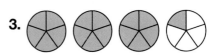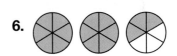

Set E (pages 356–357)

Write an improper fraction and a mixed number for each picture.

1.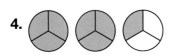

2.

3.

4.

5.

6.

7.

8.

9.

Set F (pages 362–365)

Add. Write each sum in simplest form. Use fraction pieces if you like.

1. $\frac{1}{8} + \frac{3}{8}$

2. $\frac{5}{12} + \frac{4}{12}$

3. $\frac{1}{5} + \frac{2}{5}$

4. $\frac{7}{10} + \frac{2}{10}$

5. $4\frac{2}{5} + 3\frac{1}{5}$

6. $10\frac{3}{5} + 3\frac{2}{5}$

7. $3\frac{3}{5} + \frac{1}{5}$

8. $5\frac{3}{10} + 3\frac{2}{10}$

9. $\frac{3}{5} + 1\frac{2}{5}$

10. $\frac{4}{8} + \frac{0}{8}$

11. $\frac{2}{10} + \frac{6}{10}$

12. $\frac{7}{12} + \frac{3}{12}$

Extra Practice

Set G (pages 366–369)

Subtract. Write your answer in simplest form. Use fraction pieces if you like.

1. $\frac{3}{5} - \frac{2}{5}$

2. $\frac{7}{8} - \frac{2}{8}$

3. $\frac{9}{12} - \frac{2}{12}$

4. $\frac{9}{10} - \frac{4}{10}$

5. $5\frac{8}{10} - 3\frac{1}{10}$

6. $9\frac{11}{12} - 6\frac{6}{12}$

7. $8\frac{9}{10} - 8\frac{5}{10}$

8. $6\frac{5}{5} - 1\frac{2}{5}$

Set H (pages 372–373)

Use fraction pieces to find each sum. Write your answer in simplest form.

1. $\frac{1}{8} + \frac{1}{2}$

2. $\frac{1}{3} + \frac{1}{6}$

3. $\frac{3}{10} + \frac{3}{5}$

4. $\frac{5}{12} + \frac{1}{4}$

5. $\frac{3}{8} + \frac{1}{4}$

6. $\frac{1}{3} + \frac{4}{6}$

7. $\frac{5}{12} + \frac{1}{3}$

8. $\frac{1}{2} + \frac{3}{8}$

9. $\frac{2}{8} + \frac{2}{4}$

10. $\frac{3}{12} + \frac{1}{4}$

11. $\frac{1}{2} + \frac{1}{4}$

12. $\frac{2}{5} + \frac{6}{10}$

13. It took Ramon $\frac{3}{4}$ hour to prepare dinner. The dinner lasted $\frac{1}{2}$ hour. How much time did it take to prepare and eat dinner?

Set I (pages 374–375)

Use fraction pieces to find each difference. Write your answer in simplest form.

1. $\frac{1}{2} - \frac{1}{8}$

2. $\frac{2}{3} - \frac{5}{12}$

3. $\frac{4}{5} - \frac{3}{10}$

4. $\frac{7}{8} - \frac{1}{4}$

5. $\frac{2}{3} - \frac{7}{12}$

6. $\frac{7}{8} - \frac{3}{4}$

7. $\frac{1}{4} - \frac{1}{8}$

8. $\frac{3}{5} - \frac{1}{10}$

9. $\frac{6}{12} - \frac{1}{3}$

10. $\frac{7}{8} - \frac{1}{2}$

11. $\frac{7}{10} - \frac{1}{5}$

12. $\frac{7}{8} - \frac{1}{4}$

13. One book is $\frac{3}{4}$ foot wide. Another book is $\frac{1}{2}$ foot wide. How much wider is one book than the other?

Chapter Test

Write a fraction for the shaded part of each region.

1.

2.

3.

Find the fractional part of each number.

4. $\frac{1}{4}$ of 28

5. $\frac{1}{3}$ of 15

Write two equivalent fractions for each. One should be in simplest form.

6. $\frac{2}{12}$

7. $\frac{3}{6}$

Write the improper fraction and mixed number for each picture.

8.

9.

10.

11.

Add or subtract. Write your answer in simplest form. Use fraction pieces or drawings if you wish.

12. $\frac{5}{8} + \frac{1}{8}$

13. $\frac{7}{8} - \frac{5}{8}$

14. $3\frac{3}{5} + 4\frac{1}{5}$

15. $6\frac{11}{12} - 2\frac{5}{12}$

16. $\frac{5}{8} + \frac{3}{8}$

17. $\frac{3}{5} - \frac{2}{5}$

18. $9\frac{1}{8} + 1\frac{2}{8}$

19. $\frac{5}{8} - \frac{3}{8}$

20. $\quad 5\frac{6}{8}$
$\quad - \quad \frac{1}{8}$
———

21. $\quad 3\frac{4}{6}$
$\quad + 6\frac{1}{6}$
———

22. $\quad 6\frac{6}{10}$
$\quad - 5\frac{3}{10}$
———

23. $\quad 4\frac{5}{12}$
$\quad + 6\frac{5}{12}$
———

Solve.

24. Cora's family spent $\frac{1}{4}$ hour traveling to and from a fair. They spent $1\frac{1}{4}$ hours at the fair. How much time did they spend away from home?

25. You have 48 building blocks. One fourth of the blocks are red. One third of the blocks are green. How many blocks are red? How many are green?

 Self-Check Check to see if you counted the sections correctly in Exercises 8–11.

Performance Assessment

Show What You Know About Fractions

1 Write five fraction problems about the vegetables in the picture below. Include your answers.

What You Need

grid paper (optional)
fraction pieces

Self-Check Did you use fractions in your problems?

2 Al has $9\frac{1}{4}$ inches of red ribbon and $6\frac{2}{4}$ inches of blue ribbon. He wants to make a border around a square picture frame with 4 sides measuring 4 inches each.

Does he have enough ribbon?
If yes, how much is left over?
If no, how much more does he need?

Self-Check Did you add the fractions correctly?

For Your Portfolio
You might wish to include this work in your portfolio.

Extension

Expressing Probability with Fractions

Sandra and Nick planned a board game for their school's Hobby Day. They made a spinner like the one shown at the right.

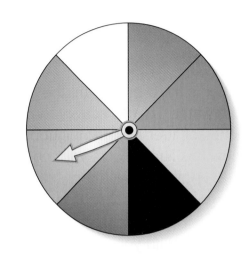

The number of spaces a player can move on the board depends on what color the player spins. Spinning blue moves a player the greatest number of spaces. What are the chances of spinning blue?

Look at the spinner. Blue is 1 of 8 equal parts. So, the chance of spinning blue is 1 out of 8. The probability of spinning blue can also be written as a fraction.

Probability
(of spinning blue) $= \dfrac{\text{number of blue sections}}{\text{total number of sections}}$

Probability
(of spinning blue) $= \dfrac{1}{8} \begin{matrix} \leftarrow \text{number of blue sections} \\ \leftarrow \text{total number of sections} \end{matrix}$

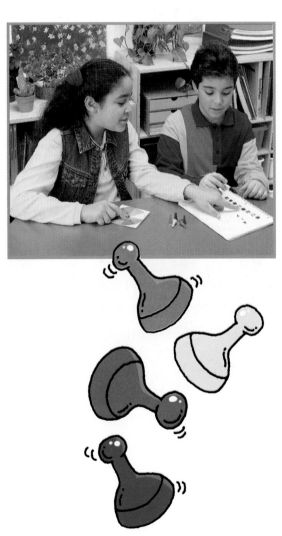

The probability of spinning blue is $\frac{1}{8}$.

Use the spinner to answer Questions 1–4.

1. What is the probability of spinning red?

2. What is the probability of *not* spinning blue?

3. What if 3 sections of the spinner were colored green? What would be the probability of spinning green?

4. Create Your Own Suppose you wanted to make a spinner for a game. How would you design it?

Using Math in Science

*Use **fractions** to investigate and **classify** the kinds of litter you find in your neighborhood.*

Taking a Litter Walk

Litter is trash thrown on the ground or in the water. Try this activity to explore the kinds of litter in your neighborhood and how this litter affects your environment.

What You Need

For each group:
  notepad
  pencil

Explore

Step 1 With your teacher, take a walk outdoors to look for litter. Make a list of 20 items you find. Each item you list should be made of only one type of material.

Step 2 Classify each item you find by the material it is made from. For example, a fast-food wrapper is made of paper; a soda can is made of metal.

Step 3 Make a chart like the one below. Show the types of materials you found and the number of items made of each type of material. Write fractions to show how much of the litter is made from each type of material. The numerator will be the number of items made of each type of material. The denominator will be the total number of items on your list.

Type of Material	Number of Items Found	Fraction of Litter Found	Fraction in Simplest Form
Paper	6	$\frac{6}{20}$	$\frac{3}{10}$
Metal	4	$\frac{4}{20}$	$\frac{1}{5}$

Analyze

1. What material was most of the litter that you found made from?

2. **What if?** Suppose a classmate told you that $\frac{1}{4}$ of their items were paper, $\frac{1}{5}$ were metal, and $\frac{11}{20}$ were plastic. How could you find which type of material was collected the most?

 For Your Portfolio

Write about how you classified the kinds of litter you found. Include the chart you made. Explain what your fractions tell you about the different kinds of litter you found.

Explore Further!

Research How does litter affect the plants and animals that share your environment? Look for examples of how litter affects living things. Write a paragraph about what you find.

Cumulative Review

★ ★ ★ ★ ★ **Preparing for Tests**

Choose the correct letter for each answer.

Number Concepts	Operations

1. Which street number shown below is an odd number?

   A. 6111 Park Street
   B. 3610 Glenview Drive
   C. 1542 Lincoln Road
   D. 4848 Milton Avenue

2. Mr. Goldberg flew one hundred two thousand, four hundred, fifty-eight miles last year. How is this number written?

   A. 100,200,458
   B. 124,058
   C. 102,458
   D. 12,458

3. What is 3,291 rounded to the nearest thousand?

   A. 2,000
   B. 3,000
   C. 3,500
   D. 4,000

4. Which picture has $\frac{2}{5}$ shaded?

   A. ○●●●○
   B. ○○●●●
   C. ●●○○○
   D. ○●●●●

5. $345 + 678 + 99 =$

   A. 2,013
   B. 1,122
   C. 1,023
   D. 922

6. Sarah wants to buy a CD that costs $13.39. She has $11.47. How much more money does she need?

   A. $2.12
   B. $2.06
   C. $1.92
   D. $1.76

7. Which is a reasonable remainder when a number is divided by 5?

   A. 9
   B. 6
   C. 5
   D. 4

8. There are 350 kids and 10 teachers in a drama club. The teachers put the students into 7 groups. How many students are in each group?

   A. 35   **C.** 45
   B. 40   **D.** 50

Patterns, Relationships, and Algebraic Thinking	Measurement

9. If 6 times a number is 72, which expression could be used to find the number?

A. 6 + 72
B. 72 ÷ 6
C. 6 × 72
D. 72 − 6

---

10. Which number sentence is in the same family of facts as 4 × 8 = 32?

A. 32 ÷ 4 = 8
B. 4 + 8 = 12
C. 16 × 2 = 32
D. 32 − 8 = 24

---

11. What is the missing number in the number pattern?

17, 34, 51, 68, ■, 102

A. 79
B. 82
C. 85
D. 97

---

12. Annie exercised for 10 minutes on Monday, 13 minutes on Tuesday, and 16 minutes Wednesday. If she continues to follow this pattern, how many minutes will she exercise on Sunday?

A. 7 min
B. 22 min
C. 25 min
D. 28 min

---

13. Mr. Rivera wants to build a fence around his back yard for his dog Max. How much fencing should he buy?

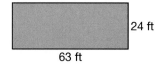

24 ft

63 ft

A. 39 feet   **C.** 174 feet
B. 87 feet   **D.** 1,512 feet

---

14. Mike gets up at 6:30 A.M. He leaves for school at 7:15 A.M. He gets to school at 7:30 A.M. How long does it take Mike to get ready to leave for school?

A. 15 minutes   **C.** 45 minutes
B. 30 minutes   **D.** 1 hour

---

15. What is the *perimeter* of the triangle below?

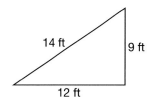

14 ft

9 ft

12 ft

A. 35 ft   **C.** 26 ft
B. 32 ft   **D.** 25 ft

---

16. Kelly adopted a puppy that weighed 3 lb 4 oz. It now weighs 12 lb 9 oz. How much weight has Kelly's puppy gained since she adopted it?

A. 28 lb   **C.** 9 lb 5 oz
B. 15 lb 3 oz   **D.** 4 lb 3 oz

Chapter 10

Decimals

Chapter Theme: "ON THE ROAD"

..................Real Facts...................

The Jesse White Tumbling Team, shown at the right, has thrilled crowds around the world. The team is from Chicago but sometimes they fly to the places where they perform. The table below shows the cost of some round-trip airfares from Chicago.

Round-trip Airfares from Chicago	
Destination	**Cost of Tickets**
Honolulu, Hawaii	$749.78
Houston, Texas	$301.00
Indianapolis, Indiana	$105.00
Miami, Florida	$218.00
San Juan, Puerto Rico	$496.55

- What do the numbers to the left of the decimal point mean? to the right of the decimal point?

- Suppose 10 members of the team are flying to Miami. How could you find their total airfare?

..................Real People...................

Meet Jesse White. In 1959 he started the Jesse White Tumbling Team. The team has performed at professional sporting events and has appeared on television and in movies. Members of the team range in age from 6 to 22. During 1999, the tumblers performed in 970 shows.

From the Farm

You will learn how fractions and decimals are related.

Learning About It

The Hall family lives on a farm in Pennsylvania. They planted 10 equal rows in a small garden. One of the rows was tomato plants.

The drawing below shows that $\frac{1}{10}$ of the crop was a row of tomatoes. A fraction whose denominator is 10 or 100 can also be written as a **decimal**.

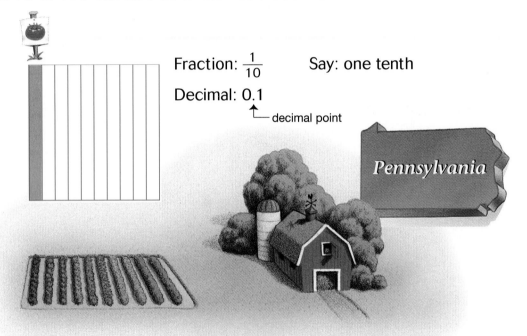

Fraction: $\frac{1}{10}$ Say: one tenth

Decimal: 0.1

⬆ — decimal point

Pennsylvania

Step 1 Work with a partner. Use grid paper to plan a 10-row garden. Make a drawing like the one above. Decide how many whole rows of corn, peas, carrots, and tomatoes you will plant. Color each row, using a different color for each vegetable.

- Label your drawing with the fraction and decimal for each kind of vegetable you will plant.

- What fraction of your garden is not made up of tomatoes? Write that fraction as a decimal.

What You Need

For each pair:
   grid paper
   colored markers or
      colored pencils

Step 2 The Halls planted two square 100-acre fields. Field A below shows that $\frac{1}{100}$ of one field was corn. Field B shows that $\frac{37}{100}$ of the other field was beans.

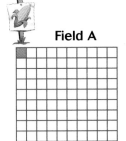

Field A

Fraction: $\frac{1}{100}$

Decimal: 0.01

Say: one hundredth

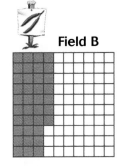

Field B

Fraction: $\frac{37}{100}$

Decimal: 0.37

Say: thirty-seven hundredths

- What fraction of Field A's crop is not corn? How did you decide? Write this fraction as a decimal.

- Use grid paper to draw a 10-by-10 square like the ones above. Use it to show a field that is $\frac{7}{100}$ corn. Write the decimal for this fraction.

- Use your grid paper to draw another 10-by-10 square. Shade $\frac{75}{100}$ of this square. Write this fraction as a decimal.

Step 3 **Equivalent decimals** name the same amount.

This square shows $\frac{3}{10}$ or 0.3.

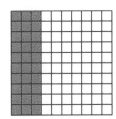

This square shows $\frac{30}{100}$ or 0.30.

- How are the two squares the same? How are they different?

- Are the decimals 0.3 and 0.30 equivalent? Why or why not?

Think and Discuss Give as many ways as you can to describe the amount shaded in the model to the right.

Practice

Write a fraction and a decimal to describe how much is shaded in each model.

1.

2.

3.

4.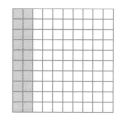

5.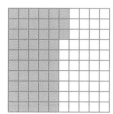

6.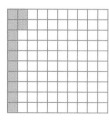

7. How are the shaded grids in Exercises 1 and 5 alike? How are they different?

Draw a model that shows each fraction or decimal.

8. $\frac{2}{10}$

9. 0.8

10. $\frac{7}{100}$

11. 0.32

12. 0.73

13. $\frac{6}{10}$

14. 0.50

15. $\frac{15}{100}$

16. $\frac{81}{100}$

17. 0.90

18. 0.03

19. $\frac{3}{10}$

20. The fractions tell how much of a garden was planted with each crop.

tomatoes $\frac{2}{10}$ 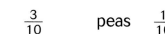 beans $\frac{4}{10}$

lettuce $\frac{3}{10}$ peas $\frac{1}{10}$

a. Write each fraction as a decimal.

b. Use grid paper to draw a model of this garden.

392

Analyze Use the drawing above to answer Exercises 21–26. Write each answer as a fraction and a decimal.

21. Which part of the harvest is corn?

22. Which part of the harvest is not corn?

23. How much of the harvest is tomatoes and beans?

24. How much of the harvest is not corn or beans?

25. How much more of the harvest is tomatoes than corn?

26. **Create Your Own** Write a problem about the harvest and exchange with your partner to solve.

Critical Thinking Corner

Visual Thinking

Shady Parts

Write a fraction and a decimal to describe how much is shaded.

1. **2.** 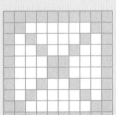 **3.** **4.**

  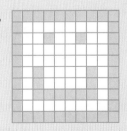

Getting Ready

You can write mixed numbers as whole numbers and decimals.

Learning About It

The Halls had their car serviced before leaving for vacation. It is $2\frac{6}{10}$ miles to the garage from their farm. Write this mixed number as a decimal.

$$2\frac{6}{10} = \blacksquare$$

You can use a model to help you.

Mixed number: $2\frac{6}{10}$

Decimal: 2.6

Say: two and six tenths

More Examples

A. Mixed number: $1\frac{3}{100}$

Decimal: 1.03

Say: one and three hundredths

B. Mixed number: $2\frac{82}{100}$

Decimal: 2.82

Say: two and eighty-two hundredths

C. Mixed number: $24\frac{8}{10}$

Decimal: 24.8

Say: twenty-four and eight tenths

Did You Know?

The prefix *deci*, as in decimal, means "one-tenth." Other words with this prefix include decimeter and decigram.

Think and Discuss Which of these mixed numbers can be written as decimals: $1\frac{5}{10}$, $2\frac{1}{2}$, $3\frac{2}{100}$, $4\frac{1}{4}$? Explain.

Try It Out

Write the mixed number and the decimal for the shaded parts for each exercise.

1.

2.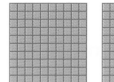

Write each mixed number as a decimal.

3. $6\frac{3}{10}$ **4.** $1\frac{47}{100}$ **5.** $5\frac{9}{10}$ **6.** $13\frac{57}{100}$ **7.** $2\frac{6}{10}$

Practice

Write each mixed number or fraction as a decimal.

8. $7\frac{2}{10}$ **9.** $\frac{3}{10}$ **10.** $4\frac{4}{10}$ **11.** $\frac{71}{100}$ **12.** $17\frac{2}{10}$

13. $\frac{25}{100}$ **14.** $8\frac{94}{100}$ **15.** $24\frac{54}{100}$ **16.** $9\frac{37}{100}$ **17.** $3\frac{6}{10}$

Write each decimal as a fraction or mixed number.

18. 0.4   **19.** 2.6   **20.** 92.05   **21.** 8.80   **22.** 35.32

Problem Solving

23. The Halls bought 3 cases of oil with 10 quarts in each case. They had 2 full cases and 7 quarts of oil left after their trip. Write a mixed number and a decimal to tell how much of the oil was left.

24. Analyze The mechanic added 2 pints of windshield wiper fluid to the car. If each half pint cost $0.50, is it reasonable to say $2.50 was enough to pay for the fluid? Explain.

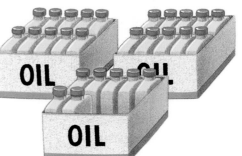

Review and Remember

Find each answer.

25. 462×34 **26.** $608 - 345$ **27.** $8\overline{)65}$ **28.** $578 + 239 + 63$

For Extra Practice, see Set A, page 422.

On the Road

You will learn how decimals show place value.

Virginia

Learning About It

The Halls stopped to buy gasoline in Virginia. Look at the pump to see the amount of gasoline they purchased.

A place-value chart helps you read and write decimals.

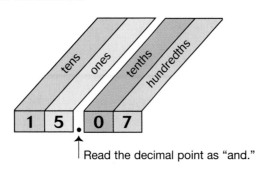

tens	ones	.	tenths	hundredths
1	5	.	0	7

Read the decimal point as "and."

15.07 Gallons

You can write this number in different ways.

- **Word form:** fifteen and seven hundredths

- **Short word form:** 15 and 7 hundredths

- **Standard form:** 15.07

More Examples

A. Write: 0.2

     tenths place

Say: two tenths

B. You can use decimals when you write money.

Write: $6.35
Say: six dollars and thirty-five cents

Think and Discuss Is the value of the digit 2 in 0.2 and 0.02 the same? Explain.

Try It Out

Write the word form for each decimal.

1. 275.14 **2.** 347.83 **3.** 194.66 **4.** 461.08 **5.** 585.4

Write each as a decimal.

6. seven and eighteen hundredths **7.** two and six hundredths

Practice

Write each as a decimal.

8. four and three tenths **9.** 8 and 2 hundredths

10. three and nine tenths **11.** 11 and 70 hundredths

Write the word form for each decimal.

12. 207.36 **13.** 182.09 **14.** 776.9 **15.** 580.19 **16.** 633.94

Tell the place value of each underlined digit.

17. 326.9<u>9</u> **18.** 835.8<u>5</u> **19.** <u>1</u>43.06 **20.** 456.4<u>8</u> **21.** 970.3<u>5</u>

22. 6<u>4</u>8.92 **23.** 421.6<u>4</u> **24.** 502.<u>3</u>7 **25.** 861.<u>6</u>7 **26.** 872.<u>3</u>2

Problem Solving

27. Analyze A decimal number has a 4 in the ones place, a 5 in the tens place, and a 9 in the tenths place. Write the number.

28. Using Mental Math A room at a motel in Williamsburg cost $49.95. Which digit is in the hundredths place? What amount of money is shown by the digit in the hundredths place?

▲ **Kid Connection** Randy James Smith of Virginia reenacts an 18th-century boat trip down the James River as he helps steer a wooden barge called a bateau (ba TOH) 120.5 miles.

Review and Remember

Choose a Method Solve by using paper and pencil, mental math, or a calculator.

29. 27 × 10 **30.** 973 − 584 **31.** $45.00 × 7 **32.** 739 ÷ 6 **33.** 6,528 + 97

Sorting Shells

Place value can help you compare and order decimals.

Learning About It

In North Carolina the Halls bought seashells that were sold by the pound. Anna's bag of shells weighed 1.83 pounds, and Zack's weighed 1.68 pounds. Whose bag of shells weighed more?

North Carolina

You can use models to compare.

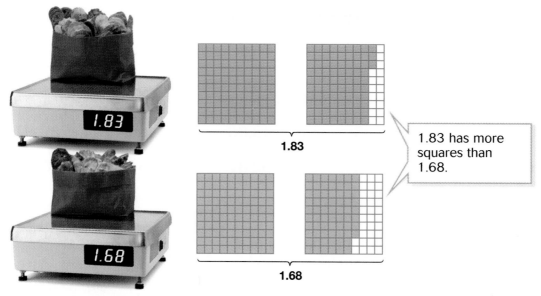

1.83

1.68

> 1.83 has more squares than 1.68.

1.83 pounds is more than 1.68 pounds. Anna's bag weighed more.

More Examples

A. 0.4 is equal to 0.40

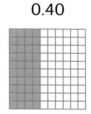

0.4   0.40

B. 0.8 is greater than 0.08

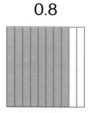

0.8   0.08

You can also use a place-value chart to compare decimals.

Which is greater, 82.58 or 82.52?

Line up the decimal points.

Begin comparing digits at the left.

When digits are the same, continue comparing the digits to the right.

82.58 > 82.52

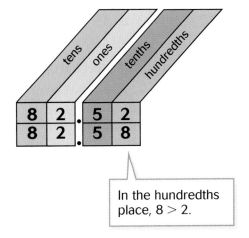

In the hundredths place, 8 > 2.

Connecting Ideas

Now that you know how to compare decimals, you can order decimals from greatest to least or from least to greatest.

Order these numbers from greatest to least: 1.6, 1.83, and 1.69.

Step 1 Line up the decimal points.

Step 2 Start at the left. Compare digits in the same place.

Step 3 When digits are the same, compare digits to the right.

Step 4 Continue until you can write all the numbers in order.

The numbers from greatest to least are 1.83, 1.69, 1.60.

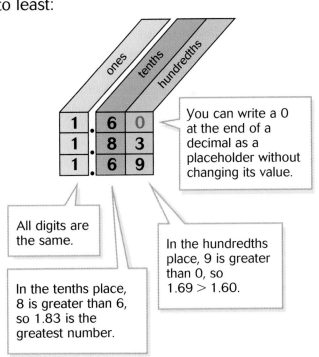

You can write a 0 at the end of a decimal as a placeholder without changing its value.

All digits are the same.

In the tenths place, 8 is greater than 6, so 1.83 is the greatest number.

In the hundredths place, 9 is greater than 0, so 1.69 > 1.60.

Think and Discuss How does knowing how to compare two decimal numbers help you order three or more?

Try It Out

Compare. Write >, <, or = for each ⬤.

1. 5.8 ⬤ 4.5
2. 35.9 ⬤ 35.93
3. 8.15 ⬤ 8.1
4. 20.86 ⬤ 20.89

Order each set of numbers from greatest to least.

5. 29.14; 29.41; 29.44
6. 6.09; 6.7; 6.49
7. 14.7; 14.07; 14.67

Practice

Compare. Write >, <, or = for each ⬤.

8. 16.08 ⬤ 16.8
9. 38.56 ⬤ 38.59
10. 56.3 ⬤ 56.19

11. 11.12 ⬤ 11.21
12. 85.8 ⬤ 85.81
13. 23.35 ⬤ 23.37

14. 44.09 ⬤ 44.9
15. 76.23 ⬤ 76.32
16. 112.52 ⬤ 112.25

17. 97.11 ⬤ 97.1
18. 9.67 ⬤ 9.57
19. 224.56 ⬤ 224.6

Order each set of numbers from greatest to least.

20. 25.91, 25.98, 25.94
21. 81.7, 81.77, 81.07

22. 73.46, 73.64, 73.56
23. 59.27, 59.75, 59.52

Order each set of numbers from least to greatest.

24. 66.04, 66.24, 66.23
25. 118.78, 118.7, 119.72

26. 36.76, 36.86, 36.96
27. 48.03, 48.3, 48.33

Problem Solving

Use the table to solve Problems 28–30.

28. Which car gets the most miles per gallon on the highway?

29. Which car gets less than 28.10 miles per gallon on the highway?

30. Which car gets twenty-eight and five hundredths miles to the gallon on the highway?

Miles per Gallon		
Type of Car	City Driving	Highway Driving
New car	26.04	28.5
Old car	26.94	28.05

INTERNET ACTIVITY
www.sbgmath.com

31. Create Your Own Make up two problems using decimals and whole numbers, about a family traveling across the United States. Ask a classmate to solve them.

32. Science Connection Kudzu is a vine that grows quickly in the southeastern United States. It can climb up to 30 cm a day. Anna found a kudzu flower that measured 28.3 cm. Zack found one that measured 28.03 cm. Who found the longer flower?

33. Journal Idea Compare and order these decimals from greatest to least: 52.65, 52.56, 52.60. Explain how you found the greatest number and the second greatest number.

Review and Remember

Find each answer.

34. $7\overline{)627}$ **35.** $\frac{3}{6} + \frac{2}{6}$ **36.** 923×70 **37.** $\frac{5}{12} - \frac{4}{12}$ **38.** $730 - 109$

39. $\frac{6}{7} - \frac{2}{7}$ **40.** $92 \div 6$ **41.** $2{,}375 \times 7$ **42.** $8\overline{)396}$ **43.** $\frac{2}{10} + \frac{6}{10}$

Time for Technology

Using a Calculator

Fractions to Decimals

You can use a calculator to find the decimal for a fraction.

Remember: $\frac{1}{5}$ means $1 \div 5$.

Press: [1] [÷] [5] [=]   Display: (0.2)

Use your calculator to find a decimal for each fraction.

1. $\frac{4}{5}$ **2.** $\frac{2}{8}$ **3.** $\frac{2}{4}$ **4.** $\frac{1}{2}$ **5.** $\frac{3}{4}$

Developing Skills for Problem Solving

First read for understanding and then focus on whether more than one step is needed to solve a problem.

READ FOR UNDERSTANDING

When President Franklin Roosevelt rode in the *Ferdinand Magellan*, he traveled at a speed of 35 miles per hour. Years later, when President Harry Truman rode in it, he traveled at 80 miles per hour.

1 How fast did the railroad car travel when President Roosevelt rode in it?

2 How fast did the railroad car travel when President Truman rode in it?

▲ **Social Studies Connection**
The *Ferdinand Magellan* is a private railroad car that was used by several U.S. presidents.

THINK AND DISCUSS

MATH FOCUS

Multistep Problems Sometimes it takes more than one step to solve a problem. Then you need to decide not only *what* the steps are, but in what *order* you should do them.

Reread the paragraph at the top of the page.

3 How can you find how far the train car traveled in 4 hours when President Roosevelt rode in it? when President Truman rode in it?

4 How much farther could President Truman travel in 4 hours than President Roosevelt? What steps do you need to do to solve the problem?

5 Why must you be extra careful when solving multistep problems?

▲ Top: President Roosevelt
Bottom: President Truman

Show What You Learned

Answer each question. Give a reason for your choice.

The *Ferdinand Magellan* has been at the Gold Coast Railroad Museum in Florida since 1959. It had been used by President Dwight D. Eisenhower 5 years earlier. Twelve years before that, it had become the official presidential railroad car.

▲ President Eisenhower

1 What can you do to find the year that President Eisenhower used the railroad car?

a. Subtract 5 years from 1959.

b. Subtract 12 years from 1959.

c. Add 5 years to 1959.

2 How can the answer to Problem 1 help you know when *Ferdinand Magellan* became the official car?

a. Add 12 years to 1954.

b. Subtract 5 years from 1954.

c. Subtract 12 years from 1954.

3 **Explain** Can you think of another way to find the year that the *Ferdinand Magellan* became the official car, using different operations?

The *Ferdinand Magellan* was taken out of the museum in 1984 so that President Ronald Reagan could use it. He made a total of 5 stops with an average of 24 miles between each stop. In 1948, President Truman traveled about 250 times farther than President Reagan.

4 What number sentence could you use to find how many miles President Reagan traveled?

a. 24 miles × 5 stops

b. 250 miles × 5 stops

c. 5 stops × 1948

5 What number sentence could you use to find how many miles President Truman traveled?

a. 250 × 24 miles

b. 250 × 120 miles

c. 250 × 5 miles

6 **Explain** What steps do you need to do to find how many miles longer President Truman's trips were than President Reagan's trip?

✔ Checkpoint

Understanding Fractions, Mixed Numbers, and Decimals

Write the fraction and decimal for each model.
(pages 390–393)

1.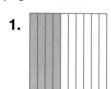

2.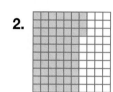

3.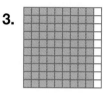

Write each fraction or mixed number as a decimal.
(pages 394–395)

4. $\frac{9}{10}$ **5.** $4\frac{87}{100}$ **6.** $\frac{1}{10}$ **7.** $\frac{92}{100}$ **8.** $8\frac{11}{100}$

Write each decimal as a fraction or mixed number.
(pages 394–395)

9. 0.8 **10.** 9.3 **11.** 0.5 **12.** 0.42 **13.** 5.77

14. 0.19 **15.** 2.25 **16.** 0.60 **17.** 0.53 **18.** 0.1

Write the word form for each decimal. (pages 396–397)

19. 482.36 **20.** 905.38 **21.** 204.91 **22.** 782.08

23. 235.2 **24.** 863.97 **25.** 606.93 **26.** 233.60

Compare. Write >, <, or = for each ●. (pages 398–401)

27. 8.3 ● 8.30 **28.** 7.9 ● 7.09 **29.** 3.16 ● 3.26

30. 4.81 ● 4.72 **31.** 1.39 ● 1.93 **32.** 32.9 ● 32.90

Order each set of numbers from greatest to least.
(pages 398–401)

33. 6.14, 6.41, 6.04 **34.** 4.38, 4.83, 8.34 **35.** 3.27, 3.37, 3.7

Order each set of numbers from least to greatest.
(pages 398–401)

36. 9.78, 9.87, 9.8 **37.** 6.18, 6.48, 6.8 **38.** 4.2, 4.12, 4.02

Problem Solving

39. The post office charges by weight to deliver packages. If a package weighs no more than 6.75 lb, it costs $3.95 to mail. If the package weighs more than 6.75 lb, it costs $5.54 to mail. How much would be charged for a package that weighs 6.57 lb?

40. Using Mental Math The veterinarian weighed 3 dogs. Sport weighed 35.14 kg, Pepper weighed 35.41 kg, and Lefty weighed 35.44 kg. Which dog was the heaviest? Which was the lightest?

What do you think?

Why do you need to line up the decimal points when you compare two numbers?

Journal Idea

Write about how you know which number is greater, 3.4 or 3.45. Then explain how you could find a number between them.

Critical Thinking Corner

Visual Thinking

Picturing Decimals

Choose the picture with the shaded area that matches each decimal.

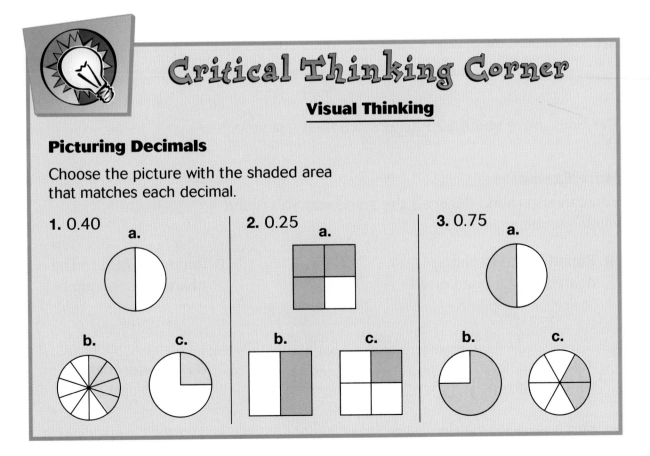

1. 0.40

a.   b.   c.

2. 0.25

a.   b.   c.

3. 0.75

a.   b.   c.

Around We Go

You can use a number line to round decimals.

Learning About It

The Halls stopped in New Orleans, Louisiana. The odometer showed that they had traveled 273.3 miles since their last stop. What is that distance rounded to the nearest whole number?

You can use a number line to help you round a decimal.

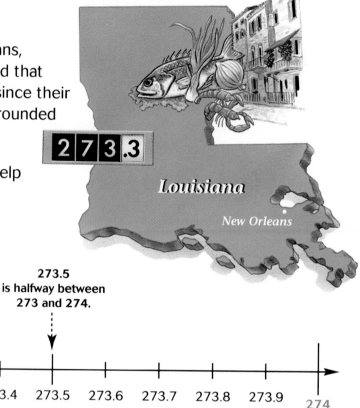

2 7 3 .3

Louisiana

New Orleans

273.5 is halfway between 273 and 274.

273.3 is closer to 273, so 273.3 rounds to 273.

273   273.1   273.2   273.3   273.4   273.5   273.6   273.7   273.8   273.9   274

The Halls drove about 273 miles since their last stop.

More Examples

You can also round decimals the same way you round whole numbers.

A. Round 273.4 to the nearest whole number.

273.4

4 is less than 5, so round down.

273.4 rounds to 273.

Look at the digit in the tenths place.

B. Round 127.84 to the nearest whole number.

127.84

8 is greater than 5, so round up.

127.84 rounds to 128.

Connecting Ideas

Once you know how to round decimals, you can use rounding to estimate sums and differences.

The Halls drove 144.6 miles before lunch and 130.4 miles after lunch. About how many miles did they drive that day?

$$\begin{array}{r} 144.6 \quad \text{rounds up to} \quad 145 \quad \text{because } 6 > 5 \\ +\ 130.4 \quad \text{rounds down to} \quad +\ 130 \quad \text{because } 4 < 5 \\ \hline 275 \end{array}$$

The Halls drove about 275 miles that day.

Another Example

Estimate the difference between 429.71 and 210.39.

$$\begin{array}{r} 429.71 \quad \text{rounds up to} \quad 430 \quad \text{because } 7 > 5 \\ -\ 210.39 \quad \text{rounds down to} \quad -\ 210 \quad \text{because } 3 < 5 \\ \hline 220 \end{array}$$

The difference is about 220.

Think and Discuss The numbers 3.5 and 4.4 both round to 4. Explain why.

Try It Out

Round each decimal to the nearest whole number.

1. 0.84   **2.** 43.5   **3.** 26.38   **4.** 19.0   **5.** 34.25

Write two decimals that round to each number.

6. 17   **7.** 25   **8.** 12   **9.** 100   **10.** 318

Round each decimal to the nearest whole number. Then add or subtract.

11. 385.46 −185.33   **12.** 815.37 +247.34   **13.** 705.3 −227.45   **14.** 345.29 +483.77   **15.** 0.69 +427.43

Practice

Round each decimal to the nearest whole number.

16. 46.8   **17.** 1.37   **18.** 78.2   **19.** 0.77   **20.** 2.91

21. 25.47   **22.** 64.3   **23.** 92.95   **24.** 49.86   **25.** 16.47

26. 21.52   **27.** 38.29   **28.** 57.18   **29.** 18.7   **30.** 68.7

31. 76.2   **32.** 84.62   **33.** 63.8   **34.** 32.55   **35.** 84.09

Round each decimal to the nearest whole number.
Then add or subtract.

36.   137.48
       + 396.12

37.   604.32
       − 187.6

38.   277.91
       − 84.33

39.   742.1
       + 106.89

40.   421.62
       + 910.81

41.   364.28
       − 219.47

42.   938.1
       − 627.72

43.   258.85
       + 632.46

44.   421.38
       + 99.7

45.   556.91
       − 218.57

46.   910.48
       − 541.63

47.   855.12
       + 97.64

Write each value as a decimal. Then round to the
nearest dollar.

	Dollars	Quarters	Dimes	Pennies	Decimal	Estimate
48.	3	2			■	■
49.		1	6	20	■	■
50.	5	2	7	4	■	■
51.	2	3	2	3	■	■

Problem Solving

52. It is about 89 miles from New Orleans to
Baton Rouge, Louisiana. If it is 49.3 miles
from New Orleans to Garyville, Louisiana,
estimate how far it is from Garyville to
Baton Rouge.

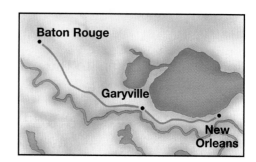

53. The Halls stopped for lunch in Lafayette, Louisiana. They spent $35.78 for food, $6.84 for drinks, and left a $7.00 tip for the waiter. Estimate how much they spent in all for lunch.

54. Breaux Bridge, Louisiana, is the Crawfish Capital of the World. One person caught 25.83 pounds of crawfish. Another person caught 31.44 pounds of crawfish. About how many more pounds were needed to make 75 pounds?

55. Analyze Zack likes mountain biking. He always practices on two trails. Trail A is 1.5 km long. Trail B is 2 km. How many practice trips does he make to reach his goal of 16 km? Explain your strategy.

▲ **Fine Arts Connection**
Zydeco is music native to Louisiana. It is played on metal washboards, spoons, harmonicas, and accordions.

 Review and Remember

Find each equivalent measure.

56. 27 yd = ▨ ft   **57.** 5 lb = ▨ oz   **58.** 6 ft = ▨ in.   **59.** 42 c = ▨ pt

60. 2 mi = ▨ ft   **61.** 68 pt = ▨ qt   **62.** 108 in. = ▨ yd   **63.** 32 oz = ▨ lb

64. 15 yd = ▨ in.   **65.** 50 lb = ▨ oz   **66.** 96 in. = ▨ ft   **67.** 144 oz = ▨ lb

 Money $ense

Souvenir Shop

1. To the nearest dollar, about how much would 2 sweatshirts and 2 T-shirts cost? About how much change would you get from $100?

2. Suppose the shop has a half-price sale. To the nearest dollar, about how much would you pay for a hat, a T-shirt, and 2 sweatshirts?

Souvenirs

T-shirts
$13.98

Sweatshirts
$34.88

Baseball Hats
$4.29

For Extra Practice, see Set D page 423.

Problem Solving
Draw a Picture

You can often solve a problem by drawing a picture.

Happy trails! Jan, Luis, Wayne, Carmen, and Tim are horseback riding on a ranch. Use the clues at the right to figure out the order in which the friends are riding.

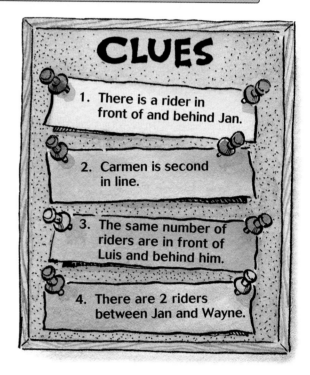

CLUES

1. There is a rider in front of and behind Jan.

2. Carmen is second in line.

3. The same number of riders are in front of Luis and behind him.

4. There are 2 riders between Jan and Wayne.

 UNDERSTAND

What do you need to find?

You need to find who is first, second, third, fourth, and fifth in line.

 PLAN

How can you solve the problem?

You can make a drawing to find the order in which the friends are riding. Draw 5 spaces to show first, second, third, fourth, and fifth. Use the clues to draw the correct friend on each line.

 SOLVE

Clue 1 This tells you that Jan must be second, third, or fourth, but you can't tell which yet.

Clue 2 Carmen is second.

Clue 3 Luis is in the middle, so he is third. That means that Jan must be fourth.

Clue 4 Wayne is first. There is one place left, so Tim must be fifth.

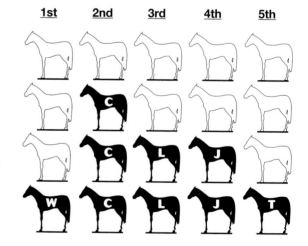

1st   2nd   3rd   4th   5th

 LOOK BACK

Does the order of the friends match the clues? Explain how you know.

Using the Strategy

Draw a picture to solve Problems 1–4.

1 A barn has 4 horse stalls belonging to Rusty, Dusty, Gusty, and Justy. Gusty's stall is next to only one other stall. Justy is in the third stall. Dusty is not next to Justy. Which horse is in which stall?

2 The fence around a horse corral is a rectangle that is 20 yards long and 12 yards wide. There are posts every 4 yards along the fence and at every corner. How many posts are there around the entire fence?

3 Breakfast on the trail is either flapjacks, oatmeal, or eggs. Monday it was not eggs, Tuesday it was not oatmeal, and Wednesday it was not eggs or oatmeal. What was breakfast on each day?

4 Ten people are going to a Texas barbecue. Tables like the ones shown are pushed together to make one long table. How many tables are needed to seat all 10 people?

Mixed Strategy Review

Try these or other strategies to solve each problem. Tell which strategy you used.

Problem Solving Strategies

- Make a List
- Draw a Picture
- Solve a Simpler Problem
- Act It Out
- Guess and Check
- Write a Number Sentence

5 Cara and Tim rode 17 miles. Tim rode 5 more miles than Cara. How many miles did they each ride?

6 Troy has 3 different pairs of boots and 4 different hats. How many different outfits can he make?

7 A fence is 15 sections long. Each section begins and ends with a post. How many posts are there?

8 Luis and Jan saddled 1 out of every 5 horses in the corral. There were 75 horses in the corral. How many horses did they saddle?

Old and New

You can add decimals the same way you add whole numbers.

Pueblo Bonito

Bike Path

Chaco Canyon

Chaco Canyon

New Mexico

Learning About It

In Chaco Canyon, New Mexico, the Halls biked about 1.5 miles. Then they continued for another 0.7 mile to Pueblo Bonito. How far did they go altogether?

$$1.5 + 0.7 = \blacksquare$$

Estimate first: $2 + 1 = 3$

THERE'S ALWAYS A WAY!

○ **One way** to find the exact answer is to use a model.

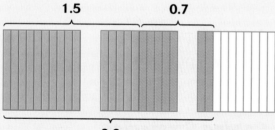

1.5   0.7

2.2

○ **Another way** is to use paper and pencil.

Step 1 Line up the decimal points.	**Step 2** Add the tenths. Regroup if necessary.	**Step 3** Add the ones. Place the decimal point.
$\begin{array}{r} 1.5 \\ +\ 0.7 \\ \hline \end{array}$	$\begin{array}{r} \overset{1}{1}.5 \\ +\ 0.7 \\ \hline 2 \end{array}$	$\begin{array}{r} \overset{1}{1}.5 \\ +\ 0.7 \\ \hline 2.2 \end{array}$

The Halls biked 2.2 miles.
The answer 2.2 is close to the estimate of 3.

More Examples

A.   4.26
      + 13.58
      —————
       17.84

B.   5.00
      + 6.76
      —————
       11.76

Think: Line up the decimal points. Write zeros as placeholders.

Think and Discuss How is adding decimals like adding whole numbers? How is it different?

Try It Out

Estimate first. Then find each sum.

1.   0.5
      + 1.3
      ————

2.   4.27
      + 0.68
      —————

3.   3.9
      + 2.3
      ————

4.   2.09
      + 1.76
      —————

5.   4.2
      + 3.85
      —————

6. 10.5 + 11.31   **7.** 4.37 + 8.91   **8.** 12.90 + 7.6   **9.** 24.04 + 1.07

Practice

Find each sum.

10.   3.78
       + 1.49
       —————

11.   6.07
       + 8.94
       —————

12.   5.5
       + 3.86
       —————

13.   8.97
       + 2.85
       —————

14.   7.77
       + 6.9
       ————

15. 24.11 + 52.42   **16.** 37.89 + 98.3   **17.** 86.61 + 38.84   **18.** 63.18 + 94.9

Problem Solving

Use the table to answer Problem 19.

19. How many miles did the Halls hike during the 3 days?

20. **Using Estimation** The Halls bought a Hopi jar for $19.56 and a Zuni necklace for $26.95. Was $50.00 enough to pay for their purchases? Explain your answer.

Halls' Hiking Diary			
	Mon.	Tues.	Wed.
Destination	Pueblo Bonito	Hungo Pavi	Pueblo del Arroyo
Miles hiked	3.75	1.7	5.3

Review and Remember

Using Algebra Solve for *n*.

21. $800 + n = 853$ **22.** $n - 450 = 50$ **23.** $n \times 7 = 63$

For Extra Practice, see Set E, page 423.

Track the Miles

You will learn how to subtract decimals.

Learning About It

Tracks at Dinosaur Valley State Park, in Texas, show that Acrocanthosaurus probably traveled at 5 miles per hour. If Pleurocoelus traveled at 2.7 miles per hour, how much faster was Acrocanthosaurus?

$$5 - 2.7 = \blacksquare$$

Estimate first: $5 - 3 = 2$

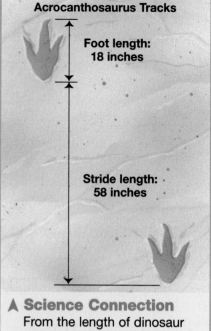

Acrocanthosaurus Tracks

Foot length: 18 inches

Stride length: 58 inches

▲ **Science Connection**
From the length of dinosaur tracks and strides, scientists have learned how fast dinosaurs moved.

THERE'S ALWAYS A WAY!

• **One way** is to use decimal models.

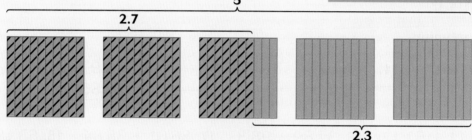

5

2.7

2.3

• **Another way** is to use paper and pencil.

Step 1 Line up the decimal points.	**Step 2** Subtract the tenths. Regroup if necessary.	**Step 3** Subtract the ones. Place the decimal point in the answer.
$\begin{array}{r} 5.0 \\ -\ 2.7 \end{array}$ Write a zero as a place-holder.	$\begin{array}{r} {\scriptstyle 4\ 10} \\ 5.\cancel{0} \\ -\ 2.7 \\ \hline 3 \end{array}$	$\begin{array}{r} {\scriptstyle 4\ 10} \\ 5.\cancel{0} \\ -\ 2.7 \\ \hline 2.3 \end{array}$

Acrocanthosaurus traveled 2.3 miles per hour faster.
The answer 2.3 is close to the estimate of 2.

More Examples

A.
$$\begin{array}{r} {\scriptstyle 5\ 11} \\ 4.6\cancel{1} \\ -\ 1.34 \\ \hline 3.27 \end{array}$$

B.
$$\begin{array}{r} {\scriptstyle 9} \\ {\scriptstyle 6\ \cancel{10}\ 10} \\ 7.\cancel{00} \\ -\ 5.72 \\ \hline 1.28 \end{array}$$

Think and Discuss Why do you need to line up the decimal points when you subtract decimals?

Try It Out

Estimate first. Then find each difference.

1.
$$\begin{array}{r} 1.9 \\ -\ 1.2 \\ \hline \end{array}$$

2.
$$\begin{array}{r} 1.84 \\ -\ 0.53 \\ \hline \end{array}$$

3.
$$\begin{array}{r} 3.6 \\ -\ 1.15 \\ \hline \end{array}$$

4.
$$\begin{array}{r} 47.25 \\ -\ 14.8 \\ \hline \end{array}$$

5.
$$\begin{array}{r} 56 \\ -\ 34.21 \\ \hline \end{array}$$

6. $44 - 13.35$ **7.** $53.21 - 47.08$ **8.** $95.3 - 76.16$ **9.** $88.41 - 65.92$

Practice

Find each difference.

10.
$$\begin{array}{r} 29.53 \\ -\ 13.85 \\ \hline \end{array}$$

11.
$$\begin{array}{r} 59.1 \\ -\ 20.09 \\ \hline \end{array}$$

12.
$$\begin{array}{r} 75.58 \\ -\ 19.73 \\ \hline \end{array}$$

13.
$$\begin{array}{r} 82.8 \\ -\ 77.52 \\ \hline \end{array}$$

14.
$$\begin{array}{r} 90.71 \\ -\ 47.83 \\ \hline \end{array}$$

15.
$$\begin{array}{r} 47.19 \\ -31.48 \\ \hline \end{array}$$

16.
$$\begin{array}{r} 19.66 \\ -\ 7.18 \\ \hline \end{array}$$

17.
$$\begin{array}{r} 68.3 \\ -\ 60.47 \\ \hline \end{array}$$

18.
$$\begin{array}{r} 32.11 \\ -\ 17.27 \\ \hline \end{array}$$

19.
$$\begin{array}{r} 76.54 \\ -\ 49.51 \\ \hline \end{array}$$

20. $60 - 28.15$ **21.** $17.08 - 9$ **22.** $84.15 - 16.48$ **23.** $25.8 - 9.37$

Problem Solving

24. In 1890, an uncle of the Halls bought 12.8 acres of land in Texas. He bought 9 more acres in 1904. Today the Halls own 42.4 acres. How many acres had been added to the land since 1904?

25. Analyze In San Antonio, the odometer in the car read 58,453.8. Exactly halfway between San Antonio and Austin, the odometer read 58,490.2. What was the odometer reading when the Halls reached Austin?

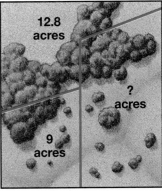

12.8 acres

? acres

9 acres

42.4 total acres

Review and Remember

Find each answer.

26. 5×38 **27.** $6\overline{)52}$ **28.** $\dfrac{7}{8} - \dfrac{2}{8}$ **29.** $\dfrac{4}{6} + \dfrac{1}{6}$ **30.** $4\overline{)365}$

For Extra Practice, see Set F, page 424.

Adding and Subtracting Decimals

Over the River

You will learn to add three or more decimals and practice subtracting decimals.

Learning About It

The Halls drove 138.6 miles from Arkansas to Memphis, Tennessee. Then they drove 21.8 miles for gasoline and another 56.3 miles to Dyersburg. How far did they drive that day?

Dyersburg

Memphis

Mississippi River

$$138.6 + 21.8 + 56.3 = \blacksquare$$

Estimate first: $139 + 22 + 56 = 217$

Then add to find the exact sum.

$$\begin{array}{r} 138.6 \\ 21.8 \\ + \ 56.3 \\ \hline 216.7 \end{array}$$

Remember to line up the decimal points.

They drove 216.7 miles that day.

Another Example

$$\begin{array}{r} {\scriptstyle 6\ 15\ 10\ 10} \\ 7\cancel{6}.\cancel{10} \\ - \ \ 28.45 \\ \hline 47.65 \end{array}$$

Line up the decimal points.

Write a zero if necessary.

Think and Discuss Explain why it is more important to write zeros as placeholders when you subtract than when you add.

Try It Out

Estimate first. Then find each sum or difference.

	1.	2.	3.	4.	5.
	4.9	76.42	46.52	8.3	117.82
	− 3.8	− 31.83	37.96	17.94	406.9
			+ 18.4	+ 58.09	+ 12.75

Practice

Find each sum.

6.	**7.**	**8.**	**9.**	**10.**
204.6	157	15.3	761.42	59.37
119.83	38.95	527.11	58.36	41.82
+ 44.5	+ 26.1	+ 83.96	+ 897.12	+ 110.65

11.	**12.**	**13.**	**14.**	**15.**
28.9	86.52	112.85	492.64	210.86
37.42	8.7	329.7	111.8	97.52
+ 81.96	+ 19.04	+ 46.11	+ 537.43	+ 173.2

**Subtract, using paper and pencil or a calculator.
Tell which method you used.**

16. 15.85 − 9.38

17. 198.52 − 77.6

18. 210.5 − 142.37

19. 376.84 − 145.92

20. 300 − 197.53

21. 876.48 − 692.8

22. 533.51 − 99.99

23. 611.19 − 256.3

24. 708.31 − 194.5

Problem Solving

25. Using Estimation The Halls recorded their expenses each day in their travel diary. Use the page to the right to decide if they spent more than or less than their budget of $80.00 a day for food.

26. Analyze Mrs. Hall bought a magnet for $4.32, Anna bought a hat for $7.89, and Zack bought a piece of petrified wood for $1.85. The total bill was $21.68. Did Mr. Hall buy the fishing bait for $5.32 or the sunglasses for $7.62?

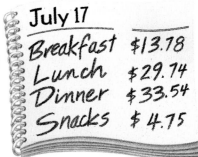

July 17
Breakfast $13.78
Lunch $29.74
Dinner $33.54
Snacks $4.75

27. What If? Suppose the Halls had a food budget of $90.00 a day. How much more money could they spend on dinner?

28. Journal Idea Explain why it is important to include decimal points when adding money. Give examples to support your answer.

Review and Remember

Find each answer.

29. 4,096 ÷ 8

30. $\frac{1}{8} + \frac{3}{8}$

31. 240 × 90

32. $\frac{8}{9} - \frac{2}{9}$

Problem Solving
Comparing Prices

Use what you know about money to solve problems.

The Harpers are visiting Carter Caves, in Kentucky. What is the least expensive way they could buy 12 postcards?

 UNDERSTAND

What do you need to know?

You need to know the different ways 12 postcards can be purchased.

 PLAN

How can you solve the problem?

Find the costs for different ways to buy 12 postcards. Then compare the costs to see which one is the least expensive.

 SOLVE

Here are 3 ways to buy 12 postcards.

- 12 individual cards
  $12 \times \$0.30 = \$3.60$

- 1 group of 10 cards and 2 individual cards
  $(1 \times \$2.00) + (2 \times \$0.30) = \$2.60$

- 3 groups of 4 cards
  $(3 \times \$1.00) = \$3.00$

$2.60 is the least amount of money.

So, the least expensive way to buy 12 postcards is to buy one group of 10 cards and 2 individual cards.

 LOOK BACK

Are there other ways the Harpers could have purchased 12 postcards? Explain.

Postcards

1 for $0.30
4 for $1.00
10 for $2.00

Show What You Learned

Compare prices to solve Problems 1–8.

CARTER CAVES
TOURS
Adults.................$6.00
Under 12..............$3.50

VISITOR'S GUIDE

1 Look at the cave tour booklet at the right. How much more does it cost for 2 adult tickets than for 2 tickets for children under 12?

2 The Jackson family has 1 adult and 4 children. But 1 of the children will turn 12 tomorrow! How much more would it cost for the family to take the cave tour next week instead of today?

3 Look at the juice prices below. How much cheaper is it to buy a 6-pack of juice than 6 separate bottles?

Juice Bottles
$0.90 each

Juice Bottles
$4.00
for 6-pack

4 **You Decide** At the rock shop, you see the prices shown below and decide to buy some polished rocks. You also find a book on rocks for $2.95 and a display case for $4. What could you get for $13?

Polished Rocks
$0.75 each
5 for $3.00
20 for $10.00

5 Cave flashlights cost $12.70 without batteries or $14.85 with 2 batteries. A pack of 2 batteries costs $2.25. Which is the cheaper way to buy a flashlight and 2 batteries?

6 Small cabins cost $37.00 a night for 2 people. There is a $5.00 charge for each extra person. Large cabins cost $50.00 for 4 people. Which is the less expensive way to rent a cabin for a family of four?

7 Ryan took 24 pictures of the caves, while Patricia took only 18 pictures. Pictures cost 8¢ each to develop. How much more will Ryan have to pay than Patricia?

8 **Create Your Own** Think of an item you would sell in different amounts. Write a problem that could be solved by comparing the prices of your item.

Problem Solving

★ ★ ★ ★ ★ **Preparing for Tests**

Practice What You Learned

Choose the correct letter for each answer.

1 Zack had 60 inches of ribbon. He used 34 inches to decorate a present. Then he used half of the ribbon that was left to decorate another present. How much ribbon does Zack have left now?

A. 13 inches
B. 17 inches
C. 26 inches
D. 30 inches

Tip

Decide what steps you need to do, and in what order you should do them.

---

2 Ryan rode his bike 8 miles on Tuesday, 12 miles on Wednesday, 6 miles on Thursday, and 11 miles on Friday. How many miles did he ride on Tuesday and Thursday?

A. 2 mi
B. 14 mi
C. 20 mi
D. 37 mi

Tip

Read the question carefully and use only the information you need.

---

3 Erin used a catalog to order some shirts. She noticed that the code numbers for the first 4 shirts were as follows: 00438, 00458, 00478, and 00498. If the code numbers continue in this pattern, what will be the code numbers of the next 3 shirts?

A. 00508, 00528, 00548
B. 00508, 00518, 00528
C. 00518, 00538, 00558
D. 00518, 00528, 00538

Tip

Use the *Find a Pattern* strategy to solve this problem. Start by adding to find how the numbers are increasing.

4 Nick mailed three packages. The weights of the packages were 21 lb, 18 lb, and 33 lb. **About** how much did the three packages weigh altogether?

A. 60 pounds   **C.** 80 pounds

B. 70 pounds   **D.** 90 pounds

---

5 A soccer team held a bake sale to raise money to buy 20 new uniforms. The uniforms cost $15 each. If the team made $224 from the bake sale, how much more money do they need to buy the uniforms?

A. $76

B. $176

C. $239

D. $300

---

6 Hal used 213 m of fence for one of his fields and 380 m of fence for another field. Which is the best estimate of the amount of fence Hal used in all?

A. 300 meters   **C.** 600 meters

B. 400 meters   **D.** 700 meters

---

7 Four people shared 3 pizzas equally. Each pizza had 8 slices. Which number sentence shows how many slices of pizza each person ate?

A. $4 \times 3 = 12$

B. $4 + 3 + 8 = 15$

C. $8 \div 4 = 2$

D. $24 \div 4 = 6$

8 A CD has 8 songs on it. The shortest song is 2 minutes long, and the longest song is 6 minutes long. Which is reasonable for the total time it takes to hear all 8 songs?

A. Less than 8 minutes

B. Between 8 and 10 minutes

C. Between 10 and 15 minutes

D. More than 20 minutes

Use the graph for Problems 9–10.

Logan made a graph to show the favorite movies of students at his school.

Favorite Kinds of Movies

Each ♦ stands for 50 people.

9 How many people chose science fiction or western movies as their favorite?

A. 25   **C.** 225

B. 125   **D.** 650

---

10 How many more people chose adventure movies than romance movies as their favorite?

A. 25   **C.** 100

B. 50   **D.** 425

Checkpoint

Adding and Subtracting Decimals

Vocabulary

Complete. Use the words from the Word Bank.

1. A number that is written as a whole number and a fraction is called a ___?___.

2. Numbers that show one or more places to the right of a decimal point are called ___?___.

3. 0.4 and 0.40 are examples of ___?___.

Word Bank

decimals
equivalent decimals
mixed number

Skills and Concepts

Round each decimal to the nearest whole number.
(pages 406–409)

4. 8.4   **5.** 3.9   **6.** 8.06   **7.** 1.08   **8.** 2.91

Estimate the sum by rounding each decimal to the nearest whole number. (pages 406–409)

9. 8.78	**10.** 9.41	**11.** 45.71	**12.** 80.92	**13.** 86.43
+ 4.18	− 6.72	+ 20.31	− 38.41	+ 71.79

Find each sum. (pages 412–413)

14. 85.67	**15.** 70.13	**16.** 49.88	**17.** 80.43	**18.** 24.53
+ 68.1	+ 17.43	+ 12.19	+ 7.95	+ 25.81

Find each difference. (pages 414–415)

19. 80.06	**20.** 69.59	**21.** 54.38	**22.** 74.63	**23.** 89.43
− 46.62	− 59.69	− 24.53	− 66.96	− 87.51

Add or subtract. (pages 416–417)

24. 5.95 + 5.39 + 4.67

25. 23.5 − 2.52

26. 0.23 + 81.2 + 85.71 + 3.42

27. 9.87 − 5.3

Problem Solving

28. **Using Estimation** Three cars measure 5.53 m, 6.55 m, and 5.42 m in length. Can they fit in a garage that is 18 meters long if they are parked end to end?

29. Find the exact answer for Problem 28. How much space is left or how much more space is needed if the cars are parked end to end?

30. Suppose you spent $20 on two books and got $2.00 back in change. How much did each book cost if one book cost half as much as the other book? Explain the strategy you used to find the answer.

Journal Idea

How is knowing how to round decimals helpful when you go shopping?

What do you think?

Why is it important to line up the decimal points when adding or subtracting decimals?

You Decide

Activity

Make a Price List

Suppose you make magnets to sell at craft fairs. If it costs $0.29 to make a magnet, how much would you charge for 1 magnet? a pack of 3? a pack of 10? a pack of 20?

Decide on a price list. Show your profit on each magnet or pack you sell. You might want to give people who buy packs a better price than if they bought magnets individually.

 You might wish to include this work in your portfolio.

Extra Practice

Set A (pages 394–395)

Write each fraction or mixed number as a decimal.

1. $\frac{7}{10}$

2. $5\frac{67}{100}$

3. $\frac{9}{10}$

4. $\frac{29}{100}$

5. $4\frac{5}{10}$

6. $\frac{9}{100}$

7. $3\frac{9}{10}$

8. $7\frac{75}{100}$

9. $\frac{20}{100}$

10. $\frac{1}{100}$

11. $2\frac{6}{10}$

12. $\frac{43}{100}$

13. $4\frac{50}{100}$

14. $8\frac{2}{10}$

15. $6\frac{5}{10}$

Write each decimal as a fraction or mixed number.

16. 9.9

17. 0.5

18. 0.4

19. 2.7

20. 4.6

21. 9.09

22. 0.03

23. 27.27

24. 4.06

25. 0.01

26. Amy rode her bicycle three tenths of a mile to school. Write this number as a decimal and as a fraction.

Set B (pages 396–397)

Write the decimal for each word form or the word form for each decimal.

1. seven and nine tenths

2. three and seven hundredths

3. one and forty-six hundredths

4. six and two tenths

5. 562.99

6. 641.96

7. 963.06

8. 234.56

9. 960.67

10. 239.8

11. 150.89

12. 952.77

13. 72.60

14. 612.05

Tell the place value of each underlined digit.

15. <u>4</u>37.51

16. 218.0<u>8</u>

17. 9<u>2</u>1.32

18. 305.27

19. 597.7<u>1</u>

20. 454.4<u>9</u>

21. 1<u>3</u>7.54

22. 943.2<u>8</u>

23. 762.<u>5</u>9

24. 388.<u>8</u>51

25. Sam wrote 7.09 to show nine tens and seven hundredths. Is his answer correct? If not, write the correct decimal number.

Extra Practice

Set C (pages 398–401)

Order each set of numbers from least to greatest.

1. 5.39, 5.36, 5.79   **2.** 8.93, 8.9, 8.33   **3.** 4.67, 4.76, 6.47

4. 1.75, 1.7, 1.78   **5.** 9.33, 9.03, 9.30   **6.** 6.24, 2.64, 4.26

7. 7.54, 7.6, 7.38   **8.** 2.28, 2.82, 2.8   **9.** 5.15, 5, 5.05

10. List three decimals between 2.01 and 2.09.

Set D (pages 406–409)

Estimate by rounding to the nearest whole number.

1. 53.66 + 84.81	**2.** 51.96 + 41.52	**3.** 94.31 − 61.16	**4.** 87.25 − 65.34	**5.** 61.25 + 53.43
6. 78.58 − 53.1	**7.** 65.01 − 35.66	**8.** 48.61 + 79.95	**9.** 35.99 + 51.46	**10.** 59.2 − 19.49

11. Mr. Lee had $50.00 to spend on two gifts. Use the chart to the right to estimate which two he could buy.

Cost of Gifts	
Item	**Cost**
Sweatshirt	$39.99
Statue	$49.95
Cap	$7.29

Set E (pages 412–413)

Find each sum.

1. 77.42 + 89.87	**2.** 68.56 + 59.21	**3.** 46.79 + 35.98	**4.** 42.01 + 94.37	**5.** 72.59 + 52.95
6. 28.6 + 39.57	**7.** 41.87 + 85.19	**8.** 60.16 + 23.7	**9.** 59.33 + 24.56	**10.** 52.36 + 60.68

11. The three sides of a triangle measure 12.5 cm, 4.9 cm and 6.55 cm. What is the total length of the three sides?

Extra Practice

Set F (pages 414–415)

Find each difference.

1. $98.16 - 55.46$
2. $82.33 - 33.55$
3. $58.19 - 29.52$
4. $71.01 - 66.98$
5. $66.98 - 52.39$

6. $67.62 - 56.85$
7. $91.66 - 87.2$
8. $79.17 - 46.76$
9. $94.23 - 58.56$
10. $81 - 78.66$

11. $75.06 - 9.47$
12. $49.3 - 24.95$
13. $80.42 - 65.84$
14. $58 - 39.08$
15. $72.15 - 70.38$

Set G (pages 416–417)

Add or subtract.

1. $11.84 + 78.94$
2. $46.28 - 9.49$
3. $46.03 - 12.13$
4. $34.57 + 63.91$
5. $31.55 + 22.76$

6. $66.3 - 35.71$
7. $59.84 + 26.44$
8. $63.4 - 16.87$
9. $47.98 - 24.91$
10. $75.94 - 50.3$

11. $94.8 - 50.18$
12. $91.78 - 57.81$
13. $40.86 + 62.85$
14. $42 - 23.57$
15. $80 - 59.88$

16. $1.59 + 8.02 + 6.79$

17. $3.61 + 5.47 + 6.6 + 1.07$

18. $6.26 + 12 + 4.4$

19. $7.45 + 3.6 + 7.38 + 2.99$

20. $1.72 + 3.15 + 6.2$

21. $4.38 + 4.2 + 9 + 8.56$

22. The Joyces set aside $200.00 for meals on their three-day vacation. Use the chart to the right to decide on which day they spent the most? the least? How much did they have left?

Cost of Meals			
Day	Breakfast	Lunch	Dinner
Mon.	$12.75	$18.00	$20.56
Tues.	$15.11	$16.48	$32.95
Wed.	$14.50	$21.35	$36.70

Chapter Test

Write the fraction and decimal for each model.

1.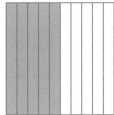

2.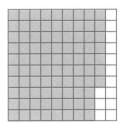

3.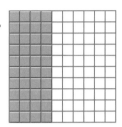

Write each decimal as a fraction or mixed number.
Write each fraction or mixed number as a decimal.

4. 0.3

5. 0.41

6. $\frac{23}{100}$

7. $4\frac{7}{10}$

8. $\frac{85}{100}$

9. $\frac{49}{100}$

10. $\frac{5}{10}$

11. 5.8

12. 0.96

13. 1.1

Order each set of numbers from least to greatest.

14. 6.41; 6.14; 6.44   **15.** 3.5; 3.55; 3   **16.** 7.82; 2.87; 8.72   **17.** 9.1; 9.0; 9.7

Estimate first. Then add or subtract.

18. 7.85 + 3.92

19. 8.12 − 5.79

20. 15.38 + 31.4

21. 29.76 − 18.44

22. 43.08 + 72.95

23. 56.9 − 31.56

Problem Solving

24. Louise wants to put a fence between two trees that are 2.85 m apart. She has three sections of fencing that measure 0.87 m, 1.20 m, and 0.84 m long. Does she need more or less fencing? How much more or less?

25. Three disks have memories of 1.46 megabytes (MB), 1.48 MB, and 1.44 MB. Which disk has the most memory? Which has the least?

 Self-Check
Look back at Exercises 14–17. Did you remember to compare digits with the same place value?

Performance Assessment

Show What You Know About Decimals

1 Make a spinner like the one shown. Spin the spinner three times. Record the numbers after each spin.

What You Need

blank 5-part spinner
paper clip

a. Find the sum of your three numbers.

b. Subtract the least number from the greatest number.

c. Could you ever get a sum of three numbers that was greater than 15? Explain.

Self-Check Did you remember to start with the ones place when you compared the numbers to find the least and greatest numbers?

2 Suppose you are on a cross-country trip. You have $12.75 to spend at a shop. You want to buy at least two items. Choose from the items at the right.

a. What will you buy? How much will the items cost?

b. How much money will you have left?

Self-Check Did you estimate first before choosing the items to buy?

Country Store

Key chains
Kentucky $ 3.95
Tennessee $ 4.15

T-shirts
Long sleeve $8.85
Short sleeve $ 6.55

Magnets
Cow $1.50   Horse $2.75
Pig $1.90   Rooster $4.25

For Your Portfolio

You might wish to include this work in your portfolio.

Extension

Finding Change with a Calculator

Yoko went to the post office to mail 3 packages to her family in Japan. She paid $17.41, $12.86, and $11.59. She gave the postal clerk two $20.00 bills and one $10.00 bill. How much change did she get back?

You can use a calculator to find out.

① Add to find how much money she had.

Press: ② ⓪ . ⓪ ⓪ ＋ ② ⓪ . ⓪ ⓪ ＋ ① ⓪ . ⓪ ⓪ ＝

Display: 50

Put this amount in memory.

② Press: M+   Display: m 50

③ Then add to find the total postage.

Press: ① ⑦ . ④ ① ＋ ① ② . ⑧ ⑥ ＋
① ① . ⑤ ⑨ ＝   Display: m 41.86

④ Press: M-

⑤ Memory recall will show you how much change she would get back. Press: MR   Display: m 8.14

The calculator subtracted   M+ 50.00
M− 41.86
8.14

Add a dollar sign to the answer. Yoko got $8.14 back in change.

Use a calculator to find the change.

1. You have $25.00. You spend $8.09, $2.36, and $4.98.

2. You have $30.00. You buy a book for $16.95. The tax is $1.02.

3. You have three $1.00 bills, one $5.00 bill, and 8 quarters. You spend $9.76.

4. You have three $20.00 bills. You spend $0.75, $14.98, and $27.60.

Cumulative Review

Choose the correct letter for each answer.

Number Concepts	Operations

1. Which is a set of even numbers?

  A. 6   12   14   20
  B. 5   8   9   11
  C. 7   13   15   19
  D. 10   21   32   43

2. An airplane flies at thirty-three thousand, five hundred fifty feet. How is this number written?

  A. 3,355   **C.** 33,550
  B. 30,355   **D.** 335,050

3. Which decimal tells how much is shaded?

  A. 20.7   **C.** 2.7
  B. 20.3   **D.** 2.3

4. Point *R* best represents what number?

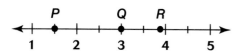

  A. 3.3
  B. 3.5
  C. 3.9
  D. 4.2

5. Brian had $20.50. He spent $3.50 on a movie ticket and $4.25 on popcorn and a drink. How much did he spend in all?

  A. $17.00
  B. $16.25
  C. $12.75
  D. $7.75

6. Kate ordered 20 boxes of pens for her office. There are 12 pens in each box. How many pens did Kate order?

  A. 2,400   **C.** 144
  B. 240   **D.** 24

7. There are 28 rows of seats on an airplane. If 6 passengers can sit in each row, **about** how many passengers can the plane hold?

  A. 130   **C.** 180
  B. 150   **D.** 280

8. Grant paid for a CD with a $20 bill. His change is shown below. How much did Grant spend?

  A. $16
  B. $14
  C. $12
  D. $5

| Measurement | Probability and Statistics |

Measurement

9. Which is the best estimate of the *area* of the shaded region?

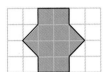

A. 8 square units
B. 10 square units
C. 12 square units
D. 24 square units

10. Samantha's fish tank holds 50 gallons of water. How many *quarts* is that? (Hint: 4 quarts equals 1 gallon.)

A. 25 qt
B. 54 qt
C. 100 qt
D. 200 qt

11. Bonnie's airplane flight took 2 hours 10 minutes. If the plane took off at 11:00 A.M., what time did it land?

A. 1:10 P.M.
B. 1:25 P.M.
C. 2:10 P.M.
D. 2:25 P.M.

12. The *perimeter* of the patio below is 34 feet. If the length is 10 feet, what is its width?

A. 23 ft
B. 13 ft
C. $10\frac{1}{2}$ ft
D. 7 ft

10 ft

Probability and Statistics

Use the graph for Questions 13–16.

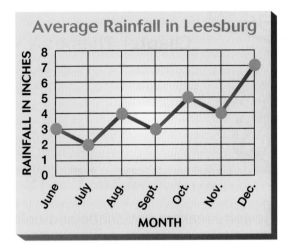

13. In which month did it rain the least?

A. June
B. July
C. September
D. November

14. How much rain did Leesburg receive in August?

A. 4 in.   C. 2 in.
B. $3\frac{1}{2}$ in.   D. 1 in.

15. How many more inches of rain were there in October than in July?

A. 7 in.   C. 3 in.
B. 5 in.   D. 2 in.

16. The largest difference in rainfall was between which 2 months?

A. June and July
B. August and September
C. October and November
D. November and December

Chapter 11 Geometry

Chapter Theme: A WORLD OF SHAPES

Real Facts

Jewelry makers use shape and color to make pleasing designs. The children pictured at the right are choosing colors and shapes for their jewelry designs.

Look for geometric shapes in the Hopi pendant shown at the right. Then use the diagram of the pendant to make a table like the one shown. Write how many of each shape you would need to make the number of pendants listed.

square

rectangle

circle

triangle

Types of Shapes Needed to Make a Pendant		
Polished Stones	Amount Needed for	
	1 Pendant	10 Pendants
Rectangles		
Circles		
Squares		
Triangles		

Real People

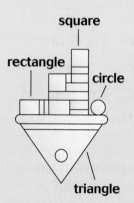

Meet Verma Nequatewa, a Hopi jewelry maker. In her studio in Arizona, she makes necklaces, bracelets, bola ties and other jewelry. A piece of jewelry can take Ms. Nequatewa up to one month to finish. The most common shapes in her designs are triangles and rectangles.

Shape Up

You can use a geoboard to make and identify polygons.

Learning About It

The world around you is filled with flat shapes called **plane figures**. Did you ever notice them on manhole or utility covers? Look at the rectangles and triangles on the manhole covers pictured above.

Rectangles and triangles are also called **polygons**. A polygon is a closed plane figure made up of three or more line segments that are connected.

Step 1 Work with a partner. Below are several polygons with special names. A point where two sides of a polygon meet is called a **vertex**. *Vertices* are more than one vertex.

- How many vertices does each polygon below have?

Word Bank

plane figure
polygon
vertex
quadrilateral

What You Need

For each pair:
  1 geoboard
  rubber bands

The Language of Geometry

Triangle	Rectangle	Square
vertex ↗		
Pentagon	**Hexagon**	**Octagon**

Step 2 Use a geoboard to make each of the polygons shown in Step 1.

- The prefix *quadr-* means "four." Another name for a polygon with four sides is a **quadrilateral**. Which of the polygons that you made are quadrilaterals?

- All rectangles have opposite sides that are equal. Is a square a rectangle? Explain.

Step 3 Record the number of sides and vertices for all the figures you made. Use a chart like the one to the right.

- What do you notice about the number of sides and the number of vertices each polygon has?

Think and Discuss Explain the statement that a polygon can have more than one name.

Type of Polygon	Number of Sides	Number of Vertices
Triangle		
Rectangle		
Square		
Pentagon		
Hexagon		
Octagon		

Practice

1. Which figures below are polygons? Explain your reasoning.

a.
b.
c.
d.
e.

2. Which figure is not a quadrilateral? Explain.

a.
b.
c.
d.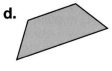
e.

▲ **Language Arts Connection** The prefix *tri-*, as in *triangle*, means "three." Other words with this prefix include *tricycle* and *triceratops*. What do you think the prefix *penta-* means?

3. Make three different quadrilaterals on your geoboard.

What's the Point?

You can use geometric terms to describe the world around you.

Learning About It

The world around you looks different when viewed from above. The table below lists some geometric terms that you can use to describe what you see in this picture of an airport.

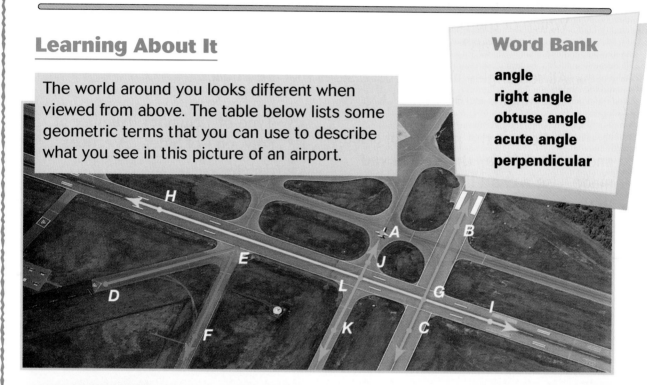

The Language of Geometry

Term	Example	Say
A **point** is an exact location in space.	A	point *A*
A **line** is a collection of points that go on and on in both directions. It has no endpoints.	B — C	line *BC*
A **line segment** is part of a line. It has two endpoints.	D — E	line segment *DE*
A **ray** is part of a line. It has one endpoint and continues on and on in one direction.	E — F	ray *EF*
Intersecting lines are lines that pass through the same point.	H, J, L, K, I	line *HI* intersects line *JK* at point *L*
Parallel lines are lines that never intersect.	J — K, B — C	line *JK* is parallel to line *BC*

Connecting Ideas

You know that two sides of a polygon meet at a vertex. Two rays can also meet at a vertex, forming an angle.

An **angle** can be named in three ways. The middle letter always names the vertex.

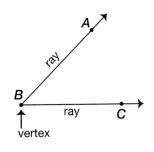

Say:	angle *B*	angle *ABC*	angle *CBA*
Write:	∠*B*	∠*ABC*	∠*CBA*

The size of the angle depends on the size of the opening between the rays. Here are some ways to classify angles.

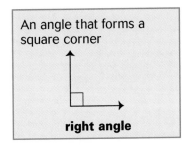

An angle that forms a square corner

right angle

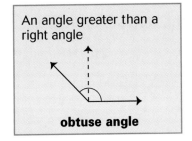

An angle greater than a right angle

obtuse angle

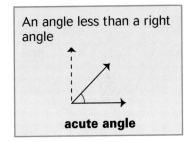

An angle less than a right angle

acute angle

Two intersecting lines that form four right angles are **perpendicular** to each other. If ∠*XYW* is a right angle, then line *XZ* is perpendicular to line *VW*.

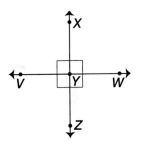

Think and Discuss Name as many angles as you can see in the photograph of the airport on page 432. Tell whether they are right, acute, or obtuse angles.

INTERNET ACTIVITY
www.sbgmath.com

Try It Out

Draw and label an example of each.

1. line *XY*   **2.** line segment *PQ*   **3.** ray *ST*   **4.** angle *LMN*

Tell whether the lines in each pair are intersecting, parallel, or perpendicular.

5. 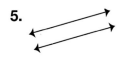   **6.**   **7.** 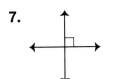   **8.**

Tell whether each angle is right, obtuse, or acute.

9.

10.

11.

12.

Practice

Draw and label an example of each.

13. line *CD*

14. line segment *JK*

15. two intersecting lines

16. two parallel lines

17. angle with vertex *B*

18. ray *GH* with endpoint *G*

Tell whether the angle is right, obtuse, or acute.

19.

20.

21.

22.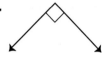

**Use the drawing at the right for Exercises 23–30.
There are many correct answers.**

23. Name a point.

24. Name two lines

25. Name two intersecting perpendicular lines

26. Name three line segments.

27. Name a ray.

28. Name a right angle.

29. Name an obtuse angle.

30. Name two parallel lines.

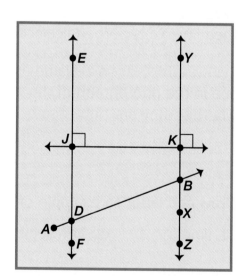

Problem Solving

31. Jennifer says that the rails of a railroad track are parallel. Is she correct? Explain.

32. Look at the clock in your classroom. What kind of angle will the hands on the clock make at 10:15? at 10:45?

33. Identify each figure at the right. How many sides, vertices, and angles does each have? What kinds of angles does each have?

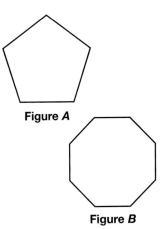

Figure A

34. Create Your Own Design a figure of your own. Then use geometric terms to describe your figure.

35. Journal Idea What is the difference between a line segment and a line? Explain your reasoning.

Figure B

Review and Remember

Using Algebra Follow the rule to complete each.

Rule: Divide by 7

	Input	Output
36.	994	▦
37.	497	▦
38.	560	▦

Rule: Multiply by 8

	Input	Output
39.	440	▦
40.	632	▦
41.	578	▦

Rule: Multiply by 4

	Input	Output
42.	749	▦
43.	▦	832
44.	▦	528

Time for Technology

Using the MathProcessor™ on CD-ROM

Lines and Angles

Use the geometry tool to explore lines and angles.

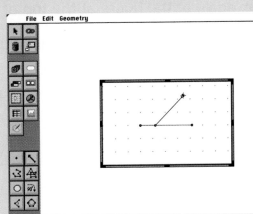

- Click ▦ to open a geometry workspace. Then click ◥ and draw a line segment 4 units in length.

- Click · and put a vertex on the line. Then click ◥ to make an acute angle. What other angle has this point as a vertex?

Use the geometry tools to make other line segments, angles, and rays. Share what you learn with a classmate.

For Extra Practice, see Set A, page 466.

Developing Skills for Problem Solving

First read for understanding and then look at figures to find shapes and patterns.

READ FOR UNDERSTANDING

*B*ecky found the figure shown at the right in a puzzle book. Her friend Rob said he counted 16 triangles in the figure. Becky thinks she can find more than 16 triangles.

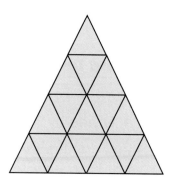

1 What geometric shape did Rob see in the figure?

2 How many of these shapes did Rob count?

THINK AND DISCUSS

MATH FOCUS

Spatial Reasoning If you look at a figure carefully, sometimes you can find geometric shapes and patterns in it. Finding these shapes and patterns can help you solve problems.

Look again at the figure at the top of the page.

3 How many triangles of this size can you find?

4 How many triangles of this size can you find?

5 How many triangles of this size can you find?

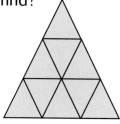

6 What is the biggest triangle you can find in the figure?

7 How many triangles can you find in the figure?

8 Why do you think Rob only counted 16 triangles?

Show What You Learned

Answer each question. Give a reason for your choice.

1 How many different sizes of squares are in the figure at the right?

   a. 1 size

   b. 3 sizes

   c. 2 sizes

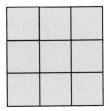

2 How many squares in all are in the figure?

   a. 9 squares

   b. 14 squares

   c. 13 squares

3 How many quadrilaterals that are *not* squares are in the figure?

   a. more than 10

   b. less than 10

   c. exactly 10

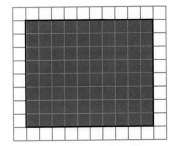

4 Which group of three shapes below could be put together to make the shaded rectangle shown at the right? The shapes may be turned.

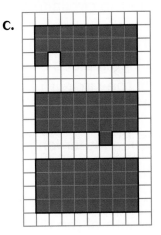

a.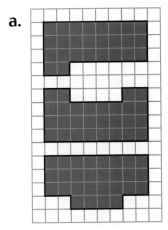

b.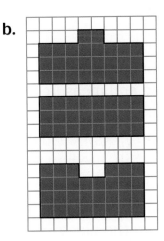

c.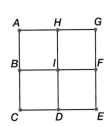

5 **Explain** Which 3 line segments could you remove from the figure at the right so that there would be only 2 quadrilaterals left?

437

Round and Round

*You can estimate the circumference of a circle
if you know its diameter.*

Learning About It

A circle is a closed curve that is made of
points that are the same distance from
the center.

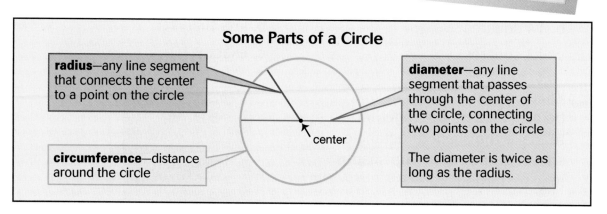

Some Parts of a Circle

radius—any line segment
that connects the center
to a point on the circle

diameter—any line
segment that passes
through the center of
the circle, connecting
two points on the circle

center

circumference—distance
around the circle

The diameter is twice as
long as the radius.

Estimate the circumference of a circle.

- Trace a circle on a piece of paper.
  Place a piece of string around the edge
  of the circle. Cut the string and measure
  it to find the circumference.

- Cut another length of string that
  measures the diameter.

- About how many times does the
  length of the diameter fit on the piece
  of string that measured the
  circumference? The circumference
  should be about three times as long
  as the diameter.

What You Need

For each pair:
  string
  ruler
  scissors
  paper
  circle to trace

Think and Discuss If a circle had more
than one radius drawn from its center, would
each radius be the same length?

Try It Out

Name the part of each circle shown in blue.

1.
2.
3.
4.

5. Explain Does a diameter always divide a circle in half?

Practice

Using Mental Math Use the circle at the right to complete Exercises 6–8.

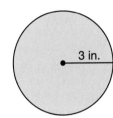

6. radius = ▓ inches

7. diameter = ▓ inches

8. The circumference is about ▓ inches.

3 in.

Find the radius or diameter. Estimate each circumference.

9. 16 in.
10. 12 in.
11. 8 in.
12. 3.5 in.

13. 14 in.
14. 20 ft
15. 3 cm
16. 16 cm

Problem Solving

17. Suppose you have 2 wheels. One is 10 inches in diameter, and the other is 20 inches in diameter. How are the diameters related? How are the circumferences related?

18. Analyze A toy's wheel has a circumference of 9 inches. The toy rolled 72 inches. How many complete turns did the wheel make?

Review and Remember

Find each answer.

19. 0.34 + 0.52   **20.** 1,561 × 44   **21.** 1.41 − 0.95   **22.** 728 ÷ 8

For Extra Practice, see Set B, page 467.

Two of a Kind

Some figures that you see are the same size and shape.

Learning About It

Geometric shapes are often used in making mobiles. This mobile has two figures that are the same shape and the same size. Can you find them?

Two figures that have the same shape and the same size are **congruent**.

Word Bank

congruent

Try to tell if the two figures above are congruent by tracing one of the figures. Then place the tracing on top of the other figure. If they match exactly, they are congruent.

Think and Discuss Are all squares congruent? Explain why or why not.

▲ **Fine Arts Connection**
You can make mobiles like this one out of clay. Mobiles are a kind of moveable sculpture invented by Alexander Calder in 1934.

Try It Out

Are the figures in each pair congruent? Write *yes* or *no*. Explain your reasoning.

1.

2.

3.

Practice

Are the figures in each pair congruent? Write *yes* or *no*. Explain.

4.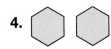

5.

6.

7.

8.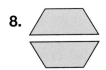

9.

Write *true* or *false*. Explain your reasoning.

10. Two circles are congruent if their diameters are equal.

11. All quadrilaterals are congruent.

Problem Solving

12. You drew a picture of a mobile. Your copy machine makes copies that are the same size and shape. Are your pictures of the mobile congruent? Why or why not?

13. **Analyze** How can you find out if two triangles are congruent if you do not want to trace and match them? What could you measure to find out?

Review and Remember

Using Estimation Estimate first. Then find the exact answer. Check that your answer is reasonable.

14. 1,603 + 129
15. 425 × 6
16. 384 ÷ 8
17. 4.36 − 2.18

18. 4,576 × 5
19. 630 ÷ 3
20. $9.02 − $7.65
21. $3.46 + $2.08

Critical Thinking Corner

Visual Thinking

Triangle Angles

Try to find a way to divide this triangle into 3 congruent parts. Then try to find a way to divide this triangle into 4 congruent parts. Can it be done? Draw or explain your answer.

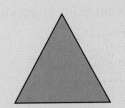

Sizing It Up

Using Algebra

Some figures have the same shape, but not the same size.

Learning About It

The fields on this farm are plowed in geometric shapes. How are the shapes that are outlined the same? How are they different?

The fields are the same shape but not the same size. Figures that have the same shape are called **similar** figures. If similar figures are the same size, then they are also congruent.

Word Bank

similar

The figures in the first pair on the right are similar because they have the same shape, but not the same size.

The figures in the second pair at the right are not similar because they do not have the same shape.

Think and Discuss Do you think the rectangles to the right are similar? Why or why not?

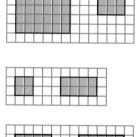

Try It Out

Write *similar* or *not similar* for the figures in each pair. Explain your reasoning.

1.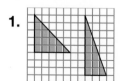

2.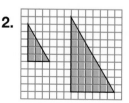

3.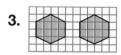

Practice

Choose the figure that is similar to the first.
Write *a, b,* or *c*. Explain your reasoning.

4.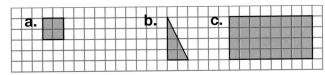

5.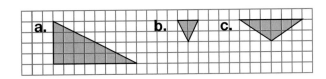

6.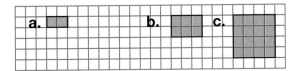

 7. **Journal Idea** Draw two figures that are similar. Draw two figures that are congruent. Explain the difference between similar figures and congruent figures.

Problem Solving

8. One kind of polygon was used for the purple shapes on the soccer ball. Another kind of polygon was used for the yellow shapes. Are the polygons similar? Why or why not?

9. You have a photo enlarged. Is an object in the enlargement photo similar to the same object in the original photo? Why or why not?

10. **Explain** Triangle *A* is similar to triangle *B*. Can triangle *A* and triangle *B* also be congruent?

Review and Remember

Add or subtract. Write each answer in simplest form.

11. $\frac{1}{5}$
$+\frac{3}{5}$

12. $\frac{7}{8}$
$-\frac{3}{8}$

13. $\frac{5}{6}$
$+\frac{4}{6}$

14. $4\frac{1}{8}$
$+3\frac{5}{8}$

15. $6\frac{4}{6}$
$-2\frac{2}{6}$

16. $8\frac{1}{2}$
$-7\frac{1}{2}$

For Extra Practice, see Set D, page 467.

To Halve and to Fold

You can find symmetry in geometric shapes.

Learning About It

Here is another way to look at the world around you. This picture of the White House can be folded along a line so that the two halves match exactly. The fold line is called a **line of symmetry**. A figure has **symmetry** if its halves are congruent.

Word Bank

line of symmetry
symmetry

Work with a partner. Here is a way you can make a symmetric figure.

Step 1 Fold a piece of paper in half. Draw half of any kind of figure out from the fold.

Step 2 Cut along the lines you drew. The cut should start and end on the fold.

Step 3 Unfold the figure you cut out.

- Do both halves match? Explain.

- Where is the line of symmetry?

- Explain why your figure is symmetric.

Think and Discuss Look around you. How many symmetric figures can you find?

What You Need

For each pair:
  scissors
  tracing paper

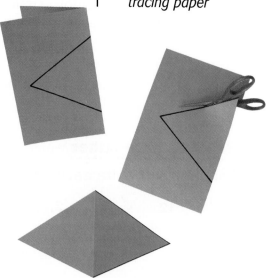

Practice

Tell if the dashed line is a line of symmetry. Write *yes* or *no*. Explain your reasoning.

1.

2.

3.

4.

5.

6.

Trace each figure. Then complete to make a symmetric figure.

7.

8.

9.

Analyze Trace each figure.
Draw lines of symmetry if you can.

10.

11.

12.

13.

14.

15.

16. **Create Your Own** Draw a figure that has no lines of symmetry. Explain your reasoning.

17. **Science Connection** Look at the three photos to the right. The top photo shows an actual face. The bottom photos were created by "doubling" the images of first the left half of the face and then the right half. From what you see in the photos, is the actual face symmetrical? Explain.

actual face

left half doubled

right half doubled

Shapes in Motion

You can use slides, flips, and turns to solve a tangram puzzle.

Learning About It

Geometry has always been part of the world around us. A tangram is a puzzle invented in China about 4,000 years ago. To solve the puzzle, put the seven puzzle pieces together to form a square.

Word Bank

slide (translation)
flip (reflection)
turn (rotation)

What You Need

For each pair:
  1 tangram puzzle

INTERNET ACTIVITY

www.sbgmath.com

Work with a partner. You can use slides, flips, and turns to form a square.

A **slide** moves a figure up, down, or over.

A **flip** of a figure gives a mirror image of the figure.

A **turn** moves a figure about a point.

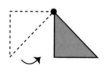

Step 1 Use slides, flips, and turns to place all but one of the triangles as shown to the right.

Step 2 Use slides, flips, and turns to place the last triangle as shown to the right. Describe each move you make.

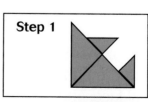

Step 1

Step 2

Step 3 Complete the puzzle.

Think and Discuss How can you use what you've learned about flips (reflections) to decide which of these figures has symmetry?

Practice

Use your tangram pieces to tell how each figure was moved from position A to position B. Write *slide*, *flip*, or *turn*.

1.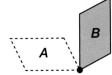

2.

3.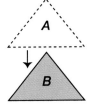

4.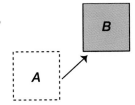

5.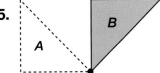

6.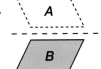

Trace each figure if you wish. Then use the tracing to find out how each figure was moved from position A to position B. Write *slide*, *flip*, or *turn*.

7.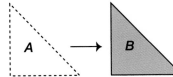

8.

9.

10.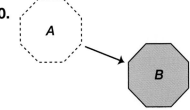

11. **Analyze** Some of the tangram pieces are congruent, and some are similar. Tell how you can decide which pieces are congruent and which are similar.

12. **Describe** How would a circle look if you turned it? if you flipped it?

Problem Solving
Use Logical Reasoning

Sometimes logical reasoning can help you solve problems.

Andrew arranged the figures shown in a line. Each figure has one more or one less side than the figure beside it. Each figure is next to a different-colored figure. The first figure is the square. How are the figures arranged?

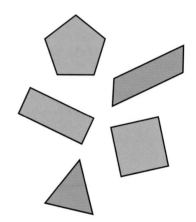

UNDERSTAND

What do you need to find?

You need to find the order of the figures.

PLAN

How can you solve the problem?

Use logical reasoning to organize what you know about the figures. Draw a picture to help you.

SOLVE

- Draw 5 lines. Put the square first.

- The 2nd figure must have 3 or 5 sides. It cannot be blue. Only the triangle works.

- The 3rd figure must have 2 or 4 sides. It cannot be green. Only the rectangle works.

- The 4th figure must have 3 or 5 sides. It cannot be pink. Only the pentagon works.

- The 5th figure is the parallelogram.

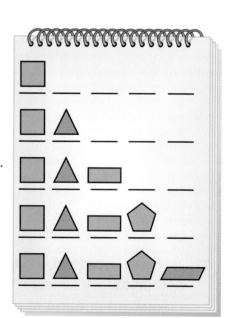

LOOK BACK

What If? Suppose you were not told that the square was first? Could you still solve the problem? Why or why not?

Using the Strategy

Use logical reasoning to solve each problem.

1 What is the mystery number?
- Its thousands digit is one half its ones digit.
- Its hundreds digit is 2 times its ones digit.
- Its tens digit is 5 more than its hundreds digit.
- Its ones digit is 2.

2 Each person gets off an elevator at a different floor. Who gets off where?
- The elevator stops at the 5th, 6th, 8th, and 10th floors.
- When Gary gets off, he says goodbye to Sam.
- Jenna is the last person to get off.
- Sue gets off 1 floor after Gary.

3 What is the mystery number? It is less than 30. If you divide it by 2, 3, 4, or 6 the remainder is 1. If you divide it by 5, the remainder is 0.

4 Use the numbers 4 through 9 to fill the circles in the triangle. Write each number only once. Each row of four numbers must have a sum of 17.

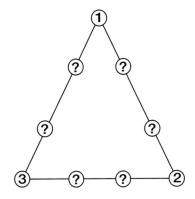

Mixed Strategy Review

**Try these or other strategies to solve each problem.
Tell which strategy you used.**

Problem Solving Strategies

- Find a Pattern
- Guess and Check
- Draw a Picture
- Use Logical Reasoning

5 How many ways can Lin arrange 12 photos in equal rows on a bulletin board?

6 Ellie's age is less than 20. The sum of the digits is even. If it is divided by 5, the remainder is 1. How old is Ellie?

7 Paper comes in packages of 25, 50, or 80 sheets. Andrew bought 315 sheets in exactly five packages. What packages did he buy?

8 Josh draws rows of shapes. The number of shapes doubles in each row. The first row has 1 shape. How many shapes are in the sixth row?

Checkpoint

Plane Figures

Name each polygon. (pages 430–431)

1.

2.

3.

4.

**Identify each figure as a line, a line segment, or a ray.
Then name each.** (pages 432–435)

5. A B

6. C D

7. E F

8. G H

Tell whether the angle is right, obtuse, or acute. (pages 432–435)

9.

10.

11.

12.

Estimate each circumference. (pages 438–439)

13. 6 in.

14. 12 cm

15. 8 ft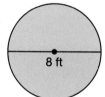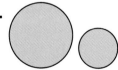

16. 20 mm

**Tell if the figures in each pair are congruent. Write _yes_ or
_no_.** (pages 440–441)

17.

18.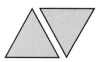

19.

**Do you need to slide, flip, or turn figure _A_ to make it
look like figure _B_?** (pages 446–447)

20.  A → B

21. 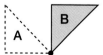 A   B

22. A   B

Using Algebra Write *similar* or *not similar* for the figures in each pair. (pages 442–443)

23.

24.

Is the blue line a line of symmetry? Tell why or why not. (pages 444–445)

25.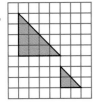

26.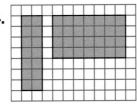

27.

28.

Problem Solving

29. From an airplane, you see two roads crossing each other. Are the roads parallel or intersecting? Explain.

30. **Explain** If you trace a picture, are your tracing and the picture congruent? Are they similar? Explain your reasoning.

 Journal Idea

Make a map of your neighborhood showing intersecting streets. Label as many geometric figures as you can.

 **Critical Thinking Corner**

Visual Thinking

What's Wrong?

The figure on the left shows a cutout made on a folded sheet of paper. The figure on the right shows a prediction of how the paper will look unfolded. What's wrong? Explain.

A.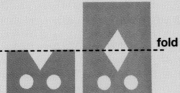

B.

C.

Around the Park

If you know the distance around something, you know its perimeter.

Learning About It

Word Bank

perimeter

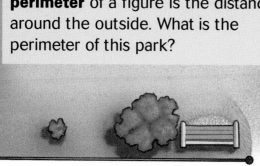

|← 45 ft →|

This park is a rectangle because it has four right angles and opposite sides that are equal and parallel. The **perimeter** of a figure is the distance around the outside. What is the perimeter of this park?

20 ft   20 ft

|← 45 ft →|

THERE'S ALWAYS A WAY!

• **One way** to find the perimeter of a polygon is to add the lengths of the sides to find the distance around.

$$45 + 45 + 20 + 20 = 130$$

• **Another way** to find the perimeter of a rectangular figure is to multiply and add.

Perimeter = (2 × length) + (2 × width)

2 × 45	=	90
2 × 20	=	+ 40
		130

The perimeter of the park is 130 feet.

Another Example

Find the perimeter of the quadrilateral to the right.

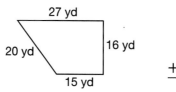

27 yd
20 yd
16 yd
15 yd

27 yd
20 yd
15 yd
+ 16 yd
78 yd

Think and Discuss How could you find the perimeter of a square by multiplying? Explain.

Try It Out

Find the perimeter of each figure.

1.
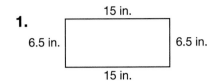
15 in.
6.5 in.   6.5 in.
15 in.

2. 27 in.   27 in.
32 in.

3.
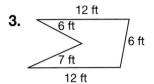
12 ft
6 ft
7 ft   6 ft
12 ft

Practice

Find the perimeter of each figure.

4.
32 in.
16 in.   16 in.
32 in.

5. 11 in.   16 in.
12 in.   17 in.

6.
11 ft
3 ft ↕   5 ft
8 ft   5 ft
16 ft

7. 10 ft   10 ft
10 ft   10 ft
15 ft

8.
22 in.
16 in.   12.5 in.
12 in.

9.
84 ft
42 ft   42 ft
84 ft

Problem Solving

10. Analyze A playground shaped like a rectangle has a perimeter of 94 feet. The length is 5 feet more than the width. How long is the playground?

11. Latoya designed the floor of her clock tower in the shape of an octagon. Suppose the perimeter is 912 inches. If the sides are equal in length, how long is each side? Explain the strategy you used to find the answer.

▲ **Kid Connection** The Kid's Crossing Playground was designed by kids in Indiana. Latoya Fitts designed the clock tower for the playground.

Review and Remember

Choose a Method Use paper and pencil or a calculator to solve. Tell the method you chose.

12. 32 + 16 + 57   **13.** 471 + 289 + 62   **14.** 5 + 750 + 245

15. 486 ÷ 9   **16.** 43 × 29   **17.** 7)329   **18.** 974 − 586

Tile It Away

Using Algebra

You can find the number of square units it takes to cover a surface.

Learning About It

In Mexico, colorful tiles can be seen in many places. The square tiles below were used to make a rectangle. The **area** of a flat surface is the number of square units needed to cover the surface. What is the area of the rectangle covered by the tiles?

Word Bank

area

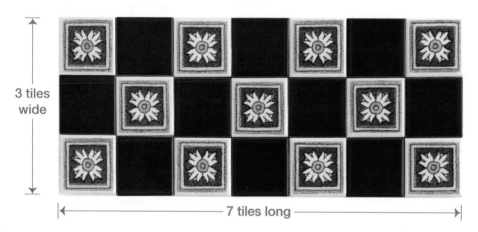

3 tiles wide

|←————— 7 tiles long —————→|

THERE'S ALWAYS A WAY!

- **One way** to find area is to count the square units. There are 21 square tiles in the rectangle.

- **Another way** to find the area of a rectangle is to multiply.
  Area = length × width
  Area = 7 units × 3 units = 21 square units

The area of the tiled rectangle is 21 square units.

Another Example

What is the area of the square at the right?

(Think: Area = length × width)

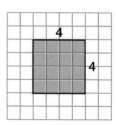

Area = 4 units × 4 units = 16 square units

The area of the square is 16 square units.

Connecting Ideas

You can use what you know about finding the areas of rectangles to help you find the area of irregular figures.

You can count square units to find the area of the irregular figure to the right.

Since each ■ is equal to 1 square unit, the area of this irregular figure is 16 square units.

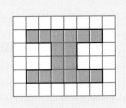

Each ■ = 1 square unit

To find the area of this irregular figure, count whole units and half units and add.

$$\underbrace{3\ \blacksquare}_{1+1+1} + \underbrace{4\ \blacktriangle}_{\frac{1}{2}+\frac{1}{2}+\frac{1}{2}+\frac{1}{2}} = 5$$

The area of this irregular figure is 5 square units.

Each ■ = 1 square unit

Each ▲ = $\frac{1}{2}$ square unit

This is how you can estimate the area of a circle. Count the ■ inside the circle. There are 16 ■. The green shapes add up to between 10 and 12 square units.

So, the area of this circle is between 26 and 28 square units.

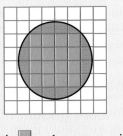

Each ■ = 1 square unit

Think and Discuss When is it necessary to count square units to find area?

Try It Out

Find each area in square units.

1.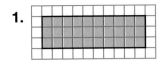

2.

3.

4.

Practice

Find each area in square units.

5.

6.

7.

8.

9.

10.

11.

12.

13.

14.

15.

16.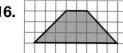

Using Estimation Estimate each area in square units.

17.

18.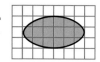

19.

20.

Problem Solving

21. Adam bought the picture to the right. It is made from square tiles. What is the area of the picture in square units?

22. **What If?** Suppose Adam makes a picture with 1-inch square tiles. The picture is 4 inches wide and 24 inches long. How many tiles did he use?

23. **Analyze** Leigh says she needs 28 square yards of carpeting for her bedroom floor. If the bedroom is 4 yards wide, how many yards long is it?

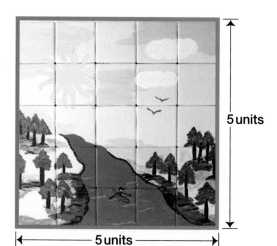

5 units

5 units

24. Suppose you paid $960 for two carpets that each measure 8 ft by 10 ft. One carpet costs twice as much as the other. How much does each carpet cost? Explain what strategy you used to solve the problem.

25. Analyze Suppose you bought 64 square tiles to cover a surface that is the same number of units long as it is wide. Describe the shape of the surface.

26. Explain You want to tile a surface shaped like an oval. Explain how you would estimate the area of the surface.

27. Predict How many different rectangles with sides that are whole units have an area of 24 square units? Use grid paper to draw and find out.

▲ **Social Studies Connection**
Some of the world's most beautiful tiles and pottery are made in Mexico. Tiles and pottery are made from clay. Then they are baked in very hot ovens, called kilns, such as this one above.

Review and Remember

Find each answer.

28. 7.3 − 1.09   **29.** 576 ÷ 8   **30.** 3,602 × 43   **31.** 53.9 − 42.45

32. 943 + 254 + 362   **33.** $7.25 + $4.97 + $8.86

 Money $ense

A Square Deal

1. Suppose you make a tile design that is 8 inches wide and 14 inches long. What is the least costly way to make the design? How much would it cost?

2. You have $10.10. Is that enough money to make a 12-inch square design? What tiles would you buy? Explain your thinking.

2 inches by 2 inches
59¢

4 inches by 4 inches
89¢

For Extra Practice, see Set F, page 468.

Problem Solving
Using Perimeter and Area

Put your understanding of perimeter and area to work.

There are two parks in Sharon's neighborhood. She thinks that North Park has about the same area as South Park because their perimeters are about the same. Is she correct?

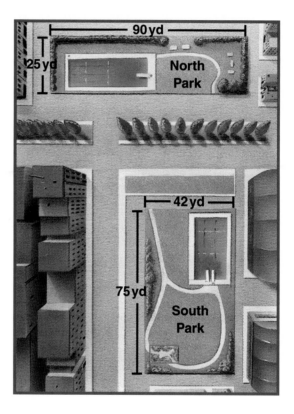

UNDERSTAND

What do you need to find?

You need to find out if the areas of the parks are about the same or if they are different.

PLAN

How can you solve the problem?

Find the area of each park by multiplying its length times its width. Then compare the two areas.

SOLVE

North Park: 90 yd × 25 yd = 2,250 square yd

South Park: 75 yd × 42 yd = 3,150 square yd

3,150 square yards is much greater than 2,250 square yards. So, Sharon is not correct.

LOOK BACK

What if North Park was 35 yards wide? What would the area be? Would Sharon be correct?

Show What You Learned

Use perimeter and area to solve Problems 1–7.

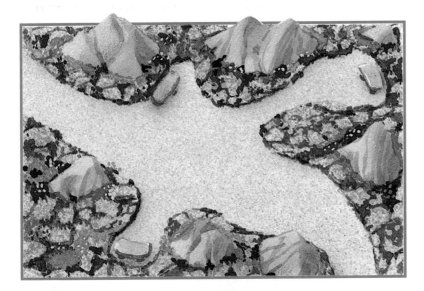

1 The perimeter of the rectangular rock garden shown above is 130 feet. If the rock garden is 25 feet wide, how long is it?

2 What is the area of the rock garden?

3 About 400 square feet of the rock garden is used for pathways. What is the area of the rock garden that is not used for pathways?

Use the chart to the right to solve Problems 4–7.

4 Alex says the area of South Park Pool is almost the same as the area of North Park Pool. Is he right? Explain.

5 **Analyze** How many times greater is the area of the West Beach Pool than the area of the East Wading Pool?

Size of Park Pools		
Pool	**Length**	**Width**
South Park	85 ft	45 ft
North Park	110 ft	35 ft
West Beach	100 ft	40 ft
East Wading Pool	20 ft	40 ft

6 **Explain** If the length of the East Wading Pool were doubled, would the area double? How do you know your answer is reasonable?

7 **Create Your Own** Write a problem about a swimming pool that can be solved using perimeter or area.

Problem Solving

★ ★ ★ ★ ★ **Preparing for Tests**

Practice What You Learned

Choose the correct letter for each answer.

1 Debbie bought 4 toy robots. The least expensive one cost $4.89. The most expensive one cost $12.73. Which is reasonable for the total amount of money Debbie paid for the toys?

A. Less than $12
B. Between $12 and $17
C. Between $17 and $24
D. More than $24

Tip

Use estimation to help you solve this problem. Start by rounding each price to the nearest dollar.

2 Pete wants to make a frame for a picture that is 4 inches by 6 inches. He plans to make the frame 1-inch wide. What will the **perimeter** of the outside of the frame be?

A. 20 in.
B. 24 in.
C. 28 in.
D. 48 in.

Tip

Draw a Picture to help you solve this problem. Sketch the picture, then sketch the frame around it.

3 It took Sherry 15 minutes to get ready for swim team practice, 10 minutes to walk to the pool, and 10 minutes to warm up before getting in the water. If Sherry got in the water at 1:15 P.M., at what time did she begin to get ready for practice?

A. 12:30 P.M.
B. 12:40 P.M.
C. 12:45 P.M.
D. 12:55 P.M.

Tip

Try *Working Backwards* to solve this problem. Start with the time Sherry got into the pool.

4 Yesterday, Frank, Oliver, and Dave each made $42 raking leaves. Which is the best estimate of the amount of money they earned altogether?

A. $40   **C.** $120
B. $80   **D.** $150

---

5 A flower shop has 37 red roses, 51 pink roses, and 23 yellow roses. **About** how many red and pink roses does the shop have?

A. 70   **C.** 90
B. 80   **D.** 110

---

6 In this diagram the green area is a garden. The white area is a stone walk. How could you find the area of the walk in square centimeters?

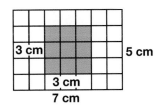

3 cm   5 cm
3 cm
7 cm

A. Subtract 6 from 12.
B. Subtract 9 from 12.
C. Subtract 6 from 35.
D. Subtract 9 from 35.

---

7 Ronald reads 8 to 12 pages of his book every day. Which is reasonable for the number of pages Ronald reads in a week?

A. Less than 8
B. Between 8 and 56
C. Between 56 and 84
D. More than 84

---

8 Debbie bought 4 pencils that cost 30¢ each, a pack of pens that cost $2.50, and some erasers that cost 15¢ each. Not including tax, what other information is needed to find the total cost of Debbie's purchase?

A. The number of pens in a pack
B. The cost of 2 erasers
C. The number of erasers Debbie bought
D. The cost of 2 pencils

Use the graph for Problems 9 and 10.

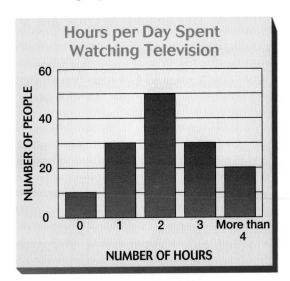

9 How many more people watch 2 hours of television a day than watch no television at all?

A. 30   **C.** 50
B. 40   **D.** 60

---

10 How many people watch less than 3 hours of television per day?

A. 45
B. 90
C. 100
D. 120

A Solid Idea

Space figures have three dimensions.

Learning About It

The world around you is filled with solid objects. Look at the sculpture to the right. It is shaped like a cube. How is a cube different from a square?

A square has length and width, so it has two dimensions. But a cube has length, width, and height, so it has three dimensions. A three-dimensional object is called a space figure or a solid. All the faces of a cube are squares.

▲ This sculpture has a cube shape. It is standing on a vertex.

Space Figures

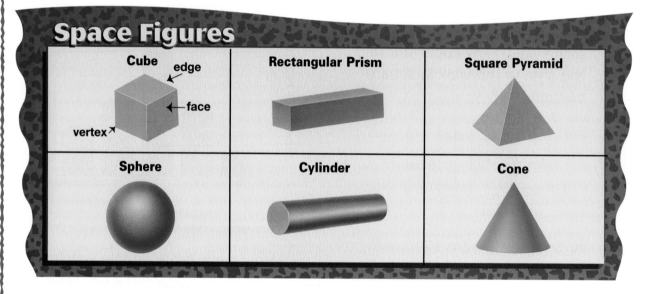

Cube	Rectangular Prism	Square Pyramid
edge, face, vertex		
Sphere	**Cylinder**	**Cone**

Think and Discuss How are a cube and a square pyramid alike? How are they different?

Try It Out

Tell which space figure each object looks like.

1.  Shoes

2.

3. Go Team!

4. TRASH

Practice

Tell which space figure each object looks like.

5.

6.

7.

8.

9.

10.

11.

12.

13. Copy and complete the chart.

Space Figure	Number of Faces	Number of Straight Edges	Number of Vertices
Rectangular prism			
Cube			
Square pyramid			
Sphere			

Problem Solving

Use the chart on page 460 to answer Problems 14–16.

14. What solid figure has a triangle as a face? a square as a face? a rectangle as a face?

15. Describe a space figure with only five faces. Make a drawing to help you.

16. Which solid shapes have curved surfaces?

▲ **Science Connection**
Minerals are often shaped like space figures. Here, many of the salt crystals look like cubes.

Review and Remember

Using Algebra Compare. Use >, <, or = for ⬤.

17. 3,384 + 926 ⬤ 4,310

18. 5 × 7 ⬤ 6 × 6

19. 16 ÷ 2 ⬤ 36 ÷ 4

20. 400 − 358 ⬤ 240 ÷ 6

21. 8 × 9 ⬤ 6 × 6 × 2

22. 1,468 + 2,890 ⬤ 2,199 + 2,039

Speaking Volumes

Using Algebra

You can use unit cubes to measure the space inside a space figure.

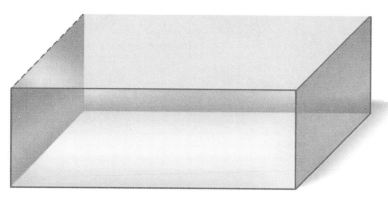

Word Bank

volume

Learning About It

Suppose you want to measure the **volume** of a space figure like the rectangular prism shown above. Volume refers to the number of cubic units that fit inside a space figure.

Work with a partner.

What You Need

For each pair:
  unit cubes or
    connecting cubes

Step 1 Use unit cubes to make a model of a rectangular prism like the one to the right.

- How many unit cubes are in each row? This number is the length. How many rows are there? This number is the width. How many unit cubes are in one layer?

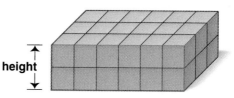

- Finish building the model as shown to the right. How many layers does it take to finish the model? This is the height.

- What is the total number of unit cubes it takes to build this model? This is the volume.

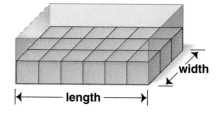

Step 2 You can also multiply to find the volume of a rectangular prism.

Volume = length × width × height
Volume = 6 units × 3 units × 2 units = 36 cubic units

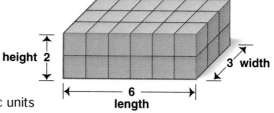

Step 3 Copy the chart below. Use your unit cubes to build at least 5 other rectangular prisms. Record your results in your chart.

Length	Width	Height	Volume
6 units	3 units	2 units	36 cubic units

Think and Discuss Can different figures have the same volume? Explain, using examples.

Practice

Find the volume of each space figure. Use unit cubes to help you.

1.

2.

3.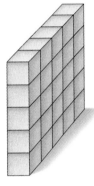

4.

5.

6.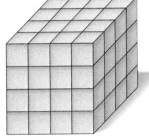

7. **Explain** How many unit cubes are in a box that has 10 rows, 10 cubes in each row, and is 10 layers high?

8. **Describe** What are the heights, widths, and lengths of rectangular prisms that each have a volume of 16 unit cubes?

Checkpoint

Understanding Perimeter, Area, and Volume

Vocabulary

Complete. Use the words from the Word Bank.

1. The distance around a circle is called the ___?___.

2. The number of cubic units that fit inside a space figure is called the ___?___.

3. The number of square units needed to cover the surface of a shape is called the ___?___.

4. The distance around the outside of a figure is called the ___?___.

Word Bank

area
circumference
perimeter
volume

Skills and Concepts

Find the perimeter of each figure. (pages 452–453)

5.
6 ft
5 ft   5 ft
6 ft

6.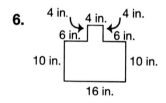
4 in.   4 in.   4 in.
6 in.   6 in.
10 in.   10 in.
16 in.

7.
35 ft
15 ft   15 ft
35 ft

Find each area in square units. Each ■ = 1 square unit.
(pages 454–457)

8.

9.

10.

Name the space figures you could use to trace the following polygons. (pages 460–461)

11. square

12. circle

13. triangle

14. rectangle

What do you think?
What happens to the perimeter and area of a square when the length of the side is doubled?

Find the volume of each space figure. Use unit cubes to help you. (pages 462–463)

15.

16.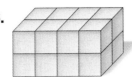

17.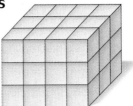

Problem Solving

18. You want to build a fence around your garden. The sides measure 4 ft, 12 ft, 10 ft, and 6 ft. How much fence will you need?

19. **What If?** Suppose you increase the size of your garden by 2 feet on each side. Now how much fence will you need?

20. **Analyze** Each layer in a box has 10 rows of unit cubes, with 10 cubes in each row. How many layers are there if there are 500 unit cubes in the box? How do you know?

Journal Idea

Write about instances in which you may need to find an area or a perimeter. Explain how this skill will be useful throughout your life.

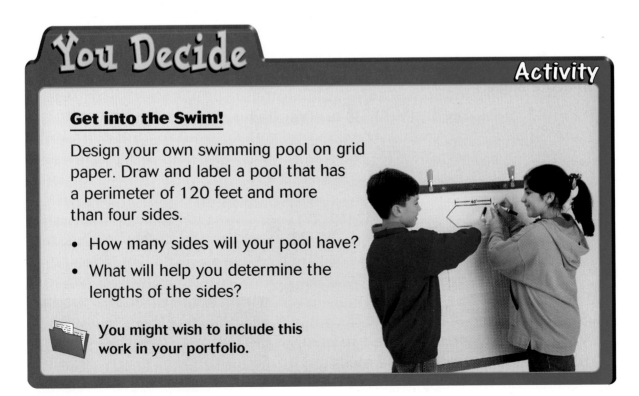

You Decide

Activity

Get into the Swim!

Design your own swimming pool on grid paper. Draw and label a pool that has a perimeter of 120 feet and more than four sides.

- How many sides will your pool have?
- What will help you determine the lengths of the sides?

You might wish to include this work in your portfolio.

Extra Practice

Identify each figure as a line, a line segment, or a ray.
Then write the name for each one.

1. A   B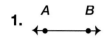

2. C   D

3. E   F

4. G   H

5. I   J

6. K   L

7. M   N

8. O   P

Tell which lines or line segments are parallel and which
are intersecting, perpendicular, or neither.

9.

10.

11.

12.

13.

14.

15.

16.

Tell whether the angle is a right angle, an obtuse angle,
or an acute angle.

17.

18.

19.

20.

21.

22.

23.

24.

25. Suppose you are in an airplane.
You look down and see these two
roads on the ground. If these roads
continue on, will they intersect? Explain.

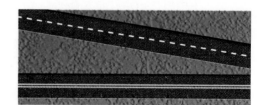

Extra Practice

Set B (pages 438–439)

Find each diameter. Estimate each circumference.

1.
2.
3.
4.

5. **Using Mental Math** The diameter of a wheel is 20 inches. What is the radius? About how many inches is the circumference of the wheel?

Set C (pages 440–441)

Tell if the figures in each pair are congruent. Write *yes* or *no*.

1.
2.
3.

4. Kim made a tracing of a picture. Are the tracing and the picture congruent? Why or why not?

Set D (pages 442–443)

Using Algebra Write *similar* or *not similar* for the figures in each pair.

1.
2.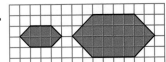
3.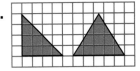

4. Jeremy used different-sized square blocks to make a path to his house. Were the squares similar? Why or why not?

Extra Practice

Using Algebra   **Find the perimeter of each figure.**

1.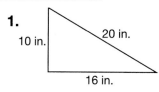

2.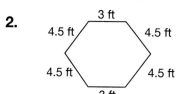

3.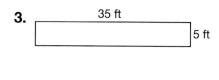

4. Sara's garden is the shape of a square. Each side is 15 feet long. What is the perimeter of Sara's garden?

Find each area in square units.

1.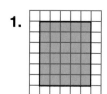

2.

3.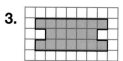

4. Suppose you want to tile a surface with 1-inch square tiles. The surface is 36 inches long and 12 inches wide. How many tiles will you need?

Tell which space figure each object looks like.

1.

2.

3.

4. Michael made a rectangular prism out of paper. How many faces did his rectangular prism have? how many edges and vertices?

 **Chapter Test**

Name each figure.

1.

2.

3.

4.

5.

6.

Are these figures congruent? Write *yes* or *no*.

7.

8.

Tell whether each angle is right, obtuse or acute.

9.

10.

Find the diameter. Estimate the circumference.

11. 3 in.

12. 5 in.

Do you slide, flip, or turn figure *A* to make it look like figure *B*?

13. A B

14. A → B

Find the area and the perimeter of each figure.

15. 6 ft
4 ft   4 ft
6 ft

16. 1 in. 1 in.
4 in.
2 in.   3 in.
5 in.

Find the volume of unit cubes in each.

17.

18.

Solve.

19. A bicycle wheel has a 22-inch diameter. What is the wheel's radius? About how many inches around is the bicycle wheel?

20. A city park is shaped like a rectangle. It is 100 feet long and 50 feet wide. What is the perimeter of the park? What is the area?

 Self-Check How would you explain to another student how to find the perimeter and the area of a rectangle that is 11 inches long and 8 inches wide?

Performance Assessment

Show What You Know About Geometry

① Describe the figure to the right. Use as many geometry terms as you can. Use the materials listed below if you wish.

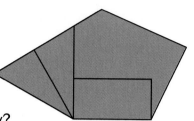

Self-Check Did you describe any angles? any congruent figures? any lines of symmetry?

② The drawing below shows a patio made of bricks. Each brick is 8 inches long and 4 inches wide. Use the drawing to answer Questions a and b.

What You Need

ruler
paper or index card
  with square corners
grid paper (optional)

a. What is the area of the patio?

b. What is the perimeter of the patio?

Explain how you found your answers.

Self-Check Did you remember to label your answers with the correct units?

For Your Portfolio

You might wish to include this work in your portfolio.

Extension

Space Figure Patterns

You can use patterns to make space figures. Predict the space figure that can be made if the pattern below is cut out and folded on the dotted lines.

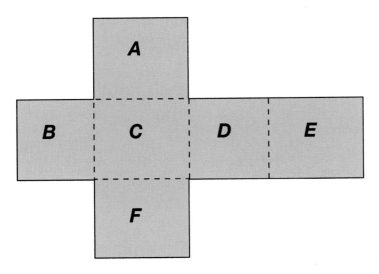

- How many faces does the space figure have?

- Are the faces A and F the same size and shape? Are faces B and D the same size and shape?

Trace or copy the pattern above. Then cut, fold, and tape your pattern to make the space figure. What space figure did you make? Did you predict the correct space figure?

Which of these patterns can be folded to make a cube? Copy the patterns onto large-grid graph paper. Cut them out and fold them to prove your answer.

a.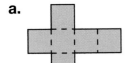
b.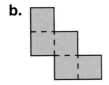
c.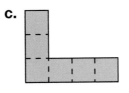
d.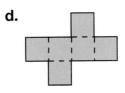

Now make a pattern for a rectangular prism of your own. Draw your pattern on large-grid graph paper. Then cut it out and fold it up.

Cumulative Review

Choose the correct letter for each answer.

Operations	Geometry and Spatial Reasoning

1. $92 \div 8 =$

   A. 11   **C.** 10 R2
   B. 11 R4   **D.** 10 R4

2. There are 22 lanes at a bowling alley. Six people can play in each lane. What is the greatest number of people who can play at one time?

   A. 22   **C.** 132
   B. 122   **D.** 142

3. $1.7 - 0.8 =$

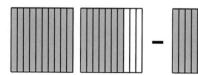

   A. 2.5   **C.** 1.5
   B. 1.9   **D.** 0.9

4. In a school election, Pam got 74 votes, Amy got 67 votes, and Zora got 119 votes. How many votes did Amy and Pam receive?

   A. 141
   B. 186
   C. 193
   D. 260

5. How many corners does an octagon have?

   A. 4
   B. 6
   C. 8
   D. 12

6. How many triangles are in the figure below?

   A. 3
   B. 4
   C. 8
   D. 9

7. Look at the shape mobile below.

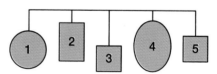

Which shapes are congruent (same size, same shape)?

   A. 1 and 3   **C.** 3 and 5
   B. 2 and 4   **D.** 4 and 1

8. Which shape has 4 right angles?

   A.   **C.**

   B.   **D.**

Patterns, Relationships, and Algebraic Thinking	Probability and Statistics

Patterns, Relationships, and Algebraic Thinking

9. Which letter on the graph best represents the ordered pair (3, 2)

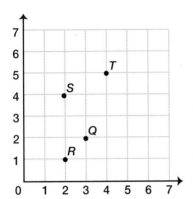

A. Q   **C.** S
B. R   **D.** T

10. What is the missing number in the number pattern?

16, 32, 64, ■, 256, 512

A. 80
B. 112
C. 128
D. 192

11. Which expression could help you solve $7 \times$ ■ $= 56$?

A. 7×56
B. $7 + 56$
C. $56 - 7$
D. $56 \div 7$

12. Which number sentence is in the same family of facts as $8 \times 3 = 24$?

A. $3 + 8 = 11$
B. $24 \div 3 = 8$
C. $8 - 3 = 5$
D. $24 \div 6 = 4$

Probability and Statistics

13. Look at the spinner. How many possible outcomes are there?

A. 2
B. 3
C. 4
D. 6

Use the graph for Questions 14–16.

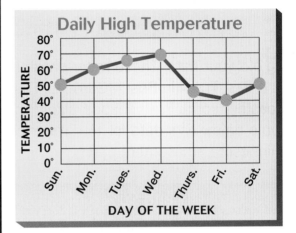

14. What was the high temperature on Monday?

A. 60°   **C.** 70°
B. 63°   **D.** 75°

15. Which day had the highest temperature?

A. Tuesday   **C.** Thursday
B. Wednesday   **D.** Friday

16. Which two days had the same high temperature?

A. Sunday and Monday
B. Tuesday and Wednesday
C. Sunday and Saturday
D. Thursday and Friday

Chapter 12

Dividing by Two-Digit Divisors

Chapter Theme: FAIRS AND RIDES

Real Facts

Hold your hats! These roller-coaster riders are on The Fast Track in Busch Gardens, Florida. Roller coasters come in all shapes, sizes, and speeds. The table below lists data for four roller coasters at a Minnesota amusement park.

Roller Coaster	Passengers per Train	Passengers per Hour	Top Speed (Miles Per Hour)
High Roller	24	1,150	50
Corkscrew	24	1,300	50
Excalibur	30	1,200	54.5
Wild Thing	36	1,700	74

Capacity and Speed of Roller Coasters

• How many passengers can 3 High Roller trains carry?

• Suppose you counted 90 passengers exiting the Excalibur coaster. How could you find how many trains ran during the time you counted?

Real People

Meet Fran Ramirez, manager of the Rides Department at a large theme park. Fran's job is to make sure the rides are working without problems so that visitors can enjoy them over and over again. Fran started working at the park when she was only 15 years old.

Using Algebra

Ups and Downs

Basic division facts can help you divide by multiples of 10.

Learning About It

A giant Ferris wheel carries 120 people in all. It has 20 cars. Each car holds the same number of people. How many people can each car hold?

Divide to find the answer.

$$120 \div 20 = \blacksquare$$

| total number of people | total number of cars | number of people in each car |

Think: **12 ÷ 2 = 6** ← basic fact

So, 12 tens ÷ 2 tens = 6

120 ÷ 20 = 6   Look for patterns of zeros.

Check: **20 × 6 = 120**

Each car can hold 6 people.

Another Example

160 ÷ 80 =   2   Use the basic fact
1,600 ÷ 80 =   20   16 ÷ 8 = 2
16,000 ÷ 80 = 200   Look for patterns of zeros.

Think and Discuss Explain how you can use basic facts and patterns to divide 90 ÷ 30 and 900 ÷ 30 mentally.

Try It Out

Use basic facts and patterns to find each quotient.

1. 80 ÷ 40 = n   **2.** 90 ÷ 30 = n   **3.** 60 ÷ 30 = n
       800 ÷ 40 = n   900 ÷ 30 = n   600 ÷ 30 = n
       8,000 ÷ 40 = n   9,000 ÷ 30 = n   6,000 ÷ 30 = n

4. 70 ÷ 10   **5.** 400 ÷ 50   **6.** 140 ÷ 70   **7.** 240 ÷ 40

Practice

**Find each quotient using mental math.
Check by multiplying.**

8. $50\overline{)350}$ **9.** $40\overline{)280}$ **10.** $20\overline{)160}$ **11.** $90\overline{)180}$

12. $80\overline{)720}$ **13.** $70\overline{)350}$ **14.** $60\overline{)420}$ **15.** $30\overline{)240}$

16. $150 \div 30$ **17.** $60 \div 20$ **18.** $540 \div 60$ **19.** $560 \div 80$

20. $210 \div 70$ **21.** $200 \div 50$ **22.** $270 \div 90$ **23.** $360 \div 40$

24. $490 \div 70$ **25.** $160 \div 40$ **26.** $300 \div 60$ **27.** $630 \div 70$

Problem Solving

28. The first giant Ferris wheel was built in Chicago by George Ferris for Chicago's Columbian Exposition. Each car held 60 people. How many cars were needed for a group of 540 people?

30. The original Ferris wheel had 36 cars that each held 60 passengers. How many people could ride at one time?

31. A Ferris wheel has 40 cars and carries exactly 360 people. Is it reasonable to say that each car holds 90 people? Why or why not?

32. Using Algebra If a Ferris wheel completes a ride every twenty minutes, how many rides can it expect to run in three hours?

29. **Using Estimation** About 16,000 people could ride the Ferris wheel during an eight-hour period. Estimate how many people could ride the wheel each hour.

▲ **Science Connection** In 1893, the Ferris wheel in Chicago was powered by steam. Early Ferris wheels were turned by horses or even people!

Review and Remember

Choose a Method Use mental math or a calculator.
Tell which method you chose and why.

33. 50×50 **34.** $1{,}091 - 892$ **35.** $473 + 897$ **36.** $5\overline{)45}$

37. $560 \div 8$ **38.** 83×215 **39.** $13 + 87 + 65$ **40.** $7{,}200 - 342$

Estimating Quotients

Step Right Up!

You can use compatible numbers to estimate quotients.

Learning About It

At the Jefferson School Fair, points were earned by playing skill games. During the first 45 minutes, 241 points were scored at the beanbag toss. About how many points were earned per minute?

241 ÷ 45 = ■

Use compatible numbers to estimate.

241 ÷ 45
↓   ↓
240 ÷ 40 = 6

> Use 240 ÷ 40 because it is easy to compute mentally and the numbers are close to the original numbers.

About 6 points were earned each minute.

Think and Discuss What other compatible numbers can be used to estimate 241 ÷ 45? Explain.

Try It Out

Use compatible numbers to estimate each quotient. Tell what compatible numbers you used.

1. 448 ÷ 52 **2.** 419 ÷ 68 **3.** 281 ÷ 31 **4.** 352 ÷ 79

5. 193 ÷ 61 **6.** 572 ÷ 84 **7.** 876 ÷ 92 **8.** 728 ÷ 83

9. 159 ÷ 75 **10.** 484 ÷ 82 **11.** 312 ÷ 98 **12.** 208 ÷ 67

Practice

Use compatible numbers to estimate each quotient.
Tell which compatible numbers you used.

13. 29)146 **14.** 18)137 **15.** 24)121 **16.** 71)500

17. 86)453 **18.** 48)345 **19.** 23)158 **20.** 92)265

21. 192 ÷ 28 **22.** 371 ÷ 59 **23.** 239 ÷ 43 **24.** 243 ÷ 63

25. 239 ÷ 31 **26.** 247 ÷ 49 **27.** 312 ÷ 78 **28.** 305 ÷ 61

Problem Solving

29. There are 178 prizes at the Fish Tank Game with 31 prizes on each shelf. About how many shelves are needed to show all of the prizes?

30. A class of 28 students earned 1,545 points playing skill games. About how many points did they average per student?

31. **Journal Idea** Explain how estimating a quotient before you divide can help you decide if your answer is reasonable.

Review and Remember

Find each answer.

32. 56 × 143 **33.** 265 − 193 **34.** 7)98 **35.** 430 + 785 **36.** 291 ÷ 6

37. 743 ÷ 8 **38.** 206 × 84 **39.** 9)126 **40.** 409 − 264 **41.** 783 + 95

Time for Technology

Using a Calculator

Estimating, Guessing, and Checking

Guess where each digit goes.
Use a calculator to check.

Hint Use multiplication.

1. 2, 8, 3, 4   82
　　　　　　　 ▨)▓▓▓

2. 1, 3, 2, 6   52
　　　　　　　 ▨)▓▓▓

3. 2, 4, 6, 8   78
　　　　　　　 ▨)▓▓▓

4. 8, 4, 9, 6   ▓
　　　　　　 54)▓▓▓

Developing Skills for
Problem Solving

*First read for understanding and then focus
on which operation is needed to solve a problem.*

READ FOR UNDERSTANDING

WATERPARK
TICKET PRICES

Adult (over 12) $18
Child (under 12) $13
Toddler (under 4) ....free

Jon and his family plan to spend the
day at Sun City Waterpark. Jon's family
includes his mother, father, brother, and
2 sisters. Jon is 9 years old. His brother
and sisters are 3, 11, and 14 years old.

1 How much does an adult ticket cost?
a child ticket? a toddler ticket?

2 How old are Jon's brother and sisters?

THINK AND DISCUSS

MATH FOCUS

Choose the Operation   Sometimes you
need to decide what operation is needed
to solve a problem. Look for clues in the
words of the problem to help you decide.

Reread the paragraph at the top of the page.

3 How much will Jon's family pay for adult tickets?
for child tickets? What operation did you use to
solve these problems?

4 How much will Jon's family spend altogether on
tickets to the park? What operation did you use
to solve the problem?

5 How did you decide which operation to use before
solving Problems 3 and 4?

Show What You Learned

Answer each question. Give a reason for your choice.

One morning, 540 people rode on the Congo Cruise. Sixty people rode on each trip.

1 How many people rode on the cruise in the morning?

　a. 60 people

　b. 540 people

　c. 600 people

2 How many people rode on each trip?

　a. 60 people

　b. 540 people

　c. 600 people

3 Which of the following should you do to find the number of trips that were made in the morning?

　a. Subtract the number of people who rode on each trip from the total number of people who rode.

　b. Divide the number of people who rode on each trip by the total number of people who rode.

　c. Divide the total number of people who rode by the number of people who rode on each trip.

The Twisting Tunnel is a fast, scary ride in a car down a dark, twisting tunnel. The ride lasts for 60 seconds. The car travels 20 feet each second.

4 Which number sentence shows the number of feet the car travels in three seconds?

　a. $60 - 20 = 40$ feet

　b. $60 \div 3 = 20$ feet

　c. $20 \times 3 = 60$ feet

5 Which sentence shows the length of the tunnel?

　a. $60 \times 20 = 1{,}200$ feet

　b. $60 \div 20 = 30$ feet

　c. $60 - 20 = 40$ feet

6 **Explain** How could you use addition to find the number of feet the car travels in 3 seconds?

✓ Checkpoint

Dividing by Multiples of Ten and Estimating Quotients

Use basic facts to divide. Check each by multiplying. (pages 474–475)

1. $250 \div 50$
2. $450 \div 90$
3. $560 \div 70$

4. $80 \div 40$
5. $320 \div 40$
6. $150 \div 50$

7. $60 \div 30$
8. $640 \div 80$
9. $240 \div 60$

10. $280 \div 40$
11. $450 \div 50$
12. $420 \div 60$

13. $360 \div 90$
14. $560 \div 80$
15. $480 \div 60$

16. $80\overline{)480}$
17. $70\overline{)630}$
18. $20\overline{)60}$
19. $40\overline{)360}$

20. $60\overline{)540}$
21. $30\overline{)270}$
22. $60\overline{)360}$
23. $90\overline{)720}$

> **What do you think?**
>
> Why is it easier to estimate $335 \div 41$ by using compatible numbers than by rounding?

Use compatible numbers to estimate each quotient. Tell what compatible numbers you used.

(pages 476–477)

24. $697 \div 78$
25. $256 \div 42$
26. $718 \div 95$
27. $310 \div 47$

28. $589 \div 83$
29. $499 \div 85$
30. $197 \div 69$
31. $345 \div 97$

32. $452 \div 48$
33. $183 \div 19$
34. $419 \div 63$
35. $161 \div 37$

Match each exercise with its estimate. Then complete the estimate by writing the estimated quotient.

(pages 476–477)

36. $423 \div 68$ a. $250 \div 50$
37. $246 \div 49$ b. $420 \div 70$
38. $159 \div 19$ c. $490 \div 70$
39. $543 \div 57$ d. $160 \div 20$
40. $501 \div 71$ e. $540 \div 60$

41. $841 \div 92$ a. $560 \div 80$
42. $182 \div 29$ b. $720 \div 80$
43. $559 \div 83$ c. $360 \div 90$
44. $358 \div 92$ d. $180 \div 30$
45. $719 \div 83$ e. $810 \div 90$

Problem Solving

46. A small Ferris wheel holds 180 people. There are 20 cars. Each car holds the same number of people. How many people can sit in each car?

47. At the Penny Arcade, 62 people spent a total of $183 in 3 hours. About how much did each person spend?

Use the table and compatible numbers to estimate answers to Problems 48–50.

48. The monorail transports people between the parking lot and the entrance to the fair. About 48 people can ride the monorail at one time. On Sunday, about how many trips would the monorail have to make to bring everyone to the fair?

Attendance at the Fair	
Sunday	1,025
Monday	489
Tuesday	510
Wednesday	535
Thursday	796
Friday	815
Saturday	1,197

49. Only school groups of about 22 each attended the fair on Friday. About how many school groups attended the fair on Friday?

50. **Using Estimation** About how many people went to the fair during this week?

INTERNET ACTIVITY
www.sbgmath.com

Journal Idea

Decide how much to charge for a ride on a Ferris wheel. Then estimate the number of times you could ride if you had $100 to spend. Explain your reasoning.

Critical Thinking Corner

Logical Thinking

Patterns

Using Algebra Draw or name the next term in each pattern.

1. R B RR BB RRR BBB RRRR BBBB . . .

2. 1, 3, 9, 27, . . .   **3.** 125, 100, 75, 50, . . .

4.

Come to the Fair

You can divide by two-digit numbers.

Learning About It

The Eiffel Tower was built in Paris for the 1889 Exposition. It was to be torn down after the fair, but became so famous that it was saved.

Suppose a ticket to the Eiffel Tower costs $21 and a group of tourists paid a total of $189. How many tourists were in the group?

$$\$189 \div \$21 = n$$

Estimate first: $180 \div 20 = 9$

Now find the actual quotient.

Step 1 Decide where to place the first digit.	**Step 2** Divide the ones. Multiply and subtract.
$\overset{X}{21)\overline{189}}$ There are not enough hundreds to divide.	Think: $180 \div 20 = 9$
$\overset{X}{21)\overline{189}}$ There are not enough tens to divide.	$\begin{array}{r} 9 \\ 21)\overline{189} \\ -189 \leftarrow 9 \times 21 \\ \hline 0 \leftarrow 0 < 21 \end{array}$
$21)\overline{189}$ There are enough ones to divide.	

There were 9 tourists in the group.

Compare the answer with your estimate. Is your answer reasonable?

The 600-foot Space Needle was built for the 1962 Century 21 Exposition in Seattle, Washington.

▲ **Science Connection** The monorail train passed the Bioclimate Sphere at Expo '92 in Seville, Spain. The 72-foot sphere produced clouds of mist so that visitors would be comfortable in extremely hot temperatures.

More Examples

A. $576 \div 82 = \blacksquare$ (Think: $560 \div 80 = 7$)

$$\begin{array}{r} 7\ R2 \\ 82\overline{)576} \\ -574 \\ \hline 2 \end{array}$$

Check.

$$\begin{array}{r} 82 \leftarrow \text{divisor} \\ \times\ \ 7 \leftarrow \text{quotient} \\ \hline 574 \\ +\ \ 2 \leftarrow \text{remainder} \\ \hline 576 \end{array}$$

If this matches the dividend, you divided correctly.

B. $326 \div 63 = \blacksquare$ (Think: $300 \div 60 = 5$)

$$\begin{array}{r} 5\ R11 \\ 63\overline{)326} \\ -315 \\ \hline 11 \end{array}$$

Check.

$$\begin{array}{r} 63 \\ \times\ \ 5 \\ \hline 315 \\ +\ 11 \\ \hline 326 \end{array}$$

Think and Discuss How do you decide where to put the first digit of the quotient when dividing by two digits?

Try It Out

Divide. Check each by multiplying.

1. $21\overline{)63}$ 2. $21\overline{)109}$ 3. $43\overline{)344}$ 4. $71\overline{)641}$

5. $99 \div 31$ 6. $91 \div 21$ 7. $888 \div 90$ 8. $386 \div 64$

9. $376 \div 53$ 10. $195 \div 59$ 11. $89 \div 20$ 12. $135 \div 32$

◄ **Social Studies Connection** Alexandre Eiffel designed the tower to show the use of structural steel. At 984 feet, the tower was once the world's tallest structure. Eiffel also designed the steel framework for the Statue of Liberty.

INTERNET ACTIVITY
www.sbgmath.com

Practice

Divide. Check each by multiplying.

13. $24\overline{)73}$

14. $31\overline{)95}$

15. $61\overline{)78}$

16. $23\overline{)92}$

17. $41\overline{)379}$

18. $21\overline{)178}$

19. $52\overline{)426}$

20. $61\overline{)491}$

21. $83\overline{)664}$

22. $32\overline{)289}$

23. $41\overline{)288}$

24. $71\overline{)599}$

25. $87 \div 20$

26. $68 \div 21$

27. $97 \div 31$

28. $95 \div 23$

29. $448 \div 64$

30. $137 \div 95$

31. $251 \div 41$

32. $630 \div 88$

33. $323 \div 53$

34. $211 \div 29$

35. $138 \div 39$

36. $504 \div 72$

Using Algebra Complete each division. Write the missing digits.

37.
```
        9 R6
   12)114
   - ▮0▮
   ─────
        6
```

38.
```
      ▮ R▮▮
   23)198
   - 184
   ─────
      1▮
```

39.
```
      5 R▮▮
   49)273
   - 245
   ─────
      2▮
```

40.
```
       6 R▮3
   ▮1)34▮
      306
   ─────
      ▮3
```

41.
```
      ▮ R10
   16)106
   -  96
   ─────
      ▮▮
```

42.
```
      7 R▮5
   29)218
   - ▮▮▮
   ─────
      1▮
```

43.
```
      8 R▮
   47)38▮
   - 3▮6
   ─────
      ▮
```

44.
```
         6
   ▮6)▮76
      ▮76
   ─────
        0
```

Problem Solving

45. The outdoor food court at HemisFair '68 could seat 325 people at 65 round tables. How many people could each table seat?

46. **What If?** Suppose the outdoor food court described in Problem 45 was enlarged enough to hold 390 people. How many more of the round tables would be needed?

47. **Using Estimation** At Expo '92 in Seville, Spain, a group of 95 people spent $775 for lunch. About how much was spent per person?

▲ HemisFair '68 in San Antonio, Texas

48. At Expo '92, Bill spent $1\frac{1}{2}$ hours in the science exhibit, on the monorail, and at lunch. He was in the science exhibit 20 minutes more than on the monorail. Lunch took 30 minutes. How much time was he in the science exhibit? Explain the strategy you used.

49. Journal Idea Without dividing, how do you know there will be a remainder in 326 ÷ 65?

Use the table for Problems 50–52.

50. Which world's fair had the most exhibits? the fewest?

51. How many more exhibits were in the Chicago fair than in the London fair?

52. Using Estimation Which fair had the fewest number of exhibits per acre?

Nineteenth-Century World's Fairs			
City	Date	Area in Acres	Number of Exhibits
London	1851	26	13,939
Paris	1867	41	43,217
Philadelphia	1867	236	30,000
Paris	1889	72	61,722
Chicago	1893	633	65,000

Review and Remember

Using Algebra Solve for *n*.

53. $140 - n = 20$

54. $72 \times 24 = n$

55. $n + 340 = 840$

56. $760 \div 9 = n$

57. $40 \times n = 320$

58. $42 \div n = 7$

Time for Technology

Using a Calculator

Finding Square Numbers

Using Algebra The two factors are the same number in each.

Use a calculator to find *n*.

Hint Guess and Check may help you.

1. $n \times n = 225$

2. $n \times n = 625$

3. $n \times n = 1,225$

4. $n \times n = 2,025$

5. $n \times n = 3,025$

6. $n \times n = 4,225$

Try, Try Again

Sometimes you may need to adjust your quotient
if it is too large or too small.

Learning About It

Work with a partner.

Step 1 Write the division exercises at the right on index cards. Choose one and use compatible numbers to estimate the quotient.

Step 2 Divide.

- Place your estimate in the quotient.

- Multiply the quotient by the divisor and write the product. Subtract if you can.

Step 3 Look at the students' work below.

- Joe's quotient is too large. How can you tell?

- April's quotient is too small. How can you tell?

What You Need

For each student:
index cards

$19\overline{)115}$

$43\overline{)295}$

$76\overline{)436}$

$52\overline{)252}$

$$7 \leftarrow \text{Think: } 280 \div 40 = 7$$
$$43\overline{)295}$$
$$-\ 301 \leftarrow 301 > 295$$

$$5 \leftarrow \text{Think: } 100 \div 20 = 5$$
$$19\overline{)115}$$
$$-\ 95$$
$$\overline{20} \leftarrow 20 > 19$$

Step 4 Look at your division exercise again.

- Decide if your quotient is correct.
  Explain how you know.

- Adjust your estimated quotient, if necessary.

Step 5 Find the quotients of the other exercises on page 486. If you need to adjust the quotients, explain why.

Think and Discuss Explain how you can tell if a quotient is too large or too small.

Practice

**Find what's wrong with the first digit in each quotient.
Correct the digit and finish dividing.**

$$\begin{array}{r} 7 \\ \textbf{1. } 24\overline{)148} \\ -168 \end{array}$$

$$\begin{array}{r} 7 \\ \textbf{2. } 59\overline{)475} \\ -413 \end{array}$$

$$\begin{array}{r} 7 \\ \textbf{3. } 18\overline{)144} \\ -126 \end{array}$$

$$\begin{array}{r} 6 \\ \textbf{4. } 91\overline{)541} \\ -546 \end{array}$$

**Estimate each quotient. Then divide and adjust your
quotient if necessary.**

5. $23\overline{)90}$ **6.** $28\overline{)84}$ **7.** $75\overline{)261}$ **8.** $57\overline{)229}$

9. $72\overline{)572}$ **10.** $51\overline{)479}$ **11.** $34\overline{)136}$ **12.** $89\overline{)374}$

 Money $ense

TICKET PRICES

Children $8.00

Adults $12.00

Senior Citizens $10.00

Group Special $60.00
(6 people)

Tickets, Please

What is the best way for each group
of people listed below to buy tickets?

1. 2 adults and 4 children

2. 6 senior citizens and 4 adults

3. 26 children and 7 adults

4. 4 children, 3 adults, and
2 senior citizens

Problem Solving
Choose a Strategy

You can choose from the many strategies you have learned to solve problems.

Kristen drives a go-cart around a track at the fastest speed possible. She drives a total of 5 miles in 15 minutes. If she continues at the same speed, how many miles can she travel in 1 hour?

 UNDERSTAND

What do you need to find?

You need to find the number of miles Kristen can travel in 1 hour.

 PLAN

How can you solve the problem?

You can **make a table** or **write a number sentence**. Your table will show how far Kristen can travel in 15, 30, 45, and 60 minutes. Your number sentence will show how far she can travel in four 15-minute periods.

 SOLVE

Make a Table

Distance Traveled				
Time in minutes	15	30	45	60
Distance in miles	5	10	15	20

Write a Number Sentence

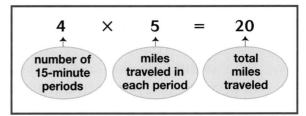

Kristen can travel 20 miles in 1 hour.

 LOOK BACK

What other strategies could you use to solve this problem?

Using the Strategies

Solve Problems 1–8 using these or other strategies to solve each problem. Tell which strategy you used.

Problem Solving Strategies

- Work Backwards
- Make a Table
- Make a List
- Use Logical Reasoning
- Write a Number Sentence
- Solve a Simpler Problem

1. There are five people waiting in line to ride the go-carts. Billy is before Lorraine but after Brenda. Lorraine is before Linda. Ricky is first. In what order are the people waiting in line?

2. Jenna, Meredith, and Kyle ride in red, blue, and yellow go-carts. Jenna is not in the yellow go-cart. Meredith is not in the yellow or the blue go-cart. Who is in each go-cart?

3. The distance around the go-cart track is 132 feet. Every 6 feet there is a flagpole. How many flagpoles are around the track?

4. Mickey, Keisha, and Sarah line up to get their pictures taken. In how many different ways can they line up?

Use the sign at the right to solve Problems 5–8.

5. How much would it cost to ride a go-cart for 15 minutes? for 30 minutes? for 1 hour?

6. Lorraine got $4 in change when she bought two go-cart tickets for $8 each. How much money did she use to pay for the tickets?

7. After 9:00 P.M., a 10-minute ride costs $4. If you spend $16, how much longer can you ride after 9:00 P.M. than before 9:00 P.M?

8. **Analyze** There are 24 people in a go-cart race. Two people race in each round. If you win, you continue to race. How many rounds will there be before there is one champion?

GO-CARTS
5 minutes for $4.00

Hold on Tight!

You can divide greater numbers.

Learning About It

Riverbank State Park in the Harlem section of New York City will be home to a carousel made of animals designed by children.

Suppose the carousel operates 27 times a day. If 864 people can ride each day, how many people can ride at one time?

$$864 \div 27 = \blacksquare$$

Estimate first: $900 \div 30 = 30$

Now find the actual quotient.

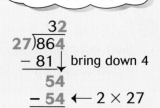

THERE'S ALWAYS A WAY!

● **One way** is to use paper and pencil.

Step 1 Use your estimate to decide where to place the first digit.	**Step 2** Divide the tens. Multiply and subtract. Then compare.	**Step 3** Bring down the ones and divide. Multiply and subtract.
		Think: $60 \div 30 = 2$
$$27\overline{)864}$$	$$\begin{array}{r} 3 \\ 27\overline{)864} \\ -81 \\ \hline 5 \end{array}$$ ← 3 × 27 ← 5 < 27	$$\begin{array}{r} 32 \\ 27\overline{)864} \\ -81\downarrow \\ \hline 54 \\ -54 \\ \hline 0 \end{array}$$ bring down 4 ← 2 × 27
There are not enough hundreds to divide. There are enough tens to divide.		

 ● **Another way** is to use your calculator.

Press: (8)(6)(4)(INT÷)(2)(7)(=)   Display: [*32* *0*]

Thirty-two people can ride at one time.

Think and Discuss Why would it be a good idea to estimate an answer before you divide?

◀ **Kid Connection** Children from New York City were asked to design animals that they would like to ride on for the carousel.

Try It Out

Divide. Check each by multiplying.

1. 41)585   **2.** 82)929   **3.** 18)296

4. 21)173   **5.** 42)982   **6.** 40)860

Practice

Choose a Method Use paper and pencil or a calculator to divide. Tell which method you chose and why.

7. 32)483   **8.** 63)791   **9.** 53)806

10. 19)733   **11.** 68)793   **12.** 14)602

13. 698 ÷ 13   **14.** 791 ÷ 46   **15.** 984 ÷ 92   **16.** 644 ÷ 34

17. 502 ÷ 38   **18.** 930 ÷ 66   **19.** 5,623 ÷ 86   **20.** 2,466 ÷ 28

Problem Solving

21. Milo Mottola, the creater of the carousel, worked 15 hours a day to make the figures. If he worked a total of 525 hours, how many days did he work?

22. **Using Estimation** Each child was promised a lifetime of free rides if his or her animal design was chosen. Explain how you would estimate how many free rides a child might receive.

23. **Journal Idea** Explain in your own words how you check the answer to a division problem when the answer has a remainder.

Review and Remember

Find each answer.

24. 74 × 96   **25.** 3,207 − 1,072   **26.** 8,921 + 475

27. 458 ÷ 6   **28.** 2,763 + 8,401   **29.** 207 ÷ 9

For Extra Practice, see Set D, page 498.

Problem Solving
Using Operations

You can use all four operations to solve problems.

The Giant Dipper is a world-famous roller coaster in Santa Cruz, California. When it was built in 1924, the ride cost $0.15. Today it costs $3.00. How much more does the ride cost a family of four today than in 1924?

 UNDERSTAND

What do you need to find?

You need to find the difference in the cost for 4 people to ride the roller coaster in 1924 and today.

 PLAN

How can you solve the problem?

Multiply to find how much it cost for 4 people to ride the coaster in 1924. Then multiply to find how much it costs for 4 people to ride the coaster today. Finally, subtract to compare the costs.

 SOLVE

- **Multiply** to find the cost of 4 tickets in 1924.
  $4 \times \$0.15 = \$0.60$

- **Multiply** to find the cost of 4 tickets today.
  $4 \times \$3.00 = \$12.00$

- **Subtract** to compare the costs.
  $\$12.00 - \$0.60 = \$11.40$

It costs $11.40 more today for a family of 4 to ride the Giant Dipper.

 LOOK BACK

Could you have solved the problem using different operations? Explain.

Show What You Learned

Solve each problem.

1 There are 1,350 light bulbs along the track of the Giant Dipper. About 120 bulbs are replaced each week. Is 6,000 bulbs a reasonable number to be replaced each year? Explain. (Remember, there are 52 weeks in a year.)

2 The roller coaster is open from 9:00 A.M. to 10:00 P.M. Each day, mechanics check the track once before the ride opens, every two hours while it is open, and once after it closes. How many times is the track checked each day?

3 The Steel Phantom roller coaster has 2 trains that ride around the track. Each train has 7 cars, and each car has 4 seats. How many seats are there altogether on the two trains?

4 **Analyze** On the Steel Phantom, one 28-seat train reloads while the other runs. The ride is 3 minutes long. How many people can ride the roller coaster in an hour?

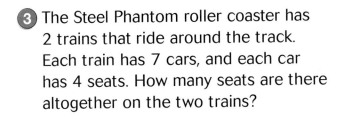

Use the table at the right to solve Problems 5–7.

5 Which is longer, Mean Streak or Desperado? How much longer?

6 **Analyze** Which roller coasters are more than twice as long as the Steel Phantom?

7 **Create Your Own** Write a problem that can be solved using the roller coaster lengths in the table. Make sure your problem can be solved using one or more math operations.

The Longest Roller Coasters	
Roller Coaster	**Length in Feet**
The Beast (Kings Mills, Ohio)	7,400
Mean Streak (Sandusky, Ohio)	5,427
Desperado (Jean, Nevada)	6,100
Steel Phantom (West Mifflin, Pennsylvania)	3,000

Problem Solving

★★★★★ **Preparing for Tests**

Practice What You Learned

Choose the correct letter for each answer.

1 Marcia wakes up at 7:00 A.M. It takes her 10 minutes to get dressed for school. Then it takes her 15 minutes to eat breakfast. After breakfast it takes her 20 minutes to walk from home to school. How long does it take Marcia to get dressed and eat breakfast?

A. 5 min
B. 10 min
C. 25 min
D. 45 min

Tip

Read the question carefully to decide what information you need to answer it.

2 Alan drove 55 miles per hour for 2 hours. Then he drove 45 miles per hour for 1 hour. How far did Alan drive in the 3 hours?

A. 45 mi
B. 110 mi
C. 145 mi
D. 155 mi

Tip

First find the distance Alan traveled at 55 miles per hour. Then find the distance he traveled at 45 miles per hour.

3 The diagram below shows a skating path in a park. John skated around the entire path one time. **About** how far did John skate?

A. 500 yards
B. 600 yards
C. 700 yards
D. 800 yards

Tip

Since the problem asks for an estimate, first round each length to the nearest hundred.

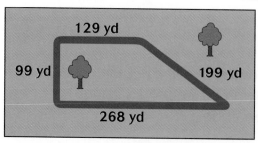

4 Tom collected 372 baseball cards. He put the same number of cards in each of 6 albums. Which number sentence can you use to find the number of cards in each album?

A. $372 - 6 =$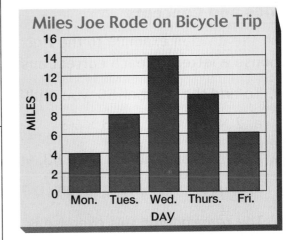
B. $372 \times 6 =$ ▩
C. $372 + 6 =$ ▩
D. $372 \div 6 =$ ▩

5 Martin is older than Allie. Shawn is younger than Allie. Roger is older than Martin. Which is a reasonable conclusion?

A. Allie is older than Roger.
B. Shawn is older than Martin.
C. Martin is younger than Allie.
D. Roger is older than Allie.

6 The fourth grade is going on a field trip. Each bus holds 32 people. How many buses are needed for 600 people?

A. 18
B. 19
C. 20
D. 24

7 On Monday the temperature was 35°F. It went up 1°F more on Tuesday, 2°F more on Wednesday, and 3°F on Thursday. If this pattern continues, what will the temperature be on Saturday?

A. 47°F C. 50°F
B. 49°F D. 51°F

8 Linda's school raised $4,500 by selling tickets to the school play. Ticket prices were $5 for children and $9 for adults. Which is reasonable for the number of tickets sold?

A. More than 1,000
B. Between 500 and 900
C. Between 300 and 500
D. Fewer than 500

Use the graph for Problems 9 and 10.

This graph shows how many miles Joe rode each day during a bicycle trip.

Miles Joe Rode on Bicycle Trip

9 How much farther did Joe ride on Thursday than on Monday?

A. 6 miles
B. 14 miles
C. 18 miles
D. 28 miles

10 Last year Joe went on a 40-mile bicycle trip. How much longer was Joe's bicycle trip this year?

A. 8 miles C. 4 miles
B. 6 miles D. 2 miles

# Checkpoint

Dividing by Two-Digit Numbers

Vocabulary

Complete. Use the words from the Word Bank.

1. In 864 ÷ 27 = 32, the number 32 is called the ___?___.

2. In 344 ÷ 43 = 8, the number 43 is called the ___?___.

3. In 504 ÷ 72 = 7, the number 504 is called the ___?___.

Word Bank

dividend

divisor

quotient

Skills and Concepts

Use the division example to the right.

Choose a letter for each correct answer. (pages 490–491)

```
          36 R▧
     23)837
      − 69
        147
      − 138
          9
```

4. To find the number 69, you multiply

   a. 2 × 48   **b.** 3 × 23   **c.** 36 × 48

5. After you subtract 69 from 83, you

   a. divide   **b.** multiply   **c.** bring down the ones

6. The remainder in this exercise is

   a. 9   **b.** 36   **c.** 138

7. To check this exercise, you use the expression

   a. 23 × 36   **b.** 36 + 23   **c.** 23 × 36, then add 9

Divide. (pages 482–485)

8. 61)435   **9.** 76)249   **10.** 32)263   **11.** 92)157   **12.** 22)44

Divide. Check each by multiplying. (pages 490–491)

13. 83)974   **14.** 67)803   **15.** 26)592   **16.** 81)966   **17.** 33)735

18. 804 ÷ 61   **19.** 829 ÷ 39   **20.** 869 ÷ 41   **21.** 644 ÷ 28   **22.** 887 ÷ 69

Problem Solving

23. A roller coaster must be given a safety check every 12 hours that it runs. In the last 6 months it ran for 540 hours. How many safety checks should have been made?

24. Once a year the light bulbs along the roller coaster track are replaced. The track is 990 feet long, and there is a light every 15 feet. How many new bulbs are needed?

25. Mr. and Mrs. Jordan and their 3 children spent $28.00 on rides, $13.50 for lunch, and $16.00 for 2 adult tickets. If they spent a total of $71.00, how much did each child's ticket cost? Explain the strategy you used to solve the problem.

Journal Idea

Is 15 R31 the answer for 376 ÷ 23? Why or why not? Explain how you decided.

What do you think?

Explain why estimating the first digit of the quotient is an important step in division. Tell what to do if your estimate doesn't work.

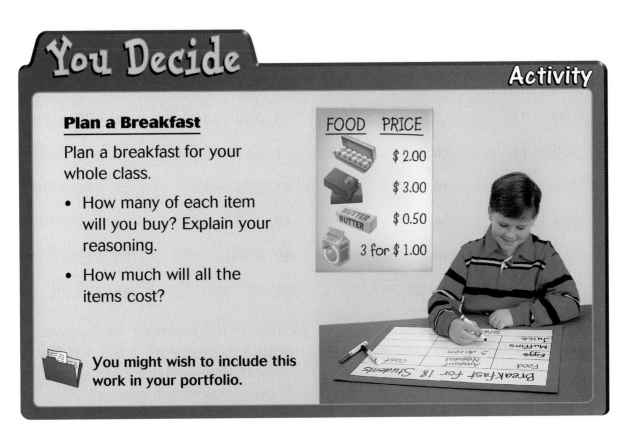

You Decide

Activity

Plan a Breakfast

Plan a breakfast for your whole class.

- How many of each item will you buy? Explain your reasoning.

- How much will all the items cost?

FOOD	PRICE
	$ 2.00
	$ 3.00
BUTTER	$ 0.50
	3 for $ 1.00

You might wish to include this work in your portfolio.

Extra Practice

Set A (pages 474–475)

Use basic facts to divide. Check each by multiplying.

1. $70\overline{)490}$
2. $90\overline{)810}$
3. $40\overline{)320}$
4. $50\overline{)250}$

5. $50\overline{)450}$
6. $80\overline{)640}$
7. $70\overline{)420}$
8. $60\overline{)360}$

9. $80 \div 40$
10. $90 \div 30$
11. $70 \div 70$
12. $60 \div 20$

13. $630 \div 70$
14. $480 \div 60$
15. $350 \div 50$
16. $240 \div 40$

17. $300 \div 50$
18. $150 \div 30$
19. $720 \div 80$
20. $540 \div 60$

21. $630 \div 90$
22. $120 \div 60$
23. $100 \div 20$
24. $240 \div 30$

25. Each car on a Ferris wheel holds 40 people. How many cars are on the wheel if it can hold a total of 320 people?

26. A parking field at the fairgrounds can hold 450 cars in nine rows. How many cars can be parked in each row to fill the field?

Set B (pages 476–477)

Use compatible numbers to estimate each quotient. Tell what compatible numbers you used.

1. $550 \div 82$
2. $209 \div 69$
3. $292 \div 48$
4. $475 \div 78$

5. $305 \div 41$
6. $120 \div 43$
7. $847 \div 89$
8. $215 \div 83$

9. $239 \div 59$
10. $321 \div 79$
11. $271 \div 32$
12. $478 \div 79$

13. $562 \div 81$
14. $179 \div 62$
15. $447 \div 92$
16. $119 \div 39$

17. $72\overline{)211}$
18. $23\overline{)138}$
19. $69\overline{)562}$
20. $51\overline{)397}$

21. $39\overline{)243}$
22. $68\overline{)352}$
23. $48\overline{)298}$
24. $71\overline{)628}$

25. There are 92 people waiting in line to ride the Ferris wheel. Altogether, they will spend $267 for tickets. Estimate how much tickets cost per person.

26. During the first hour, Becky gave out 350 programs at the 4-H Fair. About how many programs did she give out each minute?

Extra Practice

Set C (pages 482–485)

Divide. Check each by multiplying.

1. $42\overline{)85}$ **2.** $29\overline{)89}$ **3.** $51\overline{)86}$ **4.** $84\overline{)93}$

5. $63\overline{)378}$ **6.** $52\overline{)369}$ **7.** $31\overline{)248}$ **8.** $68\overline{)635}$

9. $91\overline{)776}$ **10.** $78\overline{)556}$ **11.** $49\overline{)443}$ **12.** $42\overline{)387}$

13. $168 \div 21$ **14.** $309 \div 43$ **15.** $376 \div 86$ **16.** $660 \div 93$

17. $444 \div 72$ **18.** $429 \div 69$ **19.** $231 \div 32$ **20.** $432 \div 51$

Using Algebra Fill in the missing digits.

```
        ■ R■              ■ R■               3 R■              8 R■
21. 62)315        22. 21)190        23. 93)284        24. 66)529
    − 310             − 189             − ■■■             − ■■■
       ■                ■                  5                 1


        5 R■              6 R■               3 R■■             5 R■■
25. 94)4■5        26. 38)2■9        27. 8■)289        28. 2■)136
    − 470             − 228             − 255             − 120
       ■                ■                 ■■                ■■


        8 R9             3 R36              8 R■              7 R■■
29. 36)297        30. 84)288        31. ■4)35■        32. ■7)62■
    − 28■             − 25■             − 352             − 609
       9                36                 ■                ■■
```

33. At a German restaurant, a tour group of 48 people spent a total of $384. How much did each person spend at the restaurant?

34. Analyze A ride in an amusement park lasts 15 minutes, including loading and unloading time. How many rides can be run in $1\frac{1}{2}$ hours?

35. At a recent world's fair, a total of 644 people attended an exhibit. If 92 people attended each day, how many days was the exhibit open?

Extra Practice

Set D (pages 490–491)

Copy each problem. Mark an X to show where to put the first digit of the quotient. Do not divide.

1. $54\overline{)367}$
2. $42\overline{)582}$
3. $21\overline{)329}$
4. $86\overline{)914}$

5. $63\overline{)473}$
6. $45\overline{)931}$
7. $23\overline{)247}$
8. $78\overline{)510}$

9. $94\overline{)906}$
10. $81\overline{)999}$
11. $38\overline{)390}$
12. $67\overline{)631}$

13. $51\overline{)543}$
14. $39\overline{)735}$
15. $56\overline{)486}$
16. $89\overline{)864}$

Divide. Check each by multiplying.

17. $41\overline{)597}$
18. $28\overline{)388}$
19. $53\overline{)802}$
20. $37\overline{)943}$

21. $12\overline{)152}$
22. $24\overline{)403}$
23. $36\overline{)420}$
24. $24\overline{)918}$

25. $629 \div 49$
26. $530 \div 31$
27. $436 \div 32$
28. $936 \div 72$

29. $372 \div 31$
30. $987 \div 23$
31. $715 \div 65$
32. $519 \div 12$

Use the table to answer Problems 33–35.

33. How many times must the Chieftain operate for 950 people to have a ride?

34. **Using Mental Math** A ride on the Chieftain lasts three minutes including loading and unloading. The owner runs the merry-go-round for 2 hours in the morning and 3 hours in the afternoon. How many rides can be run in this time?

35. **Create Your Own** Use the information in the chart to write a problem using division.

36. **Analyze** The owner of a merry-go-round makes $27 for every full ride he operates. How many times must his merry-go-round be filled for the owner to collect $297?

Merry-go-rounds	
Name	Number of Horses
Chieftain	25
Jumping Horses	42
Chanticleer	18
Racing Derby	64
Round Up	35
Flying Steeds	78

Use basic facts to divide.

1. 720 ÷ 90

2. 360 ÷ 40

3. 640 ÷ 80

4. 80)320

5. 50)100

6. 70)490

Use compatible numbers to estimate each quotient. Tell what numbers you used.

7. 239 ÷ 38

8. 247 ÷ 52

9. 311 ÷ 81

10. 285 ÷ 68

Divide. Check by multiplying.

11. 90)360

12. 70)280

13. 48)87

14. 19)68

15. 72)639

16. 38)348

17. 53)872

18. 36)515

19. 491 ÷ 51

20. 526 ÷ 64

21. 498 ÷ 27

22. 400 ÷ 93

Solve.

23. A ride called Shoot the Rapids holds 78 people. Two people can sit in each seat. How many rides will it take for 546 people to have a turn?

24. The ride on a miniature railroad takes 25 minutes. How many times can this ride run in 10 hours?

25. Estimate There are 9 shelves of prizes at the ringtoss game. Each shelf holds the same number of prizes. How many prizes are on each shelf if there are 630 prizes in all?

 Self-Check Did you remember to write the remainders in the answers for Exercises 11–22?

Performance Assessment

Show What You Know About Division With 2-Digit Divisors

1 Write your own division example.

908
45
3,084

a. Pick any two numbers at the right.

b. Using the numbers you picked, divide the greater number by the lesser number. First estimate the quotient. Use your estimate to check if your answer is reasonable.

c. Now divide to find the quotient. Describe the steps you used to divide.

Self-Check Did you remember to show the remainder as part of the quotient?

2 You have designed a roller coaster that can carry 135 people in 15 cars. Each car has 3 rows of seats.

a. How many people will sit in each car when the roller coaster is full? How many people will sit in each row of seats when the roller coaster is full?

b. How many cars would you use to carry 125 people? Each car must be full before you load the next car. Explain.

Self-Check Did you go back and try your answers in the problems to see if they are reasonable?

For Your Portfolio

You might wish to include this work in your portfolio.

Extension

Dividing Decimals

If you can divide whole numbers, you'll find it easy to divide a decimal by a whole number.

Be careful to

- place the decimal point in the quotient directly above the decimal point in the dividend, and

- keep your numbers carefully aligned.

37.6 ÷ 8 = n

Step 1 Place the decimal point in the quotient.	**Step 2** Divide as you would with whole numbers.	**Step 3** Continue to divide until the remainder is zero.
$$\begin{array}{r} . \\ 8\overline{)37.6} \end{array}$$	$$\begin{array}{r} 4. \\ 8\overline{)37.6} \\ -32 \\ \hline 5 \end{array}$$	$$\begin{array}{r} 4.7 \\ 8\overline{)37.6} \\ -32\downarrow \\ \hline 56 \\ -56 \\ \hline 0 \end{array}$$

More Examples

A.
$$\begin{array}{r} 0.43 \\ 5\overline{)2.15} \\ -20\downarrow \\ \hline 15 \\ -15 \\ \hline 0 \end{array}$$

(Think:) There are not enough ones to divide. Place a zero in the ones place and divide tenths.

B.
$$\begin{array}{r} 1.55 \\ 6\overline{)9.30} \\ -6\downarrow\downarrow \\ \hline 33 \\ -30\downarrow \\ \hline 30 \\ -30 \\ \hline 0 \end{array}$$
← Write this zero to continue dividing. Adding a zero will not change the value of the dividend.

Divide.

1. $6\overline{)20.4}$ **2.** $9\overline{)27.9}$ **3.** $3\overline{)15.6}$

4. $4\overline{)55.2}$ **5.** $5\overline{)3.5}$ **6.** $4\overline{)1.52}$

7. $3\overline{)2.31}$ **8.** $8\overline{)0.48}$ **9.** $2\overline{)8.1}$

10. $8\overline{)7.6}$ **11.** $4\overline{)0.2}$ **12.** $5\overline{)6}$

Cumulative Review

★ ★ ★ ★ ★ **Preparing for Tests**

Choose the correct letter for each answer.

Operations	Geometry and Spatial Reasoning

1. A boat tour lasts 20 minutes. How many rides can the captain give in 4 hours? (Hint: 60 minutes equals 1 hour.)

   A. 8   **C.** 16

   B. 12   **D.** 80

2. $3{,}300 \div 1 =$

   A. 1   **C.** 330

   B. 33   **D.** 3,300

3. Alex and his 3 friends spent $823 on vacation. If they split the cost evenly, **about** how much did each person spend?

   A. $100

   B. $200

   C. $300

   D. $2,000

4. $1.7 + 0.5 =$

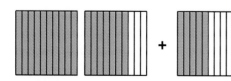

   A. 2.2

   B. 2.75

   C. 3.12

   D. 3.2

5. Which number is inside the triangle and inside the circle?

   A. 1

   B. 2

   C. 3

   D. 4

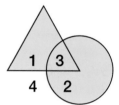

6. Which space shape could you use to draw this plane shape?

   A. cone

   B. sphere

   C. cylinder

   D. cube

7. How many more sides does an octagon have than a pentagon?

   A. 3

   B. 5

   C. 7

   D. 8

8. Which shows a line of symmetry?

   A.   **C.**

   B.   **D.**

Measurement	Probability and Statistics

Measurement

9. Matthew's dog Tip weighed 13 pounds when Matthew got him. In the first year, Tip gained 45 pounds and grew 6 inches. In the second year he grew 3 more inches and gained 40 pounds. How much did Tip weigh then?

A. 85 lb   **C.** 102 lb
B. 98 lb   **D.** 106 lb

10. Danny practiced skating for 2 hours 12 minutes. How many *minutes* did he practice skating? (Hint: 60 minutes equals 1 hour.)

A. 14 min   **C.** 102 min
B. 72 min   **D.** 132 min

11. Henry got home from school at 4:10 P.M. He made one 5-minute stop on the way home. If Henry left school at 3:20 P.M., how long did it take him to get home?

A. 50 min   **C.** 40 min
B. 45 min   **D.** 35 min

12. Abdul drank 1.5 liters of water after track practice. How many *milliliters* was that? (Hint: 1 liter equals 1,000 milliliters.)

A. 15,000 mL
B. 1,500 mL
C. 150 mL
D. 15 mL

Probability and Statistics

13. There are 4 marbles in a bag. Two are red, one is blue, and one is yellow. How many possible outcomes are there?

A. 1
B. 2
C. 3
D. 5

14. Abby's basketball team scored 43 points, 50 points, and 60 points in three games. What is the team's average score?

A. 51   **C.** 110
B. 93   **D.** 153

Use the chart below for Questions 15 and 16.

Adopted Animals				
Kind of Animal	Week 1	Week 2	Week 3	Week 4
Dog	12	10	10	9
Cat	15	17	18	20
Bird	5	6	7	2

15. How many dogs and cats were adopted in Week 2?

A. 10   **C.** 27
B. 17   **D.** 34

16. How many dogs were adopted over the 4 weeks?

A. 9
B. 10
C. 33
D. 41

Additional
Resources

Tables

MEASURES

Customary

Length

1 foot (ft) = 12 inches (in.)

1 yard (yd) = 3 feet, or 36 inches

1 mile = 5,280 feet, or 1,760 yards

Weight

1 pound (lb) = 16 ounces (oz)

1 ton (T) = 2,000 pounds

Capacity

1 cup (c) = 8 fluid ounces (fl oz), or 16 tablespoons (tbsp)

1 tablespoon (tbsp) = 3 teaspoons (tsp)

1 pint (pt) = 2 cups

1 quart (qt) = 2 pints

1 half-gallon = 2 quarts

1 gallon (gal) = 4 quarts

Time

1 minute (min) = 60 seconds (s)

1 hour (h) = 60 minutes

1 day (d) = 24 hours

1 week (wk) = 7 days

1 year (yr) = 12 months (mo), or 52 weeks, or 365 days

1 century (c) = 100 years

1 leap year = 366 days (adds one day to February)

1 decade = 10 years

1 millennium = 1,000 years

Metric

Length

1 centimeter (cm) = 10 millimeters (mm)

1 decimeter (dm) = 10 centimeters

1 meter (m) = 100 centimeters

1 kilometer (km) = 1,000 meters

Mass/Weight

1 kilogram (kg) = 1,000 grams (g)

Capacity

1 liter (L) = 1,000 milliliters (mL)

SYMBOLS

=	is equal to	$\overleftrightarrow{AB}$	line AB
>	is greater than	$\overline{AB}$	line segment AB
<	is less than	$\overrightarrow{AB}$	ray AB
°	degree	$\angle ABC$	angle ABC
°C	degree Celsius		
°F	degree Fahrenheit	(3, 4)	ordered pair 3, 4

FORMULAS

$P = (2 \times length) + (2 \times width)$ Perimeter of a rectangle

$A = l \times w$ Area of a rectangle

$V = l \times w \times h$ Volume of a rectangular prism

Glossary

A

A.M. Used to show time between midnight and noon. (p. 253)

acute angle An angle less than a right angle. (p. 433)

Example:

addends The numbers that are added. (p. 69)

Example: $7 + 8 = 15$
The **addends** are 7 and 8.

analog clock A type of clock that shows the digits 1–12 and uses minute and hour hands to tell the time. (p. 250)

Example:

angle Two rays with a common endpoint. (p. 433)

Example:

area The number of square units needed to cover a region. (p. 454)

array An arrangement of objects or numbers in rows and columns. (p. 90)

associative (grouping) property of multiplication The way in which factors are grouped does not change the product. (p. 88)

Example: $2 \times (3 \times 5) = (2 \times 3) \times 5$

average(mean) The sum of the addends divided by the number of addends. (p. 322)

B

bar graph A graph with bars of different lengths to show information. (p. 138)

breaking apart A mental math method in which a sum or difference is found by rewriting numbers so they are easier to work with. (p. 64)

Example: $26 + 13 = 20 + 6 + 10 + 3$

C

capacity The amount a container can hold. (p. 270)

center A point inside a circle or sphere that is the same distance from all points on the circle or sphere. (p. 438)

centimeter (cm) A metric unit used to measure length. 100 centimeters equal 1 meter. (p. 277)

century A unit of time equal to 100 years. (p. 258)

certain To be sure. (p. 162)

circle A closed plane figure in which all points are the same distance from a point called the center. (p. 438)

Example:

Glossary

circumference The distance around a circle. (p. 438)

closed figure A path that begins and ends at the same point. (p. 430)

Example:

clustering Using numbers that are close to a rounded number to make estimation easier. (p. 185)

common denominator A common multiple of two or more denominators. (p. 372)

Example: 24 is a **common denominator** of $\frac{1}{6}$ and $\frac{1}{8}$.

commutative (order) property of multiplication The order in which factors are multiplied does not change the product. (p. 88)

Example: $5 \times 6 = 30$ $6 \times 5 = 30$

compatible numbers Numbers that are easy to compute mentally. (p. 312)

compensation A mental math method in which a sum or difference is changed into an equivalent sum or difference to make it easier to add or subtract. (p. 65)

composite number A whole number greater than 1 with more than two factors. (p. 129)

Example: 8 is a **composite number**. Its factors are 1, 2, 4, and 8.

cone A space figure with one circular flat surface and one curved surface that form a point. (p. 460)

Example:

congruent Figures that have the same size and shape. (p. 440)

Example:

cube A space figure with six congruent square faces. (p. 460)

Example:

cup (c) A customary unit used to measure capacity. 1 cup equals 8 fluid ounces. (p. 270)

customary system A measurement system that measures length in inches, feet, yards, and miles; capacity in cups, pints, quarts, and gallons; weight in ounces, pounds, and tons; and temperature in degrees Fahrenheit. *See* Table of Measures. (p. 504)

cylinder A space figure with two bases that are congruent circles. (p. 460)

Example:

— D —

data Information that is gathered. (p. 134)

day The period of time from midnight to midnight. A day has 24 hours. (p. 250)

decade A unit of calendar time equal to 10 years. (p. 258)

decimal A number with one or more places to the right of the decimal point. (p. 390)

Examples: 0.7; 1.8; 2.06

decimal point The mark used to separate dollars from cents and ones from tenths. (p. 390)

Examples: $1.54; 1.3

decimeter (dm) A metric unit used to measure length. 1 decimeter equals 10 centimeters. (p. 277)

degree Celsius (°C) A metric unit used to measure temperature. (p. 284)

degree Fahrenheit (°F) A customary unit used to measure temperature. (p. 272)

denominator The number below the fraction bar in a fraction. (p. 338)

Example: $\frac{2}{5}$ The denominator is 5.

diameter A line segment that passes through the center of a circle and has both endpoints on the circle. (p. 438)

difference The answer in subtraction. (p. 44)

Example: 9 − 4 = 5
The **difference** is 5.

digit Any of the ten symbols: 0, 1, 2, 3, 4, 5, 6, 7, 8, and 9. (p. 3)

dividend The number to be divided. (p. 106)

Example: 6)‾36 or 36 ÷ 6
The **dividend** is 36.

divisible A number is divisible by another number if the remainder is 0 after dividing. (p. 335)

divisor The number by which another number is divided. (p. 106)

Example: 7)‾28 or 28 ÷ 7
The **divisor** is 7.

doubles Facts in which the same number is added to itself or multiplied by itself. (p. 86)

E

edge A segment where two plane faces of a space figure meet. (p. 460)

Example: edge

elapsed time The amount of time that has passed. (p. 252)

endpoint A point at the end of a line segment or ray. (p. 432)

equivalent decimal Decimals that name the same number. (p. 391)

equivalent fractions Fractions that name the same amount. (p. 344)
Example: $\frac{1}{2}$ and $\frac{2}{4}$

estimate An approximate rather than an exact answer. (p. 44)

expanded form A number written as the sum of the value of its digits. (p. 4)
Example: 1,000 + 200 + 30 + 4 is the **expanded form** of 1,234.

F

face A flat surface of a space figure. (p. 460)
Example: face

fact family Related facts using the same numbers. (pp. 41, 102)
Example: 2 + 3 = 5   5 − 3 = 2
3 + 2 = 5   5 − 2 = 3

Glossary

factors The numbers that are multiplied to give a product. (p. 88)
Example: $3 \times 8 = 24$
The **factors** are 3 and 8.

flip (reflection) To pick up and turn over. (p. 446)

foot (ft) A customary unit used to measure length. 1 foot equals 12 inches. (p. 264)

fraction A number that names part of a set or part of a region. (p. 338)
Examples: $\frac{1}{2}, \frac{2}{3}$, and $\frac{6}{8}$ are fractions.

$\frac{1}{6}$ of the set is shaded. $\frac{5}{8}$ of the region is shaded.

front-end digit The digit in the place with the greatest value, used for front-end estimation. (p. 81)

front-end estimation A method using only the front-end digits to estimate sums, differences, products, and quotients. (p. 81)

G
---

gallon (gal) A customary unit used to measure capacity. 1 gallon equals 4 quarts. (p. 270)

gram (g) A metric unit used to measure mass. 1,000 grams equal 1 kilogram. (p. 280)

graph A drawing used to show information. (p. 142)

greater than (>) The symbol used to compare two numbers when the greater number is on the left. (p. 8)
Examples: $7 > 4$, $9 > 6$

H
---

half gallon A customary unit used to measure capacity. $\frac{1}{2}$ gallon equals 2 quarts. (p. 270)

hexagon A polygon with six sides and six vertices. (p. 430)
Example:

hour (h) A unit of time equal to 60 minutes. (p. 250)

hundredths One or more of one hundred equal parts of a whole. (p. 391)

I
---

impossible Cannot occur. (p. 162)

improper fraction A fraction in which the numerator is greater than or equal to the denominator. Its value is greater than or equal to 1. (p. 356)

inch (in.) A customary unit used to measure length. 12 inches equal 1 foot. (p. 264)

intersecting lines Lines that meet or cross at one point. (p. 432)
Example:

inverse operations Two operations with the opposite effect. Addition and subtraction are inverse operations. Multiplication and division are inverse operations. (p. 100)
Example: $4 \times 8 = 32$; $32 \div 4 = 8$

kilogram (kg) A metric unit used to measure mass. 1 kilogram equals 1,000 grams. (p. 280)

kilometer (km) A metric unit used to measure length. 1 kilometer equals 1,000 meters. (p. 277)

mean The average of a set of numbers. (p. 322)

median The middle number or average of the two middle numbers in a set of data when the data are arranged in order from least to greatest. (p. 135)

meter (m) A metric unit used to measure length. 1 meter equals 100 centimeters. (p. 277)

L

leap year Every four years 1 day is added to February. That year is called leap year. (p. 258)

length The distance between two points. (p. 262)

less than (<) The symbol used to compare two numbers when the lesser number is on the left. (p. 8)
Examples: $7 < 10$, $4 < 8$

line A straight path that goes on and on in opposite directions. A line has no endpoints. (p. 432)

line graph A graph used to show change over a period of time. (p. 148)

line of symmetry A line on which a figure can be folded so that both sides match. (p. 444)

Example:

line of symmetry

line segment A part of a line that has two endpoints. (p. 432)

liter (L) A metric unit used to measure capacity. 1 liter equals 1,000 milliliters. (p. 282)

metric system A measurement system that measures length in millimeters, centimeters, meters, and kilometers; capacity in milliliters and liters; mass in grams and kilograms; and temperature in degrees Celsius. *See* Table of Measures. (p. 504)

mile (mi) A customary unit used to measure length. 1 mile equals 5,280 feet. (p. 264)

millennium A unit of time equal to 1,000 years. (p. 258)

milliliter (mL) A metric unit used to measure capacity. 1,000 milliliters equal 1 liter. (p. 282)

millimeter (mm) A metric unit used to measure length. 10 millimeters equal 1 centimeter. (p. 277)

minute A unit of time equal to 60 seconds. (p. 250)

mirror image A view of an image seen in a mirror with the left side seen as if it were the right. (p. 446)

Glossary

mixed number A number written as a whole number and a fraction. (p. 356)

mode The number or numbers that occur most often in a collection of data. (p. 135)

multiple The product of a whole number and any other whole number. (p. 95)

Example: 0, 3, 6, and so on are **multiples** of 3.

multiplication An operation on two or more numbers, called factors, to find a product. (p. 84)

Example: $4 \times 5 = 20$
The **product** is 20.

multiplication table A table that organizes multiplication facts. (p. 94)

N

noon Twelve o'clock in the daytime. (p. 253)

number line A line that shows numbers in order. (p. 24)

Example:

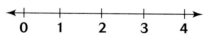
$$0 \quad 1 \quad 2 \quad 3 \quad 4$$

number sentence A fact written in horizontal form. (p. 40)

Example: $3 + 4 = 7$

numerator The number above the fraction bar in a fraction. (p. 338)

O

obtuse angle An angle greater than a right angle. (p. 432)

Example:

octagon A polygon with eight sides and eight vertices. (p. 430)

Example:

ordered pair A pair of numbers that give the location of a point on a map or a graph. (p. 150)

ounce (oz) A customary unit used to measure weight. 16 ounces equal 1 pound. (p. 268)

outcome A result of a probability experiment. (p. 164)

P

P.M. Used to show the time between noon and midnight. (p. 253)

parallel lines Lines that never intersect. (p. 432)

Example:

pentagon A polygon with five sides and five vertices. (p. 430)

Example:

perimeter The distance around a polygon. (p. 452)

period A group of three digits separated from other digits of a number by a comma. (p. 4)

perpendicular Two lines that intersect to form four right angles. (p. 433)

Example:

pictograph A graph that shows information by using pictures. (p. 142)

pint (pt) A customary unit used to measure capacity. 1 pint equals 2 cups. (p. 270)

place value The value determined by the position of a digit in a number. (p. 4)

Example: In 562, the digit 5 means 5 hundreds, the digit 6 means 6 tens, the digit 2 means 2 ones.

place-value chart A chart used to show the value of each digit within a number. (p. 4)

plane A flat surface that goes on and on in all directions. (p. 430)

plane figure A geometric figure whose points are all in one plane. (p. 430)

Example:

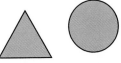

plot To locate and mark the point on a grid named by an ordered pair. (p. 151)

point An exact location in space. (pp. 150, 432)

polygon A closed plane figure with sides that are line segments. (p. 430)

pound (lb) A customary unit used to measure weight. 1 pound equals 16 ounces. (p. 268)

predict To make a statement about what might happen. (p. 162)

prime number A whole number greater than 1 with only two factors—1 and itself. (p. 129)

Examples: 5, 7, 11, and 13

probability The chance that an event will occur. (p. 162)

product The answer in multiplication. (p. 88)

Example: $4 \times 8 = 32$ ⟵ product

properties of 1 for division Any number divided by 1 is that number. Any number except 0 divided by itself is 1. (p. 110)

Examples: $6 \div 1 = 6$ $3 \div 3 = 1$

property of 1 for multiplication The product of any number and 1 is that number. (p. 88)

Examples: $6 \times 1 = 6$ $1 \times 6 = 6$

Q

quadrilateral A polygon with four sides and four vertices. (p. 431)

quart (qt) A customary unit used to measure capacity. 1 quart equals 4 cups. (p. 270)

quotient The answer in division. (p. 106)

Example: $3\overline{)24}$ or $24 \div 3 = 8$
The **quotient** is 8.

Glossary

radius A line segment with one endpoint on the circle and the other endpoint at the center. (p. 438)

range The difference between the greatest number and the least number in a set of data. (p. 135)

ray A part of a line that has one endpoint and goes on and on in one direction. (p. 432)

rectangle A polygon with four right angles and four sides. (p. 430)

Example:

rectangular prism A space figure whose faces are all rectangles. (p. 460)

Example:

regroup To use 1 ten to form 10 ones; 1 hundred to form 10 tens; 12 ones to form 1 ten 2 ones, and so on. (p. 48)

remainder The number that is left after dividing. (p. 483)

Example: 42 ÷ 8 = 5 R2
The **remainder** is 2.

right angle An angle that has the shape of a square corner. (p. 432)

Example:

rounding Expressing a number to the nearest ten, hundred, thousand, and so on. (p. 24)

Example: 43 rounded to the nearest ten is 40.

second A unit of time. 60 seconds are equal to 1 minute. (p. 250)

short word form A number written with words naming the periods. (p. 4)

Example: 20 thousand, 425

side A line segment that is part of a plane figure. (p. 431)

similar Figures that have the same shape. They are not necessarily the same size. (p. 442)

simplest form When the greatest common factor of the numerator and denominator in a fraction is one. (p. 346)

slide (translation) To move along a line without picking up. (p. 446)

space figure A figure whose points are in more than one plane. (p. 460)

Example:

sphere A space figure shaped like a round ball. (p. 460)

Example:

square A polygon with four equal sides and four right angles. (p. 430)

Example:

square pyramid A space figure with a square base and faces that are triangles with a common vertex. (p. 460)

Example:

standard form A number written with commas separating groups of three digits. (p. 4)

stem-and-leaf plot A display that shows data in order of place value. The leaves are the last digits of the numbers. The stems are the digits to the left of the leaves. (p. 158)

subtraction An operation on two numbers to find the difference. (p. 40)

Example: 15 − 3 = 12 ← **difference**

sum The answer in addition. (p. 44)

Example: 8 + 7 = 15 ← **sum**

symmetry A figure has symmetry if it can be folded along a line so that the two parts match exactly. (p. 444)

tablespoon (tbsp) A unit used to measure capacity. Three teaspoons equal one tablespoon. (p. 270)

teaspoon (tsp) A unit used to measure capacity. (p. 270)

tenths One or more of ten equal parts of a whole. (p. 390)

ton (T) A customary unit used to measure weight. 1 ton equals 2,000 pounds. (p. 268)

triangle A polygon with three sides and three vertices. (p. 430)

Example:

turn (rotation) To move around a point in a circular motion. (p. 446)

Venn diagram A diagram that uses circles to show the relationships between groups of objects. (p. 159)

Example:

vertex The point where two rays meet. The point of intersection of two sides of a polygon. The point of intersection of three edges of a space figure. (p. 430)

Example: — **vertex**

volume The number of cubic units that fit inside a space figure. (p. 462)

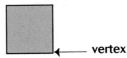

word form A number written as words. (p. 4)

Example: one hundred forty-one

yard (yd) A customary unit used to measure length. 1 yard equals 3 feet. (p. 264)

Z

zero property of division 0 divided by any number except 0 is 0. You cannot divide a number by 0. (p. 110)

Example: 0 ÷ 12 = 0

zero property of multiplication The product of any number and 0 is 0. (p. 88)

Example: 5 × 0 = 0 and 0 × 3 = 0

Index

Index

Index

Index

Credits

Becoming a Better Test Taker

You've learned a lot of math skills this year! These skills will help you with your school work and with everyday activities outside of school. How can you show what you've learned in math? One way is by taking tests.

Did you know you could do better on tests just by knowing how to take a test? The test-taking strategies on these pages can help you become a better test taker. They might also help you think of test questions as a fun challenge! When you take a test, try to use these strategies to show all you know.

Multiple Choice Questions
Know Your ABCs!

For multiple choice questions, you are given several answer choices for a problem. Once you have solved the problem, you need to choose the right answer from the choices that are given.

1 Ⓐ Ⓑ Ⓒ Ⓓ Ⓔ

2 Ⓐ Ⓑ Ⓒ Ⓓ Ⓔ

3 Ⓐ Ⓑ Ⓒ Ⓓ Ⓔ

Example

$45 \div 9 = $ ▨

A 5   **B** 6   **C** 36   **D** 54   **E** Not Here

Think It Through

Read   Did I read the problem carefully?
I need to divide 45 by 9.

Cross Out Are there any answers that are not reasonable?
54 is greater than 45, so I can cross out answer D.

Solve   What is $45 \div 9$?
$45 \div 9 = 5$

Check   Is there a way that I can check my answer?
I can multiply. $5 \times 9 = 45$

Choose   Which letter is next to my answer?
My answer is 5, and 5 is next to letter A.

Try It!

① $5 \times 12 = $ ▨
   A 17   **B** 50   **C** 60   **D** 65   **E** Not Here

② $4 \times 10 = $ ▨
   A 14   **B** 30   **C** 40   **D** 44   **E** Not Here

③ $6 \times 3 = $ ▨
   A 9   **B** 16   **C** 17   **D** 18   **E** Not Here

TESTING TIPS

▷ Estimate whenever you can before you solve a problem. You can use an estimate to check whether your answer is reasonable, or to identify answer choices that are not reasonable.

▷ Reread the question and check your work before choosing "Not Here."

▷ Make sure you bubble in the letter on the answer sheet that matches your answer.

Multistep Questions
One Step at a Time

Sometimes you need to do more than one step to answer a multiple choice question.

▷ Always look at all of the answer choices that are listed.

▷ Even if you find your answer among the choices, check your work. Answers that come from making common mistakes are usually included in the choices!

▷ If you are having trouble answering a question, go on to the next question and come back to the more difficult question later.

Example

Jen spent $11 on rides and $8 on food at the fair. Then she spent $14 on souvenirs. If Jen came to the fair with $35, how much money does she have left?

A $2   **B** $19   **C** $33   **D** $40   **E** Not Here

Think It Through

Read Did I read the problem carefully?

I need to find how much money Jen has left.

Cross Out Are there any answers that are not reasonable?

Jen came with $35 and spent money, so she can't have $40 now. I can cross out answer D.

Solve How much money does Jen have now?

$11 + $8 + $14 = $33, so Jen spent $33.
$35 − $33 = $2, so Jen has $2 left now.

Check Is there a way that I can check my answer?

I can check by adding all the amounts.
$2 + $11 + $8 + $14 = $35

Choose Which letter is next to my answer?

My answer is $2, and $2 is next to letter A.

Try It!

1 Lou is twice as old as Gene. Gene is 3 years older than Deb. Deb is 5. How old is Lou?

A 6   **B** 9   **C** 16   **D** 31   **E** Not Here

2 Mary is drawing figures in this pattern: triangle, square, circle, rectangle, triangle, square, circle, rectangle. What is the 20th figure Mary will draw?

A Triangle   **B** Square   **C** Circle
D Rectangle   **E** Not Here

Measurement Questions
MEASURE UP!

Sometimes you can use pattern blocks or a ruler to help you solve a multiple choice question.

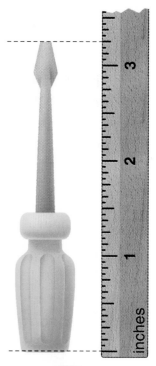

Example

Use the inch side of a ruler for this problem. Tom needs a small screwdriver to build a model. Measure the screwdriver shown here to the nearest quarter of an inch. What is the length of the screwdriver?

A 3 in.　　**B** $3\frac{1}{4}$ in.　　**C** $3\frac{3}{4}$ in.　　**D** 4 in

Think It Through

Read　　Did I read the problem carefully?

I need to use the inch side of the ruler.

Cross Out　Are there any answers that are not reasonable?

The screwdriver is between 3 in. and 4 in. long, so I can cross out answers A and D.

Solve　　What can I do to solve the problem?

I will use the ruler to measure the screwdriver. It measures $3\frac{1}{4}$ inches.

Check　　Is there a way that I can check my answer?

I can measure again.

Choose　　Which letter is next to my answer?

The letter B is next to $3\frac{1}{4}$ inches.

Try It!

Use the centimeter side of a ruler for this problem.

1 John is using different size screws as he builds his model. Which screw is between 3 and 4 centimeters long?

A 　　B

C 　　D

> Make sure you are using the correct side of the ruler when you are measuring. You may be asked to measure in inches or in centimeters.

> Make sure you line up the 0 mark on the ruler with one end of the object you are going to measure.

> Check to see how precisely you need to measure the object, such as to the nearest $\frac{1}{2}$ inch or the nearest $\frac{1}{4}$ inch.

Short Answer Questions
The Write Stuff

Sometimes a test question asks you not only to *solve* a problem but to show *how* you solved the problem. For questions like these, you need to be able to write your thoughts on paper.

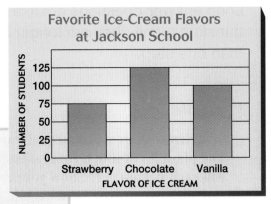

Favorite Ice-Cream Flavors at Jackson School

Example

The bar graph at the right shows favorite ice-cream flavors at Jackson School.

If you could only order one flavor of ice cream for a party, which flavor would you order? How many cups of that flavor would you order? Explain.

Think It Through

Read
What am I being asked to write about?
I need to find which is the most popular flavor of ice cream.

Plan
What can I do to solve the problem?
I can compare the bars on the graph to determine the most popular flavor. Then I can add the number of students shown by each bar to find how many students there are in all.

Solve
What is the answer to the problem?
I'd order 300 cups of chocolate ice cream.

Explain
How did I get my answer?
The bar graph shows a total of 300 students and that chocolate is the most popular flavor.

Try It!

Use the graph to answer Questions 1 and 2. Explain.

1. What flavor ice cream would you probably see the most students eating in the cafeteria?

2. 20 students who liked chocolate before like vanilla now. Does this change your answer for Question 1?

TESTING TIPS

▷ Be sure to follow the directions carefully. Sometimes you will be asked to write an explanation in words. Other times you will be asked to show your work in numbers or with drawings.

▷ Be prepared to take more time to answer short answer questions than to answer multiple choice questions.

▷ You can usually get partial credit for an answer. So, even if you can't solve the whole problem, write what you can.

Long Answer Questions
In Your Own Words

Long answer questions are like short answer questions, only they are longer and often have more than one step.

Example

Six friends share a pizza equally with no pizza left over. The pizza is cut into 8 equal slices. How much pizza will each person get? Show your answer in numbers and with a drawing. Then explain your answer.

Think It Through

Read   What am I being asked to write about?
I need to find how 6 friends will share a pizza equally.

Plan   What can I do to solve the problem?
I can divide a circle into 8 equal parts and divide the parts equally among the 6 friends.

Solve   What is the answer to the problem?
Each person will get $1\frac{1}{3}$ slices of pizza.

Explain   How did I get my answer?
I gave each person one slice. Then I divided each of the other 2 slices into sixths. So, each person got 1 whole slice and $\frac{2}{6}$ of a slice, or $1\frac{1}{3}$ slices.

Try It!

For Questions 1 and 2, use numbers and drawings to show your work. Be sure to explain how you got your answers.

1. Jim is going on a 2-week trip. He takes yellow, green, and red shirts. He takes black, brown, and blue pants. Can he wear a different combination each day?

2. Four friends are in line in order from youngest to oldest. Their ages are 7, 8, 9, and 12. Keesha is before Paul. Derek is after Paul. Ana is between two people, but she is not next to Derek. How much older is Paul than Keesha?

Becoming a Better Test Taker

TEST PRACTICE FOR THE
CONTENT STANDARDS AND LEARNING EXPECTATIONS

Using the Format of the

CTBS®
TerraNova

The mathematics skills you are learning this year are important in your schoolwork and also in your everyday life. The following pages will give you some test items that will show you how well you've learned your math skills. These problems will also help you become a better test taker when it's time to take the Comprehensive Test of Basic Skills.

Remember these
Testing Tips

Multiple-Choice Questions

▷ Estimate whenever you can before you solve a problem. You can use an estimate to check whether your answer is reasonable, or to identify answer choices that are not reasonable.

▷ Even if you find your answer among the choices, check your work. Answers that come from making common mistakes are usually included in the choices!

▷ If you are having trouble answering a question, go on to the next question and come back to the more difficult question later.

▷ Reread the question and check your work before choosing "Not Here."

▷ Make sure you fill in the letter on the answer sheet that matches your answer.

1
$$26$$
$$+\ 39$$

A 55
B 56
C 65
D 66

5 $3 \times 220 =$

A 60
B 550
C 660
D 1,100

2
$$258$$
$$+\ 381$$

F 588
G 529
H 539
J 639

6 $2.76 + 0.39 =$

F 2.05
G 2.06
H 3.05
J 3.15

3 $7 \times 6 =$

A 35
B 40
C 42
D 56

7
$$\frac{7}{6}$$
$$-\ \frac{2}{6}$$

A $\frac{5}{7}$
B $\frac{5}{6}$
C $\frac{6}{7}$
D $\frac{9}{6}$

4 $99 \div 8 =$

F 11
G 12
H 12R3
J 13

8 $\frac{2}{12} + \frac{5}{12} =$

F $\frac{7}{24}$
G $\frac{7}{12}$
H $\frac{7}{10}$
J $\frac{3}{4}$

9 This table shows the number of points scored by 5 players. Which 2 players scored a total of 45 points?

Player	Number of Goals Scored
Peter	21
Scott	19
Jack	24
Ralph	20
Kareem	26

A Peter and Ralph
B Scott and Jack
C Scott and Kareem
D Jack and Kareem

10 The Saturday afternoon games of a basketball tournament were seen by 819 spectators. The Saturday evening games were seen by 1,304 spectators. How many more spectators saw the evening games than the afternoon games?

F 485
G 515
H 595
J 2,123

11 Which of these shows 0.40 shaded?

A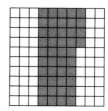

B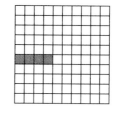

C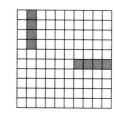

D

12 Which number sentence belongs to the same family of facts as 9 + 5 = 14?

F 14 + 9 = 23
G 14 − 9 = 5
H 9 − 5 = 4
J 14 + 5 = 19

13 Which number has the digit 9 in the hundredths place?

A 0.97   **C** 405.09
B 91.3   **D** 2,978.2

14 Which number goes in the ❑ to make the number sentence true?

33 − ❑ = 16

16   17   23   27
F   **G**   **H**   **J**

15 Which number goes in the ❑ to make the number sentence true?

6 × ❑ = 6

A 36   **C** 1
B 12   **D** 0

16 Which is another way to write 6 + 6 + 6 + 6 + 6?

F 6 + 5
G 6 × 6 × 6 × 6 × 6
H 30 + 6
J 5 × 6

17 Which expression is equal to 8 + 2?

A 2 + 8
B 8 ÷ 2
C 10 ÷ 2
D 2 × 8

18 Which of these is another way to write six thousands, two hundreds, two ones?

F 622
G 6,022
H 6,202
J 60,202

19 What part of this figure is shaded?

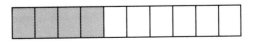

A 0.4   **C** 0.04
B 0.6   **D** 0.06

20

Fruit	Pounds Produced
Oranges	8,733
Lemons	6,550
Tangerines	6,052
Grapefruit	7,930

Which list orders the fruit from the least to the greatest number of pounds produced?

F Oranges, Lemons, Tangerines, Grapefruit

G Lemons, Tangerines, Grapefruit, Oranges

H Tangerines, Lemons, Grapefruit, Oranges

J Oranges, Grapefruit, Lemons, Tangerines

21 What part of this figure is shaded?

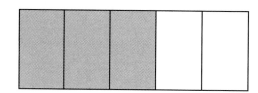

A 0.35

B $\frac{3}{2}$

C $\frac{3}{5}$

D 3.5

22 Which two figures show equivalent fractions?

R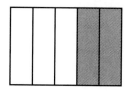

S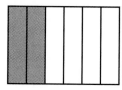

T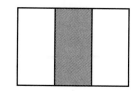

V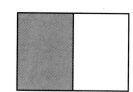

F R and S

G R and V

H S and T

J S and V

23 Which number is equal to $(8 \times 1,000) + (1 \times 1)$?

A 8,111

B 8,110

C 8,001

D 811

Directions

For Questions 24–26, you do not need to find exact answers. Use estimation to choose the best answers.

24 The librarian has 2,183 books to put into boxes. Each box will hold about 20 books. *About* how many boxes will the librarian need to use?

F 1,200   **H** 100

G 1,000   **J** 10

25 Estimate the length of a librarian's desk.

A 6 gallons   **C** 6 inches

B 6 feet   **D** 6 pounds

26 Eric purchased 3 books. Each book cost from $20 to $30. Before sales tax is added, what is a reasonable estimate of the cost of the books?

F Less than $45

G Between $45 and $60

H Between $60 and $90

J More than $100

27 On this map, what is the length of the marked path the bus will take to the library bus stop?

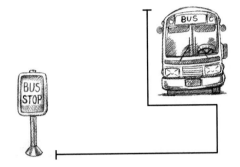

A 3 in.   **C** 4 in.

B $3\frac{1}{2}$ in.   **D** 5 in.

28 Use your inch ruler to help you answer this question. What is the area of this rectangle in square inches?

1	2	4	8
F	**G**	**H**	**J**

29 Every day after school, Jo picks lemons. Jo made the chart below to show how many lemons she picked last week.

Day	Lemons Picked
Monday	10
Tuesday	4
Wednesday	8
Thursday	11
Friday	11
Total	n

Which shows the total number of lemons Jo picked last week?

A $n - 11$
B $5 \times n$
C $10 + 4 + 8 + 11 + 11 = n$
D $44 \div n$

30 Which number sentence best describes the picture?

F $24 \times 4 = 96$
G $24 + 6 = 30$
H $4 \times 6 = 24$
J $4 + 12 = 16$

31 A pitcher of lemonade serves 4 people. Which number sentence can you use to find how many pitchers are needed to serve 12 people?

A $12 \div 4 = \square$
B $12 \times 4 = \square$
C $12 + 4 = \square$
D $12 - 4 = \square$

32 Debbie used these coins to pay for a lemonade. Which other group of coins has the same value as Debbie's coins?

F 6 dimes, 2 nickels
G 3 quarters, 7 pennies
H 1 quarter, 3 dimes, 2 pennies
J 3 quarters, 1 dime, 1 nickel

Directions

Carl has used a grid to identify the location of each house in his neighborhood. Use his grid to answer Questions 33 and 34.

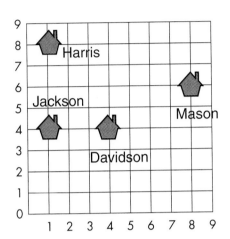

33 Which house is located at (1, 4)?

A Jackson

B Harris

C Davidson

D Mason

34 Which gives the location of the Mason house?

F (1, 4)

G (6, 6)

H (8, 5)

J (8, 6)

35 Carl told Amy that he knew a secret number. He could multiply his house number, 10, and her house number, 4, by this secret number and have the same result. Which is the secret number?

☐ × 10 = 4 × ☐

A 0   **C** 5

B 3   **D** 15

36 Anna has $382 in her savings account. What is $382 rounded to the nearest hundred dollars?

F $40

G $300

H $380

J $400

Directions

Howie, Jenny, and Keisha have been setting up bowling pins for a game in Keisha's backyard. Answer Questions 37–39.

37 Howie placed the bowling pins in rows for the game. He placed 2 in the first row, 4 in the second row, and 6 in the third row. Howie continued the pattern. How many pins did he place in the fourth row?

A 4 **B** 8 **C** 12 **D** 18

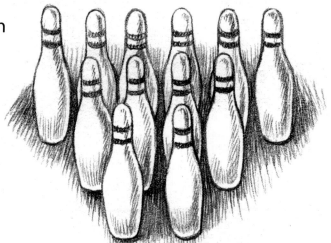

38 For the first 8 frames that Jenny bowled, she knocked over a total of 48 pins. How many pins did she average each frame?

$48 \div 8 = \square$

F 6 **G** 7 **H** 8 **J** 12

39 Howie bowled three games, doubling his score each time. In the first game, he knocked over 30 pins. How many did he knock over in the third game?

A 120 **B** 90 **C** 45 **D** 15

40 Which number will come next in this pattern?

32, 28, 24, 20, ___

F 14
G 16
H 18
J 20

41

Any number that goes into the machine is multiplied by 3 before it comes out. If 27 came out, which number went in?

A 3
B 8
C 9
D 17

42

Any number that goes into the machine is multiplied by 3 before it comes out. If 8 went in, which number will come out?

F 38
G 21
H 24
J 38

43 Which set of figures continues this pattern?

▲   ▲▲▲   ▲▲▲▲▲

A ▲▲

B ▲▲▲

C ▲▲▲▲▲

D ▲▲▲▲▲▲▲

Directions

The following chart shows how many runs five of the players on the Cincinnati Reds scored in 1996. Use this chart for Questions 44 and 45.

Name	Runs
Morris	80
Larkin	89
Davis	83
Greene	63
Boone	69

44 Which was the median number of hits made by these five players?

F 89

G 80

H 77

J 69

45 What was the average number of runs scored by the top three players?

A 252

B 240

C 84

D 10

46 The snack bar at the stadium sells 3 different snacks and 2 different drinks. How many ways can Jill choose a snack and a drink?

F 6   H 3

G 5   J 2

47 The bar graph shows the number of votes each snack received in a class survey.

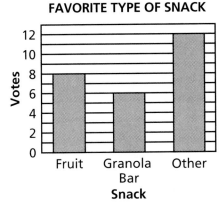

Which tally chart was used to make the bar graph?

A

Fruit	ⅢⅢ ⅢⅢ ‖
Granola Bar	ⅢⅢ ‖
Other	ⅢⅢ ‖‖‖

B

Fruit	ⅢⅢ
Granola Bar	ⅢⅢ ‖
Other	ⅢⅢ ‖‖

C

Fruit	ⅢⅢ ‖‖‖
Granola Bar	ⅢⅢ ‖
Other	ⅢⅢ ⅢⅢ ‖‖

D

Fruit	‖‖‖‖
Granola Bar	‖‖‖
Other	ⅢⅢ ‖

48 Neil asked students what they ate for breakfast this morning. She recorded the results in this tally chart.

BREAKFAST	
Cereal	ⅢⅢ ⅢⅢ ‖‖‖‖
Eggs	ⅢⅢ ‖‖‖‖
Bagels or Muffins	ⅢⅢ

How many more students ate cereal than ate bagels or muffins?

F 4   **H** 9
G 8   **J** 13

49 Suppose you spun this spinner many times.

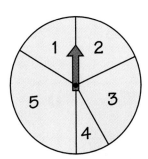

Which number are you likely to spin most often?

A 1   **C** 3
B 2   **D** 5

50 Which number is inside the triangle, outside the oval, and inside the rectangle?

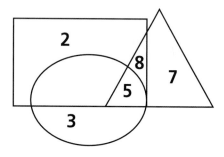

F 8   **H** 5
G 7   **J** 2

51 I have exactly 2 sides that are the same length. What am I? Which shape below is an answer to this riddle?

A

B

C

D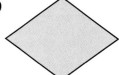

52 Which shows an angle less than a right angle?

F

G

H

J

53 The drum is shaped like which figure?

A Cone
B Cylinder
C Sphere
D Cube

Directions

Use the following art to answer Questions 54 and 55.

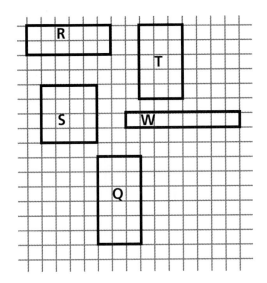

56

This postcard will be turned upside down. Which choice shows the postcard turned upside down?

54 Which two polygons do not have a perimeter of 16 units?

F R and T   **H** W and Q
G S and W   **J** R and W

F

G

55 Which polygon has the greatest area?

A R   **C** W
B T   **D** Q

H

J

57

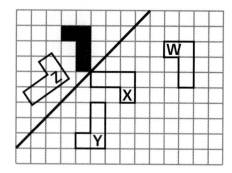

Which unshaded figure shows where the shaded figure would be if the graph paper were folded along the heavy dark line?

W   X   Y   Z
A   **B**   **C**   **D**

58 Which numeral can be folded in half so that the two parts match exactly?

2   4   7   8

F 2
G 4
H 7
J 8

59 Which rectangle is congruent to rectangle *WXZY*?

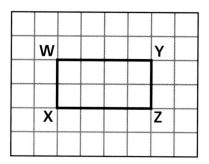

A

B

C

D